Great Letters for Every Occasion

ROSALIE MAGGIO

PRENTICE HALL PRESS

Library of Congress Cataloging-in-Publication Data

Maggio, Rosalie.
    Great letters for every occasion   / by Rosalie Maggio.
       p.   cm.
    Includes bibliographical references and index.
    ISBN 0-13-082782-7. — ISBN 0-7352-0081-5 (pbk.)
      1. Letter writing—Handbooks, manuals, etc. 2. English language—Rhetoric—
Handbooks, manuals, etc. I. Title.
    PE1483.M25 1999
    808.6—DC21
                                                 99-10586
                                                  CIP

Acquisitions Editor: *Tom Power*
Production Editor: *Sharon L. Gonzalez*
Formatting/Interior Design: *Robyn Beckerman*

© 1999 by Rosalie Maggio

Printed in the United States of America

10 9 8 7 6 5 4 3 2 1

ISBN 0-7352-0081-5 (p)

ATTENTION: CORPORATIONS AND SCHOOLS

Prentice Hall books are available at quantity discounts with bulk purchase for educational, business, or sales promotional use. For information, please write to: Prentice Hall Special Sales, 240 Frisch Court, Paramus, New Jersey 07652. Please supply: title of book, ISBN, quantity, how the book will be used, date needed.

PRENTICE HALL PRESS
Paramus, NJ 07652

On the World Wide Web at http://www.phdirect.com

To DAVID
Liz, Katie, Matt

Acknowledgments

Many of the model letters are taken from my own bountiful collection of letters received over the years. Thanks and love to all my favorite correspondents. You know who you are. Special thanks to Shelley Sateren, who generated some of the model letters, and to those who contributed letters, support, or advice: David Koskenmaki, Mary Maggio, Donald Cunningham, Frank Gargano, Mary Sweeney, Frank Jensen, Steve Sikora, Susan Berkson, Kristina Hoefer, Tom Jones, Colleen D. Taylor, and the wonderful librarians at the St. Paul Public Library, particularly its Lexington Branch.

Contents

Introduction

Every page of this book has been crafted with a specific goal in mind: to make it easy and satisfying for you to write effective letters. You may be surprised to find the book not only practical and helpful, but entertaining as well. Relevant, humorous, and useful quotations are sprinkled throughout each chapter, and lively, appealing, and simple model letters will show you how to write the kind of winning letters that people enjoy receiving—and that you actually enjoy writing!

One important message of this book, delivered indirectly throughout its pages, is that there is rarely "one right way" to write a letter. Instead there are guidelines that we are free to follow or not. We know more about our situation and our readers' situations than any letterwriting manual, which means that with a little thought, common sense, and effort, we can write—and write well—any letter we need to write. Except for someone like Napoleon, who apparently wrote more than 50,000 letters in his lifetime (and nobody ever said to him, "Get a life!"), almost everyone can use this book to write eloquent, compelling, and powerful letters.

Now and then we read that letters are going the way of the dodo. Not true. According to the United States Postal Service, "Direct mail is still one of the most appealing ways to get a message to a buyer. Households still open, read, and respond to direct mail advertising at a steady rate."

In "The Art of the Letter" published in *The Los Angeles Times*, John Balzar reports that in one recent four-year period in the United States, we wrote and mailed 100 million *more* personal letters to each other than previously. He points to evidence like the sales of writing tools. "A generation ago, the idea of a successful retail store specializing in fine writing instruments was quaint to the extreme. Just a few existed. Today, pen stores thrive in most major cities. . . . In the past 15 years, U.S. sales of fountain pens have increased from 6.4 million to 25.4 million, according to the Writing Instruments Manufacturers Association." Balzar concludes, "Whimsy, mysticism, nostalgia, rebellion, practicality, and a healthy dollop of egotism all figure in somehow in the resurgence of writing. People say they are reaching for a personal touch in an impersonal culture, something warm against the chill."

That new trend is a very old trend. In the tenth century, Sei Shonagon wrote, "If letters did not exist, what dark depressions would come over one! When one has been worrying about something and wants to tell a certain person about it, what a relief it is to put it all down in a letter! Still greater is one's joy when a reply arrives. At that moment a letter really seems like an elixir of life."

User's Guide

To make the best use of *Great Letters for Every Occasion,* first glance at the Index in the back. Close to one thousand entries guarantee that you will find the help you need, no matter what kind of letter you're writing.

Next, flip through the Appendixes to familiarize yourself with the assistance available there. Appendix I deals with the *mechanics* of letterwriting: what kind of stationery to use, how to address an envelope, the four most common ways to set up a letter on the page, and helpful postal service guidelines. Appendix II deals with the *content* of your letter: writing tips, grammar and usage, names and titles, respectful people language, frequently misspelled words, redundant words and phrases, correct forms of address.

To write a letter, find your topic among the fifty types of letters listed in the Contents. Turn to that chapter for a brief introduction followed by a list of "Do's" and "Don'ts" for your letter.

The useful "Getting Started" section offers appropriate opening sentences that you can borrow or adapt for your own letters. William Cowper wrote, "When one has a letter to write there is nothing more useful than to make a Beginning. In the first place, because unless it be begun, there is no good reason to hope that it will ever be ended, and secondly, because the beginning is half the business, it being much more difficult to put the pen in motion at first, than to continue the progress of it, when once moved." You'll find he's right. Once you have started the letter, the rest will be surprisingly easy.

The model letters illustrate for you a range of styles and patterns for your letters. At the end of the chapter, a list of related topics directs you to additional assistance.

After skimming the highlights of the chapter on your letter topic, write a rough draft. Check it against the list of "Do's" and "Don'ts." At that point, you may have a question about format or grammar or a social title. Go to the Index to quickly locate your question in one of the Appendixes.

Your final draft is minutes away.

Writing in the *St. Louis Post-Dispatch,* Elaine Veits said, "For most of us, letter-writing is a painful duty. We squeeze out an occasional Christmas note, but it's as much fun as an IRS audit."

After writing your first few letters using this book, you may find that you are not, after all, "most of us."

1

Acknowledgments and Letters of Confirmation

INTRODUCTION

Letters of acknowledgment and confirmation closely resemble each other. A letter of acknowledgment says, "I received your letter, telephone call, gift, informational materials." A letter of confirmation says, "I received your letter, proposal, telephone call and we are in agreement with each other." (This type of letter can serve as an informal contract.)

Sometimes a letter of acknowledgment also serves as a "thank you" and sometimes it says that you received the message or materials but will respond later or that you passed them on to the appropriate person. Sometimes, too, "acknowledgment" letters are really sales letters that use the excuse of acknowledging something (an order, a payment) to present an additional sales message.

You will always want to acknowledge expressions of condolence. You will usually want to acknowledge anniversary or birthday greetings, congratulations, an apology, or a divorce announcement. See Weddings for information about acknowledging the receipt of a wedding gift when you are unable to write the thank you immediately.

Most business transactions require no acknowledgment: orders are received, merchandise is delivered on schedule, payments are sent. You would, however, acknowledge receipt in unusual situations, for example, when the previous order went astray and you want the sender to know that this one arrived, or when you receive payment from someone to whom you've been sending collection letters and you want the person to know that payment has

1

been received (and, by implication, that there will be no more collection letters). You may want to acknowledge large or important payments, orders, and shipments—or those from first-time customers or suppliers. Acknowledge any letters, requests, orders, manuscript submissions, or complaints that cannot be responded to immediately so that the person knows their material was received and action is under way.

> In acknowledgment lies depth. Thank you.
> Thank you.
> Just this.
>
> —DAVID K. REYNOLDS

DO

- Write promptly. A letter of acknowledgment is, almost by definition, a letter that is sent immediately. (An exception is the acknowledgment of expressions of sympathy; because of the hardships involved, responses may be sent up to six weeks later.) If your acknowledgment is late, apologize briefly.
- Refer to the letter or items you are acknowledging ("I have just received the sheet music").
- Describe what action, if any, is being taken.
- Tell when the reader will hear further from you or from someone else.
- Explain briefly why you are unable to respond fully at the moment.
- Express appreciation for whatever was sent or for the kindness of the person in sending it.

> Life is not so short but that there is always time enough
> for courtesy.
>
> —RALPH WALDO EMERSON

DON'T

- Don't give lengthy explanations of why you can't respond immediately; letters of acknowledgment are among the briefest.

> Hail, ye small, sweet courtesies of life!
> for smooth do ye make the road of it.
>
> —LAURENCE STERN

HELPFUL HINTS

- Mail that arrives in someone's absence should be acknowledged by staff members. It is necessary only to mention the absence, not to offer apologies or explanations. No course of action should be promised or implied. An assistant should acknowledge a death or serious illness if an absent supervisor would normally send a sympathy letter.

- Organizations receiving memorial donations acknowledge receipt of the contribution and also notify the family so that they can thank the donor themselves.

- Expressions of condolence should always be acknowledged. However, it is acceptable for a close relative of the bereaved to write the acknowledgment: "Mother has asked me to tell you how much she appreciated the loving letter of sympathy and the memorial you sent for Dad. She will be in touch with you herself as soon as she is able."

- If acknowledging letters, reservations, appointments, orders, and shipments is frequent and routine, have your message printed on a supply of acknowledgment postcards (depending on your use, they could have blank spaces so you can fill in dates, order numbers, etc.). Leave space at the bottom for a handwritten note in case you need to add information.

- When someone writes you about an issue handled better by someone else, acknowledge their letter and suggest they contact the appropriate person (include name, address, telephone number, if possible). You can also pass the letter along to the proper department and notify your correspondent that you've done so.

- Apologies generally need to be acknowledged to let the other person know that their apology was received and accepted.

- Printed acknowledgment cards are sent when a complete response is not immediately possible. In this way, you can advise a number of people that you have received their gifts, manuscripts, or expressions of sympathy and that you will respond as soon as you can. Printed or engraved cards or foldovers may also be sent (with no personal follow-up) in the case of a public figure whose death inspires numerous messages of sympathy, many of them from people personally unknown to the family or deceased.

- If a friend writes to tell you of a divorce, it is best to avoid expressing either congratulations or sympathy (unless you know for certain which is called for); in most cases, simply acknowledging the information is the appropriate response.

> Custom is a mutable thing; yet we readily recognize the permanence of certain social values. Graciousness and courtesy are never old-fashioned.
>
> —EMILY POST

GETTING STARTED

Thank you for your payment of $1,165.43.

We have received your letter of August 3, in which you kindly thanked the claims adjustors at Eynsford-Hill Family Insurance for their efficiency and helpfulness after the recent floods.

We hereby acknowledge receipt of the grain inspection contract, which will be signed and returned within the next week.

Thanks for the Anstruthers credit files—and for getting them here so quickly.

This is to confirm our telephone conversation today, in which we agreed on a September 1 closing date.

Thank you for the interim report on the Bentinck-Jones merger. We'll look forward to the final report on July 1.

This is just a note to let you know that I've received the personal injury information you sent and I'll get back to you as soon as I can.

I received your letter this morning, but will not be able to get the figures to you until after April 15.

This is to acknowledge your letter of January 14 and to let you know you will hear from us as soon as a decision has been reached.

Thank you for requesting a copy of our annual report—it will be mailed to you in approximately three weeks.

Thank you for the fabric samples—I'll call as soon as my client has made a decision.

This is to acknowledge your order # 88632 for three dozen task chairs, catalog # CH1102.

Thank you for your kind letter. The family of Somers Denzil is grateful for your thoughtfulness and sympathy.

The children and family of Stephen Cheswardine wish to acknowledge with gratefulness your kind expression of sympathy.

I sincerely appreciated your loving expression of sympathy.

Your expression of sympathy on the death of our Founding President and CEO, Neda De Ham, is much appreciated.

Thank you for your letter of September 7, which I have referred to Ms. Hervey-Bonham, Special Events Director of the National Canine Institute.

I'm looking forward to meeting you Friday, June 19, at 3 p.m. at your branch office in Esmond.

This will confirm the agreement made yesterday during our meeting for our landscape consultant to assist you in drawing up a plan for your property; as long as you buy all materials from us, there is no charge for this service.

> The degree of miscommunication regarding what's been agreed upon in a business deal tends to increase in direct proportion to the amount of money involved.
>
> —ROBERT J. RINGER

MODEL LETTERS

Dear Mr. Kipling,

As we agreed in our telephone conversation this morning, a limousine will be waiting for Vidal Benzaguen inside the security gate at the Celebrity Lines airfield at 7 p.m. on December 14 to escort her to her hotel. Her assigned chauffeur will remain on call for all Ms. Benzaguen's transportation needs until the following Monday at 10 a.m.

We at Village Royal Valet guarantee that all precautions will be taken to ensure Ms. Benzaguen's complete privacy during her stay.

Yours truly,

Dear Harold Etches,

Thank you for your letter of October 12 and for the sample of foreign material that you found in our last shipment to you of cleaning compound. Both have been forwarded to our manufacturing department. You will be hearing from them as soon as they have identified the extraneous product and determined how the situation developed. In the meantime, we are replacing that shipment; you should have it by October 20.

Sincerely,

Cyril Povey
Consumer Relations

Dear Mr. Canty,

Thank you for your nice letter containing your suggestion for jelly made with our Prince Edward Grape Juice.

As a matter of company policy, however, we cannot examine your suggestion unless you sign and return the enclosed general release. We hope you will understand that such a policy is necessary.

It is always a pleasure to hear from customers who enjoy our products and we do appreciate your interest.

Very truly yours,

Prince Edward, Inc.

Miles Hendon
Counsel

MH:slc
Enc.

Dear Mr. Machin,

Thank you for your letter of November 11 addressed to Mrs. Codleyn. She will be out of the office for the next two weeks, but she will contact you when she returns.

Sincerely,

Arnold Bennett

Dear Esteban,

The birthday briefcase arrived just now, 45 minutes before I'm due to fly to Houston for a week. My effusive and detailed thanks will follow—for the moment, I just had to let you know it arrived! More later . . .

Manuel

Dear Ms. Bindon-Botting:

Your recent communication is appreciated, and it has been referred for review and appropriate action. We value you as a customer and ask your continued patience while a response to your communication is being prepared.

Office of Consumer Affairs

Dear Ms. Gargery,

This will acknowledge your letter of June 24 applying for a position as senior transportation planner with Great Expeditions, Inc. Your letter and résumé have been forwarded to the planning department. You will be hearing directly from the department director, Philip Pirrip, in about two weeks.

Sincerely,

John Wemmick
Human Resources

All doors open to courtesy.

—Thomas Fuller

Dear Hermann Heijermans,

We were pleased to receive your letter of April 29.
Normally we would answer your inquiry at once, but our Board of Directors is currently drawing up a change in our policy with respect to motorized fishing boats.
We will be able to give you a response by May 15.

Dear Andrew Fairservice,

We have received your order # 406A, dated April 18, for four dozen climbing hydrangeas. Because of climate variables this year, you will be receiving your order on May 17 instead of May 3.
Thank you again for your order. We look forward to serving you.

Dear Mrs. Munnings,

Thank you for your grandfather's emigration story, which I received yesterday. I have been able to spend only about an hour skimming through it as I am swamped with other editing projects at the moment. However, I am interested in helping you create a book out of your family's fascinating rags-to-riches-to-rags-to-riches-to-rags-again history. My workload will lighten by the end of August, at which time I can give your manuscript a thorough read.

I will contact you the first week in September with editing and desktop formatting suggestions and we should be able to pull together a fine, finished book by Thanksgiving. I hope this schedule works for you.

Sincerely,

> Be pretty if you can, be witty if you must,
> but be gracious if it *kills* you.
>
> —ELSIE DE WOLFE

RELATED TOPICS

Follow-up
Responses
Sales
Thank You
Travel
Weddings

Letters of Adjustment

INTRODUCTION

A letter of adjustment is written in response to a customer's letter of complaint or claims letter. A well-written adjustment letter can change a disgruntled customer into a gruntled one. Dealing with customer complaints promptly and conscientiously is excellent public relations.

An adjustment letter may serve to: (1) correct errors and make good on company inadequacies; (2) grant reasonable full or partial adjustments in order to maintain good customer relations; (3) deny unwarranted claims so tactfully that the customer's goodwill is retained.

In his classic *Handbook of Business Letters*, L.E. Frailey advises treating a complaint with as much respect as an order, letting customers know you are as eager to serve them as to sell them.

You will know if you have written a good letter of adjustment when the customer returns for repeat business.

If you are writing to request an adjustment, see Complaints; this chapter deals with making adjustments.

> A reputation for handling customer claims quickly and fairly is a powerful public relations tool for any firm.
>
> —L. Sue Baugh, Maridell Fryar, David Thomas

DO

- Be prompt in responding to customer complaints; this goes a long way toward establishing your good intentions.

- Open with a courtesy, an expression of sympathy and understanding, or a pleasant statement ("Thank you for your letter of June 3").

- Identify the error or problem and specify details: dates, amounts, invoice numbers.

- Say your reader was correct, if this is so. In any case, reassure the person that telling you about the problem was the suitable thing to do.

- State your regret about the confusion, mix-up, or error.

- Explain your company's policy of dealing with customer claims, if appropriate.

- Describe how you propose to resolve the problem or what you have already done. Sometimes you will give customers a choice: do they want a replacement, a refund, or a credit to their accounts? You may want to consider a goodwill gesture: a discount coupon or gift certificate or a price reduction on their next order. Be specific about the steps you are taking; vagueness may leave the customer expecting more than is offered and disappointed when it doesn't eventuate.

- When you must deny the requested adjustment (a complete refund, for example), explain why: an investigation of the matter did not support it (include documents or itemize findings); standard company policy does not allow it (and violating the policy in this case is not possible); the item is no longer under warranty; the item was used in a specifically prohibited manner. Be gracious but firm. Express your sympathy for the customer's point of view, explain that their letter was considered carefully, appeal to their sense of fair play, and close with a positive statement (offering a discount coupon, expressing your appreciation of past business and cooperation, saying that this was a difficult letter to write but the only possible response consistent with your values of fairness and responsibility).

- Mention a date by which you expect the problem to be resolved, even if it is only "immediately," "at once," or "as soon as possible."

- Restore confidence and regain goodwill by saying that this error is rare, that the company works hard to satisfy customers, and that you expect future transactions to be correct.

- Close by thanking the customer for their patience, asking for continued customer loyalty, offering further cooperation, reaffirming the company's good intentions and the value of its products, or expressing your expectation that the customer will continue to enjoy your services and products for years to come.

> Keeping an old customer is just as important as gaining a new one.
>
> —N.H. AND S.K. MAGER

DON'T

- Don't repeat all the details of a problem. Refer to it in passing and hope that it will soon be a vague memory for the customer.
- Don't use the words "claim" or "complaint" even though these customer letters are referred to as "claims" and "complaints." The terms sound accusatory and judgmental, and the majority of customers honestly believe they are due an adjustment. Instead of "The damage that you claim was due to improper packing" or "Your complaint has been received," substitute a word like "report" for "claim" and "complaint."
- Don't be overly apologetic. Something simple like "We regret the error" suffices for small matters. Serious errors may require something more, but most successful businesses are careful to avoid these.
- Don't say how "surprised" you are or how rare the problem is ("I can't believe this happened"; "Not once in twenty years have we encountered this problem")— unless, of course, it truly is an exceptional occurrence. Customers will immediately discount your goodwill, figuring if the error happened to them, it could happen (and probably has) to anyone.
- Don't overstate company culpability or indicate in writing that the company was negligent. When negligence is involved, your lawyer can suggest the best approach for your letter.
- Don't over-explain how the error happened; your letter should emphasize the solution rather than the error. The customer is primarily interested in obtaining an adjustment, not in learning about your difficulties with suppliers, employees, shippers, or order-takers. An explanation of several words ("due to power outages last week") is sufficient.
- Don't make an adjustment in the customer's favor grudgingly, angrily, impatiently, or condescendingly. Do it with grace or you will undo the positive public-relations effect of righting the error. Even when the customer is angry or rude, your attitude must be one of friendliness and understanding; the "high road" always leads to greater goodwill and customer satisfaction.

> If American industry continues to sow contempt for the
> consumer, it will reap contempt from the consumer.
>
> —BETTY FURNESS

- Don't blame "computer error." By now people know that human beings run the computers, not vice versa, and this weak and obviously untrue excuse only irritates people. Similarly, don't say that these things are bound to happen from time to time. Although this may be true, saying so indicates a certain laxness in tolerating error.

- Don't end your letter by mentioning the problem ("Again, we are so sorry that our Great Southwest Hiking Holiday was such an unpleasant experience for you") because it leaves the problem, not your goodwill and adjustment, uppermost in the reader's mind.

> Every unhappy customer will tell ten others about a bad
> experience, whereas happy customers may tell three.
>
> —LILLIAN VERNON

HELPFUL HINTS

- Sometimes the customer is partly at fault or you suspect that they are (failure to read installation instructions, excessive or inappropriate use). If you decide, for whatever reason, to grant the adjustment (most companies give customers the benefit of the doubt), do so without assigning any blame to the customer; it is counterproductive to the goodwill you are establishing.

- When neither the company nor the customer is completely at fault, suggest a compromise adjustment or offer several solutions ("Because this item is not manufactured to be fire-resistant, we cannot offer you an exact exchange, but we would be glad to replace the fielder's glove at our wholesale cost, offer you a 30% discount on your next purchase, or repair the fire-damaged nylon-mesh back if you wish to ship the glove to us").

> A compromise is the art of dividing a cake in such a way that everyone believes that he has got the biggest piece.
>
> —Ludwig Erhard

- Before sending out a product recall notice, consult with your attorney since the wording of your notice may be important. Most recalls are announced in a form letter that describes the recalled product, tells what the problem is, and explains how the consumer can receive an adjustment, replacement, or refund.

- Your adjustment letters will be many times easier to write if your company has a codified strategy for managing customer complaints. This will allow you to follow and appeal to policy and to handle similar situations evenhandedly; you will not have to reinvent the wheel for each claims letter.

- An excellent resource for those who must write letters of adjustment is Cheryl McLean, *Customer Service Letters Ready to Go!*, MTC Business Books, 1996.

> The customer is always right.
>
> —H. Gordon Selfridge

GETTING STARTED

We appreciate the difficulties you have had with your Deemster Steam Iron, but all our appliances carry large-print, bright-colored tags alerting consumers to the safety feature of the polarized plug (one blade is wider than the other and the plug can fit into a polarized outlet only one way).

We regret the difficulties you had with your last toner cartridge.

We are pleased to offer you an additional two weeks, interest-free, to complete payment on your formal-wear rentals.

Thank you for your letter telling us about the damaged Wedekind floor lamp you received from us.

You will receive immediate credit for the faulty masonry work, and we will be sending someone out to determine the best way of replacing it.

Thank you for bringing to our attention the missing steel pole in the tetherball set you ordered from us.

Thank you for notifying us of the pricing error on the Hansai Zoom Binocular—enclosed is a check for the difference.

I am sorry that your order was filled incorrectly. The correct posters are being shipped today.

Thank you for your telephone call about the defective laser labels—you should receive replacement labels within two to three business days.

Thank you for giving us the opportunity to correct the erroneous information published in the last issue of Tallboys' Direct Mail Marketer.

We were sorry to learn that you are dissatisfied with the performance of your Salten personal paper shredder.

We were sincerely sorry to hear that the merchandise you ordered on July 2 (order # A78110) has not yet arrived.

You're right, the self-repairing zippers on your Carradine Brent Luggage should not have seized up after only two months' use.

You certainly have a right to a fully functioning cordless screwdriver, and we apologize for the experience you've had.

Thank you for responding to our recall notice and returning your last shipment of asphalt. If you have not already received the replacement shipment, please call our 800 number.

We have read with consternation your account of the Walpurga Great Outdoors Stores sailing classes you took.

Although we are continuing to investigate the matter, we apologize for the exchange you had with our dispatch operator last week.

After carefully reading your letter of August 4, I consulted with our shipping department and pulled your records—it appears, however, that we did comply with the terms of the contract (documents enclosed).

Please accept our sincere apologies and the enclosed refund check for the inkless calculator ribbon.

Customer service [is] a constant state of awareness, at every level of operations, that the customer is at the heart of your business, and that being responsive to—even anticipating—customer needs will keep you ahead of the competition.

—Cheryl McLean

MODEL LETTERS

Dear Ms. Osbaldistone,

We regret your dissatisfaction with the Rob Roy giant wrecker truck you bought for your son. We would like to comply with your request for a replacement, but we have fairly strict guidelines on replacements.

It appears that this truck has done some hard living and suffered some of the effects of it, but our technicians could trace none of its injuries to defects in our manufacture.

As a goodwill gesture, we are supplying the missing wheels and returning the truck to you. It should still provide your son with many hours of enjoyment.

Thank you for buying Rob Roy toys.

Dear Gabriel Bagradian,

Thank you for your letter of July 7, appealing the $50 charge for the non-emergency use of the Werfel Community Hospital emergency room.

You were correct. A review of the records shows that your son Stephan visited the emergency room on March 19 with a collapsed lung, not for treatment of acne. We regret the error that was made in coding the reason for the visit and have made an adjustment to your account.

We appreciate your spotting the error and letting us know about it so courteously.

Sincerely,

T. Haigasun
Billing Department

Dear Ms. Duddon,

Foster WeldRite, Inc., is sorry to hear about the loss of your seven-foot Chinese paper kite. We understand it was destroyed, while hanging in your office, when ceiling fire sprinklers were activated due to an overabundance of welding smoke from our crew's work site.

As the Customer Service Department at Foster WeldRite, Inc. is unable to locate a replacement for you, will you please purchase another Chinese paper kite and send us the receipt? We will promptly reimburse you.

Foster WeldRite, Inc., has improved work-site ventilation to prevent similar unfortunate occurrences.

Thank you for your understanding and your continued patronage of Foster WeldRite, Inc.

Sincerely,

Dear Mr. Jerome,

We have received your letter and the socket wrench set you were unhappy with. Hooley Salvage will be pleased to exchange your set for the two smaller socket wrench sets that, together, are of comparable value. Fortunately, we recognized the wrench you returned as one that we stocked, so you do not need to search out your canceled check. And since we have carried that model only for the past four months, we know that your warranty is still in effect so it doesn't matter if you can't locate it.

We note that you have been ordering from us for some time, and we are always happy to be of service to our special customers.

Dear Ms. Jordan,

This will confirm the arrangements made by telephone this morning. We apologize for your conference tables arriving with a center inlay color of Vanilla Illusion rather than the Blackstar Aggregate that you ordered.

The correct order will be delivered on June 7, and the other conference tables will be picked up at that time. As I understand it, only one table of the first shipment was unboxed. If you can have that one reboxed or protected enough to be returned to us, we would appreciate it.

There will, of course, be no charge, and in recognition of the inconvenience to you, we are enclosing a coupon good for $100 off your next order. We have always appreciated your business and look forward to serving you again.

Dear Mr. Luther Fliegler,

You are entirely correct—you were billed for an extra night's stay at the Samara Resort Hotel. Enclosed is your refund. Please accept along with it our sincere apologies and a certificate good for one free night the next time you are in Burbank.

Dear Philip Quarles,

We regret your experience with the Weekend College class, "Pottery and Wheelwork." When the wheels and kiln failed to arrive before the first class, we should have canceled instead of expecting them to arrive at any time. We are, as you know, still waiting.

Ms. Tantamount hoped that students would feel the class was worth their time and money if she provided them with discussions, demonstrations, and visiting artists. But, as you say, that was not why you enrolled in the class. We are refunding your tuition fee; I understand the equipment fee was refunded earlier.

I'm enclosing a catalog for the spring session. If you decide to take the "Pottery and Wheelwork" class the next time it is offered (should the equipment have arrived!), we will be happy to give you a 10% discount on tuition.

Dear Jabez Stone,

We were upset to hear of your experience with the office assistant Webster's Staffing Services placed with you last week—and even more upset to discover, upon investigating your report, that credentials and references had both been falsified. The person no longer works out of our office, and criminal charges are pending.

We are happy to refund the fee for her two days with you. Unfortunately, our policy (and the contract we have with you) clearly states that we are not responsible for damages caused by a temporary employee while under your supervision. Therefore, we cannot reimburse you for the monitor, the task chair, the elevator service repair charges, or problems resulting from the shredded checks.

I'm putting our attorney in touch with you in case you would like to pursue your own charges against the individual.

We've been sending you talented and efficient office workers for 17 years and we have very much enjoyed our association with you. I hope you understand the uniquely egregious nature of this incident and that you will continue to take advantage of the large pool of talented office professionals we can provide to you.

Dear Mr. Magnus,

We were unhappy to hear that you felt the installation of your fiber-optical cable was "sloppily done" and the electricians "unprofessional."

We now have the report of two inspectors, one from our company and one from an independent oversight bureau, who visited your offices on November 11 and 12. Their evaluations indicate that the installation was meticulously done, that code standards were met or exceeded, that site cleanup was faultless, and that, in fact, there was no findable cause for objection.

Interviews with your staff members who had contact with the electricians turned up no negative information about their behavior.

In light of these reports, we are unable to offer you the requested deep discount on our services.

Dear Mr. John Ridd,

We are happy to stand behind our money-back guarantee and refund to you the purchase price of our book, "Twenty Easy Ways to Age-Proof Your Body Naturally." As mentioned in our original offer, you may keep the book with our compliments.

Enclosed is our current catalog of materials for healthful living, along with brochures that you may find instructive, inspiring, and helpful.

Thank you for your interest in our products.

Dear Malcolm Bryant,

We have received your signed copy of the major medical insurance waiver for this school year. The charge of $535 for student health insurance that was included in your fall tuition payment will be credited to your account.

Dear Ms. Carfax,

We are sorry that the flowers you ordered for your holiday office celebration arrived in an unacceptable condition. Thank you for the dated photograph; it was helpful to us in assessing the problem.

It appears that somewhere between our premises and yours, the flowers were exposed to the below-zero temperatures we had that week. This would result in the wilted, browned appearance shown in the photograph. We are following up on this matter with our delivery people.

It is too late to save your holiday celebration, but we would like to make amends by, first, crediting your charge card for the entire amount of the flowers and, second, offering you complimentary flowers of equal value for your next occasion. We appreciate your business and hope to be of service to you again.

> Always do right. This will gratify some people, and astonish the rest.
>
> — MARK TWAIN

RELATED TOPICS

Acknowledgments

Apologies

Belated

Complaints

Credit

Refusals

Responses

3

Requesting and Giving Advice

INTRODUCTION

Obtaining advice from qualified people can be highly beneficial to your personal and business life. The secret is to ask for advice only when you are truly open to it and only when the person you're asking has been carefully chosen.

A letter giving advice may be solicited or unsolicited. If someone has asked you for advice, respond only to the questions they've asked you, without venturing further afield. If your advice has not been requested, you are on less firm ground. Mary Lamb once wrote, "It is well enough when one is talking to a friend to hedge in an odd word by way of counsel now and then, but there is something mighty irksome, in its staring upon one in a letter where one ought only to see kind words and friendly remembrances."

> Advice is like snow; the softer it falls, the longer it dwells upon, and the deeper it sinks into the mind.
>
> —SAMUEL TAYLOR COLERIDGE

DO

- Be brief and clear when asking for advice. Leave any other issues for another letter or your request for advice may get lost in the general news.

19

- Tell why you have chosen to ask that person for this particular advice.

- Mention that the person is in no way obliged to respond; indicate that you respect their time.

- Begin a letter offering advice by rephrasing the other person's request ("You wanted to know what advice I had about finding a job in this area") or by explaining why you are writing (the other person or some third party asked you to write, something occurred to you that you thought might be of interest).

- Follow your opening sentence with a compliment or upbeat remark so that your advice is received in a positive context.

- Give brief opinions, advice, or suggestions. If the other person wants to know more, they will ask. In most cases it is best to be somewhat restrained at first.

- Offer any appropriate reasons or explanations for your views.

- Suggest what, if any, actions you think the person could take.

- Include a disclaimer such as "This is only my opinion, you know," "I hope you will use your own judgment," or "This was just something for you to think about."

- End with an encouraging statement expressing your confidence that the reader will make the best decision, manage the situation, be successful.

- Be tactful. Mary Pettibone Poole said, "Tact is the ability to describe others as they see themselves." Although this line usually gets a laugh, it speaks to a profound truth. Read your letter as though you were the other person. Can you fit it into what you know of that person's self-image? You might want to ask someone else to read it to make sure you have avoided being critical, abrasive, or patronizing.

- Be positive and appreciative when rejecting the apparently sincere and heartfelt advice someone has given you. However inappropriate or unwanted the advice was, you must assume—if nothing else, for politeness' sake—that the other person meant well.

- Write a thank-you note or letter, whether you took the advice or not.

> One way to find out the steps necessary to get to the next position you want is to ask people already there to tell you how they made it.
>
> —BARBARA PATTERSON, NANCY MEADOWS, CAROL DREGER

DON'T

- Don't ask for advice when you already know the "advice" you want to receive. It isn't fair to the person who spends time trying to put together a response and you may be unpleasantly surprised. Ask for advice only when you really want it.

> Don't ever take advice from anyone who starts a sentence with, "You may not like me for this, but it's for your own good—" It never is.
>
> —Lois Wyse

- Don't over-explain or try to defend your advice. It is enough to tell what you think in a few sentences.
- Don't use the words "should" or "ought" ("I think you should..."). An advice seeker is not so much seeking solutions as possibilities. In any case, you have only one limited view of the person's life, so it is, theoretically at least, impossible for you to know for certain the one best thing for that person to do.
- Don't give advice warning others about specific individuals or companies or products; you could create legal problems for yourself. It is generally not a problem to advise others in favor of someone or some organization, although if you are a public person, you could get asked to explain why you *didn't* mention others.

> How could advice be successful? If it turns out right, the adviser is ignored and the advisee takes all the credit. If it proves mistaken, the adviser receives all the blame.
>
> —Carolyn Wells

HELPFUL HINTS

- If the advice is about a sensitive matter or you are unsure what effect it might have on your relationship with the person, consider a referral to someone else. Advice that is unwelcome from a parent may be given some credence if it comes from a third party. Advice from a superior may be better received from a colleague—or vice versa. If you can, find a quotation that says essentially what you would have said—for example, "Starting out to make money is the greatest mistake in life. Do what you feel you have a flair for doing, and if you are good enough at it money will come" (William Rootes). Quoting someone else gives your advice a certain neutrality and distance that makes it more acceptable.
- When giving unsolicited advice, be tactful, respectful, and low-key, phrasing your words simply as suggestions the person might want to think about. In this instance the passive voice or indirect phrasing is acceptable ("If the loans could be

consolidated" instead of "If you would consolidate your loans"). You might say something like "I noticed that . . ." or "Do you need any help?" and, without giving advice then and there, indicate that you are willing to do so.

- If the advice you are requesting involves investing money or a situation that could have significant consequences for you, emphasize that the person will not be held responsible for any outcome. State this very clearly; with a written absolution, the other person might feel easier about giving advice. Remember, however, that you get what you pay for, and you might be better off paying for advice that is so important to you (seeing a financial counselor, psychologist, etc.).

> Here is what to do with hot tips. If you get a hot tip, make a note of it and pretend to be very interested. But don't buy. If the thing takes off, listen a little more closely the next time this fellow has a tip. If it gets mauled, look bitter the next time you see him. He will assume that you bought the stock; he will feel guilty; and he will buy you a very nice lunch.
>
> —ANDREW TOBIAS

- In letters of professional advice (a lawyer advising a client, a doctor outlining a suggested program of patient healthcare, a teacher suggesting special testing for a child), the advice must be professionally defensible and should perhaps include references or sources for the advice. Keep copies of the letter (copies should also sometimes be sent to third parties). On occasion, another person's opinion should be sought to reinforce the advice and protect yourself.
- Depending on the situation, a letter asking for or giving advice may be handwritten or typed. A handwritten note to an employee might be perceived as too personal or apologetic, where a typewritten message conveys a certain matter-of-factness. On the other hand, writing a personal note in some sensitive situations indicates that you are writing as a friend as well as a customer, client, or supervisor.

> The true secret of giving advice is, after you have honestly given it, to be perfectly indifferent whether it is taken or not, and never persist in trying to set people right.
>
> —HANNAH WHITALL SMITH

GETTING STARTED

I'm writing to you for advice.

I'm having a hard time deciding whether to start my middle-aged musical career taking guitar lessons or banjo lessons—do you have any thoughts on the subject?

I'm thinking of switching from the technical to the management ladder. Can you spare a few minutes to discuss this with me?

I hope this is not an imposition, but I thought you might be able to give us some advice about finding a realtor in Atlanta.

I'm in a rather difficult position at the moment and I'm wondering if you have any advice for me—and, no, that is not a euphemism for your time or your money or your circular saw—it's truly only advice I need!

You were kind enough to ask my advice about the landscaping budget, so here it is.

You wanted to know what I thought about a company-wide switch in word-processing software.

Although I liked what you wrote about adding a room onto your house, I have one idea you might want to consider.

You have not asked for advice but because it involves us to some degree, we must say how concerned we are about the calls we receive from bill collectors looking for you.

I took your advice—one of the smartest things I've done—and I'm grateful.

Thank you—your advice was just what I needed.

Whatever advice you give, be brief.

—HORACE

MODEL LETTERS

Dear Valeria and George,

I'm writing to ask for advice. The twins will start kindergarten in Pequot Landing next fall, and we still can't decide if they should go to the same school and, if so, if they should be in the same classroom. You two have done a great job with Niles and Holland, so I thought you might have some ideas. How did you handle this situation? Can you suggest anything to help us make the decision?

I hope everything's fine with you. Hello to the boys!

Russell

Reuven,

Just a note to ask if you've heard about the proposed change in sponsors for the team. What do you know about this? What would you do in my place? Let me know. Thanks!

Sidney

Dear Father Gilbert,

You've known me all my life, and there's nobody who knows more about United Services College than you do, so here's my question: would you advise me to apply there? Do I have a chance of getting in? Once there, would I fit in?

Thanks for any advice you can give me!

Stalky

All of us, at certain moments of our lives, need to take advice and to receive help from other people.

—ALEXIS CARREL

From: Wolf Larsen
To: Humphrey Van Weyden

Would you like me to set up a three-way meeting with Thomas Mugridge to discuss some of the friction I have noticed between you? If that seems unsuitable to you, perhaps you would like to set up an appointment with me. I might have some suggestions for you.

Dear Mr. Dorset,

Johnny seems to be adjusting well to life here and, in fact, appears to be quite happy. We are, however, having some problems with such normal childhood issues as bedtime, manners, hitting others, etc.

Could you please call or write and give us any advice you think pertinent? For example, how were these issues handled at home?

Looking forward to hearing from you, I am

Sincerely,
Bill Driscoll

Dear Stephen Brice,

You wanted some advice about practicing law in St. Louis. I have two practical suggestions: Judge Silas Whipple is looking at present for a law clerk and oftentimes those positions lead to something permanent. In addition, Comyn Carvel has an opening for a stock boy at his dry goods store. It's possible you could handle one or both jobs while waiting for your bar exam results. I hope this information is helpful.

Please give your parents my warmest regards.

Sincerely,
Clarence Colfax

Dear Mr. Warrington,

On our evening walks, we've been admiring the attractive changes you've made to your yard—the brick walkway, the edged flower beds, the new sod, and the serviceberry bushes along the east side. We would appreciate your advice since we're planning some improvements of our own.

Our dilemma was how to ask you for even 45 minutes of your time when you are obviously so busy with your regular job and your after-hours landscaping. May we take you and your wife to dinner some evening? Perhaps we could cut your grass the next two times in return for taking your time.

It is possible too that 10 or 15 minutes on the telephone (555-1234) would be sufficient for the few questions we have.

Thanks for considering our request and congratulations on the beautiful landscaping!

Hetty and Theo Lambert

Dear Dr. Bartoli,

Hello, and how is everything at the Bartoli Small Animal Clinic? I have such wonderful memories of the years I worked there while I was getting my D.V.M. degree.

I'd like to ask your advice. As you know, I'm moving back to Everdene. I was disappointed to learn that you have no openings in the foreseeable future. However, I've been offered positions at the North Everdene Animal Hospital and at the Oak Street Small Animal Clinic.

Both clinics are very fine and have much to offer in the way of a varied clientele and competent staff. Do you have any sense as to where I would fit in better, which clinic would better match my interests and work temperament? I'm having a hard time choosing between them, and would appreciate any advice you can give me.

Thanks!

Fanny Robin

Lena,

If I picked up the cues correctly yesterday, you seemed to be asking for advice about what to do about Donald's unsatisfactory work. I know it's a difficult situation for you.

What would you think of the three of us having lunch together? I could introduce a few work issues and the relaxed atmosphere might be helpful in allowing all of us to express ourselves. Let me know.

Quentin

Dear Amelia,

I would like to ask your advice about what is involved in getting promoted from a T-2 to a T-3. I noticed that you were recently promoted to T-3 (congratulations!) and I thought you might have a few helpful ideas.

Would you be free for lunch or even for a cup of coffee some time to discuss this?

If this isn't something you choose to do, don't give it another thought. I'll look forward to seeing you and your family at the company picnic next week.

Amos

> It's awfully important to know what is and what is
> not your business.
>
> —GERTRUDE STEIN

RELATED TOPICS

Employment

Instructions

Refusals

Requests

Sensitive Issues

Thank You

4

Anniversary Letters

INTRODUCTION

With the ready availability of greeting cards—and a growing number of gracious and artistic ones—few people today convey their anniversary wishes by way of personal notes or letters. However, anyone who has ever received an anniversary card with only a signature at the bottom knows how much pleasure could have been added with a handwritten line or two.

Anniversaries that may call for notice include: wedding anniversaries (with wishes being sent to your spouse, parents, family members, friends); anniversary of a business or of a business association; anniversary of an important personal achievement (for example, quitting drinking or smoking); anniversary of a death.

For invitations to an anniversary celebration, acknowledgments of anniversary gifts or cards, announcements of anniversaries, congratulations messages, or goodwill messages, see the Index for page numbers of the specific information you need.

> There is nothing more lovely in life than the union of two people whose love for one another has grown through the years from the small acorn of passion to a great rooted tree. Surviving all vicissitudes, and rich with its manifold branches, every leaf holding its own significance.
>
> —VITA SACKVILLE-WEST

DO

- Mention the occasion specifically (if you don't know the number of years, at least refer to "your service anniversary," "your wedding anniversary," or "the anniversary of Beryl's death").

- Include, whenever possible, an anecdote, a fond memory, good-hearted humor, or some acknowledgment of why the receiver is important to you.

- Keep track of service anniversaries in your company; sending a note marking the date is generally much appreciated, especially if you add a complimentary remark about the person's work. It creates good morale and company loyalty. In the case of colleagues, personalize the note with a recalled shared experience. Occasionally it is an excellent goodwill gesture to mark the anniversary of your relationship with suppliers or companies you do a great deal of business with.

- End your note or letter with assurances of your best wishes, affection, love, admiration, warmth, interest, delight, pleasure, continued business support, or whatever emotion is most appropriate. You can also end with good wishes for another anniversary period.

- Write close friends and relatives who have lost someone on the anniversary of the death. Don't worry about "bringing up sad memories." In one of her columns, Ann Landers wrote, "I was among those who had the mistaken notion that it was painful for family members to hear references to a loved one who had died. Many readers called me on it, and I know better now." The person will hardly be unaware of the date, and will be grateful for the supportive note that says somebody else also remembers. When someone close to you has lost a spouse after many years of marriage, you might want to send the survivor a special note on the couple's wedding anniversary date.

> The holiest of all holidays are those
> Kept by ourselves in silence and apart;
> The secret anniversaries of the heart.
>
> —Henry Wadsworth Longfellow

DON'T

- Don't detract from your anniversary wishes by including other information or news; remain focused on the anniversary.

- Don't include in your wedding anniversary congratulations any "joking" references to advancing age, incapacity, passing years, boredom, the difficulties of married life, marital squabbles, etc. Clever cracks about marriage may bring a reluctant smile, but they carry little warmth or love.

> Often the difference between a successful marriage and a mediocre one consists of leaving about three or four things a day unsaid.
>
> —Harlan Miller

HELPFUL HINTS

- If you find yourself at a loss for words, most wedding anniversary wishes can be personalized with a quotation on love. For example, Sam Levenson wrote, "Love at first sight is easy to understand. It's when two people have been looking at each other for years that it becomes a miracle." Or quote Pearl S. Buck: "Nothing in life is as good as the marriage of true minds between man and woman. As good? It is life itself."

- Most newspapers will print (usually for a fee) anniversary announcements. A couple can make its own announcement or family and friends can have their congratulations published. Often this is done in conjunction with an open house or reception to celebrate the anniversary.

- Although it isn't necessary to write a thank-you note to someone who has sent you an anniversary card or letter, a note of acknowledgment or appreciation is always welcome.

- If you receive gifts at an anniversary celebration, you will want to thank each friend warmly for gifts as they are opened, but thank-you notes are still required. The party host should receive a special thank you as well as a small gift.

- If anniversary gifts arrive early, do not acknowledge them or write thank-you notes until after the day.

> My wife thinks it's romantic the way our neighbor kisses his wife good-bye every morning at the front door. She said, "Why don't you do that?" I replied, "I don't even know her name!"
>
> —Bruce Lansky

GETTING STARTED

Best wishes for a happy anniversary to a couple we have long admired and loved.

Congratulations on your tenth wedding anniversary!

On the occasion of your 25th wedding anniversary, we send you our best wishes for continued love and happiness together.

How wonderful that you're celebrating your 50th wedding anniversary!

Congratulations on the first anniversary of the Gruensberg Leather Company—you've been a welcome addition to the downtown area.

It's a great pleasure to send you my very best wishes for ten years of doing business together!

Today marks the twenty-fifth anniversary of our productive and happy business association and I want to tell you how much we have appreciated every year of it.

Sunday is the first anniversary of Emily's death, and I couldn't let the day go by without writing to see how you are getting along and to tell you that all Emily's friends here in Groves Corners miss her very much.

You made our day with your warm and loving letter and the funny drawing—do we really look like that?

Thank you for remembering my ten-year anniversary with Lamb and Company—I didn't think anyone would notice but me!

Teddy and I accept with pleasure your kind invitation to a celebration of your parents' fiftieth wedding anniversary on Saturday, December 28, at 7:30 p.m.

Simon and Polly Tebrick invite you to help Silvia and Richard Tebrick celebrate their Silver Wedding Anniversary at a reception on Sunday, May 25, 1:00 to 4:00 p.m., at Fox Hall.

You are cordially invited to an Open House on March 16 from 5:00 to 8:00 p.m. to celebrate the fiftieth anniversary of the Crummles Theatrical Company.

On the occasion of Tidenet Fishing Company's first anniversary, we want to show our appreciation of our many fine and loyal customers with an open house July 15 and a free gift for everyone who joins us that day!

We will celebrate Mother and Dad's twenty-fifth wedding anniversary with a dinner-dance at The Coach and Horses Inn on January 15 at 7:00 p.m. and we would love to have you join us.

> It was only long after the ceremony
> That we learned
> Why we got married
> In the first place.
>
> —LOIS WYSE

MODEL LETTERS

Hi Len!

Just a note to say congratulations on six years with MacGregor High-Performance Cars! We try not to remember what the accounting department was like before you came and we hope we never have to think about what it'd be like if you left!

Here's to the next six years, and the six after that . . .

Dear Aunt Amelie and Uncle Johann,

Congratulations to the two of you on your 50th wedding anniversary! I wish I could be there to celebrate with you. I know a couple of the cousins will be taking photographs the whole time, so will you send me one or two if you have any extras?

I found a poem entitled "For a Golden Wedding" by Katharine Lee Bates, and it reminded me of you:

Dawn love is silver,
Wait for the west:
Old love is gold love—
Old love is best.

I wish you good health, continued happiness, and many small daily pleasures.

Love,

Dear Grandma Annie,

I know you and Grandpa Oliver would have been married 65 years today—and that you still miss him. I love my photograph of the two of you taken at your 60th wedding anniversary party. I think about him—and about you—a lot.

I hope this day isn't too sad for you. Fortunately you have a lot of happy memories—maybe they'll be some comfort.

Just thinking about you . . .

Love from,
Monica

Dear, dear Joan,

A very large truck appeared in our driveway fifteen minutes ago to deliver FIFTY pink and yellow and purple and green helium-filled balloons! The living room is practically impassible as the balloons fill it floor to ceiling. Such bounty! And so like you in its abundance and generosity and love of life!

A big gift box also came today with your return address but Reuben and I are waiting for our anniversary party next Saturday to open it.

We will send along additional gratitude to you, but I had to write immediately to let you know that these beautiful and light-hearted balloons have brought loads of sunshine to our anniversary week!

Love,

Maudie

Dear Lizy,

Congratulations on ten years of sobriety! Knowing you and watching you deal with this tiger has brought a lot of light to my life and inspired me in hundreds of ways. I'm proud and happy to know you. Thanks for being my friend.

TO: All employees
FROM: Martin Poyser, General Director
DATE: May 15
RE: Anniversary reception

Donnithorne Transportation Development Corporation invites you to celebrate with us the 25th service anniversary of Hetty Sorel at an informal reception in the Arthur Donnithorne Lounge on May 23, 4:30 p.m.

Hired on May 21, 1975, as a paralegal, Ms. Sorel later obtained her law degree and was admitted to the bar while working full-time. As you know, she now heads the Corporate Legal Division and has made many important contributions to DTDC's growth and progress.

Please join us on the 23rd to honor a fine lawyer, valuable employee, respected colleague, and good friend.

Dear Ephraim,

I don't know if you've noticed but we've been doing business together for ten years now, and I thought this was a good time to let you know how much I appreciate being able to rely on your good line of business furniture, timely deliveries, quick solutions when problems crop up, your obvious efforts to keep costs reasonable, and the courtesy and cheerfulness of everybody we deal with at Cabot and Sons.

Congratulations on running one of the finest businesses in the area. I hope you know I recommend you right and left!

Dear Mr. Dragomiroff,

It's a year today that you've been catering our weekly lunch meetings, and I want to let you know what a success it's been. This arrangement was one of the best moves we ever made!

To our continued happy association . . .

Dear Pierre Bezuhov,

Congratulations on thirty years as an independent publisher! Two Rivers Press has enriched not only the world of readers, writers, booksellers, and publishing but also the immediate world of everyone who lives in this community. We have access to visiting writers; young people see the value we place on books; and new ideas are constantly bubbling and churning among us. You have been yeast for a bread we all hunger for.

Thank you.

Dear Ivy and Syd,

Happy 1st Anniversary! I have such lovely memories of your wedding day. I hope you have been gathering many happy memories of your first year of married life.

I'll look forward to seeing you when you next come home for a visit.

My little anniversary offering is a line from Arlene Dahl: "Take each other for better or worse but not for granted." I feel sure you each still feel you are a very lucky person!

Love,

Auntie Burtt

> The marriages we regard as the happiest are those in which each of the partners believes that he or she got the best of it.
>
> —SYDNEY J. HARRIS

RELATED TOPICS

Acknowledgments

Announcements

Birthdays

Congratulations

Family and Friends

Goodwill

Invitations

Love Letters

Thank You

Announcements

INTRODUCTION

Announcements, whether formal or informal, make an art of stating essential facts in the fewest words possible. These brief notices herald personal landmarks (birth or adoption, graduation, engagement, marriage, significant wedding anniversaries, separation or divorce, moving to a new home, death) as well as business landmarks (new business or career; new location, branch, subsidiary, or division; mergers and acquisitions; new partners, executives, associates, employees; employee resignations and retirements; business anniversaries; promotions, raises; new products and services; changes in schedules, procedures, policies, benefits; price or rent increases; product recalls; meetings, workshops, conferences, open houses, upcoming events; layoffs).

For engagement and wedding announcements, see Weddings.

> It is good news, worthy of all acceptation! and yet not too good to be true.
>
> — MATTHEW HENRY

DO

- Send your announcement as soon as possible after the event; it should, in theory, reach people before they hear the news some other way.
- Begin with an expression of pleasure in making the announcement.
- List the key details of the news or event: who, what, when, where, why.

> News is only news for so long, so be sure to send your announcement promptly.
>
> —ROBERT AND ELAINE TIETZ

DON'T

- Don't include unrelated information or news. Although there are some exceptions (changes in company policy, for example), an announcement is not meant for lengthy explanations, instructions, or descriptions. When you combine an announcement with a sales message, your letter is still narrowly focused. An announcement can become lost or diluted when it is part of a longer communication.

> Give to a gracious message
> An host of tongues,
> But let ill tidings tell
> Themselves when they be felt.
>
> —SHAKESPEARE

HELPFUL HINTS

- To announce a meeting include: the name of the organization, subcommittee, or group; the date, time, place, and purpose of the meeting; a request to notify a contact person if unable to attend. This can be done by preprinted postcard or by in-house memo or e-mail. To announce a directors' meeting, you must often follow the format fixed by corporate by-laws or by state or federal laws; a waiver of notice or a proxy card is often enclosed along with a postage-paid reply envelope.

- Announcement of changes in company policies, benefits, procedures, or regulations should include: an expression of pleasure in announcing the change; a specific description of the change; a reference to the old policy, if necessary for clarification; an explanation of what the change will mean for employees or customers; printed instructions or guidelines if appropriate; the reason for the change and why it is an improvement; the deadline for implementing the change; the name and telephone number of a contact person for further questions; appreciation for help in effecting the change; and an expression of your enthusiasm about the change.

- To announce the opening of a new business or store, you may want to use an invitation format to ask customers to an open house or a special sales event.

- To announce a birth or adoption with engraved, printed, hand-lettered, commercial, or specially-designed-by-you notes, include: the baby's full name and, if not obvious from the name or if still unnamed, whether it is a girl or boy; birthdate (and time, if you wish) or age (if the baby is adopted); parents' names; siblings' names (optional); some expression of happiness ("pleased to announce"). Birth and adoption announcements are joyfully made today by married couples with the same or with different last names, single parents, unmarried parents, and same-sex couples. Newspaper birth announcements include: the date of birth; sex of child and name if known; parents' names and hometowns; grandparents' names. Some newspapers allow weight and height information and such sentiments as "welcome with love" or the mention of "many aunts, uncles, and cousins" in listing the baby's relatives.

- To announce a graduation, it is simplest to use the printed announcements available through most high schools and colleges. Since space at graduation ceremonies is often limited, announcements are much more common than invitations. There is no obligation to send a gift in response to an announcement (a congratulatory card is usually sent instead), but since many people feel so obliged, it is kinder to send announcements only to those who are closest to the graduate.

- To announce a separation or divorce to family and friends (which is a personal decision), state the news briefly ("We regret to inform you that our divorce was finalized on December 1") or frame the news as a change of address, telling where each person (and the children) will be living after a certain date. (If the woman is resuming her birth name, simply identify her that way.) You are not obliged to explain what has happened; if people sense from your announcement that you are retaining some privacy, it will be easier to deal with them the next time you see them. It is often good business to notify banks, businesses, charge accounts, and creditors of the changed circumstances.

- To announce a name change (legal change to a preferred name, woman resuming her birth name, the adoption of a pen name), state simply that the person will be known by the new name as of a certain date. No reasons are necessary, especially in business, but you may add a handwritten note to friends and relatives if you like.

- To announce a change of address, use forms available from the United States Postal Service, commercial change-of-address notes, or printed cards: "As of July 1 Sybil Knox (formerly Sybil Coates or Mrs. Adrian Coates) will be living at 15 Morland Drive, Houston, TX 77005, 713/555-1234."

- To announce a death, one or more of the following may be done: (1) a death notice, for which there is sometimes a fee, is published in the obituary section of the newspaper; (2) a news article describes the person's achievements or contributions to the community; (3) printed announcements are sent to out-of-town friends and acquaintances; (4) handwritten notes are sent to close family and friends who live out of town. The deceased person's address book is a good source of people who should be notified of the death. The newspaper obituary notice includes: full name of deceased, including a woman's birth name if she wasn't already using it; address; date of death; age at time of death; names, relationships, and hometowns of survivors; affiliations; personal or career information; date and place of services and interment; whether services are private or open to friends and relatives; suggestions as to the appropriateness of flowers or memorial contributions; name, address, and telephone number of funeral home. Since the death announcement goes in the newspaper almost immediately, hand deliver it or read it over the phone if possible.

- A news release announces information of interest to the general public (product recall; annual or quarterly financial report; business anniversary; fundraiser; new programs, policies, executives; company achievements, mergers, or acquisitions). Sent to newspaper editors and to radio and television station news directors, the news release includes, along with the announcement, your organization's name and address and the name and telephone number of a contact person. Address the news release to a specific person; call and ask for a name if you don't have one. Double or triple space, leaving wide margins, and answer the who-what-when-where-why-how questions in the first paragraph. Doublecheck the accuracy of your facts and explain any unfamiliar terms. News releases traditionally have "more" typed at the bottom of each page except the last, which has "- 30 -" or " # # # " to indicate the end.

- Formal announcements are printed or engraved in black on white or cream-colored cards with matching envelopes; stationers and printers can show you sample announcements from traditional to modern in a variety of type styles, papers, inks, and formats. Informal announcements can be handwritten on foldovers or personal stationery. Newspaper announcements are submitted typed, double-spaced, with roomy margins (check with the paper about any specific guidelines). Interoffice announcements (new benefits package, change in flex-hours procedures) generally use a memo format. Form letters are often used for business announcements. Postcards are convenient for announcing changes of address, meetings, and special sales. Announcements may also be made in newsletters or as part of an invitation.

> News is like food; it is the cooking and serving that makes it acceptable, not the material itself.
>
> —ROSE MACAULAY

GETTING STARTED

Effective July 10, our area code has been changed from 612 to 651—please modify your records.

Because of a recent ruling by the Board of County Commissioners, your garbage hauling fee will be increased by $1.60 per month beginning June 1.

It is a pleasure to announce the appointment of George Bonover as Principal of Whortley Elementary School.

The Reverend Malachi Brennan has been named Director of the Lorrequer Human Services Center.

We're proud to announce a new kind of management training for a new kind of manager.

We are pleased to announce even more favorable auto insurance rates for good students.

Broadbent Civil Engineering, Inc., is proud to announce the opening of offices in Denver and Salt Lake City.

We regret to announce that the annual company picnic will not be held this year, due to scheduling conflicts.

Humphrey Chimpden Earwhicker announces that by permission of the court of James County, NH, he will now be known as Haveth Childer.

Please be advised that as of June 1 your D.C. Life Insurance automatic monthly payment will be debited to your checking account on the twenty-first day of every month.

Araminta and William Brown and their children Edwina, Malvolia, Meredith, and Donald have the great happiness to announce the birth of their daughter and sister Velvet on October 12.

Ed Condon and Norman Lorenz take pleasure in announcing the adoption of Margaret Maddy, born March 25, 1994.

Emine and Kiz Tevfik are proud and happy to announce the birth of their daughter Rabia on June 29.

I am sorry to have to tell you that Dad died quietly in his sleep on February 3—he spoke so highly and so often of you that your name was a household word for all of us.

We regret to announce a recall of our Bauersch Circular Saw Kit, Model No. 38A—please return your kit as soon as possible to the store where you purchased it or call the toll-free number below for instructions.

Vanderhof Industries, Inc. is pleased to announce the acquisition of the Connelly-Smith-Dulcy Energy Group, a Gordon-area company with ninety-seven employees that specializes in energy development services.

Blakeney Information Technology Services announces that it has reached a distributorship agreement for its Extra! digital graphics software with Paris-based Chauvelin-St. Just, granting them exclusive marketing rights in the European Economic Community.

Bridgenorth Plastics is pleased to announce the expansion of its industrial plastics division to include plastic scrap pick-ups.

Important notice of change in terms: Effective January 1, 1999, your credit card agreement will be amended as follows.

> Many a small thing has been made large by the right kind of advertising.
>
> —MARK TWAIN

MODEL LETTERS

PUBLIC MEETING

Community Notification of Sex Offender Release

In accordance with the Community Notification Act, the Wingfield Police Department announces a meeting to notify the public of a Level 3 Sex Offender Release.

This offender relocated on February 16, 1999, and will reside in the 800 block of Williams Street.

The offender has a history of victimizing known females.

Complete information on this offender will be available at a public meeting to be held as follows:

    Date: February 20, 1998
    Time: 7:00 p.m.
    Place: Wingfield Community Center
           941 Williams Street

Dear Bartle-Connor Customer,

To remain competitive with other wholesale book dealers, we are obliged to change our author discount policy. As the author of any book we carry, you are still entitled to a 40% discount on your own books. We are unable, however, to continue to offer you a 40% discount on other titles. We were proud to be one of the last wholesalers in the country to offer this discount, but we think you will understand that our policy presented unfair competition to bookstores in the area as well as a significant loss of revenue for us.

Cowperwood Financial Services International
is pleased to announce
that Lillian Semple
has been named
Manhattan Regional Director and
Executive Vice President
effective January 1, 1999

July 9, 1998

Dear Client:

Effective August 1, 1998, my new address, telephone, and fax numbers will be:

Patrick J. Maggio
811 South Tejon Street
Colorado Springs, CO 80903
Telephone: 719-555-1234
Fax: 719-555-1235

We will be in a new two-story Victorian-styled building on the east side of Tejon near the corner of Tejon and Mill Streets (five blocks south of Cimmaron).

For each of you with pending matters, I will be proceeding as planned. For those who don't have current legal matters, I will look forward to hearing from you should you have a need for legal services.

Thank you for your business, past and future, and I wish you each a pleasant Colorado summer.

Kindest personal regards,

Patrick J. Maggio

Three times the wonder,
Three times the love,
Three times the joy!
And yes, three times the diapers,
Three times the formula,
Three times the lost pacifiers
But who's counting? We are!
We're seeing everything in threes!
Caroline Seeley and John Faraday
welcome with overwhelming pride and awe
Julia, Catherine, and William
4 lb. 2 oz., 4 lb. 5 oz., and 5 lb.1 oz.
born September 11
now home from the hospital,
happy and healthy.
And so now we are five!

Charmian Piper Colston and Godfrey Colston regretfully announce the dissolution of their marriage, effective March 3. They retain great affection and respect for each other, and wish to thank all those family and friends who have been such a loving and supportive part of their memories of fifteen years of married life. They wish things could have been different, but hope that you will continue to offer each of them your love and friendship.

FOR: Immediate Release

We are pleased to announce that the Eustace Dabbit Job and Career Information Center has been awarded a $75,000 grant from the Young Idea Community Fund to support its job-placement services for recent high school graduates.

Death Notices

John P. Wintergreen, age 78, of Kaufman Estates. Survived by wife Mary Turner Wintergreen; daughter Diana Devereaux; sons Alexander and George; also nieces and nephews, and colleagues from Ryskind, Inc. Member, Trinity Lutheran Church, Rotary International, Kaufman Estates Business Association. Special thanks to the staff at Trinity Lutheran Hospital. Memorial service Sunday at 2:00 p.m. at the Alexander Throttlebottom Funeral Home. Family will receive friends one hour prior to service. Interment at the Pulitzer Memorial Cemetery, with reception following in the Pulitzer Memorial Community Room. In lieu of flowers, please send contributions to the Southern Poverty Law Center.

Clara Clayhanger and Albert Benbow
joyfully announce
the birth of a son
Rupert Bennett
on Sunday, January 9, 2001

Letters are expectation packed in an envelope.

—SHANA ALEXANDER

RELATED TOPICS

Goodwill
Sales
Weddings

6

Apologies

INTRODUCTION

A letter is often better than a face-to-face or telephone apology because you can take all the time you need to get the words right. It is also better to write when you are not sure if the other person is ready or willing to speak to you. A letter does not oblige the other person to respond immediately; it allows time to absorb the message and decide how to react.

Whether you think of apologies as etiquette, as ethics, as justice, or even as "good business," they are an inevitable by-product of being alive and human. Because we all make mistakes, people are generally less bothered by your errors than you are; write your apology with dignity and self-respect.

Social apologies are written for damaged property, inappropriate remarks or behavior, children's misbehavior, a pet's damage or nuisance, failing to keep a promise, omitting someone from a guest list, betraying a secret.

Business apologies are indicated for late payments, delayed shipments, billing errors, employee rudeness or poor service, defective merchandise, out-of-stock products, order mix-ups, missing components, missed appointments or deadlines, incorrect information, and incomplete or unsatisfactory work.

For situations involving belated apologies, see Belated.

> An apology is the superglue of life. It can repair just about anything.
>
> —Lynn Johnston

DO

- Write as soon as you realize an apology is called for. Procrastination turns writing an apology into a major effort and you then end up apologizing twice, once for the infraction and once for the delay.

> Late repentance is seldom true, but true repentance is never too late.
>
> —R. Venning

- Thank the person for writing or calling, as well as for bringing the problem to your attention (if you were unaware of it): "Thank you for advising us of the error."
- Briefly specify the fault and apologize for it ("I'm so sorry about the damaged book") or, in the case of a customer complaint, summarize the problem ("I understand that you were twice given incorrect information").
- Explain the error briefly, if there are truly mitigating circumstances and if you think the person would appreciate knowing them. For example, a delayed shipment may be due to a strike or to a flu outbreak, and the customer should know this. At other times, however, explanations weaken or invalidate your apology. This is true, for example, when you try to explain why you were rude or why a child said something tactless but undeniably true.
- Admit that you have no excuse for the incident, if this is true ("There is no excuse for what I did"). It is much more sincere and effective than trying to make up an excuse.
- Convey some understanding of the other person's position: "I know how disappointed you must be"; "You have every right to be upset with the situation"; "I understand how frustrating it must be."
- Tell what corrective action you are taking (if appropriate) or offer to make amends. You could suggest several possible solutions and ask which the person prefers.
- Offer assurance that you'll do better in the future: "I have taken steps to ensure that this doesn't happen again"; "The problem is being corrected"; "The situation has been rectified, and a check is being sent."

- When writing an apology to a customer, end with a positive statement: "We look forward to continuing to serve you" or "We value your patronage and your friendship."

> Two words will get you through many bad times in the business world: *I'm sorry.*
>
> —MARY A. DE VRIES

DON'T

- Don't end up apologizing for more than the specific incident. There is no need to get into generalities about what a klutz you always are or how these things always happen to you.

- Don't overdramatize your behavior, failure, or error ("I wish I were dead after what I did"; "You will probably never want to see me again"; "I am very, very, very sorry"; "This is the worst thing I have ever done in my whole life"). Profuse apologies over relatively minor incidents sound patronizing and insincere. On the other hand, indifferent apologies for major incidents sound rude and insincere.

- Don't indulge in agonizing about your error or behavior; it is uncomfortable and unappealing for the reader. Apologize clearly and briefly; don't end up apologizing many times in different ways.

> A general rule of etiquette is that one apologizes for the unfortunate occurrence, but the unthinkable is unmentionable.
>
> —JUDITH MARTIN

- Don't imply that the other person is at fault; some people's apologies read more like accusations. For a business apology, it is probably better not to write at all than to insinuate that the customer is at fault. With a little ingenuity, you can express regret without accepting responsibility for a situation that is not, after all, your fault. When the other person is partly responsible for the problem, apologize only for your share of it. Don't mention anything else.

- Don't try to defend or excuse yourself, justify your actions, or hedge on an apology ("I'm sorry, but I still think I was right"). If you are going to apologize, do so cheerfully and wholeheartedly. If you can't, perhaps you aren't ready to apologize yet or an apology isn't called for.

> A stiff apology is a second insult.
>
> —G.K. CHESTERTON

- Don't blame computers for errors. By now everyone knows that some human had its fingerprints all over the guilty computer; this weak and patently untrue excuse only irritates people. And don't say that these things are bound to happen from time to time. This may be true, but saying so indicates a certain company laxness in tolerating error.

> A multiplicity of explanations undermine their own credibility.
>
> —COMTESSE DIANE

HELPFUL HINTS

- A well-written apology replying to a business complaint can make a satisfied customer out of an unsatisfied one. You may sometimes be able to add a refund, discount, free pass, or some other material apology for your customer's inconvenience.

- Form letters are helpful in apologizing for such minor and routine matters as a brief shipping delay or temporarily out-of-stock merchandise. They should not be used, however, to apologize for more serious problems.

- Although some commercial cards deliver charming "I'm sorry" messages, you will still want to add a handwritten note. A personal apology should be handwritten. A business apology is typed unless the situation has personal overtones (rudeness, for example), in which case a handwritten note is appropriate.

- Certain apologies can be potentially troublesome. To acknowledge in a letter of apology that your company was at fault or negligent could later support a lawsuit; when in doubt, consult with your attorney, who will suggest the best approach to take in your letter. You want to offer an apology that is acceptable to the other person, but not susceptible to building a legal case against you. In a serious personal situation (for example, your dog attacks someone who requires medical attention), you may want to consult an attorney before writing your apology in case it affects your liability. In his article, "Saying You're Sorry in a Litigious Society" (in *The International Journal of Medicine and Law*, no. 7/8, 1992), Ralph Slovenko advises doctors to be careful about how they sympathize on a patient's death. An expression of sympathy at a funeral, for example, "could lead to an utterance which, in the hands of a skillful lawyer, might be turned into an admission of wrongdoing." Putting on paper anything that sounds like an apology for the death would be unwise.

- Parents of a child who annoys or hurts others or damages their property should write a note of apology. However, the child should also apologize in some age-appropriate manner, and it can be mentioned in the adult's note that "of course, Lennie will want to apologize to you himself."

> Apology is a lovely perfume; it can transform the clumsiest moment into a gracious gift.
>
> —Margaret Lee Runbeck

GETTING STARTED

We owe you an apology.

I want to apologize for keeping your hedge clippers for so long.

I apologize for having misspelled your name in my last letter.

I deeply regret the way I behaved last night.

Although I apologized to you yesterday for our guests blocking your driveway, I want you to know how sorry we are and to assure you that it won't happen again.

I really goofed, and am I sorry!

Is my face red!

There is no good excuse for what I did.

I can't tell you how sorry I am about my carelessness with the candleholders you so kindly lent me.

You were right, I was wrong, and I'm sorry.

I can't blame you for being angry—I would also be angry if I were you.

We sincerely regret that our Bundle of Joy bouquet was delivered to the wrong hospital.

We are sorry that your printer was packaged without the instruction manual.

Thank you for your letter of July 15 telling us about the unfortunate remark made by one of the security guards.

As you correctly pointed out, we made a mistake on your last statement.

We certainly owe you an apology for the experience you had with one of our recruiting specialists.

We are sorry for any inconvenience caused by the error in our bridal registry—you will, of course, receive the china you originally chose.

We were very sorry to hear from our sales representative that you are not pleased with the quality of our fresh produce.

Thank you for letting us know about the condition of the dining room at one of our franchises.

Please forgive us for erroneously charging you for a missed visit.

I wish to offer my most sincere apology for the repeated errors you encountered on your last order.

Please accept my apology for the delay in filling the position of training coordinator.

I am so very sorry about telling everyone in the office your news before you could tell them—I can't imagine what I was thinking.

I didn't realize until afterwards how completely tactless and inappropriate my remarks were yesterday—I'm sorry for my thoughtlessness.

I was totally out of line yesterday when I insisted on knowing what your salary is—I can only hope you will forgive my poor taste and insensitivity.

> It is little consolation, and no compensation, to the person who is hurt that the offender pleads he did not mean to say or do any thing rude: a rude thing is a rude thing—the intention is nothing—all we are to judge of is the fact.
>
> —MARIA EDGEWORTH

MODEL LETTERS

Dear Ms. Belvawny,

All of us at Little World Sing Along were extremely distressed to hear that you received an inappropriate adult horror video inside the packaging sleeve of our children's sing-along video. We deeply regret the embarrassment, confusion, and disappointment this caused during your family's holiday gift opening.

We have traced the incident to a disgruntled employee who is no longer with the company. We are enforcing stricter control procedures to ensure that something like this never happens again.

Please accept the replacement video along with your choice of any other three videos from the enclosed Little World Sing Along catalog.

Thank you for your continued loyalty to our mail-order company, which is devoted to bringing your family the finest music produced for young children today.

Sincerely,

Dear Philadelphia Bucksteed,

We at Kipling Instant Dinners apologize for the missing spice packet in the box of Kipling Instant Spaghetti Bolognese that you purchased. We can understand how irritating this must have been for you during your dinner preparations to discover only the pasta portion of the dinner.

Mistakes on our production line are rare but we deeply regret any inconvenience this one has caused you. Please accept the enclosed coupons for two free instant dinner mixes. We hope you will continue to place your full trust in Kipling Instant Dinners in the future.

Sincerely,

Dear Leora,

I don't like being on the outs with you, particularly since it is entirely my fault— I can finally admit that. I made far too many assumptions, and I am sorry.

Can we meet for breakfast some morning before work, as we used to? I'd love to see you.

Joyce

Dear Marius Rennepont:

We sincerely regret the damage your package received during handling by Rogolette Express, Inc. We realize your deliveries are important to you, and you have every right to expect them to arrive in good condition.

As happens in almost every endeavor, particularly when huge volumes of materials must be handled under time pressures and the employment of mechanized equipment, occasional accidents occur. Even so, we consider this one mishap too many.

Be assured that we are constantly improving our processing and handling methods to avoid incidents such as this.

Please accept our apologies.

My dear Melibea,

I owe you two apologies—one for allowing my hawk to stray into your garden yesterday and the other for trespassing when I came to find him. Please be assured that this will not happen again.

However, in all the confusion, I left my hat behind. May I stop by tomorrow to pick it up?

Again, sincerest apologies from your

Calixto

Dear Mr. Hipcroft,

Thank you for your phone call this morning, letting us know you received the wrong fencing. By now your Canadian Western Red Cedar should have arrived and the erroneous shipment should have been picked up for return.

We appreciate your business and were most happy to make amends, as you said, "within the hour." We don't like mistakes any better than you do.

We apologize for the error (which we've traced—it won't happen again), and we thank you for being so gracious about it.

> **An error gracefully acknowledged is a victory won.**
>
> —CAROLINE L. GASCOIGNE

Dear Sid,

I'm sorry. I've been sitting here for five minutes trying to think how to apologize for having forgotten our meeting earlier this afternoon, but I don't find any better words than "I'm sorry."

I hope you know this isn't like me and that I feel terrible.

All day today I was following my agenda for tomorrow. Only when I showed up for a meeting where I wasn't due for another 24 hours did I realize what I'd done.

Can we reschedule?

> **If you haven't made any mistakes lately, you must be doing something wrong.**
>
> —SUSAN JEFFERS

Dear Bryan,

I'm sorry about your frustrating and fruitless visit to the formal wear store. Yes, the average person would probably think "a tuxedo is a tuxedo is a tuxedo," and, yes, there is actually a dizzying array of choices to be made.

Since they now have your measurements, I called and had them reserve what you'll need in the way of jacket, shirt, tie, cummerbund, and studs for the 24th. So you're all set, but I'm sorry I didn't think to be more helpful.

Incidentally, here's the answer to the question I know you're going to ask: You wear the cummerbund with the pleats facing upwards. In the old days, men used to keep their theater tickets, keys, etc., in there—can you imagine?

Dear Netta,

I feel terrible about my carelessness in giving you the outdated national directory of funeral home directors. I'm just glad you discovered the problem before the mailing went out.

My most abject apologies . . .

Ellen

Dear Mr. Parker,

I apologize for the cursory job I did on the retirement-package outline for Portugais-Steele, Inc. I was thinking more in terms of a rough draft than you had intended. As you know from seeing the Chaudière Imports retirement package, which was completed last week, I am generally thorough, detailed, and precise.

I will have the desired preliminary proposal on your desk Friday morning.

> The person who can meet an apology more than halfway and forgive with a graciousness that makes the aggressor feel almost glad that the trouble occurred, but very certain that it shall never occur again, is the one who will make beautiful and lifelong friendships.
>
> —JULIA W. WOLFE

RELATED TOPICS

Acknowledgments

Adjustments

Belated

Complaints

Responses

Sensitive Issues

7

Letters of Application

INTRODUCTION

There are three ways to persuade a prospective employer to invite you for an interview:

1. You fill in one of the company's application forms and submit it either alone or with a cover letter, which is a brief letter stating that the application is enclosed and perhaps mentioning a point or two that indicate you would be a good candidate for the job.

2. You send a résumé, a businesslike and detailed summary of your work and educational history, your skills, and your career goals, also with a cover letter.

3. You write a letter of application, which is a combination cover letter and résumé—longer than a cover letter, shorter and less formal than a résumé. (The letter of application is also sometimes called a broadcast letter.)

How do you know which approach is appropriate? The first clue is the employer's directions: "Fill out an application form"; "Send or fax a résumé"; "Apply to the following department." In addition to applications that are solicited (there is a definite opening being advertised), there are unsolicited applications (you know of no opening but you would like to work for that company). In the latter case, with no directions from the employer as to how to apply, a letter of application may be the best choice. In these cases, a powerful one-page letter that includes résumé material can be more effective than a conventional résumé and cover letter.

The object of an application letter (also occasionally called a letter of interest) is to attract and hold the attention of the prospective employer who is skimming through great piles of mail trying to identify the few suitable candidates who will receive a phone call or letter inviting them for an interview. A letter of application is thus a sales letter in which you are both seller and product.

Letters of application are also written to camps; clubs and organizations; colleges, universities, and trade schools; franchise organizations; private elementary and secondary schools; and for volunteer positions. The content differs from that of job application letters, but the general guidelines in this chapter are still useful.

> The nearest to perfection most people ever come is when filling out an employment application.
>
> —KEN KRAFT

DO

- Address your letter to a specific individual, after having doublechecked the spelling of the name (even if it's simple—"Gene" could be "Jeanne," "John" could be "Jon") and the person's correct title.

- Open with an attention-getting sentence or paragraph.

- Tell why you are seeking this position, why you have chosen to apply to this particular company, why you feel you are qualified, and why you left your previous position. (The latter should be included only if it is helpful to securing an interview and reflects favorably on you.)

- List the skills you have that are appropriate to the job and summarize your education and experience. A letter of application is never meant to be an exhaustive list of everything you know and have done. Select the most important items (and those most relevant to the opening) and leave the rest for the interview. Tell enough to show that you are qualified for the job and tell it in such a way that the person wants to interview you. Don't cram in too much because the reader will have to work too hard to discover the important points.

- Be concise. The letter of application should be no longer than one page.

- Emphasize how your abilities can benefit the company. Instead of the message "Here is what I can do," fashion the message to say "Here is what I can do for you."

- Use action verbs when detailing your abilities and accomplishments (see Résumés for a list of effective verbs).

- Tailor your message to a specific company. Employers can spot a generic or boiler-plate letter, and it tells them you are more interested in a job, any job, than in a job with them. Personalize your letter. When prospective employers receive a letter that has obviously been written especially for them, they will give it more than the sixty seconds most such letters get.

- Request an interview ("I will be in Sacramento next week—can we arrange for an interview?").

- Provide an address and daytime phone number.

- Close with a pleasant or forward-looking statement: "I appreciate your time and consideration"; "I look forward to discussing this position with you."

- Reread your letter before mailing to see if it sounds confident, professional, and persuasive. If you were the employer, would you want to interview the person who wrote this?

> Work is not, primarily, a thing one does to live, but the thing one lives to do. It is, or it should be, the full expression of the worker's faculties.
>
> —DOROTHY L. SAYERS

DON'T

- Don't emphasize how much the company can do to further your career goals.

- Don't refer to negative aspects of your present or past employment.

- Don't belittle your own qualifications. It is good to be modest, but not unhelpfully so.

- Don't indulge in generalities, especially the vague "etc."; specify exactly what you can do or have done.

- Don't use your present company's letterhead stationery for your letter of application.

- Don't use gimmicks, fancy language that you don't normally use, a humorous approach, or any attention-getting device that could well backfire. Conservative (which is not the same as boring) is better here.

- Don't mention salary in your letter (even perhaps when an ad asks you to state salary requirements); save that discussion for the interview.

- Don't refer to yourself as "the writer" ("The writer has had six years' experience as a heavy equipment operator").

- Don't base your request for a job on your need for the job or on an appeal to sympathy ("I am the only support of my family"); base it only on your abilities and what you have to offer.

- Don't offer to work for very little or for less than anyone else; it is poor psychology (and poor economics) to try to sell yourself as a bargain.

Those who aim low usually hit their target.

—DENIS WAITLEY AND RENI L. WITT

HELPFUL HINTS

- The most critical factor in getting an interview is how closely you match the prospective employer's needs. You already know what you have to offer; now you need to know what the company wants of you. To emphasize this match, you need to learn about the company: call the company and ask questions; research the company at the library; speak to people who work there or who know the company. By presenting as clear a picture of yourself as you can, you make it easy for an employer to determine quickly whether there is a possible match.

- Some want ads now suggest that applicants fax materials to prospective employers. Unless a résumé is specifically requested, you may fax a letter of application, either with a cover sheet or with space at the top of the letter for the faxing information (see Faxes).

- To apply for a franchise, pay close attention to FTC guidelines. You may also want a lawyer to help you with some of the correspondence.

- Most individuals apply to colleges or universities or to community colleges or trade schools without too much difficulty. If, however, you are a student at the very high or very low end of your graduating class or if you have special needs (for financial assistance, for example), look for special help in this area beginning with the high school counseling office, private counseling services, and some of the numerous publications available. For some students, the process of applying for admission to college can take many months and requires much specialized information.

- Letters of application are always typed. Avoid spelling or grammar errors, low-quality paper, smudged or hard-to-read print, and poor spacing on the page.

- If you are on the other side of the desk and are asked to design a job application form, familiarize yourself with state and federal antidiscrimination laws. You may not ask applicants for such information as: age, race, sex, height and weight, color of eyes, hair, or complexion; birthplace; dates of public school attendance; arrest record, type of military discharge, past workers' compensation claims; whether they own their own home, have ever been sued, or had a surety bond or government clearance denied; work transportation arrangements; non-job-related handicaps; activities, memberships, and hobbies not directly related to the job. Have a lawyer check the rough draft of your application form for possible state or federal discrimination violations.

> Always be smarter than the people who hire you.
>
> —LENA HORNE

GETTING STARTED

I am applying for the position of credit research analyst that you advertised in today's paper.

According to this morning's paper, you are seeking a storm restoration contractor.

I was pleased to see your advertisement in this morning's paper for a floral designer because I have just moved here and am looking for a position after having worked as a floral designer in Chicago for the past six years.

The skills and duties outlined in your advertisement in today's paper are almost a perfect match for the position I held until recently at Geoffrey Bentley Publishers, Inc.

I understand from Dr. Demetrius Doboobie that you have an opening for a medical records supervisor.

I was happy to learn that there is an opening for an insurance underwriting coordinator at the Roger Brevard Marine Insurance Agency.

Dr. Breuer has informed me that you are currently looking for a part-time veterinary technician.

I understand that there is currently no opening in your office, but I would like you to keep my résumé on file and to be considered for any openings that occur.

After eight years as a senior analog engineer at Blayds-Conway, I am seeking a position in this area because of a family move.

Daffyd Evans told me that you are looking for a real-time software engineer.

Because I believe you would find me to be an efficient, experienced, and dedicated legal administrative assistant, I am applying for the position at Wilson & Bean.

At the suggestion of Wilhelmina Douglas-Stewart, I am writing to request an interview for the project leader position in your long-haul fiber-optic communications department.

My eight years as a food microbiologist at Samuel Braceweight, Inc., make me eminently suitable for the responsibilities of the position you are currently advertising.

I have been managing the Boulder branch of your Sixth Chamber Bookstore for three years. I understand that you plan to franchise several of your bookstores, and I would like to apply for the franchise for this store if it is available.

> When someone says "Opportunity only knocks once," what in the world are they thinking? Opportunity exists virtually everywhere you look.
>
> —RICHARD CARLSON

MODEL LETTERS

Dear Mr. Hartright,

I heard about your internship through the film scoring department at Berklee College of Music, where I'm currently in my eleventh semester.

Although I will graduate next semester with requirements fulfilled for the four-year program with three majors (film scoring, songwriting, and jazz composition), I intend to specialize in film. I view this internship as one of a number of significant steps in bettering my skills and adding to my experience.

If selected, I can guarantee that you will be pleased with me as an employee. I've been a paid and unpaid composer, music director, and performer, and no one for whom I've worked has ever been less than highly satisfied. I tend to work harder than anyone else in the vicinity, turn out twice whatever the goal or assignment is, and am perfectionistic, creative, responsible, and knowledgeable.

My experience with studio work is limited, but I thoroughly understand the function and use of the equipment involved.

Enclosed please find an unofficial transcript, work samples, and letters of recommendation.

I look forward to speaking with you about the internship.

Sincerely,

Dear Ms. Werle,

Your neighbor, Gina Gregers, who is a good friend of mine from high school, told me yesterday that you're currently on the lookout for a lunch-hour delivery driver for your catering company.

I have a valid driver's license, have never had a moving violation or even a parking ticket, and am very familiar with the city and suburbs.

I am a freelance photographer by trade but my income is fickle and highly seasonal (I'm overbooked in the spring, starving by fall, eating again at Christmas during the Santa-at-the-mall photo shoot frenzy, and quite hungry again by spring when fortunately wedding and graduation shoots begin again). I am interested in a steady part-time job to supplement my photographer's spotty income.

I am dependable, courteous, and friendly. I would enjoy making catering deliveries and could even stay for setting up at catered parties when necessary. It would be fun to have a T-shirt made with your company logo and photo on it (my photographer skills to be employed here).

I will call you next Monday, July 16, to see if we could meet for an interview.

Thank you for considering me.

Sincerely,

Hjalmar Ekdal

P.S. Working for a catering company would also be most reassuring during my "lean" months. What do you do with the party food leftovers?

Dear Mr. Kringelein,

Please consider me as an applicant for your advertised part-time position as clerical assistant in your business office.

My word-processing and business computer skills, which you require, are excellent: I am completely at home with Windows 98, Office 97, and Microsoft Word 6.0.

Before moving here last month, I was employed for the past six years as assistant to the manager of Baum Office Products in Philadelphia (references available) on a part-time basis. My duties there included all office word processing, mailing list management, transcription, and such general office functions as telephone answering, faxing, and photocopying.

I look forward to hearing from you.

Dear Ms. Rondabale,

I would like to apply for the position as surgery scheduler for your ophthal-
mology practice.

I received a two-year degree in office administration from Beckford Business
College in 1996. Since then I have worked full-time for Alasi Surgical Associates as a
surgery scheduler.

The work here has been more than satisfactory to me, but your clinic is half an
hour closer to my home and I would like to shorten the commute.

I can come for an interview any Saturday or any weekday during the lunch hour
or after 5:30. If you leave an interview date and time on my home answering machine
(555-1234), I will call to confirm.

Thank you.

Dear Ms. Saverne,

As the result of a telephone call to your office this morning, I learned that Duval
International is seeking someone to manage the security operations of its office complex and that you are the person to contact about the position.

I have eleven years' experience as a security services supervisor and broad experience with access control and with most security systems, including CCTV alarms. I
also have an AA degree in law enforcement.

I was employed by Stanislas & Sons from 1989-1994, and by Barr Associates
from 1994 to the present. Favorable references are available from both companies.

I would like to set up an interview to discuss the position with you. I have
24-hour voice mail at 555-1234.

Dear Ms. Gebbie,

The requirements listed for your opening for an accountant almost exactly
match my qualifications.

I have a two-year accounting degree from Holland Community College (1992)
and four years' experience as Assistant Accounting Manager with Stevenson Hotel
and Lodging, Inc. One of my responsibilities was the payroll, so I am familiar with
and knowledgeable about payroll operations. I also worked extensively with account
reconciliation and analysis, with accounts payable, and with general ledger.

I am proficient with 10 Key, Excel, and Microsoft Word 6.0. My previous
employer particularly appreciated that I am able to work independently as well as to
function productively as a team member.

References are available upon request.

I am very interested in discussing this position with you.

Six months of looking for a job had made me an expert at picking out the people who, like me, were hurrying up to wait—in somebody's outer anything for a chance to make it through their inner doors to prove that you could type two words a minute, or not drool on your blouse while answering difficult questions about your middle initial and date of birth.

—Gloria Naylor

Dear Ms. Jocelyn,

I am looking for a position as an electrical engineer. Several people have mentioned your employment agency as being outstanding in placing people in this field.

I have an M.S. in electrical engineering and seven years' experience in the design of lighting and power systems; the last two years I was also project manager.

I believe my qualifications make me someone you can place, both to my satisfaction and to a future employer's satisfaction.

I assume the next step is to call for an appointment and to bring in my résumé, list of publications, and references. I will check with your office next week.

I'm looking forward to meeting you.

Sincerely,

Dear Mr. Artworth,

We are responding to your opening for a full-time resident manager team for your 100-unit townhouse community.

We have experience with all aspects of on-site management and maintenance: six years as caretaker of the Roland Arms Hotel (we shared the one position, which required more work than one person could do); eight years as resident managers of the Beaker Estates; and the last three years as resident managers of the Burkin-Jones Assisted Living Community, all in the St. Louis area (references are available).

We are moving here to be near a daughter and her family, and would like to find work and salaries commensurate with our work history.

We would enjoy discussing this position with you.

Dinah and Roland Delacroix

Dear Mr. Brandon,

I am interested in your opening for a cargo agent. I meet or exceed all the qualifications given in your classified ad (I have a high school diploma and a perfect driving record, I am able to lift up to 75 pounds, and I can work well without supervision). I am also willing to work nights, weekends, and holidays.

I have been working for Dashwood Warehouse, Inc. for the past eighteen months, unloading rail cars and being responsible for various other warehouse duties. However, Dashwood is downsizing and will be letting go of eight employees, including myself, as of November 1. I expect to receive a very positive reference from Dashwood.

I am available for an interview at your convenience.

Dear Mr. Squales,

As someone with three years' telemarketing experience and two years' experience as office manager of a small business, I think I am a good candidate for your convention sales and marketing coordinator position.

My strengths include effective oral and written communication skills and an aptitude for interpersonal business relationships. I am considered a good team player and am precise and detail-oriented in my work.

I would like to bring in my résumé and references and discuss this opening with you.

The pitcher cries for water to carry
and a person for work that is real.

—Marge Piercy

RELATED TOPICS

Cover Letters

Faxes

Résumés

8

Letters of Appreciation

INTRODUCTION

Letters of appreciation are some of the easiest, most delightful letters to write: you are never obliged to write them, there is no deadline, and the only rule is sincerity. It is one of life's small pleasures to be able to be kind and generous with very little cost to yourself.

Letters of appreciation are sent to employees who are doing "ordinary" work, but doing it very well; to strangers you encounter who, in the course of simply doing their job, have demonstrated above-average efficiency and service; to friends and relatives who have gone the extra mile; to people who have referred work or clients to you; perhaps to people you've read about in the newspaper who have contributed something to our world.

A letter of appreciation is different from a thank-you letter in that it isn't really called for, and the person is in no way expecting it. If Aunt Estrella gives you a gift, you will want to send her a thank you. If Aunt Estrella sends your son a thoughtful gift for graduation, he will want to thank her, but you may want to write her a letter of appreciation, saying how much her faithful support of your children has meant to you over the years.

> Everyone wants to be appreciated, so if you appreciate someone, don't keep it a secret.
>
> — MARY KAY ASH

DO

- Write when the idea occurs to you. It is too easy to think these letters are "unnecessary." Letters of appreciation make the world go round.

- Be sincere. If you find yourself exaggerating or using flowery language, stop and ask yourself what you're really trying to say. Then use your own everyday words just as if you were speaking to the person.

> The deepest principle of Human Nature is the *craving to be appreciated*.
>
> —WILLIAM JAMES

DON'T

- Don't be embarrassed to say nice things. Our culture more often rewards the snappy put-down (with laughter and renewed contracts for TV sitcoms, for example) than it does the positive remark or the compliment. As long as they are sincerely meant, compliments rarely fail to please.

- Don't use letters of appreciation to customers as an excuse to solicit more business or to "butter up" someone for future advantages; a letter of appreciation should have only one message.

> The victory always remains with those who admire, rather than with those who deride, and the power of appreciating is worth any amount of the power of despising.
>
> —A.C. BENSON

HELPFUL HINTS

- When someone writes you a letter of appreciation, reflect on what pleases you about it and what, if anything, doesn't. Then remember this the next time you write one.

- Enormous goodwill can be generated for your business by writing brief, sincere notes of appreciation to employees, customers, or suppliers. Once you start looking for ways to appreciate people, you will see them everywhere; make a habit of sending off appreciative notes several times a month.

> Praise keeps productivity and quality high. This works especially with those who do routine jobs over a long period of time. We all appreciate recognition. No one can ever get too much approval.
>
> —PRISCILLA ELFREY

GETTING STARTED

I'm impressed!

Can you stand one more compliment?

To show our thanks and appreciation for your prompt payments this past year, we are raising your credit limit to $3,000.

I want to tell you how much I appreciate what you are doing for the recycling program in our neighborhood.

The Ridley County School Board would like to add its thanks and appreciation to those of the recipients of the scholarships you made possible.

As principal of such a large elementary school, you may not know what goes on in every classroom, but I wanted to tell you that Miss Eurgain is an absolute treasure.

You probably don't remember me, as I was just one of Aunt Avis's many nieces and nephews in and out of her hospital room, but I wanted to express my appreciation to you for your excellent care those last weeks.

I would like to express my appreciation for the knowledgeable and sympathetic care you gave me during my hospitalization for knee surgery.

What would we have done without you?

How thoughtful of you to let me know you appreciated the interim report—I'm glad it's what you wanted.

I want to express my appreciation to all of you for the extra hours and hard work you put in last week to secure the Gryseworth contract.

> There is as much greatness of mind in acknowledging a good turn, as in doing it.
>
> —SENECA

MODEL LETTERS

March 29, 1998

Dear Dr. Koskenmaki,

I just wanted to take a moment to thank you for your kindness and compassion in helping me deal with the loss of my beloved sheltie, Stevie.

Your reassuring attitude actually made the agonizing reality of Stevie's euthanasia bearable for me. I'm sure that forcing him to continue living on in his compromised and diminished state would have been a mistake.

So thank you, Liz, for being there for Stevie and me. You took one of life's more sorrowful and unpleasant tasks, and dignified it with your caring and professional demeanor. I'll always be grateful for that.

Yours very truly,
Donald R. Cunningham

November 5, 1973

Public Relations Department
North American Van Lines
Box 988
Fort Wayne, IN 46801

Subject: Successful move!

North American Van Lines has just moved us from Ames, Iowa, to Middletown, Ohio, and I would like to tell you that it was a pleasant experience all around. I would have thought the odds were against having so many efficient people in one company, but apparently not.

The reason I chose North American in the first place was because the woman who answered my initial phone call seemed so professional and alert—I decided that if you had the sense to choose someone like her for the front office, the rest of the company couldn't be too bad. And they weren't!

The estimator, packers, loaders, drivers, unpackers, warehouse people—all did a great job. Some 8,000 pounds of household goods were moved with all the care and know-how I would have given them had I been able to do it myself. A 100-year-old stained-glass window, my collections of Christmas plates and Occupied Japan porcelain, and several other valued treasures arrived intact.

The North American agent in Ames was Sevde Transfer and the Middletown agent was Miles Moving and Storage. If the rest of your agents are as good, your stock ought to keep on rising!

Sincerely,

Nanda Brookenham

July 3, 1994

Dear Matti,

Thanks for having the house so nice and clean when we got home. It really made a big difference.

Thanks, too, for driving carefully to and from the Twin Cities. It was a worry to me, but only half as big a worry as usual because I knew you would be careful.

It was so great to see you when you walked into Nonna's cabin last night. And I am impressed that you remembered to get Grandpa a birthday card. That was a classy thing to do. I was so proud of you.

Love,

Mom

Dear Ellen Goodman,

This is a "like" letter. It's almost a love letter. Thank you so much for saying the things that need to be said in such an accessible, memorable, persuasive way. I wonder if you know how many of us start our day by discussing your column. Your February 5 column on the rush to judgment of the Clinton administration was nothing short of brilliant. That's only my opinion, mind you, but, hey, take it anyway. Day after day, you're wonderful, but that column was so good I had to write and tell you so.

No response to this letter is necessary. I'd rather see you working on your next column than answering mail.

I send my best wishes for the continuation of your important work and for your health and happiness.

August 1, 1993

Kathy / Suture Nurse
c/o Emergency Room
United Hospital
333 North Smith Avenue
St. Paul, MN 55102

Dear Kathy,

I hope this reaches you; leaving a message via telephone didn't seem to work. I wanted to thank you for the superb job you did of suturing a fingertip cut on Tuesday, July 27, around 3 a.m. for the 16-year-old who needed to play the piano for musicals that week.

I've never seen anything heal so well or so quickly. He got through the week of performances pounding on the piano for all he was worth, thanks to your advice and bandages. We also both appreciated your professionalism and your warmth. This was a very minor injury, but it's wonderful to know that people with serious injuries will receive this kind of expert, compassionate care. It's a fine thing to be so good at what you do.

Very best wishes to you for personal and professional happiness.

Sincerely,
Varena Tarrant

May 28, 1994

Richard Charles Levin, Ph.D.
President, Yale University
43 Hillhouse Avenue
New Haven, CT 06511

Dear Dr. Levin,

The baccalaureate address that you gave on May 22 was simply stunning. Part of me says you already know this and don't need to hear it from a stranger, but another part of me says we're always glad to know that what we intended was what we in fact delivered.

I can't imagine anything graduates need to hear more than the message based on the words of Hillel and your emphases on critical thinking skills and service to others. I don't quite know how to tell you that I felt your speech was brilliantly and tightly constructed without sounding as though I'm giving you a grade on it. Perhaps I'll just say that your address was an intense pleasure to me. Thank you.

There is no need to respond to this letter. With all good wishes for health and happiness to you and your family, I am

Yours truly,

Dear Bickerton,

Just a note to tell you how delighted I was to see that the first two books you edited for us received starred reviews in the *Gazette*. That's a sensational debut! I know how hard you've been working on your manuscripts and it's paying off for all of us here at Pall Mall Press. I appreciate your diligence, creativity, and expertise.

I knew the day you walked into my office a year ago for an informal interview wearing that gargantuan pin "I am a workaholic and proud of it!" that I should create a vacancy for you in the editorial department immediately. I'm glad I did!

Dear F.R.S. Bensington,

It is a pleasure to learn of the issuance on January 31, 1999, of United States patent 1,234,567 showing you as sole inventor of the food product known familiarly as "boomfood." Congratulations from Redwood-Skinner, Inc. management on this official recognition of your scientific achievements.

As we mark the 8th patent assigned to Redwood-Skinner in your name, be assured that your contributions are much appreciated. Please accept my best wishes for your future successes.

Sincerely,

Edward Redwood

Senior Vice President
Research and Development

Dear Yerba,

Several years ago you wrote a letter supporting my nomination by the Department of History as a Distinguished Professor. I am happy to inform you that I was conferred this title on May 27. I am deeply appreciative of your kind support. Many thanks.

It was a thrill to find myself among people I have admired for years. I feel I don't deserve this honor, but as Jack Benny once said, "I have arthritis and I don't deserve that either."

I'll look forward to seeing you at the next national convention.

Sincerely yours,

Kate

> Next to beauty is the power of appreciating it.
>
> —Margaret Fuller

Dear Ms. Hexam,

During your presentation at the Amorphous Metals Forum, I was impressed by the depth of your knowledge and your creative and constructive applications of it. I am aware of your work in other areas, and it is inspiring to know that you are contributing in several related fields.

Thank you for your many contributions.

Bella Wilfer

Vice President
Research and Development

> Kind thoughts, kind words, kind deeds, how brightly they always shine in our memories!
>
> —Mary Anderson

RELATED TOPICS

Congratulations

Goodwill

Thank You

Belated Letters

INTRODUCTION

One of the hardest letters to write is the one that is overdue. Each day that goes by increases our guilt and our resistance to writing it; too often we end up not writing at all. The most common belated letters are thank-you notes for gifts that we didn't like or gifts that were so generous we were overwhelmed by them; letters of sympathy; letters of refusal or rejection; letters to family or friends who have written us such a lovely, long, newsy letter that we don't know where to begin to answer it; and letters dealing with sensitive issues. (For help with a particular topic, check the Index.)

> Better late than never.
>
> —Titus Livius

DO

- Avoid the situation in the first place by organizing letters to be answered in order of importance. Don't respond to less difficult letters until you have taken care of those on top of the pile.

- Briefly acknowledge your tardiness and then get right to the main message.

> The path of later leads to the house of never.
>
> —DONALD E. WALKER

DON'T

- Don't go into a long song and dance about how sorry you are for your tardiness, or an even longer explanation of exactly why you couldn't get the letter written sooner. This only takes the spotlight off the other person and focuses it rather ego-centrically on you. One of the most charming brief acknowledgments of belated-ness came from my good friend Tom Jones in 1991: "Our Christmas greetings are late this year, frankly for no good reason."
- Don't imply that the reason for the tardiness is somehow the other person's fault ("I'm always nervous about writing you because you write such beautiful letters and I don't" or "I didn't want to hurt your feelings with our rejection of your proposal, so I put off writing").

> Don't fill *more* than a page and a half with apologies for not having written sooner!
>
> —LEWIS CARROLL

HELPFUL HINTS

- Keep a selection of interesting postcards on hand. When you realize you're going to have trouble writing a letter, send a brief note on a postcard acknowledging the issue and saying you'll be writing soon. This greatly reduces the sense of something hanging over you and you'll find the letter twice as easy to write when you get to it because you will feel virtuous for having sent the postcard earlier.
- Address an envelope to the person. Then open a computer file or pick up a pen and paper. You'll feel the weight of a half-begun task pulling at you and you will find it easier to finish it, just to get that envelope off your desk.

- A late thank you is harder to defend than any other kind of delayed message, but it is still much better to write late than not at all. Don't take more than a phrase or a sentence to apologize for the delay ("My thanks are no less sincere for being so unforgivably late"; "I am sorry not to have told you sooner how very much we enjoyed your homemade chutney"). Then go to the expression of your thanks.

- Reading other people's letters will inevitably improve our own skills. For example, Oscar W. Firkins (in Ina Ten Eyck Firkins, ed., *Memoirs and Letters of Oscar W. Firkins*, 1934) had some particularly gracious ways of apologizing for belated letters:

> "I want to write a word to you this morning to thank you for the kind letter I received some months ago, and to assure you that my silence has meant neither forgetfulness nor indifference."

> "Again delay has overtaken me in the matter of response to your letter. Examination time and the preparations for my trip must shoulder part of the responsibility, and the rest must be referred to that immemorial scapegoat, human nature."

> "I have long had in mind a letter to you, postponed by the foolish wish we all have to write more and better tomorrow instead of less and worse today."

Sylvia Townsend Warner (in William Maxwell, ed., *Letters: Sylvia Townsend Warner*, Viking Press, 1982) also did her share of apologizing:

> "It is disgraceful that I have meant for so long to write to you, and put it off for equally long."

> "I have begun many letters to you in my mind, and some even on paper, but never finished them."

> "I have been a Hog with Bristles not to have written to you before—though I got back ten days ago I have not had a moment to turn around in since, not to turn around with any feelings of leisure and amplitude, such as I would want when I write to you."

> "You must have thought me very ungrateful in not writing before to thank you for taking so much trouble about my poems. My time has been taken up with visitors."

We always feel some difficulty in addressing those whom we are not in the habit of addressing frequently; we feel that the letter which is to make up for long silence, and epitomize the goings on of a good many months, ought to be three times as kind, satisfactory, and newsful as if two others had preceded it.

—SARA COLERIDGE

GETTING STARTED

Please forgive the delay in responding to your letter of June 14.

Our best wishes for your 75th birthday are no less warm and heartfelt for being so late.

Please forgive me for not writing sooner to thank you for the lovely and useful fleur-de-lis letter opener.

I've been writing you in my head for weeks. It's time to get it down on paper.

I'm sorry for the delay in getting back to you. I've been out of town the past three weeks.

Please accept our apologies for this late response to your inquiry about space availability in the 1099 Kenyon Road building.

We are unfortunately unable to deliver your order by the agreed-upon date.

We apologize for the delay in scheduling your tree trimming—the cleanup after the May 30 storm has left us shorthanded for everything else.

My tardiness is due to bouts of extreme busyness and bouts of extreme laziness—I don't know which is worse.

I'm sorry—this letter is badly overdue.

"A day late and a dollar short." One of these days I mean to get organized. In the meantime, my apologies.

I hope my tardiness in responding to your inquiry has not greatly inconvenienced you.

I've wanted to answer your letter ever since it came.

I imagine that everyone but me has written by now to congratulate you on your promotion and exciting move to Los Angeles.

I apologize for not having responded sooner.

My delay in acknowledging the touching gift of your father's stamp collection is simply inexcusable.

> Half the good intentions of my life have been frustrated by my unfortunate habit of putting things off till tomorrow.
>
> —MARIA EDGEWORTH

MODEL LETTERS

Dear Ms. Lessways,

Cyril Povey passed on to me your request for information about buying a home in the Bursley area the same day he received your letter; the delay is entirely my fault and I apologize.

If you have not yet made other arrangements, I would be happy to show you some lovely homes. We currently list seven properties in your price range that meet or exceed your requirements.

I would be happy to help you find "your" house. Should I be out of the office when you call for an appointment, please speak to Janet Orgreave, who will set something up.

Sincerely,

Edwin Clayhanger

Dear Ursula and John,

There is no adequate excuse for not having written sooner. We were stunned by the news of Muriel's death—please know that we are grieving with you. Any death is difficult to understand, but a child's death is simply not something we know how to accept.

The last time we visited you, I spent some time reading to Muriel and I was enchanted with her quick mind and her loving heart. I will never forget that moment at the door, when we were leaving, and she insisted on giving me her favorite book. I don't know that I've ever seen a child capable of that kind of generosity. And when I sent her a copy of the book, so that we could *both* enjoy it, she had you send me yet another from her personal "liberry."

If anything could comfort you at this time (which I doubt) it would be that you loved Muriel as few children are privileged to be loved, and you saw that her life was nearly perfect in every way. She was a thoroughly happy child.

Can you come to us for a weekend soon?

With all our love and sympathy,

Maud and William

Dear Walter Morel,

Please excuse the delay in sending you your copy of the signed contract. Mr. Lawrence will be calling you next week about the schedule.

Sincerely,

Gertrude Coppard

Dear Mr. Cuff,

You will receive the ten (10) hanging pedestals (model # 233-1010) for your workstation modulars this week. We apologize for the delay in getting this part of your new workstations to you, especially since you received the other modulars some time ago. Our supplier had an unexpected shortfall of the hanging pedestal.

I hope the delay has not inconvenienced you too much. You are one of our four-star customers and we look forward to doing business with you for many more years to come.

Sincerely,

Rachel Verinder

P.S. Enclosed is a certificate good for $200 off on your next order—our way of saying, "Sorry for the delay!"

Dear Mrs. Carthew,

Please forgive our tardiness in thanking you for your most generous and valued donation to the Community Affairs Treasure Chest. Because moneys received in our current fund drive are being matched, your contribution is a very significant one to us.

Thank you for being one of our most consistent and openhanded supporters.

Dear Mala Tarn,

Six weeks ago you requested information about filing deadlines for the current round of state artist-in-residence grants.

I regret very much my delay in responding. You will know how much I deplore my oversight and how deeply sorry I am when I tell you that the deadline was August 1, two days ago.

I have no way of making my negligence right with you. I can only hope you will accept my apologies.

I have put your name on our mailing list so that from now on you will automatically receive all news of grants, and their deadlines.

> The obligation to express gratitude deepens with procrastination. The longer you wait, the more effusive must be the thanks.
>
> —Judith Martin

Dear Mrs. Tuke,

I apologize most sincerely for the delay in getting our estimate to you. You should have had it within days of our estimator's visit to your office. I'm sorry to say that it's entirely my fault (I put the estimator's notes in the wrong file). I hope I have not, by my delay, caused you to lose interest in Trevor Floor Coverings as the best company to install your hardwood flooring.

Attached please find an itemized estimate of all materials and labor plus information on installation services, site cleanup procedures, and our company lifetime guarantee.

Our policy is to match wherever possible any other estimates you might have received. To discuss this, please call Alban Roche, Manager of Trevor Floor Coverings, at 555-1234.

Thank you.

Dear Sylvia and Austin,

My warmest wishes to the two of you for a long and happy married life are no less fervent for being so very late. I hope you will accept my belated good wishes (and an equally tardy package I'm mailing separately).

Knowing how kind you both are, I expect that you will overlook the fact that my habitual disorganization got the best of me (once again!).

Think about a trip to Florida. I have a lovely bedroom with a private entrance and your name on the door! (Well, it'll be on the door if you give me a couple of days' notice!)

Love,

Aunt Dorothy C.

Dear Ms. Otley,

I said I would notify you as soon as we made a decision on filling our executive chef position. I imagine that, not having heard from us, you assumed correctly that we had offered the position to another candidate. However, I am sorry to be so late letting you know myself.

We were impressed with your credentials, especially with your employment at the Talvace Country Inn and with the references from Ralf Isambard and Edith Pargeter. We felt you would be a welcome addition to Harry's. In the end, however, we decided in favor of the candidate with more experience in our specialty areas.

Best wishes to you for continued success and happiness in your career.

Dear Mrs. Wix,

I am sorry to be so tardy thanking you for the extraordinary quilt. After studying each square carefully, I realized you had "written" the story of my life. No wonder you asked for any rags or cast-off clothing I might have! It is such a stunning gift that I have dithered for days about how to properly thank you for it, how to let you know that I am deeply touched and grateful. There is no way to do it adequately, so I hope you will accept my simple but heartfelt "Thank you, dear Mrs. Wix!"

Would you be able to come to dinner one night this week so that you can tell me all about the making of the quilt and we can admire it together?

Much love,

Maisie

Sometimes I can scarcely understand how I can postpone the writing of certain letters. Strangely enough they are always the letters I want most to write, and herein lies the little seed of my big sin! It is because I am not willing to write a routine letter to certain persons whom I love and esteem, that I fail to write any at all. I keep believing there will come a quiet day . . . when I can quietly say what is in my heart: important things to me simply because I believe them or am troubled by them or want to tell some one who will understand what I am saying. Well, the quiet days are stuff of which only dreams are made.

—LILLIAN SMITH

RELATED TOPICS

Apologies
Sensitive Issues

10

Birthday Letters

INTRODUCTION

Commercial birthday cards have multiplied to such an extent that it is possible to find a card oriented toward a specific person ("to someone who has been like a mother to me"; "to my son-in-law"; "to Grandpa") with almost precisely the message we ourselves would have written if we had spent several hours working on it. As a result, few letters or notes are written today solely to commemorate a birthday.

Even the best greeting card, however, is not as warm as a few handwritten lines with personal sentiments. And for most people, finding a birthday letter enclosed in the card is as good as or better than receiving a gift.

Some businesses (most commonly insurance companies) send birthday cards to their customers as a goodwill gesture.

Ellen Glasgow once wrote to friends, "It is lovely, when I forget all birthdays, including my own, to find that somebody remembers me." Birthday greetings are some of the easiest and most gratifying letters we write. If you are short of self-improvement strategies, you might add to your list the resolve to send birthday wishes to more people.

Let every birthday be a festival, a time when the gladness of the house finds expression in flowers, in gifts, in a little fête. Never should a birthday be passed over without note, or as if it were a common day, never should it cease to be a garlanded milestone in the road of life.

—MARGARET E. SANGSTER

DO

- Add a note on the usually blank page of the card opposite the inside message, or at least add several lines under your signature. If you have ever received a birthday card with only a name at the bottom, you know what a flat feeling it is. You're grateful that someone remembered you, but you wonder for a moment why they bothered. A card should include a handwritten message, even if—in the case of someone you don't know well—it is only one sentence.

- Mention the birthday briefly if you are writing a letter and then continue with your usual news and reflections. The long, newsy birthday letter to family or friends is an exception to the general advice to focus on the recipient's situation when you are congratulating someone.

- Sign an individual's, rather than a company's, name when sending a goodwill birthday card to customers. This is usually the individual who handles the client's business. William B. Dudley, financial adviser, says sending birthday and anniversary cards is a way of keeping in touch with people; he actually sends more cards to people with whom he has not done business at all than he does to clients. "It is one way of marketing my services and keeping my name in front of people. You would be surprised at how often someone will call me who was referred by someone because the person making the referral had received my cards."

The great thing about getting older is that you don't lose all the other ages you've been.

—MADELEINE L'ENGLE

DON'T

- Don't make "joking" references to age, incapacity, diminished faculties, sagging bodies, etc. The "humorous" put-down of age is the stuff of many commercial greeting cards. It's difficult to find one that is lighthearted and funny but doesn't have a slighting sting in it. It's equally unsettling to see cards for 21-year-olds assuming they can hardly wait to get to a bar, cards indicating that "The Big 4-0" is depressing, and cards telling 50-year-olds that they are "over the hill."

- Don't use clichés such as "You're not getting older. You're getting better!" Take a minute to think how you would feel if you were receiving your message instead of sending it.

- Don't include unpleasant news in a birthday letter if you are writing a long, newsy one; save it for later.

> Years in themselves mean nothing. How we live them means everything.
>
> —Elisabeth Marbury

HELPFUL HINTS

- Keeping a supply of greeting cards on hand is the best way to ensure that you will follow through on the thought that someone is due for a birthday. When you set out to buy one card, buy three or four instead, adding the extras to your stockpile.

- At the beginning of the year, note birthdays on whichever calendar you use most. Although this takes a few minutes, it will save you a great deal of time throughout the year. The dates can be copied from the old year's calendar onto the new year's, so that only the first gathering and noting of birthday dates is time-consuming. If you work regularly on a computer, use it to keep track of special dates.

- People who send birthday greetings to many people may want to take time at the beginning of each month to choose and address a card to all those having birthdays that month. On the upper right-hand corner of the envelope, which will later be covered by a stamp, pencil in the date of the birthday. Arrange them in order and send each one off a few days in advance of the penciled date. You may want to write all your letters and seal all the cards at the beginning of the month or you may want to write each one at its proper time. In any case, doing a month's worth of card selecting, addressing, and dating will make the letterwriting part more enjoyable—and there's no danger of forgetting anyone.

- Although it isn't necessary to write a thank-you note to someone who has sent you a birthday card or letter, a note of acknowledgment or appreciation is always welcome.

- If you receive gifts at a birthday party, you should thank each friend warmly for gifts as they are opened, but thank-you notes are still required. If someone hosts a party for you, they should receive a special thank you as well as a small gift.

- If you find yourself at a loss for words, most birthday wishes can be personalized with a quotation; some are even age-specific: "I was grown up at ten, and first began to grow young at forty" (Madge Kendal); "I can't actually see myself putting make-up on my face at the age of sixty. But I can see myself going on a camel train to Samarkand" (Glenda Jackson); "Age puzzles me. I thought it was a quiet time. My seventies were interesting, and fairly serene, but my eighties are passionate. I grow more intense as I age" (Florida Scott-Maxwell); "I'm a hundred-and-one years old and at my age, honey, I can say what I want!" (Bessie Delany).

- In her book *The Bestseller*, Olivia Goldsmith points out, tongue-in-cheek, that it is considered very bad form to wish authors on their birthdays "many happy returns" since to a writer "returns" signifies books that are unsold and returned to the publisher.

- Collect small, flat, useful gifts that can be inserted in a birthday card: handkerchiefs, bookmarks, postage stamps, lottery tickets, art postcards, dollar bills. You can also plump up a birthday card with photographs, newspaper clippings, or recipes.

> The fact was I didn't want to look my age, but I didn't want to act the age I wanted to look either. I also wanted to grow old enough to understand that sentence.
>
> —ERMA BOMBECK

GETTING STARTED

Happy Birthday!

I hope today is a memorable and happy one for you.

It's your day—enjoy!

I hope your birthday is especially happy; you deserve the best.

Here's a loving birthday greeting to a nephew who means a lot to me.

I'm sending this birthday note to reach you, I hope, on the important day.

Congratulations and all good wishes on your 32nd birthday!

It is always a pleasure to say "Many happy returns of the day" to someone as dear as you.

With best wishes to you for many more years of love and health and happiness.

I hope you celebrate your birthday properly—fireworks, brass band, balloon ascension, and three roller coaster rides!

I wish you love, tranquillity, small daily joys, and a few good surprises.

A very happy birthday to a real sweetheart!

Happy birthday, my dear and good friend Suke.

I wish I were sending you something lovely and unique and meaningful for your birthday—instead there is only this card, my love, and, in the bottom of the envelope, a big hug.

How old would you be if you didn't know how old you were?

—RUTH GORDON

MODEL LETTERS

Dear Muriel Joy,

Happy birthday! I'm sending you 6 quarters, 6 colored bows for your hair, 6 teddybear stickers, and 6 tiny horses for your collection.

How old did you say you are today?

Love,

Aunt Dinah

Dear Uncle Ashley and Aunt Melanie,

Happy birthday to one of you and happy unbirthday to the other one (you'll have to sort that out for yourselves; I can't do *every*thing!). Here's the thing, Uncle Ashley—I had a choice between a birthday card with pale flowers and rather sticky sentiments and this one. I thought to myself, "Which one would he prefer?" I hope I was right.

How are you? I think of you much oftener than I write. What I need to do is call sometime—then you can tell me what's been going on and how you are.

We're fine. Charles is fishing in Canada for ten days. Tara has moved to California! She graduated from vet school this month and took a job as a racetrack veterinarian. The practice treats only horses—racehorses or otherwise Very Expensive Horses. She had her own horse shipped out there and last week I put her two cats on a plane—can you imagine? When I look up in the sky and see a plane flying overhead, I hardly ever think, "There go 300 passengers and a couple of cats."

Birthday hugs from

Margaret

Dear Gil,

Happy 19th birthday! Do you believe it? It sounds even older than 18 for some reason, heh heh.

I hope you have a good day—celebrate yourself!

I wish I were the kind of person who would hop in the car, drive to Bridger's Wells, hide myself in a birthday cake, and at the appropriate moment jump out to surprise you. I think this would make a good movie actually—you don't have very many old godmothers jumping out of birthday cakes anymore.

So what's new and what's happening and what's coming down the pike for you? (I show a distressing failure to grasp current slang, but it all seems so largely unprintable that I must resort to the dated, but clean, stuff.)

The washing machine is going, the dryer is going, the dishwasher is going, and pretty soon my printer will be going. I love having all my machines working when I'm not. Yay. I'm varnishing the dining room buffet and my fingers are all sticky and I'm going to hate myself later for using this keyboard with varnishy fingers.

Gil dear, have a good birthday—I hope to see you one of these days. If you ever come up here for a concert or whatever and want to stay overnight, you are always welcome.

Love,

Jenny

My dear Brenda,

Belated but loving birthday wishes to you! How can you stand me, with my laggard ways? I hope you give me credit, however, for the tasteful blending of my holiday greetings with your birthday. Subtle, no? It took me a while to organize this, especially the little Santa tie-in on the birthday card—that was a nice touch, I thought.

I hope your day was lovely and I wish I could have been there as I feel sure you celebrated it in some offbeat and memorable way. I'll never forget the year you invited us to your birthday party and had a bus waiting out front. Your friends immediately divided into two groups: the one that leaped onto the bus, ready for the adventure, and the rest of us, who sounded like six-year-olds: "But where are we going? When will we be back? Is there a bathroom on the bus?"

Whatever you did, I hope it was grand!

Love,

Minna

Dear Debbye,

Happy 30th birthday, my wonderful dear! I get such a feeling of delight and pride and satisfaction in thinking what you have managed to do with your thirty years! Your life is a work of art—your own sweet self, your rare relationship with Jeff, the indefatigable young Mason who is worth a lifetime in himself, your work, your lovely home, that great dog, your friends, etc., etc. Way to go, Debbye! I hope you have enough time on your birthday to really FEEL how good it all is. I love knowing you!

Give Jeff and Mason hugs from me, will you? And Happy Birthday, Sweetie!

Happy Birthday, Mother!

I'll be thinking of you all day today—with lots of love. You might be wondering where your birthday present is, so let me tell you. Go up to the attic and look on my old blue dresser (behind the clothes bags). I hope it is still there! I couldn't help but buy your present over the summer, so I figured I'd just hide it away instead of carrying it out here with me. The only bad thing with my sly plan is that between August and November I realized that it was something you probably didn't really need. Oh well.

I have work and then a meeting and then class and then another meeting on your birthday, but I will call you when I get in—probably around six my time. I hope you have a good birthday until then! I love you, Momma!

Katie

Dear Victor,

Happy Birthday to you and best wishes for many, many more. Just because you never let us have an office birthday party for you doesn't mean I can't send a card, I hope.

It's been great working with you these past eight years, and I look forward to more of the same.

Waldman

Dear Mrs. Gadsby,

We've never met (I just moved into the neighborhood last week) but while chatting with your daughter on the sidewalk, I learned that today is your 80th birthday. I couldn't let the occasion pass without sending you my best wishes for health and happiness.

I'm looking forward to meeting you—perhaps we could have coffee or tea together sometime. Until then, Happy Birthday!

Emma Deercourt

> We are always the same age inside.
>
> —Gertrude Stein

Darling Liz,

This will be your first birthday away from home. Although we never made a major event of it, you were always here at the kitchen table for at least part of your birthday—and I always got to bake your cake! Poor us. Maybe poor you, but I suspect you'll be fine. Actually, I think it's wonderful that we were able to spend 26 of your birthdays together. We certainly were spoiled, having you nearby all that time. I knew we were lucky!

Love,

Mom

Dear Rabbi Wasserman,

On behalf of the members and officers of the Adath Women's League, I send you best wishes for a joyous birthday and a happy, healthy year!

Karen Engelschall

President
Adath Women's League

It's not how old you are but how you are old.

—MARIE DRESSLER

RELATED TOPICS

Belated
Congratulations
Family and Friends
Invitations
Thank You

11

Letters About Clubs and Organizations

INTRODUCTION

Although club and organization correspondence is often mostly about membership (letters applying or recommending for membership and those granting or denying membership) and dues, it also includes: letters of welcome to new members; invitations to club members for organization events or to potential speakers; announcements of group activities, meetings, changes, reminders; requests for volunteers, equipment, or funds; letters of thanks or appreciation for contributions of time and resources or to guest speakers; letters of resignation. Examples and guidelines for each specific type of letter can be found elsewhere in the book (Thank You, Congratulations, Announcements, Invitations, Fundraising).

Most club or organization correspondence is brief, routine, and fairly easily written. But since each letter or notice represents the organization to its members and to the public, it needs to be accurate, neatly presented, and enthusiastic.

Some 20,000 national and international organizations are listed in the *Encyclopedia of Associations* (Gale Research Company), and many other clubs, societies, and groups function in less formal ways to provide people with ways of sharing interests, goals, lifestyles, professional information, and recreational activities. Within some groups, the orientation is primarily social, with members viewing each other as friends. Other groups operate more like businesses, and members view each other primarily as acquaintances. The social or business climate of your organization will dictate the tone of your correspondence.

> To associate with other like-minded people in small purposeful groups is for the great majority of men and women a source of profound psychological satisfaction.
>
> —ALDOUS HUXLEY

DO

- Be brief and organize your information from most important to least important so that busy recipients can see at a glance what the message is, and read down far enough to determine its interest to them.

- Be friendly and tactful; some warmth and good cheer are expected in an organization or club that people choose to join.

- Include in any correspondence about organization events: the name of your organization; the kind of event (annual picnic, monthly meeting, fundraiser); the date, time, and place of the event; a phone number for further information; at least one reason why a person would want to attend the meeting (celebrity guest speaker, awards, special election, panel discussion, book signings, door prizes).

- Keep letters to members businesslike and somewhat formal unless you are writing on behalf of a small, casual group.

- Include the following information when inviting someone to speak to your group: your organization's name; the date, time, and place of the event, with directions or a map, if necessary; the topic you would like addressed; the reason or focus for that particular event; a description of the group's interests and backgrounds so the speaker has some sense of the audience; an estimate of the size of the audience; approximate length of the talk and your expectations of when the speaker would arrive and depart; whether you are paying a fee and/or the speaker's travel expenses and lodging; what equipment (microphone, overhead projector) is available; the name and phone number of a contact person (if this is not you) who can give the speaker additional information.

> A small group of thoughtful people could change the world. Indeed, it's the only thing that ever has.
>
> —MARGARET MEAD

DON'T

- Don't misspell members' names. People lose confidence and interest in an organization that can't even get their names right.

- Don't be negative—at least not on paper. Personality conflicts, disagreements and disputes over policies, and shifting allegiances all give groups their dynamism and distinct character, but they are best handled face to face. Committing delicate situations to letters that go in public files is unwise.

> The length of a meeting rises with the number of people present and the productiveness of a meeting falls with the square of the number of people present.
>
> —EILEEN SHANAHAN

HELPFUL HINTS

- Unless your club is a primarily social one in which the members know each other very well, club or organization business correspondence should be typed.

- Meeting notices, announcements, less formal invitations, and short messages can be conveniently sent on postcards.

- Most organizations of any size find computerized mailing lists indispensable both in keeping costs down and in simplifying correspondence with members. To further reduce mailing costs, check with the United States Postal Service about the requirements and procedure for applying for Third Class mailing privileges, which may be advantageous to you, depending on the size of your mailing list. Organizations with nonprofit status may enjoy further benefits.

- Many clubs and organizations have their own newsletters. While nominally a "letter," newsletters are different enough and challenging enough to merit their own book. Libraries and bookstores carry such helpful books as *Editing Your Newsletter*, 4th ed., by Mark Beach, Writer's Digest Books, 1995; *Starting and Running a Successful Newsletter or Magazine* by Cheryl Woodard, Nolo Press, 1997; *Everyone's Guide to Successful Publications: How to Produce Powerful Brochures, Newsletters, Flyers, and Business Communications, Start to Finish* by Elizabeth Adler, Peachpit Press, 1993. Older books that nonetheless cover important basics include *Publishing Newsletters*, rev. ed., by Howard Penn Hudson, Charles Scribner's Sons, 1988; *The Newsletter Editor's Desk Book*, 3rd ed., by Marvin Arth and Helen

Ashmore, Parkway Press, 1984. You can also find good suggestions in related books such as *Start Your Own Newsletter Publishing Business*, Prentice Hall, 1994; *The Upstart Guide to Owning and Managing a Newsletter Business* by Lisa Angowski Rogak, Upstart Publishing, 1995; and *Home-Based Newsletter Publishing* by William J. Bond, McGraw-Hill, 1992. You might also want to contact the editor of a local newsletter and offer to help out in any way (or suggest a donation) in exchange for learning firsthand how a good newsletter is put together.

> Communication is the essential life blood of
> organizational life.
>
> —ANN HARRIMAN

GETTING STARTED

If you are interested in the Leonardo da Vinci Society, I would consider it a privilege to put your name forward for membership.

As a member and the current secretary of the San Luis Rey Numismatic Society, I'm always interested in finding other coin collectors who might like to join us.

Your name has been suggested to me by Joe Starks as someone who might be interested in joining the Eatonville Business Alliance.

It is my pleasure to propose Dr. George Bull for membership in the New Winton Professional Society.

I recommend Jessica Lovell for membership in the Shore Club.

I would like to present Helena Richie for membership in the Old Chester Composers Forum.

We have received your membership application and we will notify you as soon as we have completed the admissions process.

The St. Sampson Complainers' Club takes great pleasure in inviting you to become a member.

I am happy to notify you that you have been elected a member of the Executive Board of the Plattsville Bonsai Society.

The Board of Directors of the Deerfield Horse Council is pleased to notify you of your election to the office of president for the coming year.

I am pleased and honored to accept the nomination to the Board of Directors of the Ingolstadt Teachers Guild.

I accept with great pleasure your invitation to join the Stanstead Singles Gourmet Club.

I appreciate the honor and kindness of being nominated for membership in the Midlothian Investors Club, but I am unfortunately unable to accept as I am being transferred out of the city.

It is with much regret that I resign my position as Treasurer of the Stepney Dressmakers' Association.

I am sorry to inform you that illness obliges me to step down from the club presidency, effective immediately.

Notice: The Zenith Street Rod Association will not hold its regularly scheduled meeting on April 9 at 8:00 p.m.; the next meeting will be held May 8 at 8:00 p.m. in the Floral Heights Community Center.

Your letter of resignation was read to the Board at the last meeting, and as Secretary I have been asked to convey to you both our regret at losing you and our sympathy for the circumstances that make it necessary.

> **Please accept my resignation. I don't care to belong to any club that will accept me as a member.**
>
> —GROUCHO MARX

MODEL LETTERS

To: Selina, Abby, Clara, Monica, Alexis, and Rachel

From: Damaris

Have any of you met Amy Parker yet—our new neighbor in the house directly across the street from us? She has a son, Ray, who is 18 months old. I'm wondering if we wouldn't want to invite her to join our babysitting co-op.

She seems awfully nice and I see pure patience and tenderness in her dealings with her son. She has worked in a day-care center and is presently pursuing an elementary education degree at the U.

What do you think?

To: Hudson Valley Investment Group
From: H. James
Date: June 25
Re: Next meeting date and agenda

Next meeting: Thursday, July 9, 7:00 p.m., Hudson Valley Bank Community Room.

Agenda: Cecilia Mallet will present half a dozen or so good electronics stock offerings.

Note: We have to be out of the Community Room by 9:00 p.m. sharp so we'll start on time and move right along.

Dear Junior High members of the Pendexter Gymnastics Club,

Remember when you were preschoolers and kindergarteners enrolled in your very first gymnastics class—the fun, the excitement, the thrill of improving your strength, coordination, and self-confidence?

We need *you* to volunteer to be spotters during our preschool and kindergarten classes this summer. If you put in 15 hours of volunteer time, we'll thank you with an all-day pass to The Fortress Amusement Park.

So please, join our teaching team this summer and help these young ones grow, learn, and blossom the way you have!

Dear Marian Forrester,

As an employee of The Ellinger Corporation, you are entitled to membership in the Ellinger Athletic Club for a nominal monthly fee.

To allow you to experience the benefits of Club membership, I'm enclosing a one-month trial membership card along with a color brochure describing the Club's many offerings. No matter which method of keeping fit suits your interests and lifestyle, you will find it at the Ellinger Athletic Club.

I hope to see you there!

Dear Members of the Board of Directors,

For health reasons, I must resign as president of the Greater Chicago Oratorio Society. This resignation is tendered with much regret and is effective immediately.

I have enjoyed my long association with the Society and will continue to attend meetings when possible, but for at least some months to come, I will be unable to carry out the responsibilities of the office of president.

Although I am somewhat restricted as to activities at the moment, I will be glad to do anything I can to help with the transition to a new president.

Sincerely,

Dear Laurence Seldon,

Each year we invite interested candidates to join the Newland Association for Tax Justice. We work to make our federal tax system more equitable, to encourage helpful responses to citizen inquiries, and to convert the present complicated and convoluted tax forms to something more accessible to the average taxpayer.

You have been suggested for membership by Ellen Osenka. I am enclosing a brochure that describes the Association and its activities, a membership application form, and a copy of a recent newspaper article detailing some of our efforts.

I look forward to hearing from you.

Dear Mr. Bluntschli,

Thank you for your letter notifying me of my nomination to the Board of Directors of the Northwest General Contractors Association. I accept the nomination with pleasure and pride.

I look forward to attending the meeting of the Board of Directors to be held on September 18 at 7:30 p.m. in the Association meeting room.

Dear Carrie Meeber,

On behalf of the members of the Hurstwood Business Association, I thank you for the informative, witty, and thought-provoking speech you gave at our November 15 meeting. All who heard you were delighted and several people have already asked that you be invited back.

I'm enclosing the agreed-upon honorarium, along with a small gift that I hope you will find useful.

With our thanks and best wishes,

Hurstwood Business Association

Sondra Finchley, Secretary

The intangible duty of making things run smoothly is apt to be thankless, because people don't realize how much time and trouble it takes and believe it is the result of a natural and effortless function.

—A.C. BENSON

Dear Member,

Enclosed is the agenda for the next meeting of the Petroleum Council, to be held April 21 at 7:30 p.m. in Room 203 of the Drouet Building.

Also enclosed is a survey on the effectiveness of Council activities. Please complete it and bring it to the meeting.

Thank you!

TO: Members of the Upper Midwest Racewalkers Association
FROM: Niel Herbert
DATE: May 29
RE: Regional meet

Our next competitive regional meet will be held at 10:00 a.m. on June 30 at the Linstrum College Stadium (map enclosed).

Although most of the arrangements are well in hand, we still need two judges (call Ivy Peters at 555-1234 if you are able to do this).

See you there!

> Any group has a sense of who it is and what it values, but this sense often remains beneath the surface. A wise leader can discern these unspoken beliefs and articulate them.
>
> —DIANE DREHER

RELATED TOPICS

Announcements

Fundraising

Invitations

References

Refusals

Requests

Welcome

12

Complaints

INTRODUCTION

Some complaints can be handled by telephone. In general, however, a letter of complaint (also known as a claim letter or sometimes as a consumer action letter) is much more effective. First, you have something tangible sitting on a desk—eventually someone has to do something about it. Second, you can often be more tactful in a letter. Third, you are assured that all the details have been conveyed in an accessible form (it is hard to imagine someone on the other end of the telephone taking down dates, names, and invoice numbers as carefully as you would arrange them in a letter). Fourth, you now have a record of your complaint.

For assistance with complaints sent to government agencies or representatives, see Public Officials. For a complaint that you want to have a wider readership, see Letters to the Editor. If you are responding to a complaint, see Adjustments or even Apologies.

> The wheel that squeaks the loudest is the one that gets the grease.
>
> —JOSH BILLINGS

DO

- Write promptly: the facts of the problem will be easier to recall or assemble, and your chances of getting a favorable response are greater.
- State the problem: what it is, when you noticed it, how it has inconvenienced you, what you have done, what needs to be done to correct it.
- Be brief: a one-page letter has the best chance of being read.
- Be courteous: the person to whom you are writing may have had nothing to do with the error and will be more willing to help you if you are not hostile or accusatory. When appropriate, include positive remarks: why you chose that product, how long you have used the company's services or products, that you think this incident must be an exception to the rule.
- Use language and a tone that conveys that you are reasonable, fair, objective, unemotional, commonsensical, and positive.
- Provide all factual details. For a problem with merchandise: give date and place of purchase, sales slip number, description of product, serial or model number, amount paid, name of salesperson involved (if appropriate), your account number or charge card number. For a problem with a rude or inefficient salesclerk, a driver, a belligerent or threatening stranger: give date and time of the incident, the name of person involved (if you know it), where it occurred, names of witnesses, and other relevant details. For a problem with printed inaccuracies, misstatements, or incomplete information: identify the offending article by date, section, page, and column; supply correct data, proof of it (if necessary), and your phone number. For a problem with the airlines: give flight number, dates of flight, points of origin and termination, description of problem or incident, where and when it occurred, what you want done about it.
- Provide complete and accurate names and addresses—your own and that of the person to whom you are writing. Also include your home and work telephone numbers.
- Include photocopies of your documentation: sales slips, proofs of purchase, warranties or guarantees, previous correspondence, pictures of damaged item, repair or service orders, canceled checks, contracts, paid invoices.
- Tell why you think it's important that the complaint be taken care of.
- State clearly and firmly what you expect from the person or company: refund, replacement, exchange, repair. If you want money, state how much. Request a reasonable, possible solution.
- Suggest a deadline for the action requested.
- In closing, express your confidence in the other person's desire to do the right thing and ability to take care of the problem to your satisfaction ("I am sure you will find a solution for this problem"; "I am confident that you will want to replace this defective answering machine"). Assume that the person who receives your complaint letter is going to be helpful and let this assurance show.

> The world is disgracefully managed, one hardly knows to whom to complain.
>
> —RONALD FIRBANK

DON'T

- Don't indulge in sarcasm, accusations, abuse, recriminations, blame, smart remarks, exaggerations, or emotional outbursts—unless, of course, your only aim is to vent your anger on someone. If you want an adjustment, an apology, or other positive response, avoid antagonizing the very person who is in the best position to help you. Negative letters are not only ineffective, they make you look foolish (and feel foolish later, when you think about it).

- Don't use subjective phrases like "I want," "I feel," and "I need." Figures, dates, facts, photographs, and documentation are more persuasive.

- Don't threaten to sue. This is generally seen as a bluff; people who are going to sue leave this sort of talk to their lawyers. You might—if you mean this—say that you are going to take the case to small claims court, which is one way of achieving a quick, inexpensive resolution. (Note that there are time limits on certain legal actions.)

- Don't hint for free products or "compensation" beyond what you are due.

> Savignano's Mail-Order Law: If you don't write to complain, you'll never receive your order. If you do write, you'll receive the merchandise before your angry letter reaches its destination.
>
> —ARTHUR BLOCH

HELPFUL HINTS

- To whom, in general, should you address your complaint? Some authorities recommend starting with a phone call, or with the lowest-ranking person authorized to help you, or with someone at the local level who may be closest to the problem. Only after failing to get satisfaction do you contact higher-ups. Other sources recommend going straight to the top—to the president, CEO, owner, manager—where people have the authority to act. However, many companies have customer relations personnel, and because their principal goal and their skills are oriented to satisfying customers, they may be most effective in resolving your problem. If you receive no satisfaction from the company, you may want to pursue the matter with: your local Better Business Bureau; a local, county, or state consumer agency; the consumer division of the state attorney general's office; your state representatives; a relevant consumer group; a trade association; the appropriate regulatory government agency. When appealing to one of these groups, include a brief statement of the issue as well as a list of all the steps you have taken along with the names and titles of those you've contacted.

- To whom, in particular, should you address your complaint? The short answer is: to a person with a name. When your letter is addressed to nobody in particular, it's too easy for it to end up on nobody's list of responsibilities. If you don't know a name, there are several options. For corporations, telephone the company to determine the name of the person best able to help you. Addresses and telephone numbers can be found in one of the following: *Consumer's Resource Handbook* (available free—see bullet below); *Standard & Poor's Register of Corporations, Directors and Executives; Standard Directory of Advertisers; Thomas Register of American Manufacturers;* and *Trade Names Directory* (all available in the reference section of your library). For lawmakers or government officials, check listings in *U.S. Government Manual* (new edition every year, usually available in the reference department of your library); *Who's Who in American Politics;* various state and federal handbooks and directories; and *Federal Information Centers* (available free—see bullet below). If, in the end, you fail to find a specific name, use an appropriate-sounding title: "Dear Customer Relations Manager"; "Dear Community Affairs Representative."

- For a free copy of *Consumer's Resource Handbook* or *Federal Information Centers,* published by the United States Office of Consumer Affairs, write: Consumer Information Center, Pueblo, CO 81009. *Consumer's Resource Handbook* is designed to help you communicate more effectively with manufacturers, retailers, and service providers. It is also a self-help manual for resolving individual consumer complaints and for improving the way businesses, governments, and other groups respond to consumer inquiries and complaints. It's an excellent resource. *Federal Information Centers* lists centers across the country to contact when you need assistance from the federal government

- Type all letters of complaint. If this is impossible, they must be written legibly and neatly.

- Keep the originals of all correspondence, canceled checks, sales slips, and supporting documents. Make an extra set of copies for yourself, and send a set with your letter. In addition, keep a record of every phone call, letter, or other action you take, along with the dates, the name of those you dealt with, and a summary of the results.

- Don't send copies to third parties when you first write a company; give it a chance to settle the problem. If you receive no satisfaction, subsequent letters can be copied to regulatory agencies, trade associations, or consumer advocate offices. On your letter to the company, indicate with "cc:" those who are receiving a copy of the letter.

- Focus on one complaint or one issue per letter. When you report in the same letter a rude salesperson, insufficient parking, a mispriced item, and a can opener too dull to open anything, you are likely to get (at most) a blanket apology and no particular action on any of the individual problems.

- Place more emphasis on how the problem can be resolved and less emphasis on the details of the mix-up, your reactions and feelings, and what a disaster it has all been. Your letter should be oriented toward resolving the problem or arriving at a solution.

- When you are involved in a dispute about something you bought with a credit card, you will want to write to your credit card company as well as to the company you bought the items from. Ask them to withhold payment while the problem is being resolved (read the information on the back of your statement for details). Give the credit card company all details: your name, account number, credit card statement reference number, amount, store where purchased, and description of the item.

- To protest a rent increase or an increase in auto, medical, or homeowner insurance, include: name, address, telephone number, apartment or policy number, years you have been renting or insured with that company, history of rates, reasons for your objection. Ask firmly that someone call you to discuss the matter.

- When you are one of a large group protesting an action, product, service, or corporate behavior, it is better to write individual, personalized letters than to send form letters or group-generated complaints. Organizations are more likely to respond to one well-written, original letter than to hundreds of mimeographed postcards. In some cases, the great number of complainants may be persuasive, but in general you may be wasting time and postage on mass-produced complaints.

> One quarter of what you buy will turn out to be mistakes.
>
> —DELIA EPHRON

GETTING STARTED

We have been having intermittent problems with your Brill-Oudener multifunction office machine.

I like your products, but I seriously object to your ageist advertising.

I was distressed to witness the rudeness of one of your waiters to an older couple who evidently didn't order or eat their dinners as quickly as the waiter would have liked.

I would like to alert you to a potential problem with your Barr-Saggott tanning bed.

I feel certain you would want to know that we are receiving a number of complaints from customers about the incomplete and confusing instructions accompanying your electronic organizer.

It is with both reluctance and concern that I write to tell you that your son and one of his friends have been setting small fires in the alley.

The luggage alarm that I bought from you on October 3 (copy of sales slip enclosed) shrieks not only if a stranger picks up my luggage after I've set the alarm, but for random, unprovoked, and unpredictable reasons.

I wonder if you are aware that one of your sales staff apparently doesn't know that today it is considered unfortunate, if not highly sexist, to address adult women customers as "dearie" and "honey" and to inquire about their plans for the evening (even when accompanied by a jovial "ha ha," this does not pass for charm or humor or sales ability).

I am becoming increasingly concerned about the way performance reviews are conducted here at Shorthouse Laboratories.

I am writing to inform you of an error on my July 14 statement.

Having received no satisfaction from the employees at your Boston store, I am writing directly to you, as President of Bellamy's Wedding Gown Preservation Company, to ask for replacement of the pearl button that was missing from my gown when it was returned to me.

I wish to register a complaint about the carelessly shoveled (it is barely legal, I believe) and thus dangerous sidewalk in front of your store.

I appreciate your time on the telephone yesterday and your willingness to look into this matter (documentation enclosed).

I'm not sure what could have happened, but the ship-in-a-bottle kit that I have just received from you arrived with a broken bottle and several broken ship parts (see enclosed Polaroid photo).

Of the 1500 ladybugs I received from you this morning, approximately half were dead.

As a tenant in your building at 548 Park Drive, I want to remind you that additional security measures that were promised last year have yet to be implemented.

The later school start times are working a serious hardship on at least one family that I know of—us.

The statement I received from you for my daughter's six-day resident wilderness dance camp does not reflect the fact that I already paid an enrollment fee of $100 (see the enclosed photocopy of the cashed check).

Can you please tell me if it is true, as my son reports, that there is no longer such a thing as an excused absence?

We would like to alert you to a problem we noticed with your heated outdoor pool when we stayed at the Steptoe Ski Resort last week.

I appreciate the work you did for me on the family genealogy, but I must ask you to recheck some apparently incorrect information.

The two weeks' delay in shipping the halogen lamps has now turned into four weeks and I am not happy with the explanations given for the delay.

I find it irritating in the extreme to be addressed by my first name by tellers at the drive-up bank because (a) they don't know me, (b) I have not invited them to use my first name, and (c) it is a nonreciprocal situation since I don't know *their* first names.

This is the second time I have requested the return of my security deposit, which is puzzling since you agreed to return it to me when I moved out on August 31.

I am sorry to have to tell you that your otter hound, Bite'm, has been getting out at night again (none of the others do, which I can't figure out).

Complain to one who can help you.

—Yugoslav Proverb

MODEL LETTERS

Dear Franklin Finer Fotos,

I received the enclosed photographs and developing packet yesterday. Although these are my negatives, the prints are not mine.

I've been sending film to you for over ten years and this is the first time there has been a mix-up. I am satisfied with a record like that. Your past good business practices make me certain that you will straighten out this situation quickly.

Sincerely,

Rosanna Spearman

TO: Federal Communications Commission
     Common Carrier Bureau
     Consumer Complaints
FROM: Undine Spragg
DATE: April 12, 1996
SUBJECT: Operator Assistance Services (800/555-5000)

I would like to file a complaint about Operator Assistance Services (OAS).

I have been billed by OAS for a 31-minute collect phone call made on Saturday, February 17, 1996, from San Miguel, GU, Mexico, in the amount of $180.14 (including tax).

I was unaware that it was a collect call. I heard a foreign language, which I didn't understand, followed by my brother's voice. Only after I investigated the charges did I realize I had inadvertently accepted a collect call. This should have been made clear, perhaps by an operator who speaks the language of the country where the call will be accepted.

For a collect 31-minute call from that city on a Saturday, AT&T's highest tariff would have been $39.31 + tax. Although most of us accept a certain amount of immoderation in fees, I think that charging *four and a half times* the very highest rate is unconscionable.

In the course of speaking to three OAS employees, a lawyer at the state attorney general's office, and several employees of my local telephone utility, I learned that (a) there are many complaints about companies such as this one; (b) most of these companies deliberately use voices and "bells" to resemble familiar long-distance carriers. Most people hearing "operator assistance services" and the familiar voice and chimes will assume they have reached, for example, an AT&T operator.

I urge you to implement some controls on such unruly and greedy companies. I am particularly outraged as I "bought" a service I had no idea I was buying because of the foreign language. Had I known I was buying, I would still have had no idea that I was buying at such vertiginously high prices. It's all very well and good to say caveat emptor but where the deception is clever, intentional, and protected by law, I think the FCC needs to involve itself and tighten the rules.

Please add my letter to your thick (I hope) file of complaints on these fringe-lunatic carriers.

TO: Igen Travel Agency
ATTN: Barbara

Please send me a refund of my check for $50 dated March 22, 1989, which your agency cashed without providing any service or value for it. I would also like repayment for my telephone calls to you during the past two months.

Today, in a matter of ten minutes, I booked our party of three into a Budapest hotel. My first choice was already booked for the dates we needed, but my second choice was available. I am appalled and outraged that you delayed our plans for two full months for no apparent reason. Had you made the reservations two months ago, when you agreed to, it's possible that our first choice would not have been booked.

You did not return any of my phone calls, and whenever I was able to get you on the line, you couldn't talk, but promised to call me back "in five minutes," "by Tuesday," or "immediately"—none of which you ever did.

I fail to see how such a small matter as booking three people into a hotel could take two months.

I will expect a check by return mail.

Sincerely,

Monday July 29 85

Dear Tolstoy Company

I bought a T.N.T. Blazer set today. What a disappontment. I've bougt lots of tolstoy toys but none of them that didn't realy work! for my birthday (April 9) I got the T.N.T. Hazard set that was so cool I thougt all the T.N.T. things would be neat. Thats when I started to want to by the Blazer Blast set. Anyway I mowed the entire lawn twice for 4$ each time so I got 8$ and I had 2$ so I went and bougt it with 10$ and it costed 899 plus tax = $9.53 and it all got wasted. Im seding you the recet and the price tag. Please write back. (P.S. are lawn is Huge.)

Sincerly,

Matt David Koskenmaki

Dear Public Relations Department,

I thought I would add my two cents' worth to my son's letter.

We've been trying to teach our children the value of a dollar, and Matt has gotten pretty good at recognizing what's worth what. I agree with his assessment of the value of this item—it's cheap and flimsy and doesn't work—and I want to say that this isn't worthy of you, Tolstoy. We've been some of your greatest fans for years. I can't remember how many times we've taken the tour through the Tolstoy factory (when they used to give them) or how many Tolstoy cars, trucks, and horse trailer sets I've bought over the years for our own and other children.

I tried to discourage my son from spending his money on this item. It didn't seem to me to be a toy with many possibilities, which is one of the criteria I use in buying toys. However, in the end, I saw the Tolstoy name and thought—for my sins!—it can't be too bad if it's Tolstoy. And that's why I feel a bit cheated.

I don't know what you can do about this, but there were a lot of strong feelings around here today so we had to write. I would like to hear what you think about all this.

Sincerely,

R. Koskenmaki

There is hardly a problem, no matter how complicated it is, that when looked at in the right way doesn't become still more complicated.

—Peg Bracken

Dear Customer Service,

Re: All-Purpose Economy Cart, Model # MA-129
    Invoice # 667-8910
    September 19, 2000

We have just received the thermoplastic all-purpose equipment cart, which was to have had heavy-duty swivel casters, two of which were locking. However, none of the four casters appear to lock, which makes it difficult and awkward to maneuver the cart.

Should we return the entire cart for an exchange (I assume you will pay the cost of returning it), or are there caster assembly parts that can be sent to us to replace the ones we have? Something needs to be done as this spanking new cart handles worse than our old one. And costs a good deal more.

I look forward to hearing from you promptly.

To: Customer Services

Last week I purchased a Contemporary office wall clock, model # 1200B (photocopy of barcode, store receipt, and credit charge slip are enclosed).

I bought this particular clock because I had previously owned the same model and liked it. My former clock "died" last week, although its death was somewhat perplexing. The battery was still good, the second hand continued to move, but only in a hiccupping manner. The other hands stopped at 8:43. The clock would work when placed flat on a desktop, but would resume its 8:43 position when remounted on the wall.

Imagine my astonishment when my brand-new Contemporary office wall clock also stalled out at precisely 8:43. Once again, the battery worked, the second hand fluttered minutely in place, and the hour and minute hands had only one thing to say. As nearly as I can tell, nothing is caught or stuck. I can only assume there is some design error that causes this model to stop at 8:43.

I now own two identical, lovely, but useless Contemporary wall clocks.

What do you suggest?

> While not exactly disgruntled, he was far from feeling gruntled.
>
> —P.G. WODEHOUSE

To: Conrad Lyte
From: Archibald Purdy
Re: Simplex Wrench II
Date: September 3

Field tests of the Simplex Wrench II are turning up a few problems. In analyzing the scaling-up process, it has become clear that we received far too little feedback from your sector. Information that should have been made available to Production was never conveyed to them.

Please analyze the role of your sector with respect to the Simplex Wrench II, discuss the situation with your staff, and then let me know what you think could have been done differently and what we can do to avoid similar problems in the future.

Dear Hezekiah Biles,

As you know, we require that rent be paid by the 5th of each month. In the eight months you have lived at 548 Tower Avenue, we have not yet received your check by the due date.

In the past, we have found a solution to our bookkeeping problems is to request an additional month's rent deposit from late-paying tenants. In that way, we always have the current month's rent in hand.

Unless we receive your next rent payment by September 5, we will need an additional month's rent deposit. Please reread your lease for the terms under which we can ask you to vacate the apartment—one of them is nonpayment or late payment of rent.

Thank you for your immediate attention to this matter.

Dear Mr. Blazey,

We are becoming increasingly dissatisfied with the industrial machine maintenance service supplied by your company.

Although our contract specifies weekly inspections, our records show there were no inspections during the following weeks: April 12, May 3, May 17, June 14, June 28.

In addition, we have had two machine breakdowns serious enough to halt work. They had to be dealt with on an emergency basis. We have a maintenance service contract to avoid this very situation.

Although we understand the occasional unforeseen problem, we are seeing a pattern of inadequate service.

We are prepared to see how the next month goes. If service has not improved as of September 1, we will have cause to void our contract and seek another maintenance service company. It is more convenient for us, of course, to avoid doing that, so we hope you can provide the kind of service we originally contracted for.

Dear Mr. Blackmore,

I generally receive the interest statement on my Bundelcund Bank home-equity line of credit loan on the 25th of each month. The interest is due by the end of the month. This means I must get the payment in the mail the same day to assure its delivery by the due date or, if I am feeling insecure about an intervening weekend or postal service delays, I must drive it over to the bank to avoid paying interest on the interest.

I receive no other bill that expects payment by return mail.

Please adjust my billing cycle to allow for reasonable delays, for late postal deliveries, for the possibility that I might be out of town for a day. Most companies allow at least two weeks between the arrival of a bill or invoice and its due date.

Sincerely,

Dear Mrs. D. Barley,

Your check # 15178, made out to Dunbury Florists in the amount of $57.83, has been returned by your bank. Normally we assess a $15 charge in addition to collecting the face amount of the check. However, I see that you notified us about your stolen purse and the possibility that your check might be returned.

You have been a frequent customer at Dunbury Florists for some years and I am pleased to waive the $15 charge in your case.

Thank you for replacing this check as soon as possible.

> When people cease to complain, they cease to think.
>
> —NAPOLEON I

July 29, 1985

To: Medical Benefits
From: Godfrey Ablewhite
Date: January 12, 1995
Re: Employee ID # 484941530

Enclosed is a check for the current monthly payment covering the period 2-1-95 to 2-28-95.

Also enclosed is a photocopy of my last check, cashed by you—of which you apparently have no record. Please verify that our account has been credited with the $188 sent you in December.

I look forward to receiving either written or telephone confirmation that our records agree.

RELATED TOPICS

Acknowledgments
Adjustments
Apologies
Neighbors
Orders
Responses

13

Congratulations

INTRODUCTION

Some of the most delightful mail we receive—right up there with "I love you"—is the letter that begins, "Congratulations!" Because it is rarely obligatory and because its contents are wholly positive, the congratulations letter adds a glow to any personal or business relationship. You don't have to wait for big news—small landmarks and successes have a sweetness all their own, and the recipient of your note will long remember your thoughtfulness.

There is no dearth of reasons to send a congratulations letter: birth or adoption of a baby; bar mitzvah or bat mitzvah, confirmation, ordination, religious milestones; graduation; engagement, marriage; successful game, sports season, play, concert, art exhibit; new home; award, honor, election, appointment, achievement; speech, publication, public recognition; new business, account, contract, product, store, location, merger; good business year, company success; new job, position; business or military promotion; retirement.

Sometimes a "congratulations" approach is used in sales letters, but this is more sales than congratulations since the congratulations are impersonal (see Sales).

For birthday, anniversary, or engagement and wedding congratulations, see the appropriate chapter.

> If you think a complimentary thought about someone, don't just think it. Dare to compliment people and pass on compliments to them from others.
>
> —CATHERINE PONDER

DO

- Write as soon as possible after hearing the news. Congratulations are best served up warm. (If you're late, write anyway; people always enjoy this type of mail. Apologize only briefly for the delay.)

- Mention the specific reason for your congratulations (graduation, new business, promotion, honor, baby, accomplishment).

- Tell how happy, pleased, proud, or impressed you are—and why.

- Stay focused on the good news. Save other issues, questions, information, sales messages, or work matters for another day. Don't compare the recipient's news to something you once did or to something you read in the paper; let the person enjoy a moment in the sun—alone.

- If appropriate, tell how you heard the good news (if you saw it in the newspaper, you may want to enclose the clipping).

- Relate an anecdote, shared memory, or reflection that has some bearing on the occasion.

- In closing, wish the person continued success and happiness, express your confidence in a bright future, or assure them of your best wishes, affection, love, admiration, warmth, interest, delight, pleasure, continued business support, or good wishes.

> A little praise is not only merest justice but is beyond the purse of no one.
>
> —EMILY POST

DON'T

- Don't put a negative spin on your congratulations. Instead of "I never would have thought you could do it" or "After all this time, you finally did it," say "I'm so impressed with your energy and determination" or "Congratulations on your hard work and perseverance."
- Don't exaggerate the situation or indulge in unrealistic and excessive flattery ("watch out, Corporate America—here she comes," "I can see that I'll soon be writing to congratulate you on the Nobel Prize"). It makes people uncomfortable. A simple congratulations and a few personal remarks bring quite enough joy on their own.
- Don't talk about "luck" when congratulating someone; it implies that chance rather than talent and hard work was responsible for the success.

> Everybody knows how to utter a complaint, but few can express a graceful compliment.
>
> —WILLIAM FEATHER

HELPFUL HINTS

- Written congratulations are required only when you have received an announcement of some personal news (for example, a wedding or a graduation).
- Commercial cards are available for almost every occasion that calls for congratulations. However, add more than your signature, even if it's just a promise to call or write later. Best of all is a personal message of shared pleasure and admiration. The classic message of congratulations is a handwritten note on personal stationery. Congratulations to people with whom you have a business or more formal relationship may be typed.
- Promotion congratulations to an employee should emphasize that the promotion is the consequence of outstanding work and also point to future responsibilities, challenges, or satisfactions.
- It is good public relations to write notes of congratulations to customers, clients, suppliers, colleagues, and other business associates when there is good news (births, weddings, promotions, new business). It is one of the few times you contact such individuals without requiring something in return and is thus effective in establishing business loyalty.

- In the case of an adoption, don't write or imply, "I'll bet you get pregnant now." People adopt for reasons other than fertility, and adoption is not a cure for infertility (pregnancies after adoption occur at about the same rate as in couples dealing with infertility). Don't ask about the child's background or biological or birth parents (never write "real parents"; you are writing to the real parents). Don't say you admire your friends for adopting anymore than you would admire a biological parent for having a child. Instead, ask the parents to tell you all about the child and the great arrival day, say that you can't wait to come visit, and wish them all much happiness.

- In the case of multiple births, don't ask if she took fertility pills and don't say or imply, "You poor things!" Just say "Congratulations!" In the case of a premature baby, send congratulations, gifts, and warm wishes as you would normally; do not wait to see how the baby does.

- In the case of the birth of a child with defects or a disability, write that you've heard they have a new little one, that there seem to be some problems, that you are thinking of them. Avoid commercial "new baby" cards and conventional congratulations on the one hand, and expressions of sympathy on the other. Some of the unfortunate remarks that these new parents have had to hear from "friends" include: "You're not going to keep it, are you?" "I think you should sue the hospital." "Is one of you a carrier for this?" "Maybe the baby won't live; that would be best all around." "Whose fault was it?" "Did you drink while you were pregnant?" "I guess it could have been worse." "God only sends burdens to those who can bear them." Until you know how the parents are feeling (devastated, concerned but optimistic, happy to have the child at any price), do not reveal your own feelings—they may be wide of the mark. Later, when you know how the parents are feeling, you can respond on a more emotional level.

- Many newspapers offer opportunities for family, friends, or business associates to make public their congratulations.

- Congratulations are often appreciated on the anniversary of some significant personal achievement—abstaining from smoking or drinking, for example—but be certain you are on close enough terms to offer them. It is rarely appropriate in the case of business acquaintances or casual friendships.

> To rejoice with one's neighbor's joys is no less a duty . . . than to grieve with his grief.
>
> —LADY KATIE MAGNUS

GETTING STARTED

Congratulations on your election to the Leys College Board of Directors.

I am almost as delighted as you must be about the birth of your beautiful daughter—congratulations to you both and best wishes to the three of you!

Congratulations on the birth of your son—may he have much health, happiness, and love in his life.

Congratulations on an outstanding first year at Langdon Towne Graphics.

I couldn't let this happy occasion go by without wishing you both many years of health and happiness in your new home.

Congratulations on your promotion to division credit manager!

Congratulations to you as project leader on the outstanding success of the new desalinization technology.

This is to extend to you and your staff my heartiest congratulations on last month's sales record.

Your department certainly hasn't let any grass grow under its feet—congratulations to all of you on the rapid completion of the Bourchier project.

I was pleased to hear that you are now Supervisor of Information Systems in the Colleton Public Schools—congratulations!

Anthony just told us the wonderful news about your research fellowship—good for you!

I've just heard from Choi Nam-Sun that two of your poems will be included in the next issue—congratulations!

It was a pleasure to read in last night's paper of your being named president of Otway-Bethel Creative Expressions—my heartiest congratulations!

Please accept the congratulations of everyone here at Avonia-Bunn Title Insurance Company on your Outstanding Service Award.

Congratulations on your landslide election to the Calaveras County Board of Examiners.

Congratulations on opening your own chiropractic office!

May your first twenty years of business success and community service serve as the inspiration for the next twenty.

Well done!

I am so impressed!

What terrific news!

My hat's off to you!

You've done it again!

Good news travels fast!

I wanted you to know how proud and happy I was to hear that your short will be shown at the Brooklyn Film Festival.

Eph and I are so proud of you!

I've just finished reading the wonderful article in the paper about your new composition, "Amalgamations," and I wanted to congratulate you on your talent, hard work, and success!

The news about your promotion to agency manager just made my day!

Congratulations on forty years of outstanding contributions to Heaslop-Moore Plastics.

I was delighted to receive the announcement of your graduation from the University of Minnesota School of Veterinary Medicine—congratulations!

Aunt Evalina told us about your "dramatic" success—congratulations on what was evidently a stunning performance.

> Nothing makes people so worthy of compliments as occasionally receiving them. One is more delightful for being told one is delightful—just as one is more angry for being told one is angry.
>
> —KATHERINE FULLERTON GEROULD

MODEL LETTERS

Dear Buckie,

Congratulations on receiving your medical degree! None of us understands how you survived such a grueling course, especially as the single mother of three. We still miss Eric, and I know you do, too—that's been another very hard thing for you these past few years. I know he would be happy and proud to know what you've accomplished.

I'm sending your name and office address to everyone I know in the Santa Fe area, in case they need the services of a very fine physician.

All the best,

Dear Gavin,

I was pleased to hear the news of your promotion to Director of Development. We'll miss you here in the marketing department, but everyone is delighted for you.

Although Ralph Waldo Emerson said, "The reward of a thing well done is to have done it," I always think it never hurts to get a little recognition and maybe a promotion! Congratulations on this most appropriate and well-warranted one.

Hi Paul!

I heard that you're working on a sensational collaboration with Jacques Dechartre. I've admired his sculpture for years and I can see why he would appreciate your work. Congratulations, and best wishes on the completion of the project!

Dear Sheila,

Congratulations on the opening of The Dublin Walk! I wish you all the best of luck with this exciting new venture. Your location couldn't be better, the time is right for an Irish gift shop in this area, and you are so creative and hardworking that I know the store will be a runaway success.

If you have any extra flyers, I'd be glad to pass them on to friends.

Dear Friends at Auerbach Motors,

Congratulations on your first ten years in business! May you have ten more, and ten more, and ten more. . . . The write-up in the paper about those first years was very interesting.

We have always appreciated your business, and look forward to many more years of serving you.

Dear Janna,

Congratulations on your first year with SkiHill, Inc. We have all appreciated your many talents and contributions, especially your successful computerization of the accounts department.

We hope you will be with us for many more years. I'm enclosing a gift certificate for two to Mario's Ristorante with thanks from all of us for your outstanding work.

> I can live for two months on a good compliment.
>
> — MARK TWAIN

Dear Winnie and Ed,

Congratulations to you both on the twenty-fifth anniversary of Leitner's Heating & Plumbing. As you know by now, you're our best (our only!) supplier, and the reason is simple: you're a class act. Quality and competence have paid off for you, and nobody could be happier for you than I. Best wishes with the next twenty-five years.

Dear Adela,

Congratulations on your retirement! I'm as happy for you as I am sad for us. At last you'll be able to do some of the things you've talked about doing for years, especially the fishing up north. But I don't know how we're going to get along without you around here. Dr. Aziz may think he runs the department, but everybody knows that when you really want to find something or get anything done, Adela's the one to see.

Enjoy yourself, but stop back often to check on us, will you?

Dear Professor Emanuel,

Allow me to congratulate you on your recently published research work on mathematics education in our elementary schools. Those of us who have been unhappy with the status quo have long needed solid research such as yours on which to base our proposals for change.

The long-range benefits of your research are incalculable, and I hope you will continue to bring your undoubted analytical gifts to this area.

Dear Lila,

I was so very pleased to hear of baby Savannah's arrival! You and Henry must be delighted. I hope you will soon be feeling your usual energetic self again, and that Savannah brings you joy, laughter, and quiet satisfaction all the days of your life.

When you are ready for visitors, I want to be one of the first in line! (Do you have any pictures yet?)

Dear Jefferson,

The newsletter is splendid! Congratulations on a first issue that is bright, funny, informative, and well presented. I can't imagine not subscribing—enclosed is my check.

Everybody likes a compliment.

—ABRAHAM LINCOLN

Dear Fleda Ringgan,

Congratulations! Your outstanding credit rating and your superior financial management have earned you an offer of an impressive credit line of $50,000 and a low ongoing 9.4% fixed APR, one of the best rates available today!

Other benefits of the WETHERELL GOLD CARD include no annual fee, travel accident insurance, auto rental insurance, online account management, consolidated year-end purchase summary, and 24-hour-a-day personal telephone service.

Return your Acceptance Certificate today (be sure to include your special invitation code) and begin reaping some of the benefits of your financial reliability!

Dear Lucie,

Congratulations on your blue ribbon in the state science fair! It was such a thrill for all of us to see your picture in the paper and to realize what a tremendous achievement this is.

We're hoping you can come for dinner some night and explain your project to us. It sounds fascinating, but complicated. Until then, give yourself a pat on the back for your good work.

> To hear how special and wonderful we are is endlessly enthralling.
>
> —GAIL SHEEHY

RELATED TOPICS

Appreciation

Employment

Family and Friends

Goodwill

Sales

Weddings

14

Cover Letters

INTRODUCTION

Cover letters (also called transmittal letters) are short and to the point, serving primarily to accompany and identify résumés, application forms, manuscripts, documents, product literature, payments, charitable contributions, contracts, reports, samples, data, or other materials. They may also highlight important points in the enclosures or explain something that is not immediately obvious. Their purpose is to orient the recipient quickly to the nature of the enclosed materials.

When a cover letter is sent with a résumé, it is a sales tool with a twofold purpose: to make the reader want to read your résumé and (along with the résumé) to sell the reader on you as someone who should be invited for an interview. See also Résumés and Applications (a combination of a cover letter and résumé).

Distinct from a cover letter is the cover sheet that accompanies a fax. It simply lists the person sending the fax, the person receiving it, the fax number, and the number of pages included (see Faxes). Cover letters that accompany samples or product literature are essentially selling something (for more information on this type of letter, see Sales).

> It is estimated that the average piece of business correspondence gets less than thirty seconds of the reader's attention. Even a truly great cover letter will not get much more.
>
> —Martin Yate

DO

- Be brief. A cover letter is usually only a paragraph or two and rarely more than one page. Except when the cover letter is actually a sales letter accompanying samples, product literature, or catalogs, the purpose of the cover letter is to make the reader want to move quickly on to the enclosures.
- Check all names, titles, and addresses for accuracy; this is particularly crucial when applying for a position.
- State what is enclosed, attached, or mailed under separate cover. If appropriate, state number and type of items, amount of payment, or other description that will allow recipients to verify that they have received what you said you sent.
- Mention, if appropriate, why you are sending the material (in response to a request, to introduce the person to a new product, for their information).
- If necessary, explain what the item is and how to read, interpret, or use it.
- Summarize briefly the main points of a document, highlight strong qualifications on your résumé, or otherwise orient the reader toward the salient issues of your material. Keep this section brief and avoid repeating the enclosed material unnecessarily.
- Tell what response you are expecting from the other person or specify what future actions you will be taking.
- Close with an expression of appreciation or a forward-looking statement. In *Cover Letters That Will Get You the Job You Want* (Better Way Books, 1993) Stanley Wynnett says, "The last two words of every cover letter I have ever written are *thank you*." In the case of a letter accompanying a résumé, close on a strong note: "I will call you next week after you have had a chance to go over my résumé"; "After reviewing my enclosed résumé, please call me for an interview."

> Very seldom will you write a letter more important to you than that accompanying a résumé.
>
> —Margaret McCarthy

DON'T

- Don't close on a weak note. Words like "hope," "wish," "if," "should," "could," and "might" signal a lack of confidence: "I hope to hear from you"; "If you wish, I could come for an interview at your convenience"; "Call me if you're interested."

- Don't mark envelopes containing your cover letter and résumé "personal and confidential"; it is outdated and rarely respected.

- Don't send a one-size-fits-all cover letter when applying for a job. Tailor each cover letter carefully to the specific company; recipients often look to see if there is anything related to their company and will not be impressed by a mass-produced letter. On the other hand, a form letter is perfect for writing routine cover letters that accompany, for example, requested information. When you don't need an individualized cover letter but you want to give your boiler-plate message a more personal appearance, use good quality paper, address the person by name (instead of using "Dear Friend" or "Dear Subscriber"), and sign each letter individually.

- Don't try to attract attention with "cute" stationery, humor, multiple question marks or exclamation marks, smiley faces, or other gimmicks. On the other hand, you want to personalize your letter and make it stand out. There is a fine line between an enthusiastic, energetic, confident letter and one that makes the reader wince in vicarious embarrassment. If you are in any doubt as to which your letter is, have someone evaluate it for you.

I do loathe explanations.

—J.M. BARRIE

HELPFUL HINTS

- A well-constructed cover letter accompanying your résumé is a powerful selling instrument. A few do's and don'ts specific to this type of cover letter: Personalize your opening paragraph by mentioning the person who referred you, the ad you are responding to, some facet of the company you're applying to (and the more specific you are about what you like about the company, the more effective it is). Identify the position or kind of work you are applying for. Mention specific accomplishments (but without the dates and other information that will be found in your résumé) that match the job opening. State what action you will take next ("I will call for an interview appointment after you have had a chance to review my résumé"). Don't focus on what you want, but instead generate interest in you by telling how you can contribute to the company. Don't write more than one page; you may think you must include everything, but a long cover letter is offputting to a busy person and may not get read at all.

- Cover letters aren't necessary with routine orders, payments, shipments, recommendations, references, or when the recipient has requested or is expecting your enclosure; write a cover letter if the materials do not speak clearly for themselves or if you wish to attach a sales message.

- A note that accompanies a gift has a purpose similar to that of a cover letter. Identify the enclosure ("a little something for your birthday") and include your greetings and best wishes.

- The cover letter that accompanies a report should identify the report by title; mention why it was prepared, who authorized it, and who wrote it; provide a summary (based on the report's introduction, abstract, or summary). If the report is formal, the transmittal letter is placed after the title page and before the table of contents.

- The cover letter that accompanies a manuscript submission is brief; its sole purpose is to introduce yourself and your submission and then get out of the way so the person can get to the manuscript. A good cover letter tells what you're enclosing and why, explains a little about yourself, and concludes with a courtesy.

- For more assistance with cover letters, see the excellent *Cover Letters That Knock 'Em Dead* by Martin Yate, 3rd ed. (Adams Media Corporation, 1998) and *Cover Letters* by Taunee Besson, 2nd ed. (John Wiley & Sons, 1996). For cover letters specific to accompanying résumés, see *The Perfect Cover Letter* by Richard H. Beatty, 2nd ed. (John Wiley & Sons, 1997) and for cover letters specific to manuscript submissions, see *How to Write Attention-Grabbing Query & Cover Letters* by John Wood (Writer's Digest Books, 1996).

> We never get a second chance to make a first impression.
>
> —Joan Kennedy

GETTING STARTED

I thought you might like to have a copy of the recommendation I wrote for you. I sent the original on in the envelope you provided.

Here is the set of deck plans I promised you.

Enclosed is a completed application form. Please note my four years' experience as an installation technician.

For the past four years, I have been working as senior research scientist for a leading manufacturer of biologicals.

As a June graduate of Cleveland College with a B.A. in business, I am looking for employment and wanted to check first with you because I so enjoyed working for The Clement Group as an intern in your marketing department.

Under separate cover I'm sending you samples of our new line of Natural Solution products for the hair.

Thank you for your patience—enclosed please find the replacement part for your Noyes Intercommunication System.

Enclosed please find everything you need to know about the recent changes to our pension plan.

At your request, I am sending you a brochure describing our seminars on building your own patio, walks, and paths with pavers.

We are pleased to enclose the sample fireproof file folder that you requested.

After you have reviewed the enclosed proposal, please call me (or Bess Beynon if I'm out of town) to discuss it.

For your consideration, I am enclosing a brochure that describes solutions for all your communications needs.

Our check for $15,223.92 is enclosed and constitutes full payment for all items listed on Invoice # 68-331982.

Please sign and date all copies of the enclosed contract, keep one copy for your files, and return the others to us.

Here are molding samples we'd like you to evaluate.

I would like to direct your attention to the enclosed summary of changes in the organization of our graphic production department.

Enclosed is a copy of my March gas and electric bill in the amount of $134.12 along with my check for $114.12 (let me know if you do not agree that there was an error of $20).

I am enclosing the damaged belt from my twenty-year-old Bannister vacuum in the hopes that you can locate a replacement for it.

Will you please look over the enclosed rough draft of your will and let me know if it needs any changes or corrections?

Your Old Chester Urban League membership renewal is enclosed.

Beatrice Chavender, Director of Environmental Services, has asked me to forward the enclosed environmental assessment worksheets to you.

I'm sending you a copy of the article on vascular intervention that we discussed last week.

Enclosed is a copy of the survey on equipment rental in the six-county metro area.

Enclosed please find the complete medical records for Enoch Drebber from the office of Dr. Julian B. Emory.

Gautier Lighting appreciates your interest in our landscape light systems and we are pleased to send you the enclosed materials describing our products.

> The old aphorisms are basically sound. First impressions *are* lasting.
>
> —JESSIE FAUSET

MODEL LETTERS

Dear Maud Dolomore,

Enclosed is the substantially revised manuscript for "The Widow of Traunstein." It is, I believe, much better than the earlier version, and I'm grateful that you obliged me to push the story further. Also enclosed is a SASE for your response.

To make up for my last overlong letter, I will keep this one overshort. I hope all's well with you.

Harold Biffen

Re: Embarrassing senior photos

Enclosed is, I hope, a sufficiently, but not overly, embarrassing "early years" photo of Katie Koskenmaki, CC'94, for your senior album. The underwear on the head is the embarrassing part. I think.

Also enclosed is a SASE for the photo's return (for which, many thanks).

If this isn't quite what you had in mind, please call collect and I'll send something else.

Dear Dr. Cheesewright,

Your office manager, Ms. Sheriff, mentioned to me that you might soon have an opening for a dental hygienist. She suggested I send you my résumé.

You may not remember, but I was a patient of yours when I was growing up here, and even as a youngster I thought it would be "fun" to work in your office! I've been living in Chicago for the past ten years, but am planning to move back here because of my father's health.

After you've had a chance to look at my résumé, you can reach me at 555-1234 if you would like to schedule an interview.

TO: Classifieds, *Harcourt Morning News*
FROM: Acting Regional Director, Emergency Management Systems
DATE: July 26
SUBJECT: Legal Notices

Enclosed is a Legal Notice advising the public of reimbursements being offered to eligible local governments and state agencies for the costs of repairing publicly owned facilities damaged in the recent severe storms.

Please publish this Notice three times in the *Harcourt Morning News*, on August 5, 12, and 19. Send your invoice to this office.

Thank you.

Dear Acquisitions Librarian, Randolph AFB,

Enclosed is a copy of my novel, *The First Fall*, published by Nine Ten Press. I'm sending it to you because I think it is interesting to and appropriate for military personnel and base libraries. It focuses on returning veterans after World War II, many of whom suffered from what we then called battle fatigue, but what is now called post-traumatic shock syndrome.

The influx of veterans onto college and university campuses in 1946 changed both those colleges and our society in ways we are still trying to understand.

The book has sold over a thousand copies so far in our area—and without advertising. Major bookstore chains list it on their computer systems, and the book can be found on the shelves of such bookstores as The Hungry Mind in St. Paul and the Tattered Cover in Denver.

Comment sheets and a complimentary review by the Minneapolis *Star Tribune*'s book editor are also enclosed.

I hope you like the book and believe as I do that it belongs in your library system. Enclosed is an order form and postage-paid reply envelope.

Dear Students, Parents, Alums, and Friends,

It is with great pride and pleasure that we send you the enclosed newsletter bringing you up to date on activities, accomplishments, and news at the Harrington School of the Dramatic Arts.

You'll read about standing ovations, scholarship winners, innovative classes, student productions, a new wing, top ratings in dramatic competitions around the state, and profiles of some of our outstanding teachers.

Many alums and friends of the school have chosen to share in the exciting things going on at Harrington by contributing to the school's financial needs. We receive contributions marked "for the Tuition Aid Fund" or "for whatever you most need at this time." A number of supporters have named the school as beneficiary in their wills and life insurance policies.

In addition to the newsletter (see page 6 for a particularly exciting story), we're sending a "News About You!" form (classmates and friends enjoy knowing what you're doing), a networking survey (so that alums and students can share information about professional opportunities), and a "Gift That Keeps on Giving" form to help you find a way of supporting Harrington that suits your budget.

Enjoy!

Dear Mr. Scott,

Thank you for your interest in the Waverly Inn for the Scott Family Reunion. We have recently completed a $5 million renovation of the entire hotel. Our gracious rooms, suites, and meeting facilities will provide every comfort for your group, while our full-service restaurant and lounge, Olympic-sized pool, game room, sauna, Jacuzzi, and exercise room will help make your stay enjoyable, convenient, and entertaining.

Enclosed is a folder with complete information on the Waverly Inn, a Calendar of Area Events for the period of your projected stay with us, and several colorful brochures to distribute to members of your family.

Please review the attached proposal, which reflects our telephone discussion of September 3. If it meets your approval, please sign one copy and return it to me.

I look forward to the possibility of hosting your family.

Dear Mr. and Mrs. Caswell,

Enclosed is the free information you requested on homeopathic first aid in the wilderness. The color chart will make it easier for you to identify useful plants and the mini-first aid guide is designed to be carried in a pocket while hiking.

I am also sending you a copy of our most recent Wentworth Homeopathic Remedies catalog and our Wentworth Home Health Appliances catalog, along with a $10 coupon good for your first order from either catalog.

We look forward to being of service to you.

Dear Reverend Bashaw,

According to the item in this morning's paper, you are setting up a fund to provide food, shelter, and other necessities for those members of your congregation whose home burned yesterday.

Our family once found itself in almost identical circumstances. Enclosed is a check for $500, which I hope you will put to good use on behalf of the family.

Thank you.

> A dynamic cover letter can give you an edge in the competitive world of job-hunting.
>
> —KATHARINE HANSEN AND RANDALL S. HANSEN

TO: Supervisors of New Intern Employees
FROM: Minna von Barnhelm
SUBJECT: Intern Employment
DATE: August 30

As the potential supervisor of a new intern, you will want to review the attached guidelines governing the employment of an intern.

When you are ready to extend an offer to a candidate, please call with your requisition number and I will prepare the offer letter for you.

Once you have hired an intern, it is essential that the new employee be fully trained in safety and security procedures.

Dear G.E. Challenger,

I was intrigued with the ad in Sunday's paper seeking someone experienced with high-pressure liquid chromatography—first, because there aren't that many openings in this field and, second, because my experience and background match almost precisely what you appear to need.

I was further intrigued when I called the number given in the ad and discovered that this is your company. I have never forgotten several of your research papers that were required reading when I was in college.

After you have had a chance to read my résumé, I hope you will agree that an interview might be interesting to us both.

Some writers, new and experienced, sabotage submissions through the cover letter. For example, promising the editor that the story enclosed is a "gothic, techno-horror, psychological, noir thriller" promises way too much, and virtually guarantees a submissions editor's disappointment.

—Pam Cully

RELATED TOPICS

Applications
Queries
Résumés
Sales

15

Letters About Credit

INTRODUCTION

A great deal of the paperwork involved in financial, credit, collection, and money matters has been standardized and codified into forms. There will always be exceptions and difficulties and changes, however, and these often require that letters be written.

To refuse credit or loan applications, you may find additional helpful suggestions in Refusals.

> The business community and society at large are both strongly credit oriented. The amount and variety of credit correspondence generated as a result are staggering.
>
> —MARY A. DE VRIES

DO

- Provide accurate information and then check and doublecheck it. Identify all names, addresses, amounts, payment dates, and terms precisely and in full. This serves as a record for you, and offers the other person the opportunity to correct any erroneous items.

- Keep in mind that credit and financial matters are, theoretically at least, confidential. Make every attempt to safeguard the credit information you give or receive.

- Be tactful. Even people with poor credit histories often feel they are doing a good job given their circumstances.

> The object of collection letters is to get the money without losing the customer.
>
> —N.H. AND S.K. MAGER

DON'T

- Don't use words like "failure" ("your failure to respond," "failure to pay"); "ignore" ("you have ignored our letters"); "insist" or "demand" ("we insist that you send payment at once"). They make the other person feel small, which is not conducive to facing up to responsibilities.

- Don't use negative tactics (insults, name-calling, bullying, sarcasm, arrogance, threats, and verbal wrist-slapping) as they only produce negative results: debtors can make you the bad guy. Don't threaten customers with a collection agency or legal action until you are prepared to do so.

- Don't send collection letters to a person's place of business where others might open the mail. For the same reasons of privacy, don't use postcards to send collection messages.

> We all know that when a business sends its customers "friendly reminders," it really means business.
>
> —JUDITH MARTIN

HELPFUL HINTS

- If you find yourself unable to make a loan payment or installment credit payment on time, write the company at once. Apologize for being overdue, state your intention to pay as soon as possible, and enclose whatever portion of the balance you can. If you have a good reason for being overdue (illness, layoff), you could mention it. Otherwise, don't go into details; your creditor is principally interested in knowing that you are taking responsibility for the account.

- When writing to approve a loan application or grant credit, state that the request has been approved; indicate the amount approved and the effective date; explain credit or loan payoff procedures. Enclose forms needing signatures along with instructions on how to complete them properly. Welcome new customers to your lending institution or business, express appreciation for their business, and suggest they bring all their credit needs to you.

- To request correction of an inaccurate credit record, identify yourself by full name and address, state the incorrect portions of the record, and explain why they are incorrect. Include copies of any documents (statements, loan papers, tax returns, paycheck stubs) substantiating your position. Ask that a corrected copy of the report be sent to you. Thank the person for their assistance; they most likely were not responsible for the errors and can, in fact, be of help to you.

- Collection letters can reach levels of high art in their quest to collect on an overdue bill without losing the customer's goodwill. They are always courteous and, in the beginning at least, they assume that the customer intends to pay but has been a little lax or forgetful. Each letter sent to an overdue account is written as though it will be the last; it is optimistic, appreciative, confident. Always include a customer, order, or invoice number; date and amount of purchase; original payment due date; date by which you now expect payment; references to previous letters about the outstanding balance; suggested payment plan; any other descriptive information. Leave enough time (two to three weeks) between letters to give the customer a chance to pay. And close each letter with a statement that tells the customer to ignore the letter if payment has already been sent. Including a postage-paid reply envelope is often effective.

  Collection letters begin with a mild *reminder* that a bill is overdue. They escalate through a series of letters of *inquiry*, *appeal*, and *demand* to a final letter stating that the account is being turned over to a collection agency. A possible sequence of messages might look like this: ➤ The regular monthly statement is stamped with a "Past Due" or "Second Notice" message. ➤ A brief, friendly letter points out the overdue payment ("May we call your attention to the fact that your account is currently past due?" or "You are usually so prompt in your payment of bills that we are sure you overlooked your December statement"). ➤ You write a little more insistently, and firmly remind the customer that payment still has not been received. In a second paragraph, you might ask for explanations or suggest several face-saving reasons why the person hasn't paid (bill was overlooked or lost in the mail, customer was away). Close with an expression of your confidence that the payment will be sent at once. If you are using a form letter, try to personalize it in some way; people tend to think you aren't really serious yet if you're sending a form letter. ➤ Write a longer, more urgent letter, giving one or more reasons why sending payment would be a good idea: the person's credit rating and reputation might be adversely affected; it is a matter of fairness and justice; it is the responsible thing to do; the customer will be relieved to have the matter taken care of. You might suggest several payment schedules (weekly, semi-monthly, monthly, or two lump-sum payments) and ask the customer to choose one. ➤ You are becoming somewhat stern now, and you present additional arguments for payment: you have carried out your obligations by providing the service or shipping the goods and now the customer must carry out their obligation by sending payment; the amount is too small to risk losing a good credit rating; the customer would not wish to be placed on your delinquent list; they would certainly not wish to be reported to the trade credit bureau; they will not be able to place any future orders with you. For the first time, you mention the possibility of turning the account over to an agency or an attorney for collection. ➤ By now you are fairly certain that the customer is deliberately choosing not to pay. In a strongly worded message, you announce that you are obliged to turn the account over either to an agency for collection or to a lawyer for legal action. (If you opt for legal action, you will be wording your letter with your attorney's advice.) Even now, however, give the customer ten days in which to make arrangements to settle the account before taking action. Be clear that the action can be avoided if the customer responds at once. Some companies give this letter the appearance of an official document coming from an outside agency. ➤ Your last letter reflects your belief that this particular customer is going to pay only if forced to do so. You announce that the account is being transferred to a named collection agency or to a named law firm as of a stated date. This letter is a simple announcement of the action you are taking; you no longer attempt to get the customer to pay.

Note that when trying to collect from a customer who reports adverse circumstances (illness, unemployment, financial reverses, bankruptcy), work out a feasible payment program even if it is an extremely generous one. A background check should give you a sense of whether the person is actually experiencing difficulties that merit special attention. Reducing a bill by even a small amount is a success for both creditor and debtor and deserves your efforts.

> Beautiful credit! The foundation of modern society.
>
> — MARK TWAIN

- Loans between family members or friends often come with hidden costs, both financial and personal. When requesting a loan like this (presumably because it is the only option you have), choose the individual carefully (you may have to answer the question "Why me?"). Be businesslike and factual; do not plead or try to play on their sympathies. Suggest a repayment plan and tell how much interest you will pay. Offer a convenient excuse for not agreeing to the loan ("This may not be a good time for you" or "Perhaps this isn't something you feel you can do"). Thank the person for previous support and express your appreciation for their accessibility. When refusing a request for a loan from a family member, be very brief: "I wish I could help you, but it's not possible just now." Do not overexplain or apologize or hedge in any way. If you like, you can close by asking if there is some other way you could help. When granting a request for a loan from a friend or family member, put it in writing: state the full loan amount, the terms and dates of repayment, the interest, and any other important information. Send two copies of your letter and ask that the person sign and date one of them and return it to you. When you need to remind a friend or family member of an overdue loan, send a gentle reminder and help the person save face by including an excuse ("I know how busy you are . . ."; "I wonder if you forgot about . . ."; "Am I mistaken, or did we agree that you'd repay the loan September 1?"; "I know what a procrastinator you are!"). If you have to write a second time, include a photocopy of your original agreement letter.

- When writing to deny credit or a loan: thank the person for their interest; express regret that you are unable to extend credit; assure them that you gave thorough consideration to their request; suggest an alternate course of action (layaway, paying cash, smaller loan) that will allow a continued relationship; encourage them to reapply later. If asked, explain the denial by listing your credit criteria and mention the problems presented by the person's credit background. Be tactful and express goodwill; the applicant is still a potential customer. For smaller, more routine credit requests, many banks and lending institutions use forms stating simply "Your request for a loan has been denied," followed by a check-off list of possible reasons: length of employment, lack of information, excessive credit obligations, newcomer to the area with no credit record, poor payment record, garnishment, and so forth. You may want to leave a blank to fill in the name of the credit bureau where you obtained your information.

- When asking a credit bureau to run a check on yourself: state your name, address, social security number, telephone number; use letterhead stationery or enclose a business card to substantiate your identity. When asking a credit bureau to check on another person's credit history: supply the person's name, address, and social security number; give a legitimate business reason for asking (you are renting them an apartment, selling them a car, co-signing a loan with them). When asking an individual or a business for a credit reference: give the name and address of the person under consideration; politely request any pertinent credit information; explain briefly why you want it ("we are discussing a partnership"); reassure the person that you will treat the information confidentially; express your appreciation for the information, and enclose a self-addressed stamped envelope for their reply. In some cases you might want to mention how you were referred to them (for example, by the person under consideration) or you may want to ask specific questions: How long have you known the person? In what capacity? What kinds of credit have been extended? What is the current balance? The person's payment pattern? How long has the person been employed there? At what salary? When discussing another person's credit history, say nothing that cannot be substantiated. Doublecheck names and account numbers to be certain you have the right person's credit history.

- Letters dealing with credit are almost always typed on letterhead stationery. Form letters are useful for the first few collection letters in a series.

> Creditors have better memories than debtors.
>
> —Benjamin Franklin

GETTING STARTED

Thank you for sending your credit references so promptly—they all supplied complimentary reports.

Thank you for applying for a charge account with Heath & Gerard. We are pleased to extend credit to you at any of our eight metropolitan stores.

I would appreciate your raising my credit limit from $10,000 to $20,000.

Because of your excellent credit record over the past two years, we are pleased to announce a raise in your credit limit from $5,000 to $10,000.

We noticed that you have not used your Randall Charge Card for some time now.

Please close my Fortis-Pryde account, effective immediately.

I apologize for the delay in paying this bill and I appreciate your patience.

Thank you for your courtesy and patience in allowing me to pay off the balance of my Irving Products, Inc. account in small installments.

We are puzzled that our application for a home equity line of credit has been refused—please send us a copy of our credit report, if that was the problem, or your explanation of this refusal.

Please cancel my credit card, #4128 1234 5678, immediately, and send me confirmation that you have closed the account; I have destroyed both our cards.

We noted a persistent pattern of nonpayment in your credit history and would like to suggest that you reapply for a credit card when you have resolved some of these problems.

We regretfully advise you that we are unable to open an account for you at this time because your current financial condition does not entirely meet our requirements.

I'm writing to notify you of an error in our credit history and to request an immediate correction—please see enclosed documentation.

We are disappointed not to have heard from you about your overdue balance of $1,785.97.

> We all know how the size of sums of money appears to vary in a remarkable way according as they are being paid in or paid out.
>
> —Julian Huxley

If you haven't already mailed in your payment, won't you take a moment to send it today?

The amount of $459.11 is still unpaid. As you will recall, our bills are payable on the 15th of the month following a purchase.

Our records show that this bill is overdue. If it has not already been paid, please send us your check. Thank you.

Just a reminder: a past due amount is included in your balance on the enclosed statement.

We don't like to remind a good customer like you that a bill is overdue, but perhaps you just forgot.

Your account is now ninety days overdue in the amount of $1,208.54. As you are one of our longtime customers with an excellent credit rating, we assume this is a simple oversight.

We regret that we will not be able to fill your current orders until your account has been brought up to date.

We would appreciate your sending us a check for the unpaid balance on your account, $5,498.44, by return mail; payment is now three months overdue.

Your account is seriously in arrears and we have as yet had no response from you to our repeated reminders.

If you are unable to pay the entire balance, we would be glad to accommodate you if you would like to suggest an appropriate payment plan.

Because the collection of small amounts entails considerable expense for us, we would appreciate your remitting this amount promptly (invoice enclosed).

It is important that you take some action before this unpaid balance affects your credit rating.

Although we prefer not to place your account in the hands of a collection attorney, we will be obliged to do so unless we receive payment by August 31.

This letter will serve as notice that Antonio Poppi has turned your account over to us for collection because of a balance of $944.30, which is now 9 months overdue; collection proceedings will begin 10 days from the date of this letter unless you contact us to make arrangements for payment.

Thank you very much for your recent remittance, which has allowed us to reactivate your account.

We appreciate your payment of $1,104.67, which we received today. We are happy to be able to remove you from our collection system and to reestablish your line of credit.

Your letter of October 3 asking for payment of our July bill has just been brought to my attention. I apologize that you had to write us several times about this—it was completely overlooked.

We will appreciate any credit information you can give us about the Reverend John Gillett.

We regret to report—confidentially, of course—that our business experiences with Van Tassel Distribution, Inc., have been less than satisfactory to us.

Yankele Ben Yitzchok has had an excellent credit history with this company, and we recommend him highly as a credit customer.

Trina Sieppe McTeague, 1899 Norris Street, Frank, MI 49946, has applied to the Miners Credit Union for a loan, and gave us your name as a reference.

> Debt is the sort of Bedfellow who is forever pulling all the Covers his way.
>
> —MINNA THOMAS ANTRIM

MODEL LETTERS

Dear David Herries,

We received your payment coupon that referenced a payment of $3,099.25. However, a payment of this amount has not been posted to your account.

If you have sent a payment that was cashed by your bank, please send us a photocopy of the front and back of the canceled check or money order. Or, if the payment was not cashed, please send us a replacement check.

We apologize for any inconvenience this may have caused.

We look forward to serving you.

Christine Paull
Customer Service

TO: Yonge Credit Services
FROM: Charles Cheviot, Cheviot-Rivers State Bank
DATE: September 3, 2000
RE: Averil Ward

Will you please run a credit check for us on:

> Averil Ward
> 1856 Ernescliffe Road
> Hector, OH 45042

Ms. Ward is applying for a home equity line of credit with us, and we wish to verify the information she has given us with regard to her credit history. Thank you.

Dear Jed,

Sorry to remind you again, but it's been three months since I lent you $1,500 "for just a few days." I'd like to be able to just write it off, but as it happens we need that money ourselves—right away.

I can stop by your place after work on Friday to pick it up. Or you could drop it off at the house. Let me know.

Dear Crocker-Harris Electronics Corp.

Re: Account # 18145-99782

Because of flooding at our main store three months ago, we have been experiencing some temporary financial difficulties and have fallen behind on our payments to you. We expect to resume regular payments as of August 1. In the meantime, please accept the enclosed check on account.

We thank you for your understanding.

Dear Mrs. Lanier,

We at Parker Investment Mortgage, Inc. understand and appreciate how very difficult this past year must have been for you.

However, given your history of missed payments (June 1997, September 1997, November 1997, and February, March, and April 1998), the fact that your account is now three months past due, and our inability to arrange a meeting with you to discuss solutions, we are unable to grant you any additional time.

Unless we receive your unpaid balance by May 15, you will receive a foreclosure notice.

Sincerely,

Dear Abel Beechcroft,

On March 1, your account (#1842-1995BE) will be transferred to the Ainsworth Collection Agency for recovery of the past-due amount of $1,291.96. If you contact us before then, we would be glad to determine a plan of repayment. Otherwise, you will be hearing directly from someone at Ainsworth.

Sincerely,

Dear Lavinia Penniman,

Please be advised that as of today's date, the above-referenced account reflects a zero balance and has been closed to any further purchases as per your request.

If we can be of any further assistance, please contact us. It has been a pleasure to serve you.

Very truly yours,

Cardholder Services

I don't like money, actually, but it quiets my nerves.

—Joe Louis

Dear Mr. and Mrs. Archibald Craven,

Thank you for your letter of November 30, disputing the payment of interest charges on your "12-month interest-free" purchase of furniture from us.

When you purchased your sofa, chair, and ottoman last November 18, we offered to carry the full amount of the purchase, $1,574.97, interest-free for one year—and you accepted our offer. The terms of the offer were explained at that time.

Each month thereafter you received a statement from us, noting the amount of the original purchase, the accruing finance charges, and stating very clearly, "If you pay the payoff amount by the expiration date listed below, you will be credited for the amount of interest accumulated on that purchase."

You did not pay the payoff amount by the expiration date of our agreement, November 19 of this year; thus you now owe the payoff amount plus the accrued interest of $272.61.

Please note that interest will continue to accrue until all charges are paid.

For further questions, call Mary Lennox in the Accounts Due Department at 555-1234.

Dear Werfel Credit Advisors, Inc.,

I believe I need a credit counselor to help with my current financial goals: to reestablish a good credit rating, to set up a workable debt repayment plan, to analyze and prioritize my present spending patterns, to learn how to budget, and, in general, to get my finances under control.

Would you please send me complete information on your services, including fees? I would also like the names of several people with whom you have worked who would be willing to recommend you. What I absolutely do not need at this time is more delay and confusion in my money life.

Thank you.

> The world is a puzzling place today. All these banks sending us credit cards. . . . Imagine a bank sending credit cards to two ladies over a hundred years old! What are those folks thinking?
>
> —SADIE DELANY

Dear Avery,

I'm enclosing a self-addressed stamped envelope along with the form below. I hope to hear from you by return mail.

Please mark one of the responses below and enclose this form in the self-addressed stamped envelope along with your check, money order, or cash.

____ Whoops! I was just about to send you the $300. Here it is.

____ The kids need shoes and we don't have any food in the house, but, what the heck, I owe you!

____ Are you SURE it was $300? Let me check. Yup, I guess it was.

____ WHAT $300??!! Heh heh, just joking.

____ I don't know why you should get paid before the dentist, Sears, and the kid who cuts the grass, but, here, take it!

When you think no one cares if you're alive, try missing a couple of car payments.

—Anonymous

RELATED TOPICS

Acknowledgments

Announcements

Apologies

Complaints

Orders

Refusals

Requests

Responses

Thank You

16

E-mail

INTRODUCTION

With a computer, a modem, a telephone line, and a subscription to an electronic-mail (e-mail) network, you can type and send a message and receive an answer in minutes. Less intrusive than the telephone, far simpler and quicker than writing a letter, e-mail has been adopted by millions worldwide. It's not farfetched to think that it, or one of its even more sophisticated descendants, will be more common than the telephone before long. It is already used by the majority of businesses, educational institutions, and federal and state agencies.

The hardware and software—"how to do it" and "how it does it"—of e-mail belong in another book; the emphasis in this chapter is on the letter-writing aspects of electronic mail.

The hallmark of e-mail style is its conversational tone. Because questions and answers can be sent back and forth very rapidly, it resembles a dialogue while a regular letter resembles a monologue. One consequence is that senders tend to dash off e-mails, knowing that if they make a mistake or leave out a piece of information, they can send another e-mail in seconds.

E-mail has actually inspired a surge in communicating. People who haven't written a letter in years find e-mail suits them because of its simplicity, directness, and speed. Another advantage is being able to communicate with people in another time zone or on another biorhythmic pattern without fearing you'll wake them with a phone call. When you're working late, you can still send information to another person's electronic mailbox for retrieval first thing in the morning. E-mail is particularly useful when you have a thirty-second message to send someone who usually involves you in a fifteen-minute phone call. It also encourages the sending of quick notes that wouldn't, in themselves, warrant the effort of a regular letter.

E-mail is new enough that conventions and guidelines are still in process, being formulated primarily by those who most use it.

> Admitting you don't have an e-mail address these days is almost like admitting you still listen to eight-track tapes.
>
> —Tom McNichol

DO

- Doublecheck every e-mail address before sending your message. The system is absolutely unforgiving. "Almost correct" doesn't cut it.

- Use a subject line—a word or phrase to let your reader know instantly what the e-mail is about. It must be brief (you are usually allowed only a limited number of spaces). There is generally a special space for the subject—some mailers will automatically insert "Re:" (for "Regarding") or "Subject." Examples of subject lines include:

    Re: Welcome back!

    Re: newsletter error

    Re: benefits hotline

    Subject: the check's in the mail

    Subject: fundraising meeting

    Subject: new corporate library hours

- Start with "Hi," "Hello," "Greetings," or the person's name followed by a comma or dash. The "Dear" convention of letters is generally too formal for e-mail.

- Be brief, direct, and clear. E-mails are more like memos than letters and more like conversations than letters or even memos. Get to the point as quickly as possible.

- Use language that is natural and comfortable for you. Where in a letter you might write "I will" or, more formally, "I shall," in an e-mail you write "I'll."

- Be discreet. E-mail can show up in odd and embarrassing places. People you never expect to read your message may see it.

- Try to limit your message to one screen, which is usually less than 25 lines of text. When your message is longer, you might send it using the "attachment" function along with a brief cover message.

- Follow the same rules of good writing (spelling, grammar, punctuation, usage) that you would use in any correspondence. However, you can be a great deal more informal, simple, and brief on e-mail. Use of first names and even nicknames is common.

- Mark your message "urgent," if it truly is, or it may get lost in a series of e-mail messages.

- Send copies of your e-mail message only to those who need to receive them. It does not endear you to others to fill their electronic mailboxes with irrelevant material. It's estimated that much of the e-mail received in large companies is unnecessary and inappropriate to the receiver.

- End by stating what action you expect. Do you want a response? Is the e-mail FYI (for your information) only and thus no response is needed?

- Close with your last thought. It is not necessary to have a formal closing ("Sincerely," "Truly yours," etc.). Type your name, however, as the person's system may give only your e-mail address, which might not be identifiable to everyone.

- Do check for accuracy before transmitting; once it's gone, it's gone. And it all happens in an instant.

- Acknowledge e-mail as soon as you read it. If you are unable to provide an answer or appropriate response at the moment, at least send a reply saying the message was received and you will send the requested information later. Most e-mail software has a "reply" feature, which simplifies acknowledging messages.

> Be bold. Be fast. Get to the point right away. The best e-mail communication is simple and clear. E-mail isn't good for really nuanced communication.
>
> —CONSTANCE HALE

DON'T

- Don't expect e-mail to be private; it is easily forwarded or misrouted. Be especially careful what you say about others.

- Don't fire off e-mails when angry or upset; given the medium, it's extremely easy to do this and regret it afterwards.

- Don't use e-mail to send an urgent message; there is no guarantee it will be read immediately. Some people check their e-mail frequently and many offices are set up so that users are notified when e-mail comes in, but other people may not read an e-mail for days.

- Don't use e-mail to send high-impact news (death notice, new company president, serious illness); a letter, phone call, or meeting is the appropriate choice here.

- Don't use all capital letters unless you want the recipient to understand that you are YELLING. Capitalize as you would normally.

- Don't forward any e-mail without the original sender's permission. Similarly, do not share others' e-mail addresses without checking with them first.

- Don't give your password or user ID to anyone you don't know very, very well.

- Don't waste people's time with unnecessary or trivial e-mails. This method of communication is so quick and easy that we are often tempted to send something along that we'd never think of typing up, signing, and sending through the regular mail.

> The shortest works are always the best.
>
> —JEAN DE LA FONTAINE

HELPFUL HINTS

- When replying to an e-mail, you are usually given a choice between including or not including the other person's message in your reply. It is useful sometimes to include the message you're answering because you can respond to questions as they occur with a brief "yes" or "no," and the recipient knows what you're talking about. In e-mail, quotations look like this: < >, so the other person's words will be in "quotation marks"; yours won't be.

- In *The Argument Culture*, Deborah Tannen states that while e-mail has brought us tremendous benefits, "it also enhances hostile and distressing communication. . . . It is easier to feel and express hostility against someone far removed whom you do not know personally, like the rage that some drivers feel toward an anonymous car that cuts them off." Being aware of this tendency (so common that there is a word—"flaming"—to describe angry, hostile messages) will help you avoid it and recognize it for what it is.

- You may encounter "emoticons" in your e-mail. They are used to express emotions. For example, :-) stands for a happy face (look at it sideways).

- Abbreviations are also used much more commonly in e-mail than in standard letters. FYI (for your information) is familiar to most people. Not so familiar are BTW (by the way), TIA (thanks in advance), and LOL (laughed out loud).

- Some e-mail is simply read on the screen and then either deleted or filed on the person's hard drive. Although an e-mail can also be printed out by the person who receives it, it won't be a thing of beauty. If you want your recipient to have a decent-looking hard (paper) copy, you may want to send one by mail.

- E-mail addresses usually end with a code that identifies the mailer by type: .com (commercial); .net (network); .gov (government); .st (state government); .edu (educational institution); .org (organization—usually nonprofit); .mil (military).

- Because e-mail is sent solely in ASCII text, certain options—like italics, underlining, and foreign accents—don't work. To indicate underlining or italics, put asterisks before and after the word or phrase ("I'm sending you *two* instead of three").

- If you use e-mail at work, familiarize yourself with your company's policies on e-mail usage, privacy, security, and archiving. The e-mail system is company property and most organizations have fairly comprehensive guidelines about its use by employees.

- For more complete information about electronic mail, check your library or bookstore for titles such as *Effective E-mail* by Bradley F. Shimmin (1997); *The Three R's of E-mail: Risks, Rights, and Responsibilities* by Diane B. Hartman and Karen S. Nantz (1996); *The Elements of E-mail Style* by David Angell and Brent D. Heslop (1994); *Using E-mail* by Dave Gibbons (1994).

- There is information about using e-mail on the Internet—for example, at http://www.webfoot.com/advice/email.top.html you'll find Kaitlin Duck Sherwood's "A Beginner's Guide to Effective E-mail."

> When you make a phone call there's a 50 percent chance it will come back but when you send e-mail for some reason it's like you're on a level playing field and everyone sends messages back. It's a different culture. You're never put on hold. The answers are always relevant. There's no chat; no small talk.
>
> —ALANA KAINZ

GETTING STARTED

Thanks for notifying me of the new meeting time. You didn't say, but is it still going to be held in Room 306?

I've lost Miriam Ephraim's address. Do you have it?

Are you available to judge a race walk a week from Saturday?

This is to let you know that your order (#08554) was received and will be shipped this afternoon.

Did you see the article about elder law in today's *New York Times*?

Forgot to ask—is it their 37th or 38th anniversary?

You asked if I knew of a good book about Leonardo da Vinci—actually I do.

Here are this week's airfare bargains.

I read about the tornado that went through your area—are you OK?

Are you checking your e-mail these days? This is the third time I've written.

Good to hear from you!

Is there any recent news about how Cressida is doing?

When you have a minute, will you fax me a copy of your most recent patent application?

I'm trying to round up some people to hike through New England for two weeks this fall—are you interested?

Just a note to say I really enjoyed your op-ed piece on hog confinements. Have you had much feedback?

I've just mailed you the material for your audio presentation. You should have it Monday or Tuesday.

I'll be gone for the next two weeks—if anything comes up, just e-mail me and I'll get back to you after the 3rd.

Thanks for forwarding the specs—I AM interested.

Is it my bookkeeping or am I missing a check for the last job?

I had a note from Mrs. Hook Eagles asking about a vacancy in the 1330 building—do we have one, do you know?

Feel free to forward the following to anyone who might be interested.

Computers are incredibly fast, accurate and stupid; humans are incredibly slow, inaccurate and brilliant; together they are powerful beyond imagination.

—ALBERT EINSTEIN

MODEL LETTERS

From: maggiokm@email.com
To: maggio1@email.com
Date: Thu, 26 Feb 1998 20:35:29 EST
Subject: thesaurus

Hello again. I've been meaning to ask you which thesaurus you recommend. I've decided I need to invest in one (might find it at a used bookstore). I don't have any confidence in the one on my word-processing program, but I don't know much about thesauruses other than that they're in the dinosaur family. Thanks. Love - K

From: drlizk@email.com
To: maggio1@email.com
Date: Thu, 13 Nov 1997 21:43:17 EST
Subject: my new computer!

This is my very first e-mail letter. So what does "Cc" mean in the box next to the "To" box in which I wrote "mom"? Perhaps it means "from." It's going to take me awhile to get used to this deal. Not to mention that I haven't typed anything in years. Already my left wrist hurts.

From: sjberkson@email.com
To: maggio1@email.com
Date: Fri, 3 Jul 1998 14:36:01 EDT
Subject: !

A journalist had done a story on gender roles in Kuwait several years before the Gulf War, and she noted then that women customarily walked about ten feet behind their husbands. She returned to Kuwait recently and observed that the men now walked several yards behind their wives. She approached one of the women for an explanation. "This is marvelous," said the journalist. "What enabled women here to achieve this reversal of roles?" Replied the Kuwaiti woman: "Land mines."

Have a good weekend. We're off to MC tomorrow for a week. Who knows where you are.

Love, Susan

From: slz3@email.edu

To: maggio1@email.com

Date: Mon, 9 Dec 1996 15:48:00 (EST)

Subject: WHM Contract

Hi. I'm filling out the contract for women's history month right now and I have a couple of questions. We've decided on an honorarium of $150—is that agreeable? Should we have books there for signing? My advisor is checking out how much the housing is here and I'll let you know as soon as I find out. Thanks, Samara

Subj: e-mail!

Date: 96-09-05 21:52:29 EDT

From: kk278@email.com

To: maggio1@email.com

Hey, look at this! I finally got my e-mail to work! All through the efforts of a very nice fellow named Jerry who also happens to be a screenwriter doing research at Columbia who also happens to be very cute who also left his terminal to set me up on the appropriate computer who also gave me his phone number. For now, got to go! Hugs and kisses! I love all your mail! Katie

Subj: Just keepin' in touch

Date: 96-05-05 13:43:52 EDT

From: md@email.com

To: rm@email.com

Hi mom. Of course I'm alive. Had you doubts? I hardly think that three days without hearing from me justifies using capital letters on me.

> Everywhere e-mail is enhancing or even transforming relationships. Parents keep in regular touch with children in college who would not be caught dead telephoning home every day.
>
> —DEBORAH TANNEN

Subj: Friday morning
Date: 96-02-23 13:24:46 EST
From: md@email.com
To: rm@email.com

I will medley for you when I plane in to the Cities. Who's going to car me home from the airport? I'm going to go CD now.

From: pg@email.com
To: johnny@email.com
Date: Mon, 21 Sep 1998 16:31:31
Subject: Bonjour!

Comment etait ta classe de francais? Tu etais superbe, je suis sure! Cette machine est difficile; elle n'a pas d'accents!

I mailed you a French dictionary and two books, which are not wonderful, but which were the most succinct I could lay my hands on. When I have a minute, I'm going to photocopy a couple of pages of verb declensions for you because you really don't need a whole book of verbs—I saw one at Half Price, but it was just too much (not money, verbs).

From: nick@email.com
To: hartmore1@email.com
Date: Mon, 28 Sep 1998 19:26:34 EDT
Subject: Paris tomorrow!

Hey! I just got a job today as National Sales Manager for Oliphant Books, a trade publisher here in San Fran.

We're leaving for Paris tomorrow morning, for a week's stay. Hope to reside at a small hotel in the Marais. Any last minute tips/advice?

Yes, this is the SAME trip we had planned when I got sick 50 weeks ago, and twice since then. The tix expire on 10/13, so the timing was a little too close on this one.

Hope you're well,
Nick

From: selamlek@email.com
To: pat@email.com
Date: Mon, 28 Sep 1998 03:38:19

Hi and how is/was the trial?? Just a note to say thanks SO much for the pictures from the reunion. You chose very well for me—thanks!

I'm looking forward to seeing you on Friday. Am I losing my mind and did you already give me your flight number and arrival/departure times, or have I just lost them along with my mind? If the latter, will you forgive me and send them again? S.

From: hop@email.com
To: maggie@email.com
Date: Thu, 17 Sep 1998 09:03:35
Subject: your layover on Oct. 12

Because of the ridiculous parking situation, we won't meet you at the gate. Stay on the ticketing level and walk straight out the main doors. (There's a baggage level and a ground transportation level, but if you don't go down any stairs you'll be fine.) We'll be waiting out front to take you to dinner and we'll get you back in plenty of time to catch your connecting flight. See you then!

From: bc@email.com (Baldassare Calvo, Ph.D.)
To: ced@email.com (Members of Continuing Education Network)
Re: "Modern Business Writing: Creative Expressions"
Date: April 3, 1999

"Modern Business Writing: Creative Expressions" is a series of weekly distance education classes available to your location via videotape or video teleconferencing. This series of four seminars will cover the main forms of business writing (letters, reports, proposals, e-mail, etc.) with guidelines and practical examples for each.

Each live teleconference is limited to the first 15 locations to register. Fees are $50 per videotape or free teleconferencing to member sites.

For detailed information, reply by typing INFORMATION in the subject line. To receive educational credit, a list of attendees' names and employee numbers must be faxed to 608/555-1234.

> Effective communication is the cement that binds an organization together. It is the foundation upon which successful teamwork and good customer relationships are built. It is no accident that employees who can communicate effectively and assertively soon find themselves in leadership roles.
>
> —CONNIE PODESTA AND JEAN GATZ

From: harrys@email.com
To: 66078.67647@email.com
Date: Wed, 16 Sep 1998 15:57:43
Subject: Unsubscribe

Please remove my e-mail address from your list immediately. I do not appreciate your unsolicited messages.

From: gordy@email.com
To: cary@email.com
Date: Wed, 30 Sep 1998 11:21:21
Re: amorphous metals symposium

Sept. 16 is fine with me. Sorry to be late with my response—I've been out of town. I hope all's well with you. Gordy

From: rmay@email.com
To: cdodge@email.com
Date: Mon, 14 Sep 1998 14:09:30
Subject: your article on infoshops

Just a word: congratulations! I'm sending copies of your good article to everybody I know. Way to go! R.

From: jen_perne@email.com

To: linda_conway@email.com

Date: Wed, 19 Aug 1998 14:02:30

Re: new books

Five years ago, I'd've sent you a handwritten thank-you note on my monogrammed stationery or an attractive commercial thank-you card with a personal message at the bottom. Today: e-mail!

Will you accept my sincere but e-mail thanks and appreciation for your invaluable input on the new books? I am so impressed by their high quality, gorgeous designs, endpapers, typography, colors, type of paper, and their finishes, etc. They are a good example of book art at its finest and I feel lucky to be associated with a publisher that can produce books like that.

Thank you for all you contributed to these beautifully turned-out books. I could not be more pleased. J.P.

From: kenlake@email.com

To: cl@email.com

Date: Wed, 16 Sep 1998 18:25:23

Hi Colleen! I'm back at the office and have dug out from under mail, phone calls, e-mail—YOU know what it's like—and now I want to make good on whatever I promised you while under the influence of fresh mussels!

I remember you taking notes and thinking how smart that was, but I figured, "I'll never forget any of THIS." Ha!

Under separate cover, I'm sending the outlines and mailing addresses, both in hard copy and on disk. I'll also go through the Rattigan file to see if there's anything else useful to you.

But WHAT ELSE DID I SAY I'D SEND? Duh.

It was a pleasure seeing you. Thanks again for lunch!

From: clara@email.com
To: newmoon@email.com
Date: Mon, 21 Sep 1998 06:51:57
Attn: Joe Kelly

Hi Joe! I'm mailing you hard copies this morning (for italics, etc.), but I thought it might be easier for you to get most of the material electronically. I hope a couple of these will be useful to you.

As far as attribution goes: if you use only a couple of quotations, just use them. Should you use more than a few, or should you put a bunch of them together in a column or something, then I suppose there should be an "Excerpted from . . ." line.

Hope you're well. Don't worry about responding—I know you're always in the middle of fifty things.

From: ch@email.com
To: clayton1@email.com
Date: Fri, 25 Sep 1998 11:54:03
Subject: diversity conference

Hi! How "diverse" can our schedules be? After a meeting with the diversity symposium group this week, we decided that the 22nd of February would probably be better for us. Friday nights are difficult events to fill, compared to Monday nights. Are you able to do that? If so, I'll begin to work on flights and lodging. Have a good weekend! Cary

From: kjk33@email.com
To: susieq@email.com
Date: Mon, 14 Sep 1998 10:24:49

Hey Susan! How are you? What's new? I'm back, but sort of tentative about it at the moment—shoveling out, you know. D. said you called, but I didn't get the idea there was a message. I hope all's well.

The trip was wonderful: the drive out with the top down, stars overhead, music playing; pinball and pool games in Boston plus movies and Matt's good cooking and his personable tidy little cat; flying over flyover country to LA; time with darling Liz, horseback riding in the foothills of the Sierra Madre, Hollywood gawking, lots of time for reading, thinking, writing, vegging out. Really a luxury and I loved every minute of it. So.

Talk to you soon!

If you would be pungent, be brief; for it is with words as with sunbeams—the more they are condensed, the deeper they burn.

—ROBERT SOUTHEY

RELATED TOPICS

Acknowledgments

Family and Friends

Follow-up

Information

Memos

Pen Pals

17

Letters Dealing with Employment

INTRODUCTION

Robert Orben once said, "Every morning I get up and look through the *Forbes* list of the richest people in America. If I'm not there, I go to work." Most of us go to work.

While we're there, in-house correspondence has a great deal to do with workplace morale, efficiency, and congeniality. Courtesy and professionalism should mark every exchange of letters or memos.

This chapter deals with letters to and from employers and employees. For useful related material, check the Index. Or, when writing letters to obtain employment, see Applications, Cover Letters, References, and Résumés. For business announcements (changes in policy, personnel, organization), see Announcements.

> To love what you do and feel that it matters—how could anything be more fun?
>
> —KATHARINE GRAHAM

DO

- Date every in-house communication.
- Be brief. Your memos and letters will be more popular (and more quickly answered) if they are concise. Get in the habit of checking your correspondence specifically for words, sentences, and paragraphs that can be cut without loss of meaning.
- Be professional. Even when writing someone you know well, maintain a certain businesslike tone. Anything that gets put on paper can be saved and reread. Where a careless remark is soon forgotten, a carelessly written sentence lives forever.

> The ability to take pride in your own work is one of the hallmarks of sanity. Take away the ability to both work and be proud of it and you can drive anyone insane.
>
> —Nikki Giovanni

DON'T

- Don't put into writing anything to employees or prospective employees that could be considered actionable. Common sense provides some guidance, but consult with an attorney on the phrasing of sensitive letters (reprimands and terminations, for example).
- Don't include negative emotions; negative facts may have to be outlined, but the discussion should be objective rather than emotional (angry, vengeful, irritated, judgmental, hurt, contemptuous).

> The brain is a wonderful organ; it starts working the moment you get up in the morning, and does not stop until you get into the office.
>
> —Robert Frost

HELPFUL HINTS

- Some guidelines for responding to job applicants include: (1) When you are unable to make an immediate decision among applicants, acknowledge receipt of their materials or thank them for their interviews. If possible, tell them when you will notify them of your decision. Thank them for their interest in your company. (2) In the case of a rejection, express appreciation for the applicant's time and interest and state simply that you are unable to make an offer. If you think it is appropriate or helpful, you can briefly explain the decision. Close with positive comments on the person's application, an invitation to reapply at a later time (if appropriate), and your confidence of success in the person's search for a suitable position. (3) When offering someone a position, open with congratulatory and complimentary remarks. Include any necessary information or confirmation of the job description and the name and telephone number of someone who can answer further questions. Close with an expression of goodwill about the person's employment with the company. You may want to insert some positive remarks about the company to influence the person's decision to accept the offer.

- Send goodwill notes of congratulations and commendation to: employees who have completed a project, obtained a new account, or otherwise contributed to the good of the company; co-workers and employees who have been promoted or who have received awards; workers marking service anniversaries; those who are retiring; employees, co-workers, and managers celebrating personal milestones (birth of baby, marriage). These notes are some of the least obligatory and most influential of office correspondence.

- Most in-house appointments or meetings are arranged by telephone, e-mail, or memo: explain why you want the meeting, offer possible dates and times, and express your appreciation for the person's attention to your request. If you need to change a meeting, always mention the original time and date and ask for confirmation of the new time. If you need to cancel a meeting, repeat the time and date, state that you must cancel (briefly explaining why), and apologize for the inconvenience. If you miss a scheduled meeting, write an immediate, sincere apology; ask what you can do to make amends.

- Raises and promotions are usually given on the basis of fairly standard criteria. However, if you write a letter requesting either, be brief and factual, and supply supporting documents (letters of commendation, patents, research papers, sales records, evaluations, awards). Nobody ever has a "right" to a raise; don't let this attitude color your letter. Avoid threatening to leave; you may be given the opportunity. Don't compare your salary to others'; management does not appreciate employees who compare salaries, and they may become defensive. Instead, show how your work has become more valuable to the company or speak of an "adjustment" to reflect additional hours, duties, or productivity.

- To reprimand an employee, begin with a positive or complimentary remark. Describe factually the unacceptable employee behavior and (if necessary) tell why it is unacceptable. Suggest how the employee can improve or change. If appropriate, state the consequences of continuing the behavior. Close with an expression of confidence that the situation will be successfully dealt with by the employee. A reprimand is brief, respectful, encouraging, and positive (instead of writing, "Don't send out any letters with misspellings," write, "Please use your spellcheck function followed by a dictionary check of any questionable words").

- The painful and unpleasant task of notifying employees of layoffs or terminations has become fairly codified, partly because of labor unions, partly because of legal ramifications, and partly because it is most efficient for large organizations to standardize their approach in dealing with them. When a letter is written, it is usually brief. In some situations a letter could include: a statement about the layoff or termination; an expression of regret for the necessity of taking this measure; the date on which the layoff or termination becomes effective; in the case of a layoff, the possible length of the time, if known; details on company layoff and termination policies, career counseling, letters of recommendation, available public assistance, and any other information that will help the employee cope with the layoff or termination; the name and telephone number of someone who can answer further questions.

- The common practice is to resign in person, and then to follow up with a letter. Begin with a positive remark about the position, company, or person to whom you are writing. State that you are resigning as of a specific date. In most cases, offer a reason: poor health or work-related health problems; age; greater opportunities for advancement and higher salary, or more desirable location with another company; a family transfer; career change; recent changes that have affected your position. "For personal reasons" is used when that is accurate or when you prefer not to identify the real reason. Whatever reason you present will be the one used in official announcements, so choose your words accordingly. Be brief, dignified, and somewhat formal; a letter of resignation is not the place for complaints and anger. You may need the company's goodwill for letters of reference or future associations in your professional community. If you are leaving because of illegal or dishonest practices, it would be effective to take as much documentation as you can to outside ombuds agencies. If you are leaving under pleasant circumstances, you may want to offer to train your replacement. Express your appreciation for your co-workers, management, company, or other positive aspects of your employment. In some situations, a one-sentence letter of resignation, with no explanation, is appropriate. If you have been asked to resign or have been discharged, don't mention this; simply state that you are resigning, which is then the way it will appear in the official records.

- To accept a letter of resignation, include some expression of regret, some positive comments on the person's association with the organization, and good wishes for the person's future.

- Most in-house correspondence consists of memos. More official communications (promotions and resignations, for example) or letters that go in people's files are typed on letterhead stationery.

> People are not the best because they work hard. They work hard because they are the best.
>
> —BETTE MIDLER

GETTING STARTED

Thank you for your letter and résumé, which we received today.

We have received a number of responses to our advertisement for the driver education instructor position, and we ask your patience while we evaluate them.

We are pleased to offer you the internship with the Caroline Bury Summer Youth Art Program.

Although your credentials are impressive, we have decided to offer the position to someone with more experience in microcomputer analysis and design.

Unfortunately we are not able to offer you a position with Barnabas Ltd. at this time. Our decision in no way reflects on your considerable qualifications.

Thank you for the opportunity to work for Tegeus-Chromis Learning Systems as a marketing analyst. I am delighted to accept this position with such a distinguished and forward-looking company.

I accept with great pleasure the offer to join Hastings Health Care as medical archive product manager.

I am looking forward to a long and productive association with Bolton Cork & Seal Company.

I appreciate very much your offer of the position of financial aid officer—and I'm sure you know how much I wanted the position—but I have, in the meantime, accepted a position that involves one-fourth the commute, which turned out to be a deciding factor.

On behalf of the management of Alfred Booker Publications, I am pleased to inform you that you have been promoted to Senior Editor, effective June 1.

I am writing to recommend in the strongest possible terms that Thorkell Mylrea be promoted to Associate Counsel.

Congratulations on your promotion—we are all pleased for you.

Please join me in congratulating Justine Brent on her promotion to Supervisor of the Pediatrics Unit.

Just a note to tell you that your report was thorough, well-written, and highly convincing—it could serve as a model of the effective report.

I have very much enjoyed my volunteer work at the Alexander Clues Animal Center, but for health reasons I must cut back on my activities and will not be available after August 1.

Did I have the date wrong? I thought we were meeting yesterday at 1:30 p.m. I won't be free again until late next week, but maybe we can arrange something then. Please let me hear from you.

As a follow-up to our discussions on September 3 and September 7, I am writing to formalize complaints about your lack of compliance with company safety regulations.

Your resignation has been received with regret, and will be effective June 1, as you requested.

It's that time of year—annual performance review time—and I'm looking forward to meeting with you. Please complete the attached form and call me to set up a time for us to talk.

I'm looking for a college student who would be interested in interning in the materials science lab this summer—do any of you know anyone who might be suitable?

I would like to meet with you to review the circumstances leading up to my termination notice.

May I have a few minutes of your time sometime in the next week or two to discuss the possibilities of my transferring to the Compson branch?

You are cordially invited to a lunchtime celebration in the South Banquet Room at noon on September 1 to wish Julius Beaufort well as he takes his retirement, effective September 15.

Eighty percent of success is showing up.

—WOODY ALLEN

MODEL LETTERS

TO: All employees
FROM: Human Resources
DATE: November 1, 1999
RE: Reimbursed travel expenses

A number of travel expense forms are being completed and turned in after business travel. Please note that company policy requires travel expenses to be preapproved. For questions, contact Lola Pratt, extension 341.

TO: Building 102 employees
FROM: Constance Broddle
DATE: April 3, 1999
SUBJECT: Safety Seminars

By now you are all aware of the laboratory accident that occurred in Building 102 last week. Although OSHA has determined that it was not preventable, they recommended increased employee education.

Please sign up for one of the required safety seminars listed below:

Tuesday, 2 p.m., Building 102, Room 16

Tuesday, 4 p.m., Building 102, Room 18

Wednesday, 2 p.m., Building 102, Room 18

Friday, 2 p.m., Building 102, Room 16

Dear Bettina Percival Reynaud,

Thank you for applying for the position of multimedia technologist with Constantin-Scott Graphics Corp. Your work history is noteworthy, and you made an excellent impression at your interview. As you know, however, we were looking for someone with at least five years' experience, and we did find a candidate with that qualification.

We appreciate your interest in Constantin-Scott Graphics and, in fact, would like to suggest that you reapply to us in six months when we expect to have another such position open. We will keep your application on file until then.

I am sure that you will be an asset to the company that hires you—good luck in finding the right place.

Sincerely,

Dear Jed Holland,

Thank you for coming in for the interview on Monday. We all enjoyed meeting you.

I would like to offer you the scanning and image editing position at a beginning salary of $19,500 a year. If you decide to accept this offer, you will have the option of beginning work on either September 11 or 18. Please let me know which date you prefer.

The first three months will constitute a training period, including several scheduled orientation sessions. At the end of that time, a mutual evaluation will determine whether we are satisfied with your work and whether you are satisfied with your position. If the evaluation is positive, which we expect it to be, you will be placed on the staff as a full-time permanent employee with medical and dental benefits. Until that time, however, you will be classified as a temporary employee and will not be eligible for permanent benefits.

Please let me know as soon as possible if you wish to accept our offer. We are very much looking forward to working with you.

Yours truly,

TO: Christine Brant
    Orin Mannon
    Peter Niles
FROM: E. O'Neill
DATE: June 30, 2001

Congratulations on the success of the Electra Project! The Board of Directors was impressed and pleased and asked me to pass on to you their heartfelt thanks and appreciation for the many hours of overtime you put in, for your creative solutions to a difficult problem, and for the professional and congenial way in which you worked together on a stressful project.

TO: Register personnel
FROM: Rudy Saltiera
DATE: May 3, 1999
SUBJECT: Use of demagnetizers

There has been an increase lately in the frequency of our ESA alarms being activated. Although the alarms can be triggered by pacemakers or magnetic keys or may even be giving phantom signals, they most often are activated by items that have not been properly demagnetized at the checkout counters. Please pay special attention to your demagnetizing as we try to eliminate unnecessary alarm signals.

Dear Melancthon Conant,

As you know, the last six months have been difficult for Decameron Systems as we have tried to compensate for a slow economy, increased competition, and low sales. We had hoped to retain all our employees, but it has become apparent that this will not be possible.

It is with great regret that we inform you that we are unable to continue your employment after July 1. We hope that our difficulties are temporary and that this layoff will also be temporary. We are not in a position, however, to promise anything at this time.

Please check with Personnel for information on letters of reference, company layoff policies, public assistance available to you until you find other employment, and career counseling.

Please accept our appreciation for your fine work record and our expression of regret at our necessity to take this step.

> Work itself is the reward. If I choose challenging work it will pay me back with interest. At least I'll be interested even if nobody else is. And this attempt for excellence is what sustains the most well lived and satisfying, successful lives.
>
> —MERYL STREEP

Dear Patients and Friends,

I plan to retire from the practice of dentistry effective June 1, 1998. Your records are being conveyed to my son, Dr. Matthew J. Maggio, at 1099 Kenyon Road.

I sincerely appreciate the trust and confidence you have had in me for your dental needs all these years. I have truly enjoyed the pleasure of knowing you personally and professionally.

I am positive that my son can provide you with the same care and interest in your dental health, if you so desire.

Closing with a thank you, I am

Sincerely,

Paul J. Maggio, D.D.S.

Dear Mr. Dedalus,

It is with more than a little regret that I write to say I have decided to take another position and thus will not be accepting your excellent job offer. As you know, I admire The Finnegan Companies very much and was honored to be offered the position of pension administrator. This was a difficult decision and only time will show whether I made the right choice.

In the meantime, I want to thank you for your many kindnesses to me and to wish you and The Finnegan Companies continued success and prosperity.

Dear Marjorie Daw,

Thank you for your good letter and résumé. It was a pleasure to read your very personalized and well-researched reasons for wanting to work for Delany, Flemming, and Aldrich.

We are, unfortunately, not adding to our staff at the moment, but I will keep your résumé on file. Such intelligent interest in our firm on the part of a job candidate is always impressive and intriguing to us.

Best wishes to you in finding a fulfilling and rewarding position.

Dear Mrs. McKlennar,

I am pleased to offer you the part-time position of behavior health coordinator, starting at $9.75 per hour. Enclosed is a copy of The Edmonds Clinic's Employment Policy.

This offer is contingent upon the results of a medical preplacement examination, which includes drug and alcohol tests. Please contact my secretary, Magdelana Martin (555-1234), who will make arrangements for the examination. Check back with Ms. Martin five days after the examination. If the results are acceptable, we can establish an employment start date.

If you accept our offer of employment, you will need to complete the top portion of an Employment Eligibility Form (Department of Justice Form I-9) and provide documents that certify you are a citizen of the United States. A listing of documents that are acceptable and a sample I-9 form are attached.

On your scheduled starting date, please come to the Clinic's staffing office at 7:45 a.m. for a brief orientation. (You may park in the visitor parking lot until you have been issued a sticker.)

We would appreciate having your decision about this offer within five days of the date of this letter.

If you have any questions about the position or the terms of this offer, I can be reached at 555-1111.

To: Yucca Plaza employees
From: Cherry Martin, Director of Personnel
Date: October 15

   We are sorry to announce that Dorothea O'Faye has resigned as The Yucca Plaza Director of Customer Relations effective November 1. She has accepted the position of Managing Director with Martin Pelley Holding Corp. Although we will miss her, we wish her every success in her new position. She will be replaced by Stephen R. Rojack, currently Assistant Director of Customer Relations.

> It's strange how unimportant your job is when you ask for a raise, and how important it is when you want a day off.
>
> —HOWIE LASSETER

RELATED TOPICS

Announcements

Applications

Appreciation

Congratulations

Cover Letters

Follow-up

References

Refusals

Responses

Résumés

Thank You

Welcome

18

Letters to Family and Friends

INTRODUCTION

With the advent of every new technology, the death of letterwriting is announced or at least predicted. In 1912, Agnes Repplier wrote, "Why do so many ingenious theorists give fresh reasons every year for the decline of letter writing, and why do they assume . . . that it has declined? . . . They talk of telegrams, and telephones, and postal cards, as if any discovery of science, any device of civilization, could eradicate from the human heart that passion for self-expression which is the impelling force of letters."

E-mail and inexpensive long-distance dialing have certainly taken over some letterwriting functions. Happily, in the case of e-mail, it is not an "either/or" proposition. E-mail has probably fueled writing among family and friends like nothing since the pony express. It would be highly premature to speak of the demise of letterwriting.

For special kinds of letters to family and friends, see the specific chapters (for example, Love Letters or Holidays).

> How eagerly in all times and all places, have people waited for mail from home! How wistfully have they repeated, over and over again, that old familiar question: "Any mail for me?"
>
> —LILLIAN EICHLER WATSON

DO

- Write when it is a pleasure and not a chore (unless, of course, this only happens to you with the return of the locusts). The casual guideline about letters to family and friends is that short and frequent is better than long and infrequent. However, this is a matter of temperament and the general feeling is that it is very good to get personal mail at all, never mind whether it is short and infrequent, or otherwise.

- Open with a pleasantry indicating you are glad to be thinking about the other person.

- If you're stumped for something to write about, consider these topics: what you've been doing lately; books you've read; movies, plays, sports events you've seen; local or national politics; news of family or friends that the other person knows; a joke you heard or something that made you laugh; issues you care about (gun control, the tax code, youthful violence, television programming); something new or used you just bought; plans for the summer, the fall, next year; the weather; changes at work; pets' behavior; hobbies or collections; or, choose one recent event (it needn't be terribly important) and tell it like a story.

- Include cartoons, newspaper clippings, snapshots, bookmarks, or other materials that are satisfying to receive and make your letter look like a great deal more than it is.

- Close with an expression of affection or love and with a forward-looking statement about seeing or hearing from the person.

> Will you write me immediately? Write me. When I receive your letters I feel as though they're fanning me with peacock feathers.
>
> —FEDERICO GARCÍA LORCA

DON'T

- Don't begin with an apology for not writing or with a statement that you have nothing to say. Instead, begin with something cheerful, positive, and interesting.

- Don't let your letter consist entirely of questions and comments on the other person's life and last letter ("Your remodeled kitchen sounds fantastic!"; "So how does your garden grow?"; "I'll bet you were proud of Cicely"). Mark Van Doren once said, "The letter which merely answers another letter is no letter at all." And Sigmund Freud said, "I consider it a good rule for letterwriting to leave unmentioned what the recipient already knows, and instead tell . . . something new." D. H. Lawrence said, "I love people who can write reams and reams about themselves: it seems generous."

- Don't complain or be negative (unless of course you can do it entertainingly). A cheerful, positive tone is always welcome (unless you or your reader has been facing difficulties when it might be better to be a little more realistic about your feelings).

- Don't close with "Well, I've bored you long enough" or "I'd better quit before you fall asleep." Instead, say how much you'd enjoy hearing from them when time allows or how much you miss them or how happy you were about their news.

> I am much fonder of receiving letters, than writing them: but I believe this is no very uncommon case.
>
> — Mary Lamb

HELPFUL HINTS

- Remember your writing teacher's advice to "Elaborate! Elaborate!" Instead of merely reporting that you went camping, elaborate on the theme. Almost any sentence lends itself to some kind of elaboration, and that's usually the kind of detailed writing that's enjoyable to read.

- Postcards are a great help for keeping in touch when you haven't time for a letter. Keep a stack of colorful, funny, or oldtime postcards near your letterwriting area and get in the habit of sending off a couple a week. This will make you very popular and will relieve you of the guilt that unanswered mail produces in most people.

- While it is rarely a good idea to write to unknown individuals who are incarcerated, it is generally a good idea to write family and friends who are in jail or in prison. They appreciate mail. The first several letters will be awkward, but if you can establish some neutral subjects (books, interests, hobbies, mutual friends, social issues), the letters will become easier to write with time and practice.

- Some thoughts on writing to children: Print or type your letter; it's easier for children to read. Children appreciate a stimulating, challenging, or curious statement, a bit of trivia, a thought problem, word puzzle, anecdote, or joke. Share your thoughts, discuss ideas, ask questions, talk about something that is important to you. Too often adults underestimate children, who enjoy being let into the adult world. Avoid the word "kids" ("I'm so proud of you kids!" "Do you kids still live on pizza? Here's a certificate good for a free one"). Avoid preaching or writing down to young people. Reread your letter as though someone were sending it to you or to some adult you know. Except for the reading level, does it sound okay? Many young people generally aren't fond of writing letters. Enclose with your letter a few postcards or a self-addressed envelope with an unattached stamp (so that the stamp isn't wasted in case they don't write back). Construct a humorous letter for the child to return to you that consists of boxes to check off with various made-up statements and "news." This technique will probably net you a letter at least once. When writing a child who is away from home for the first time, avoid expressing how much they are missed. You may say lightly, "We miss you!" but do not go into detail about how empty the house seems. Some children take these things seriously and feel responsible for their parents' feelings. It is also better to avoid detailing what everybody at home is doing; that too can make them sad. Instead, ask questions that will provide them with something to write back about: What time do you get up? What do you usually eat for breakfast? Do you have a swimming class? Who else lives in your cabin? Are there any animals there? Have you been in a canoe yet? What is your favorite activity? Who is your counselor? Have you made new friends? Who? Very young children appreciate mail even if they can't read. When you write remember that a parent will be reading it aloud; things sound different that way. Include a colorful drawing or cut-out picture along with their name (which many youngsters recognize early on), a picture of you, a fancy pencil, or a small toy.

• When children will be in the care of adults other than their parents or guardians, they should have with them a letter authorizing emergency medical help, if necessary. In the case of summer camps or day-care providers, a form for this purpose is generally provided. But if you are leaving your children with someone for the weekend, write: "I [name] give permission to [name of person caring for your children] to authorize any necessary medical emergency care for [name of child or children] from [date] to [date]." Sign and date the letter. If known, add a telephone number where you can be reached.

It is an unfortunate fact that the youngsters at summer camp who are the most homesick are those who have dogs at home.

—Jack Herbert

GETTING STARTED

How are you?

Where do I begin?

So much has happened since I last wrote.

I can't tell you how much I appreciated your letter.

If only I wrote as often as I thought about you!

Your letter was such fun to read—thanks!

And how is my favorite cousin?

We recently became the proud and confused owners of a personal computer, and you are about to sample our first efforts.

Thanks so much for your last great letter.

I feel like writing you an accomplished, deft, clever, witty, imaginative letter (I have been using the thesaurus option on my computer—can you tell?) but I am feeling kind of inarticulate, deficient, dimwitted, thick, dull, backward, and dense at the moment (egad, thesauri are fun).

Hello. Hello. I hope that's twice as good as Hello.

Dear Sis o' mine and spouse o' hers, Greetings! Hey, what's happening! Hey! hey! hey!

This is what I'm doing with that one extra hour I get this time of year when we switch from Daylight Savings Time to Central Standard Time—I'm writing to you.

We were so happy to hear that you'll be moving closer to us!

Just a note to say we think about you often, but not in any way that you'd know about (unless you're a mindreader).

Thank you so much for your letter. Your line, "Some days I forget exactly who the enemy is at the moment but I get over it," has stayed with me ever since. Ain't that the truth, Ruth.

Marguerite Kelly and Elia Parsons once wrote, "Each child has one extra line to your heart, which no other child can replace. That helps explain how I can love each of you 'the most.'"

> To send a letter is a good way to go somewhere without moving anything but your heart.
>
> —PHYLLIS THEROUX

MODEL LETTERS

TO: Mom, Dad, Frank, Mary, Mike M., Courtney, Anthony, Pat, Cid, Seery, Cass, Kevin, David M., Mary C., Mike P., Tom, Anna, Paul, Terry, Kalli, Lauren, Leah, Mark, Matt M., Laura, Sam, Jack, David K., Liz, Katie, Matt K.

RE: August get-together

Rooms have been reserved from Tuesday, August 4, to Sunday, August 9, at the Select Inn, which is located 1 mile from the Mall of America, near a casino, two zoos, and several dinner and improv theaters, and 1 mile from the airport—if you are flying in, a 24-hour free shuttle connects the airport and the motel.

Services and amenities include: restaurant, lounge, Olympic-size indoor pool, 7,000-sq.-ft. Health Club (which we can use), whirlpools, saunas, game room, "USA Today" delivered to your room M-F, free coffee and apples in the lobby. Two years ago they totally renovated the inn. Rooms include voice mail, hairdryers, irons/ironing boards, free local phone calls and long-distance access, coffeemaker, dataports, cable TV. One of the many features they list is "automatic revolving door" in the lobby. Just thought you'd like to know.

We are renting a hospitality room overlooking the pool, where we can have meals and hang out any time of day or night, thereby sparing rooms where people are sleeping, showering, acting weird, etc.

What you need to do:

1. Note August 4-9, 1998, on your calendars.
2. Figure out your own schedule and travel plans.
3. Call the Select Inn to hold your room with a credit card.

Please direct all questions, complaints, insults, or whining to Matt M. (I am merely his puppet). Lawsuits will be handled by Pat. For dental work, call 515/555-1981, 608/555-4794, or 515/555-4565. All other inquiries will be returned unopened.

Signed,

One of You

P.S. For those of you receiving this on e-mail, a hard copy will follow.

Dear Son,

Thanks for installing all the games on my computer. Although, well, I wasn't getting any work done so I closed down Minesweepers Sunday evening about 6:31 and I've been without it ever since. Like right now, for example, I'm without it. I will be without it again tomorrow. But I'm doing fine. I don't think about it too much. Well, a little bit right after breakfast, like when I might read the papers except that I think I could also be playing Minesweepers. I mean, IF I could play it. And then, oh, sometimes a little bit right after I read the papers. And then maybe when like, for example, somebody really chatty calls and I think, "Gee I could play Minesweepers while this conversation is just going on and on," although I probably wouldn't because that's so rude. But I think about it. But mostly I don't think about it. Well, a little bit in the afternoon when I feel sleepy sometimes and I think, "If I had Minesweepers I could play for just a little while, like, maybe only 15 minutes, or maybe an hour. Or well, I guess it could be an hour or two. Anyway, *then* I'd feel wide awake." But I guess the time I really think about it is late afternoon when I'm tired from being at my desk all day and I'd just like to kind of let down and relax with a little level-3 Minesweepers. Well, I guess the only other time I think about it is right before bedtime and I think, "Oh just one last little game." So, as I say, I'm doing pretty well without it even though it's been two whole days, well, 48 and a half hours right now actually, but I'm getting along fine without it. Just thought you'd like to know. Love from your Minesweep—no, I mean from your Mother.

Dear, dear Bob,

I wouldn't blame you if you periodically gave up on us ("What is it with those people?"), but I hope you won't. George Sand said, "It is always the best friends who are neglected and ignored."

How are you, and how, specifically, are your back and your teeth? Getting older is a bummer, isn't it? As an uncle of mine says frequently and loudly, "Nothing good happens to you when you get old!"

And what about your friend in Eau Claire? I noticed you haven't visited him yet. If you have visited him, and didn't tell us, we're going to write you right off our Christmas card list. (Yeah, I thought that'd get you!)

This last letter of yours (written in O'Hare Airport) was one of your better ones. I will save it for discussion sometime when we're all sitting around and can really get into conspicuous consumption, suicides of young people, getting set in our ways, oh, many things . . .

Matt's in the living room playing, "The No Hope, No Soap, No House, No Mouse Blues." So I'm a little distracted.

I tried to call you this afternoon but, of course, you heard it was me and you wouldn't pick up the phone. Fine. We'll have our chat some other time. 'Til then, as Sanford Berman always says, "Be well!"

Dear BonBon,

(Well, you're always playing with *my* name. . . !) What is new around your house? How was Emily's ballet début? Did you take pictures? Do you have a couple for me?

We have just been consumers and we are trying to feel good about ourselves again. We went *furniture* shopping. Us. Can you imagine? This is how bad it was: when I tried to give away our old furniture, nobody would take it—not impoverished college students, not Goodwill, not Salvation Army, not even homeless shelters. And here I used to invite guests to sit on it. The new furniture is not much of an improvement—the colors fight with the rug and the rug has always fought with the wallpaper. The sofa is way too large for the living room, but you know what? We ran out of interest before we ran into the right furniture.

Here's a picture of Liz. Is she cute or what? She just treated a dog who ate an entire roll of toilet paper—and a cat who needed Prozac. Katie's all excited about the script for her next film. All I know is that it's some horror piece set in the snow, which she says will be a production nightmare. So I say, couldn't you have horror in the grass or something? No, it's got to be snow. Fine. Matt is putting the final touches to a composition for 120 violins. Where you find 120 violins I don't know. Whatever. I sit here and listen to the three of them talking about things that sound impossible to me . . . and enjoy it!

Lots of love to you, Bonnie!

From: drlizk@email.com
To: dkoskenmaki@email.com
      kk278@email.com
      mdkosken@ma.email.com
      maggio1@email.com
Date: Fri, 20 Feb 1998 20:55:31
Subject: New address

Hello there, family member! As of the 27th, my new home address and phone number as well as the clinic address and phone number will be as shown below.

I love California. I hope each of you can visit me sometime soon! As an added incentive, my friends at the stable said that if I ever have visitors, I can borrow one of their horses so I can show you around the mountains and river valley of San Gabriel on horseback. I guess that's not much of an incentive for Dad. However, as a special inducement for him, now I can rock climb (sort of), and we can go rock climbing together! I suppose Matt wouldn't be too intrigued by the horse incentive either. Hmmm—well, Matt, I know of some very hip jazz clubs that I bet you'd love—and I promise that if you come visit me I'll never ask you another computer question as long as I live. This is truly the most beautiful time of the year to visit, you know.

I'm sure I'll talk to you soon, by e-mail or otherwise.

> Letters freeze time for us, eternalizing shared experiences so we can go back and draw strength from them. Letters are like deposits in a secret bank that can be withdrawn when they are needed. And as we look back in love, we appreciate anew the thought and time that was taken to express those feelings.
>
> —LOIS WYSE

Dear Momma!

I just finished shooting an exercise in the rain, and I was up until three last night acting in someone else's shoot (and then up at seven to work on my own shoot). I would be extremely content, except that I couldn't get my last two shots because the camera got wet and started malfunctioning. My poor actors were soaked and frozen by the time we were through.

I realized that I am surprisingly sad about my li'l bunny. I always knew she was going to die, but after she lived through last fall, I guess I figured she was invincible. It wouldn't have meant anything to her, but I feel bad that I wasn't there before she died. I don't want a new bunny, not even a little baby fuzzy one; I miss Twinky, rascal that she was. James was very sympathetic. I told two friends at work, though, and they both responded by saying, "Oh. So anyway, I had to get up at six this morning . . ." and "Where's the stapler?"

The computer is working very slowly today, so I guess that's it for my patience and message.

I loves my Mom.

Katie

Dear Elly,

I cherish your warm, thoughtful, and newsy letters. I wish that over the years a few circumstances (distance, time, and money) had allowed us to see more of each other. And yet, how can I complain? One of your letters is like visiting for weeks with anyone else.

When I see your return address on an envelope, I put my feet up on my desk, pour a fresh cup of tea, reach for the letter-opener, and prepare for a restful and enjoyable time-out.

I'll be responding to your letter with my usual pages and pages, but for the moment, I just wanted you to know what a pleasure your letters are to me.

Love,
Doreen

> I have walked on air all day since getting your letter.
>
> —Vita Sackville-West

Hey Bung!

Are you going to our 35th college reunion? Flying from Los Angeles to Boston isn't worth it to me unless you're going to be there. Let me know, will you?

Do you remember the way we spent the first night of our first day at college? If we both end up at the reunion, let's do it again for old times' sake.

Best!

W.M.

From: nn@email.com
To: daisy1234@email.com
Date: Tue, 22 Apr 1999 13:09:14

Daisy, Daisy, Daisy! It was such a treat to have you and your sibs come by! Having such appreciative and demonstrative guests for lunch was a real pleasure for us. You have four articles due May 1? Whew! Good luck! Since you mentioned romantic quotes, I'll tell you what we say when we're asked how we've stayed together so long: "It's easy! Neither of us understands the other!" Come again, please. We'll have leg of lamb next time. David wants to know (and so do I) the address of the pensione you stayed in when you were in Rome. N.

> What a treat to receive a letter from a friend! . . . I hold
> my treasure lightly and wait until I have a quiet moment
> alone before I open it. I hate to dilute the anticipation and
> appreciation of someone's thoughts and feelings by facing
> them when I'm distracted. Someone has taken the time to
> focus on me, even if only for a moment. I feel touched
> and want to savor the all-too-rare experience.
>
> —Alexandra Stoddard

From: jazzou@email.com
To: florry@email.com
Date: Thu, 24 Sep 1998 20:16:54 EDT
Subject: Hi!

Yes, ain't e-mail grand? Keeps me in touch with people I otherwise wouldn't communicate with, which is most everyone since I don't write too many letters. Glad to have your online handle.

I'll be getting into your fair city on October 27. I'll go directly from the airport to the Delta Queen, which will be docked at the steamboat landing where it usually is, I presume. It is customary for the boat to depart around 7 or 7:30 p.m., but it's been known to leave as early as 6 p.m. (doubtful, though, since we're usually awaiting straggling passengers or luggage). If you're able to come visit, we can sit and chat awhile. Announce yourselves at the gangway as the guests of Jazzou Jones and they should let you on board, or they can page me, or whatever the latest policy is. At any rate, I hope we can connect, since it's always a great pleasure just to be with you and get a little caught up with each other.

John is a senior now and busily involved in his last year of his great passion—soccer. He's the team captain and so far leading a pretty talented bunch of guys in a 3-1-0 season. Diane and I go to every game and act like typical idiotic parents. He's applying to several colleges—his interests are in coaching, psychology, and owning and operating a bar. It'll be fun to watch him combine that. I've made him promise to let me book the correct kind of entertainment for the bar so I'll always have a place to play my ragtime.

My big project right now is reissuing my tried-and-true recording "Riverboat Ragtime" on CD. This is my 20th season on the river and I'm noting the occasion by taking the original recording, which was a 33 1/3 LP and then a cassette, and adding 5 or 6 new rags and producing it as a CD and lengthened cassette. My latest new one is "Paddlewheel Rag," which will complement my other original from the record, "High Water."

Hey, this turned into a lengthy thing, and you're probably ready to get on with your life, so I'll close for now. See you on the 27th! Love to all.

> A handwritten, personal letter has become a genuine modern-day luxury, like a child's pony ride.
>
> —SHANA ALEXANDER

RELATED TOPICS

Advice

Anniversaries

Apologies

Birthdays

Congratulations

Get Well

Holidays

Love Letters

Pen Pals

Thank You

Weddings

Welcome

19

Faxed Letters

INTRODUCTION

The fax (short for facsimile machine) has become a way of life for many individuals and businesses. It scans your letter, converts the words and graphics to signals that can be sent over telephone lines, and transmits them to a machine at the other end, where the process is reversed. Like a photocopying machine, it works only with already prepared documents.

A letter written to be sent by fax is just like any other letter. However, once you have typed or printed it and signed your name, you insert it in the fax machine instead of folding it, addressing an envelope, enclosing the letter in the envelope, sealing it, stamping it—and waiting several days for it to reach your addressee.

The virtue of the faxed page is its speed, not its beauty. Some fax paper is not appealing aesthetically. The print can be blurry or at times illegible, depending on the quality of the original document and the machines used to transmit it.

> Our perception that we have "no time" is one of the distinctive marks of modern Western culture.
>
> —MARGARET VISSER

DO

- Determine whether faxing is indicated. If you and your addressee both agree that you need a speedy transferal of data or information, it is the best choice. Routinely sending letters by fax that aren't in any particular hurry is not a good idea. It costs the recipient to receive a fax, so you want to be sure the person will welcome it, not look on your letter as a nuisance.

- Write your letter as carefully as you would if you were putting it in an envelope and sending it by mail.

- Include on a cover sheet or the first page of your fax: your name along with information on how to contact you (fax number, e-mail address, company name and address, phone number).

- Indicate how many pages are being faxed. Include the cover sheet in your count. This lets recipients know whether they have received everything you sent.

- Use a readable font—at least 10-point size is generally suggested. Anything smaller is not very pleasant to read.

> Americans have more time-saving devices and less time than any people in the world.
>
> —ANONYMOUS

DON'T

- Don't fax something that has already been faxed several times; each transmission reduces its sharpness, making it hard to read and unappealing-looking. Any fax that is a little fuzzy looking when you get it is going to look worse after you send it on.

- Don't send confidential and sensitive information by fax, unless you are certain that only your intended recipient will collect it from the fax machine on the other end. Anyone can read your letter while the fax machine is printing it or while it waits to be picked up by or distributed to your recipient. Want ads may say, "Please fax confidential résumé," but it is better to assume that confidentiality is not absolute.

- Don't take stapled items into a copy center to be faxed; this is one of the most common annoyances to copy shop personnel. Pages are sent one at a time.

Desire to have things done quickly prevents their being done thoroughly.

—CONFUCIUS

HELPFUL HINTS

- Faxing résumés and application letters has become acceptable to many companies and is actively solicited by others ("Please fax or mail résumé to . . ."). Faxing a résumé or letter of application in such cases is appropriate and probably necessary since other applicants will be faxing theirs.

- Faxes can be sent to anyone who has a fax machine—and to anyone who doesn't. People who do not have a machine of their own can send and receive faxes at most photocopy centers. To send, bring in the letter or pages to be faxed while you wait. To receive, notify the person at the other end of the store's fax number and advise them to put your name and phone number at the top of the fax so the store can call you when it arrives.

- If you or your company relies on the fax machine for much of your correspondence, it is thrifty and efficient to design letterhead stationery that will accommodate information needed for faxing. You can then do away with the cover page, saving yourself and your recipient time, paper, and phone costs.

- Organizations that do a great deal of faxing would be wise to experiment with different ink colors, letterheads, and fonts, in order to find the ones that look best after being faxed.

- Faxing is particularly useful for correspondence with people in other parts of the world. Many foreign hotels now routinely request that reservations be made by fax. Businesses appreciate that transmissions are instantaneous and do not have the awkwardness of factoring in different time zones. Faxes have all the immediacy of a telephone call but they are much less expensive.

- There is thus far a bias against indiscriminate faxing of sales-oriented material. Theoretically someone could fax a sales letter to all the fax numbers they can find. However, this means recipients are paying to receive something they did not ask for. Although most of us have learned to live with unsolicited third-class mail, we would not be pleased to have to pay to receive it.

There can be too much communication between people.

—ANN BEATTIE

GETTING STARTED

Here are the figures you wanted.

This will confirm the arrangements we made on the telephone today.

Here is the missing paragraph for the op-ed piece appearing in this evening's paper.

The names and phone numbers listed below were correct as of this morning.

I'm sorry about the rush, but I'd appreciate it if you could look over this contract and let me know by noon if it's going to work for you.

We were ready to start printing when Tony Kirby pointed out that this graph doesn't look right—will you check it over and get back to us right away?

> We can outrun the wind and the storm, but we cannot outrun the demon of Hurry.
>
> —JOHN BURROUGHS

MODEL LETTERS

TO: Hotel Al Madarig
FAX # 011.39.924.33.790

Salute!

We will be in Castellammare del Golfo in October and would like to make the following reservations:

October 25–30 (6 nights—we will leave the morning of the 31st)

3 rooms: 1 with 2 beds for 2 people (144,000 lire per night)
      1 with 1 bed for 1 person (92,000 lire per night)
      1 with 1 bed for 1 person (92,000 lire per night)

If possible, could we have rooms with a view of the sea?

If you do not have an elevator, could you please see that the room with two beds is on a lower floor? My aunt has difficulty with stairs.

Thank you. We are looking forward to our stay with you. My cousin speaks very highly of Al Madarig.

Respectfully yours,

TO: Prosper Bertomy and Company

FAX # 201/555-6435

FROM: Raoul Lagors
         1432 Valentine Street
         Fauvel, NJ 06792
         201/555-2778

PAGE: 1 of 4

In response to your ad for an estimator at your headquarters office, I am faxing you my résumé.

Please note the four years' experience with another maker of precast concrete wall panels, as well as my experience working with sales engineers and project managers and preparing computer-based take-offs and estimates.

I look forward to hearing from you.

TO: G. Selden

FAX: 212/555-6367

FROM: James Hubert Saltyre

RE: Bankruptcy proceedings for the Delkoff Typewriter Company

Bettina Vanderpoel has provided us with the necessary figures and documents. Please check the attached statement for errors or inconsistencies and fax it back with your corrections as soon as you can. Before 3 p.m. today would be helpful. Thanks!

TO: Cornelia Carlyle
      Program Coordinator

FAX: 507/555-1999

FROM: Barbara Hare

TELEPHONE/FAX: 507/555-8365

I've just learned that you have an immediate opening for a counselor in your short-term high-adventure program for adolescent girls.

As you will see from the résumé on the next page, I have worked with both adolescents and wilderness adventure programs, and I have my B.A. degree in human services.

I would like to set up an appointment to discuss this position with you.

Thank you for your time and attention.

To: Kim Cameron
Fax # 307/555-7777

August 31, 1999

Dear Ms. Cameron,

While putting the final touches on our 37th Annual Investment Banking Convention brochure, I realized we don't have a professional bio for you. Can you fax us one (about a paragraph in length) as soon as possible?

Thank you.

Magnolia Hawks
I.B.C. Committee
Fax # 718/555-2222

To: Maureen Phillibrand
Fax # 555-8888

Maureen, I need to turn in the attached meeting announcement this afternoon. Is everything correct? Did I leave anything out? Thanks. Tim

Tim Cornwell
Fax # 555-4444

To: Humphrey Van Weyden
Fax # 507/555-1234

Humphrey,

I'm faxing both you and your lawyer a copy of the revised contract. If you leave a message on my voice mail or fax me back with an okay, I can overnight the original copies of the contract to you for your signature first thing Monday morning. I'm looking forward to working with you.

Maud

Maud Brewster
Fax # 212/555-4321

TO: Customer Service, Fielding Furniture
FROM: Bridget Allworthy, Allworthy Mfg.
DATE: July 10, 1999
RE: Floor Mat # 4A-668

The second sheet of this fax is the page from your catalog that describes the floor mat we recently ordered. Whoever wrote the copy for this item had never met the mat. This floor mat is NOT slip resistant, it is not forest green (we don't know what color it is, but we are certain it is not forest green), and it is impossible to vacuum, as suggested in the description. Most important, it is quite a bit shy of the 4' × 8' dimensions promised.

Please send instructions on how we can return the mat at your expense and obtain a refund. Thank you.

TO: J.L. Herlihy
        James Office Supply Co.
        Fax 651/555-1234
FROM: Townsend P. Locke
        Townsend Mfg. Co., Inc.
        Fax 312/555-1122
RE: Order # BC-800-10467
DATE: October 11, 1999

The above-referenced shipment should have arrived before noon today and did not. Are we scheduled to receive it this afternoon? Let me know. We were assured we would have it today. Thank you.

Fax 818/555-3241
ATTN: Anthony Benson
      Van Dine Printing Co., Inc.

Tony,

I'm relieved that you haven't printed the brochures yet.

Below is the paragraph that is to be substituted for the second-to-the-last paragraph on page 4:

All submitted technical papers must be publication-ready, printed on one side only, be accompanied by an abstract, summary, and bibliography, and not have been published previously elsewhere. Submission of a paper implies permission to publish.

Alvin
Fax 818/555-2314

> The more people are reached by mass communications, the less they communicate with each other.
>
> —MARYA MANNES

RELATED TOPICS

Memos

20

Follow-up Letters

INTRODUCTION

The follow-up letter, which relates to an earlier letter, mailing, conversation, or meeting, is an effective and courteous way to tie up loose ends, to encourage some action that you want, or to build on something already begun.

Follow-up letters are written: to remind someone of an appointment, meeting, favor, request, inquiry, invitation, payment, or work deadline; to inquire about an unacknowledged letter, phone call, package, or gift; to sum up the decisions made in a conference, meeting, or telephone call so that there is a record and so that your recollections can be verified by others; as part of an ongoing debt collection effort; to add new or further information or material to an earlier mailing or contact; to verify a problem has been settled to the customer's satisfaction; to express your appreciation or interest after business lunches, dinners, meetings, or conferences or following visits by prospective members, students, guests; to encourage a sale after a customer has shown some interest in your products or services, has received samples or product literature, has been given a demonstration, or has been visited by a sales representative.

Letitia Baldrige, former White House social secretary and etiquette authority, recommends following up meetings and lunches with notes. "This little personal touch, which takes three minutes, makes an enormous impression," she says. "The ones who do it regularly in business are such standouts. They're the ones who jump ahead."

Follow-up letters can also be sent as letters of thanks, appreciation, acknowledgment, or confirmation. Some follow-up letters are actually sales letters. For additional information, see those chapters.

> A follow-up letter after a job interview can often be the extra push that gets you the job.
>
> —HAROLD E. MEYER

DO

- State why you're writing.
- Thank the person for the interest shown or tie your purpose in writing to your last contact with the person. If necessary, remind the person who you are ("We met last week at the performance boats trade show") or what you were discussing.
- Offer new or further information.
- Tell what your next step is, or what you want the person to do: acknowledge receipt of merchandise, telephone you, send payment, reply to an earlier letter.
- Close with a courtesy or an expression of appreciation for the person's time and attention, or with a forward-looking statement about further business or contacts.

> Any road is bound to arrive somewhere if you follow it far enough.
>
> —PATRICIA WENTWORTH

DON'T

- Don't simply repeat information sent earlier. A follow-up letter should have an identifiable reason for being written, such as new or additional information, a request for a response, news of a special offer, thanks for a previous order or meeting.
- Don't imply your reader is thoughtless or negligent when writing about an unanswered letter or unacknowledged gift. Although the possibility of mail going astray is slim, you must allow for it. Even if the recipient is at fault, it is neither good manners nor good business to point this out.

> Much of good manners is about knowing when to pretend that what's happening isn't happening.
>
> —Mrs. Falk Feeley

HELPFUL HINTS

- A follow-up letter written a day or two after a job interview (before a decision has been reached) shows that you are thorough, courteous, and confident; lets you restate your abilities and interest in the position; places you once more before the prospective employer; allows you to provide additional information, to emphasize a strong point made during the interview, or restate something you didn't say clearly in the interview. Tell how much you enjoyed the interview and meeting the person; restate your special qualifications for the particular position; close with your thanks and a courtesy such as "I look forward to hearing from you."

- Write a follow-up letter even when you have not been offered the position you interviewed for. Thank the person for their time, tactfully express your disappointment, ask that they keep your résumé on file, and close with an appreciation of the person and the company.

- A follow-up sales letter, which is a type of sales letter, is written promptly (while the customer is still thinking about the presentation, earlier sales message, visit from a sales representative). Begin by referring to the earlier contact, thank the person for their interest or the time they gave you, add something new to the overall message, reinforce your original strong selling points, and suggest an action: place an order, call you, accept a trial subscription.

- When someone fails to acknowledge your gift, a follow-up letter can be written eight weeks after sending it. Describe the gift; business gifts are often opened by staff rather than by the intended recipient and wedding gifts can easily be misidentified. Adopt a neutral tone, emphasizing your concern about receipt of the gift rather than any negligence in acknowledging it.

- When a customer fails to respond to a statement or invoice, a follow-up letter with a brief message ("Did you forget?" or "Just a little reminder...") is often sufficient since many late payments are oversights. If there is still no response, you will want to begin a series of collection letters (see Credit).

- A meeting or event or guest speaker scheduled weeks or months in advance sometimes benefits from a follow-up note to participants a week or a few days beforehand. Repeat the date, time, place, and any other pertinent information along with a remark about looking forward to seeing the person.

- After a meeting or conference call in which decisions were made, write a follow-up letter to the other participants repeating the details in order to verify your perceptions and to provide a written record of what was said. In *The 100 Most Difficult Business Letters You'll Ever Have to Write, Fax, or E-mail,* Bernard Heller recommends writing a follow-up letter or memo when you want to be certain the ideas you contributed in a meeting are credited to you. He suggests saying that you've had some further thoughts on the ideas you submitted and that you think it's a good idea to get all of them down on paper: "This is the gist of the ideas I offered. A detailed explanation of each one is on the pages that follow."

- Successful businesses keep in touch with customers after they purchase products or services, sending follow-up letters to see how things are working out, to inform customers of new product lines, to remind them that you appreciated their business in the past and hope to serve them again.

- When a request has gone unanswered within a reasonable time, write a follow-up letter repeating your original message (or including a copy of it), emphasizing the importance of the person's response, and mentioning the consequences to you or to them if no response is received.

> Bulldogs have been known to fall on their swords when confronted by my superior tenacity.
>
> —MARGARET HALSEY

GETTING STARTED

Just a note to say that I still haven't received a copy of the year-end sales figures.

I am still interested in receiving a review copy of your book on insurance scams.

I wanted to follow up on our phone conversation yesterday with several other possibilities.

It occurred to me that I haven't received any confirmation that you received the report I mailed you on June 4—could you let me know on the enclosed, self-addressed postcard?

Have you had an opportunity to use the Austell Rental Center coupon we sent you last month?

Thank you for letting me help you with the purchase of your new car, which I hope you are enjoying very much—I'm enclosing my business card in case I can be of further service to you or to anyone you know.

I wanted to make sure you're aware of the service warranty on your new gas dryer.

On April 3, I sent application materials to you for your library information specialist position.

It's so unlike you not to have responded that I suspect you never received our invitation to spend a week up north with us this summer.

I appreciate the time you took yesterday to discuss your opening for a dental treatment plan analyst.

Thank you for taking the time this morning to describe the inventory manager position, to show me around the building, and to introduce me to other members of your staff.

I want to thank you for the courtesy you showed me yesterday when I stopped in to introduce myself as your new Midwest sales representative.

After visiting with you at the home security trade convention last week, I telephoned Norma Ashe, our representative in your area, and asked her to call on you.

I was delighted to meet you at the campaign rally yesterday after all these weeks of appreciating your effective volunteer work and seeing your name on several generous checks.

Many thanks for giving me some time yesterday to discuss our newest industrial tape products.

You may have been a member before, but you've never seen prices like these!

Several months ago, I wrote you about the introduction of our specialized counseling services at the Community Center.

The membership campaign of the Plum Creek Community Center is well under way, and hundreds of present and former members have renewed, but we have yet to hear from you.

'Tain't no use to sit and whine
'Cause the fish ain't on your line;
Bait your hook and keep on tryin',
Keep a-goin'!

—FRANK L. STANTON

MODEL LETTERS

Dear Ellen and Malcolm Graeme,

Last month we sent you a brochure and informational materials about Lady of the Lake Riverboat cruises. Now that you've had a chance to look over the color photographs of our roomy staterooms, Grand Salon dining room, Early American piano bar, and gracious decks, would you be interested in making your reservation for a one-week or two-week cruise on this elegant floating palace?

We are generally completely booked by March 1 of every year, so we urge you to make your plans soon!

Dear Lenina Crowne,

You may have misplaced our earlier notice that your subscription to the award-winning, environmental monthly *Brave New World* expires with the current issue. To avoid missing the series on new recycling technology that begins in the June issue along with our regular departments and features, please send in the enclosed postage-paid reply card today.

Sincerely,

Helmholtz Watson
Circulation Department

Dear Maria Ponto,

You must have sharp eyes to have spotted the top-of-the-line Wellesley knives at our State Fair booth!

Thank you for your interest and please accept the enclosed order form and literature.

We are on the cutting edge of knife manufacturing and we guarantee your complete satisfaction.

Order today and we'll pare down your cost by 10 percent!

Yours sincerely,

> I am a kind of burr; I shall stick.
>
> —WILLIAM SHAKESPEARE

Dear Oliver,

You were asking about the Advanced American Sign Language course I took last year. I hunted up my old materials and am sending you an informational brochure with the address and telephone number. It's a superb organization and the course was excellent. As I said the other day, I recommend it highly.

Best!
Zach

Dear Mr. Melhuish,

I notice from our records that after you arranged for your first housecleaning service by the Beresford Bucket Brigade, you were obliged to cancel.

You may have decided against a housecleaning service or made other arrangements. But knowing of your interest, I'm enclosing our brochure and a special $15-off coupon. I'd like to remind you too that every member of the Brigade is professionally trained, that we bring our own equipment and supplies, and we offer you a quality service guarantee.

Call 555-1234 to arrange a time! (And do it soon—autumn is our busiest season!)

Dear Rowland Mallet,

The last time we spoke you were considering replacing your file cabinets with our Hudson Tuff-Bilt Easy-Access file cabinets.

In case you're still considering new file cabinets, I'm enclosing our most recent catalog, plus brochures on the Hudson line of cabinets.

We recently furnished a complete set of replacement cabinets to a company in another city, and the buyer is so pleased she offered to speak to anyone considering a similar move. If you'd like her number, let me know.

Looking forward to hearing from you, I am

Sincerely yours,
Mary Garland

Dear Mr. Havern,

I appreciate the time you spent with me last week when I stopped in at Heavenly Gifts to leave you a sample Angels calendar.

I thought you might like to know that today I received the latest sales figures and we have sold 8,500 copies of the calendar in just three weeks. I think it is an item that would do very well for you. You were so right when you said anything involving angels is very popular just now.

Let me know if I can provide any further information.
Best wishes!

Dear Elizabeth Mwres-Denton,

Last week we met at the Wildlife Benefit. I enjoyed hearing about your experiences with bluebird preservation efforts.

You mentioned to me your frustration with the amount of time you spend on your business tax preparation and seemed interested in having it done by a professional tax preparer. We also spoke about auditing services that are helpful to a small business owner.

Enclosed are some materials you might find useful as you look into those possibilities.

If you'd like to come in and discuss some of your options and ask me to explain the kinds of service I offer, call for an appointment (an introductory visit is always complimentary).

Best wishes, especially with the bluebirds!

Dear Ms. Sperrit,

I'm wondering if you have received the two messages I've left this past week asking you to call me.

I would like to bring in a handmade quilt to show you the damage done when I left it for "special care" dry cleaning. I have already brought the quilt in twice and spoken to two people as you weren't there at the time, but I think you, as the manager, are the appropriate person to speak with. Since the quilt is awkward to transport, I want to be sure you are available the next time I come by.

My phone number is 555-1234. I would appreciate a call.

Dear Uncle Meleager,

Last week you offered to show me some of the family correspondence dating back 150 years. May I take you up on that offer sometime next week? I'll call to see what time is good for you.

Peter

> Diamonds are only chunks of coal,
> That stuck to their jobs, you see.
>
> —Minnie Richard Smith

RELATED TOPICS

Acknowledgments

Appreciation

Credit

Employment

Responses

Sales

Thank You

21

Fundraising Letters

INTRODUCTION

With fundraising appeals outnumbering every other kind of letter except sales letters, and with most people juggling multiple demands, a fundraising letter has to be outstanding to be successful.

Your response rate will be higher if you are writing on behalf of a long-established organization with a good reputation. Beyond that, your best strategy is vigorous writing: compelling anecdotes, easily grasped and persuasive statistics, thought-provoking metaphors, testimonials from familiar public figures, dynamic verbs, and well-worded appeals to heart and purse. One way of learning to write strong fundraising letters is to study effective sales letters.

This chapter deals solely with the writing of fundraising letters. For assistance in replying to appeals, see Acknowledgments, Refusals, or Responses. To acknowledge responses to your fundraising letters and to thank people for contributing, see Acknowledgments and Thank You. For ideas on writing invitations to fundraising benefits, balls, banquets, and other events, see Invitations.

> In the end, raising money is basically a matter of going out there and asking. There are no shortcuts.
>
> —GEORGETTE MOSBACHER

DO

- Arouse the reader's interest with an attention-getting opening.

- Clearly identify the organization and its purpose: what it does and for whom, how it is unique, what its most impressive achievements are—but establish this background quickly and colorfully enough to keep the reader's interest high.

- Establish the need and convince the reader it is real and compelling (without exaggerating the facts). Appeal to the heart by the use of anecdotes, quotations, testimonials, case histories, descriptions. Appeal to the head by use of statistics and information, but remember that appealing to the head is less effective than appealing to the heart.

- Be specific. Your support evidence should be specific (instead of "Every night in this country children go to bed hungry," write, "Every night in this, the richest country in the world, one child in four goes to bed hungry"). Make a specific request ("Please send a check today") or even ask for a specific amount ("Your $100 will plant four new trees").

- Tell specifically how the person's contribution will be used ("With your help, we want to offer college scholarships to an additional twenty students this year").

- Explain or imply what contributing will do for the reader: give personal satisfaction, alleviate suffering, improve the community, better someone's prospects, offer a tax deduction, provide entry to a select group of givers, result in recognition or publicity, impress you or some figure they admire, allow them to share some of their surplus, respond to a cause they believe in.

- Be positive. Rather than describe how bad the situation will be if the reader doesn't contribute, describe how much improved the situation will be if the reader does contribute.

- Adopt a friendly, informal, personal tone—as though you were talking to the person—but without slang or jargon. If possible, establish a bond between you and the reader or between your organization and the reader ("As a householder, you understand responsibility").

- Establish the credibility of the organization and assure the reader that any contribution will be used effectively.

- Be as brief as possible. There is a lot of competition for people's time and you probably have only seconds to make an impact.

- Convey a sense of urgency and encourage the person to take action at once—and give at least one good reason for doing so. Fundraising letters that are set aside for future consideration are rarely acted upon.

- Thank the person for their interest and concern.

- Make it easy to give by including a postage-paid reply envelope or a toll-free number where contributions can be made by credit card.

- Have the letter signed by the highest-ranking member of your organization or by a well-known public figure.

- Add a postscript. The P.S. is more likely to be read than any other part of your letter, and letters with a P.S. have a higher response rate than those without. The attention-getting P.S. should be brief (less than five lines). It can urge the person to take action immediately, express appreciation for the person's help and interest, or add one more persuasive bit of information. Note that more is not better in this case; two postscripts are weaker than one.

> The strongest word in fundraising is "you."
>
> —HERSCHELL GORDON LEWIS

DON'T

- Don't "lean on" potential contributors. People cannot be shamed or harassed or obviously manipulated into giving; they prefer believing their contribution is a free-will offering springing from their own generosity and not from your pressure.

- Don't use clichés if you can help it: "We need your help"; "Why read this letter?"; "You don't know me, but . . ."; "Send your check today!"; "Please take a few minutes to read this letter." You can distinguish clichés only by reading hundreds of fundraising letters, but it is worth your time to do so in order to study what works and what doesn't.

- Don't use gimmicks such as unusual typefaces, extensive underlining or capitalization, colorful inks, or odd page layouts. A strong message is key, and gimmicks will not help a weak one and will undercut a strong one. Fundraising appeals are, however, more commonly using strategies such as what appears to be a handwritten note on the envelope, a smaller enclosed letter, an incentive that is either enclosed or offered.

> One applauds the industry of professional philanthropy.
> But it has its dangers. After a while the private heart begins
> to harden. We fling letters into the wastebasket, are abrupt to
> telephoned solicitations. Charity withers in the incessant gale.
>
> —PHYLLIS MCGINLEY

HELPFUL HINTS

- A fundraising letter can begin by asking the reader to sign a petition, call a legislator, vote on an issue, or participate in a letterwriting campaign, and then later in the letter ask for a contribution as well.

- Divide your message into two parts. First, give the reader a vivid picture of what is possible: healthy, well-nourished children; an active community center; eradication of a disease; a new library. Second, tell the reader exactly what you plan to do to arrive at the previously painted picture. The first part of the appeal is emotional and subjective; the second is factual and objective.

- A series of fundraising letters, each with a different emphasis, is often very effective because when one angle doesn't rouse an individual, another might.

- Most serious contributors today are interested in how organizations use their money. You may want to enclose an annual report or fact sheet telling what percentage of funds goes to administrative costs and what is spent on the organization's main activities. Credibility and accountability are serious issues for fundraisers.

- Most fundraising letters today are form letters. Although the well-written ones are surprisingly effective in bringing in large sums for their organizations, the most successful letters are directed at specific groups or are personal letters written to individuals.

- For more assistance with fundraising letters, see in particular Mal Warwick, *Raising Money by Mail: Strategies for Growth and Financial Stability*, Strathmoor Press, 1995; Robert L. Torre and Mary Anne Bendixen, *Direct Mail Fund Raising Letters That Work*, Plenum Press, 1988; Kay Partney Lautman and Henry Goldstein, *Dear Friend: Mastering the Art of Direct Mail Fund Raising*, 2nd ed., Taft Group, 1991; Siegfried Vögele, *Handbook of Direct Mail: The Dialogue Method of Direct Written Sales Communications*, Prentice Hall, 1992.

> I cannot think a civilization worth having that does not encourage and enable its subjects to spend something, not extorted by governments but freely given to keep wretchedness at least from the streets they walk through day by day.
>
> —FREYA STARK

GETTING STARTED

Will you be paying higher property taxes next year? Depending on how you cast your vote, you just might be.

I would like to invite you to become a member and supporter of the East Lynne Family Assistance Network.

Margaret Mead once said, "Never doubt that a small group of thoughtful, committed citizens can change the world. Indeed, it's the only thing that ever has." We would like to invite you to be one of those thoughtful, committed citizens.

As we launch our global campaign to protect endangered wildlife, I am writing you, as a committed supporter, because your participation is essential.

I am troubled by the growing violence among children, and I know you are too.

If you've visited one of our city lakes recently, you will not be surprised at the severity of the problems we are facing.

On behalf of the Santa Eulalia Food Bank Network, I ask you and Elliot Computer System Products, Inc. to consider sponsoring a food-collection drive.

I don't like asking for money any more than you like being asked, but this is a special situation.

Before we can begin raising funds for the new annex, we need volunteers to help with the mailing—will you consider giving several hours of your time to help out?

Sophy Crewler's campaign chest consists of small individual contributions from people like you who want a senator who represents all the people, not just those with special interests.

Your past generosity to Save-the-World testifies to your concern about the environment.

If you are considering a year-end tax-deductible donation, and you are concerned about what the future holds for our children, look at what your gift could do.

I'm writing to ask you to join a very special campaign against illiteracy—one that dares to ask for more than your money.

Instead of writing a three- or four-page letter to you, I'm keeping this short and to the point.

When you contribute to the Cowperwood Foundation, you invest in the future of your community.

On behalf of the staff of The Bloomfield Home for Children, I want to thank you for your generosity and tell you about some of the programs you have supported.

If you know anyone who is living with AIDS, you know that we desperately need to find an affordable, effective cure—but that takes money, a lot of money.

Marian Wright Edelman said, "Democracy is not a spectator sport"—if you agree with her, what is your own personal game plan?

Have you got room in your heart for one more child?

Please join us, your friends and neighbors, in the exciting work of bringing a light rail transit system to our area.

We're asking you to do two things: first, sign the enclosed petition to retain the community park at Fourth and Locust Streets and, second, send a check to help with our referendum campaign.

I want to share a story with you that illustrates for me what heroism is all about.

Time is of the essence, and the well-being of countless children hangs in the balance so let me come straight to the point.

We are so grateful for your generous pledge made June 4—and we promise to be even more grateful once we receive it.

> I have tried to teach people that there are three kicks in every dollar: one, when you make it—and how I love to make a dollar; two, when you have it—and I have the Yankee lust for saving. The third kick is when you give it away—and it is the biggest kick of all.
>
> —WILLIAM ALLEN WHITE

MODEL LETTERS

Dear Friend,

Have you ever wished you could give more to help others?

In a way you can. Our home ownership program for the working poor uses a smaller percentage of your tax-deductible donation than 98% of all other registered charitable foundations. Your dollar goes further here. Because we want it that way. (Enclosed is a financial statement that will show you where every dollar went in the year just ended.)

To help others fulfill the American dream of home ownership nurtures the whole community, not just the new homeowners. Our loan counseling program helps people work their way out of poverty and into a home that they will eventually own. Homeowners make strong, stable communities.

You can be part of this satisfying and important work. Best of all, you know that your hard-earned and generous contribution is taken seriously and goes directly to the purpose for which you intend it!

Take just a minute to make your money go further and send your check today! Your community will thank you!

Dear Anne and Joseph Mair,

You are cordially invited to a black tie, white gloves, and long gown No-Ball Ball to help raise the funds needed to build our neighborhood ballpark.

Only $25 per phantom plate and space on the invisible ballroom floor! Please send your check *now*—the ballpark grounds have been cleared, the work is ready to begin, and our kids have waited long enough! The whole neighborhood will benefit from providing a supervised, safe place for our children to play their various fun and rewarding sports.

Please send your check today. Then reserve the evening of May 20, 6 to 10 p.m., for our fantasy No-Ball Ball. As soon as we receive your check, we will send you one complimentary Movie Shelf video rental coupon and one pack of microwave popcorn.

May we suggest that you rent a fun family baseball or hockey movie with your free video coupon the night of May 20? We hope you have a ball at home with your loved ones that evening, and we thank you for your support! All our kids and coaches can hardly wait—so please send your check *today*!

Sincerely,

Nothing is so contagious as enthusiasm; it moves stones, it charms brutes. Enthusiasm is the genius of sincerity and truth accomplishes no victories without it.

—EDWARD G. BULWER-LYTTON

Dear Sarah Tucker,

I am running again for office as Representative of District 54A. You may remember that as a political newcomer two years ago, I missed winning the seat by 148 votes out of more than 18,000. This time we'll do it!

I believe I can offer this district responsible, commonsensical, effective, and ethical leadership. I'm particularly interested in supporting public schools, handgun control, the environment, the working poor, the creation of new jobs, and financial aid for college students and first-time home buyers.

If this looks like your agenda, too, get on the bandwagon! Knock on doors, distribute leaflets, staff the phone lines, put up a campaign sign in your yard, and—yes—send money!

If you think you have to send a lot, think again—almost everything I raised in the last campaign was given in modest amounts—$5, $10. I'm proud of that. So send what you can, do what you can, and come November, go vote!

Dear Martin Kernahans,

How would you like to be able to support Global Health Services far into the future with a single stroke of your pen?

All you need to do is list Global Health Services as the beneficiary of a certain portion of your life insurance policy. For example, if you have a $200,000 policy, you could give 99% ($198,000) to your spouse and children and 1% ($2,000) to Global Health Services.

Call your insurance agent today and request a beneficiary change form. In just minutes you can guarantee support for Global Health Services beyond your lifetime.

Dear Mr. and Mrs. Pender,

How concerned are you about the quality of education in this country? Do you believe we are educating future employees and employers capable of earning a living for themselves and others? Are we turning out knowledgeable voters? Responsible taxpayers? Readers and thinkers and scientists and inventors?

Maybe you are only slightly concerned, say, $10 worth of concern. Perhaps you are very, very concerned, maybe all of $500 worth of concern. Like most of us, you are probably somewhere in the middle.

EDUCATING FOR THE FUTURE asks that you show your concern now—with a check. Several of our most immediate goals are to establish:

✓ Accessible programs for expectant parents, new parents, and parents of young children that will offer practical information on parenting as well as appropriate emotional and financial support.

✓ Phonics-based programs for all new readers.

✓ Incentives and pay scales that would allow our brightest college graduates to become teachers without sacrificing their own personal and financial goals.

See the enclosed brochure for program descriptions and our long-range goals.

We believe that the start-up costs of putting U.S. education back on track will be more than earned back by savings down the road in terms of decreasing illiteracy, unemployment, poverty, crime, and abuse.

Because EDUCATING FOR THE FUTURE is organized for the purpose of lobbying and influencing legislation, your donation is not tax-deductible under current guidelines. It may, however, be deductible as a business expense. If you have questions, please contact us or your tax accountant.

President Lyndon B. Johnson once said, "At the desk where I sit, I have learned one great truth. The answer for all our national problems—the answer for all the problems of the world—comes down to a single word. That word is 'education.'"

Please show your concern NOW and help us educate for the future!

Dear Mrs. Trusty,

Although this is a "begging" letter, we are not asking for money. In fact, we're not even asking for anything specific.

In the 57 years of its existence, the nationally recognized and award-winning Colman Residences have provided programs and services to hundreds of individuals with developmental disabilities.

It has been a serious struggle at times to keep our heads above financial waters, but we have been fortunate in the generous friends, family members, and foundations who have supported us over the years.

We have also been blessed by creative individuals who have shared their special resources with our residents. For example:

- a book club supplies us with dozens of pumpkin pies every Thanksgiving;
- weavers donate their time to teach weaving;
- a ranch gives us free tickets to its rodeo every year;
- a motorcycle club and a snowmobile club regularly give rides to residents;
- an auto dealership has donated a station wagon every three years for the past fifteen years;
- a local service club provides a small bus for small-group field trips;
- a restaurant owner invites residents to a special holiday meal every December;
- volunteers bring small animals to visit on Saturdays.

We're writing to ask you to think about what you could share with Colman residents. Call me at 555-1234 and let's talk about your ideas.

Dear Mrs. Ogmore-Pritchard,

One can do much. And one and one and one can move mountains.
(Joan Ward-Harris)

Will you be one of the "ones" who will help us move mountains? We have one particular mountain in mind—the mountain of unconcern, neglect, abuse, and wrongful use of many of our wilderness areas.

The enclosed copies of recent newspaper articles will give you an idea of the problems facing us today. Also enclosed is an invitation to become a member and support our efforts to move this mountain!

Dear Mr. Gamgee,

We are happy to send you the enclosed free informational literature on lymphedema. I hope the material is as helpful to you as it has been to thousands of others. I also hope you will support our Annual Fund Drive to raise money for more research in this field.

Any gift you send will help support critical research to find the causes and cures of lymphedema. Only 12% of funds received goes for organizational expenses. Your donation also funds the continuing dissemination of free information such as the brochures we're sending you.

Please help us (and ultimately yourself) today!

Dear Daphne Pleydell,

We believe, along with George Eliot, that "the strongest principle of growth lies in human choice." Choice inspired the founding of Universal College. Choice underlies our curriculum and extracurricular activities. From the moment students arrive on campus, they make choices. If you are familiar with our graduation rates, graduate employment rates, and student evaluations, you know that choice works—and works superbly.

Now we want to give YOU a choice. This year when you donate to Universal College, you can choose how your money is spent. On the enclosed form, check off the area you want to target: Scholarships, Library Collections, Salaries, Building Program, Sports Equipment. There is even an "Other" category that we will honor if possible. If you choose more than one, stipulate percentages of your donation to be used for each.

(Please indicate if your gift will be matched by your employer. Your personnel office will provide you with the necessary information and forms.)

Thank you for choosing to support Universal College!

Dear Beck Knibbs,

Please accept the enclosed special gift with our thanks for your faithful support. We think you'll appreciate this miniature address book each time you need a telephone number and you can't get to your Rolodex or your computer!

We also hope it will remind you of how critical your dedicated membership is to our successes and to encourage you to make those phone calls to your senators and representatives when tax-reform legislation is pending.

While this gift is not meant to obligate you, we can't help hoping that you will respond with a generous donation. More than ever, we need to keep up the momentum we have established to achieve an equitable, accessible, and sensible system of taxation.

Dear Charles Heath,

   Most of us would agree that no child in this land of plenty should go to bed hungry at night.

   Most of us do not agree, however, on the causes of and solutions to the reality of hungry children in our midst.

   In the meantime, while we discuss, while we debate, while we disagree, children continue to wake up hungry, attend school hungry, and fall asleep hungry.

   Feed the Children! believes that we need to keep searching for root causes and for effective longterm solutions to poverty, but that we cannot allow children to be hungry TODAY.

   One hundred percent of all donations to Feed the Children! goes directly to children, either through food shelf disbursements or through school breakfast programs.

   If you are concerned for the hungry child TODAY, please join in our work by sending a check in the enclosed envelope. With your efforts, our efforts, and the efforts of those who continue to look for longterm solutions, we *can* put an end to hunger for the little ones.

> When you put something good into the world, something good comes back to you.
>
> —MERLE SHAIN

RELATED TOPICS

Acknowledgments

Follow-up

Goodwill

Invitations

Refusals

Requests

Responses

Thank You

22

Get Well Letters

INTRODUCTION

Most of us rely on commercial get well cards where the biggest challenge is choosing just one from the hundreds of messages and beautiful designs. The most carefully chosen card, however, can't express a personal and unmistakable interest in that one person as well as several handwritten lines from you somewhere on the card.

If you have ever received a get well card with nothing but a name signed at the bottom, you know how disappointing it is. You are grateful for the kind gesture but you would have loved a distinctive message.

Some get well messages are easy to send—the illness is not serious or we don't know the person well enough to be too involved emotionally. In other cases, our feelings of helplessness, apprehension, and even pity keep us from writing or else produce letters we're not satisfied with.

The main purpose of get well letters is to remind people that they are not alone in their trouble, to offer them the undoubted power of love and friendship as a force for healing. Your "encouraging word" doesn't have to be lengthy, literary, or memorable; a few sincere sentences will do.

> What a strange distance there is between ill people and well ones.
>
> —WINIFRED HOLTBY

DO

- Write as soon as you hear the news. Although get well letters are always welcome, the prompt ones deliver a warmer, stronger message.

- Say simply and directly that you are sorry about (or sorry to hear or learn about) the illness, accident, surgery, or hospitalization.

- Express a concern for the person's well-being ("I want you to be comfortable and on the mend").

- Assure the person of your affection, concern, sympathy, encouragement, confidence in their recovery, warm thoughts, best wishes, love, or prayers.

> Illness is the night-side of life, a more onerous citizenship. Everyone who is born holds dual citizenship, in the kingdom of the well and in the kingdom of the sick. Although we all prefer to use only the good passport, sooner or later each of us is obliged, at least for a spell, to identify ourselves as citizens of that other place.
>
> —Susan Sontag

- Be pleasant, positive, and optimistic with your words of hope and comfort. If the person has a terminal illness or is critically ill, you will want to be loving and supportive without mentioning the future.

- Be brief if the person is seriously ill; later you can send a longer note or letter. And make certain your note is not a chore to read; someone just out of surgery doesn't have the interest or energy to decipher illegible handwriting. In the case of someone convalescing at home, you don't need to be brief. A long, newsy letter is usually welcome.

- Focus more on the other person's situation than on your own feelings of inadequacy. Express what you feel—if you feel helpless and upset, say so—but don't dwell on it. The situation is more about their feelings than yours.

- Reassure employees who are hospitalized or ill that their jobs are secure and that their work is being taken care of. If appropriate, you might also want to reassure them about sick leave policy and medical benefits; people often don't look carefully at the details until they are too sick to do anything but worry about them.

> People seldom refuse help, if one offers it in the right way.
>
> —A.C. BENSON

- Offer to help in a specific way: take notes at meetings for them, relay telephone messages, drive children to school, provide a meal for the family, bring a selection of library books to the hospital, cancel engagements or appointments the person had, bring mail to the hospital and help answer it, read aloud to the person, run errands. No matter how sincerely you mean it, saying vaguely, "If there is anything I can do, please let me know" is not helpful. It is difficult for someone who is ill to think of how you can help or even to call you. Good friends know they can request your help without your needing to say so. Otherwise, call a family member or neighbor to see what needs doing.

- Address the person in the same manner you did before their illness. Jean Kerr once wrote, "One of the most difficult things to contend with in a hospital is the assumption on the part of the staff that because you have lost your gall bladder you have also lost your mind." It is wounding when friends and family treat the patient as someone who is not quite what she or he used to be. The recipient of your letter is still a person, with all the usual human hopes, interests, relationships, and emotions.

- End with your hopes for less discomfort, a speedy recovery, rapid improvement, better health, a brighter tomorrow.

> I enjoy convalescence. It is the part that makes the illness worth while.
>
> —GEORGE BERNARD SHAW

DON'T

- Don't compare the person's situation, illness, or surgery to anyone else's. Even if you have gone through something almost identical, wait until the person is fully convalescent and distanced from the present discomfort and danger to bring it up. Each person's experience is unique and deserves its distinctive woes.

- Don't send a get well letter or card to someone who is not going to get well—and don't write to say how sad you are. Instead, send your love along with an upbeat note, share a warm or funny memory, or write about something positive—how well the person's children are doing, for example. Your main message is that you are thinking about the person.

- Don't offer medical advice or criticize the care the patient is receiving or the medical choices being made. Most people already have doubts about whether they are being cared for as effectively as possible; it is upsetting when friends add to them. The person closest to the sick person can act as a patient advocate, asking questions, checking test results, and conferring with doctors, but there's rarely any need for more than one or two supporters of this nature. If the patient does not have this kind of help and you are concerned, offer to sit in on the next patient-doctor visit.

- Don't catastrophize the situation with words such as "tragic," "devastating," "affliction," "torture," "nightmare," or "agony" unless they are truly appropriate. Take your cue from the patient and do not jump to conclusions as to how they might be perceiving the situation. You can be sympathetic and emotional without overstating the facts or dramatizing your own reaction to them.

- Don't use terms such as "victim," "handicapped," or "bedridden." They convey a perception of helplessness and vulnerability.

- Don't use empty phrases, clichés, and falsely cheerful messages like "It's probably for the best" (it doesn't feel "best" to the person who is ill); "I know how you feel" (no, you don't); "God only gives burdens to those who can carry them" (this is arguable); "Every cloud has a silver lining" (not when the cloud is hovering over *your* bed); "Think on the bright side—at least you don't have to go to work" (the person might prefer the office to the sickbed); "I'm sure you'll be up and around again in no time" (the patient is sure of no such thing, and the time passed in bed does not feel like "no time"). Reread your letter to see how you, in the same situation, would feel about its tone.

> Don't discuss your ailments before visitors. Visitors prefer talking about theirs.
>
> —Minna Thomas Antrim

HELPFUL HINTS

- Although most get well messages are handwritten, there is nothing wrong with a typed or printed one. The important thing is to send one.

- Those who are living with AIDS are first your friends, neighbors, and relatives, and only second someone with a usually terminal illness. Write as you would to anyone with a serious illness, and do not assume the person's time is short; medical advances are adding years of high-quality life for some people with AIDS. It is more important to be supportive and to send a card than to say exactly the right thing. However, it will help if you focus on the person, rather than on the illness. You might also suggest a visit. Because of the perceived nature of AIDS, some people distance themselves from friends living with it, adding another hardship to the illness.

- Some people advise not mentioning the specific circumstance, surgery, illness, or procedure, opting for a certain vagueness ("your surgery" instead of "your colostomy"). Others suggest not beating around the bush. Your choice will depend on how well you know the person and how you would be talking about this if you were face to face.

- Co-workers and customers or suppliers that you know personally will welcome a get well card and a simple handwritten message telling them you're thinking about them. Cards to close associates, employees, or longtime customers are also appreciated when there is an accident or illness in their families.

- Without a specific and heartfelt invitation, it is better not to visit people who are hospitalized or seriously ill at home. This is the main purpose of a get well message—to stand in for you when someone isn't well enough to see you.

- Friends or relatives in chemical dependency treatment or in treatment for depression, eating disorders, and other such conditions may also be glad to receive words of support and encouragement. A simple "I'm thinking about you" or "I care about you" is often sufficient until you know how receptive they are to discussing their situation in more detail.

- When someone has a terminal illness, it is better not to mention it in your letter or note—unless, of course, the person has broached it with you first. Some people with terminal illnesses report that their family and friends won't talk about what is uppermost in their mind, that is, the prospect of pain, dying, and death. However, telling the person you are thinking of them is always welcome. Assure them of your love for them and your support for their family. Mention the things you know they can still enjoy: visits from family and friends, home videos, books, card games, phone calls, organizing picture albums, dictating memoirs, or anything else you know brings them pleasure. You can say you were sorry to hear about the illness, and then add something positive ("I'm glad you are resting comfortably now" or "It sounds as if you are getting excellent care").

- Instead of a lengthy letter, which may be fatiguing or uninteresting to seriously ill people, enclose with your card and note an amusing or intriguing clipping from the newspaper, photographs, a pressed flower, a cartoon, a sachet of potpourri, a teabag (if appropriate), a quotation, a child's drawing, or colorful postcards. Enclosures are particularly helpful when the usual words won't come easily—in the case of the terminally ill, for example.

- When writing to a sick child, say you're sorry to hear they're sick, and then enclose something colorful, entertaining, and age-appropriate: a word puzzle, riddles, a cartoon or clipping from the paper, a story you made up or photo-copied from a magazine, a sticker book. You could also hand-letter a "coupon" good for a stack of library books that you will bring over and pick up several weeks later, a carry-in meal from a favorite fast food place (if parents have approved the idea), thirty minutes of being read to, chauffeuring of friends to and from the patient's house or the hospital. If you think the child will be writing back, help them along by asking a few questions: What's the hospital room like? Who is the doctor? What is the best thing about being sick? The worst thing? What is your day like, from morning to night? What is the first thing you're going to do when you get well?

- When a friend or relative is injured or ill enough to need constant care, you might want to write not only to the patient but to the person responsible for their care—spouse, parent, child, relative—and offer your emotional support as well as some help (running errands, chauffeuring, bringing meals, spending time with the patient so that the caregiver can have some free time).

A sick room is at times too sacred a place for a friend's knock, timid as that is.

—EMILY DICKINSON

GETTING STARTED

I hear you've been under the weather lately.

Teresa and I were sorry to hear about your emergency surgery.

We were surprised and shocked by the news—you're the last person in the office any-one would suspect of having heart trouble.

I was sorry to hear that you were in the hospital.

Here's hoping you pass all your tests—I guess they're not the kind you can study for.

Everyone at work feels so bad about what happened.

I was sorry to learn about your recent stroke.

I've just heard about your illness and want to tell you I'm thinking about you.

I'm relieved to hear that your accident wasn't as bad as it could have been—although you may feel at this point that it was quite bad enough.

I heard that you're doctoring with that troublesome foot again.

You realize, of course, that the Lorna Doone Square Dancers will be limping along until you get back!

Clementina told me what you are facing, and I wanted to send all my love and prayers.

Hearing about your diagnosis was a shock, but we are hoping for better news down the road.

You're very much on my mind and in my heart these days.

It was discouraging to learn that Zuleika is in the hospital again.

I was very sorry to hear about Saunders's accident last night.

I'm sorry you've had such a scare, but relieved that you caught it in time.

Bentley reports that you're doing well and all of us here at Drummle Auto are looking forward to your full and speedy recovery.

> A cold is both positive and negative; sometimes the Eyes have it and sometimes the Nose.
>
> —WILLIAM LYON PHELPS

MODEL LETTERS

Dear Mr. Holly,

On behalf of everyone at South Riding Bank, I send you our best wishes for a comfortable hospital stay and a speedy recovery.

Things won't be the same here until you get back.

Sincerely,

Jessy Brimsley

May 20, 1997

Flavia dear,

Your mother told us of your surgery and my prayers for you are that you may be comfortable and on the mend when my wishes reach you. We don't have all the particulars concerning your trip to the hospital but we do hope they don't make you leave too soon.

Thinking of you, honey, and please take care of yourself. We'll be in touch with your mom.

Love ya,

Aunt Helga

Dear Mrs. Berners,

I am so sorry to hear that your cancer has recurred, but I'm glad you called to let us know. We had been wondering why we hadn't seen you in your garden the last couple of days. You sounded optimistic that after your hospital stay and the outpatient treatments, you could look forward to a healthier fall and winter.

One small thing: don't even think about weeds or growing grass until then—we can easily mow your lawn when we mow ours and weed your garden when we weed ours. Next summer you can help with ours, all right?

We're looking forward to seeing you when you get home.

Love from

Your Neighbors to the West

April 3, 1998

Dear Konstantin,

What are *you* doing in a sick bed? The hospital would be the last place I'd ever expect to find you! I can be light-hearted because, from what Stiva says, you are going to be fine. I'm sorry you had to go through this though. It must've been scary (and probably still is). Once you are home and things are somewhat back to normal, I'll call because I want to know just how everything happened.

You are very much in my thoughts. Talk to you later . . .

Love,

Kitty

Wednesday

Dear Lorna,

I was sorry to hear about your accident. Carver tells me that you are getting stronger every day and that you'll be out of the hospital in about a week. I'm relieved to know that!

Love,

John

Dear Jacob,

Everyone here at Berlin Plumbing & Heating joins me in wishing you a speedy recovery. I spoke to Karen yesterday and she seemed to think you're halfway there.

Don't give a thought to work—we're parceling out things among us for the time being (but don't think that we can do this for very long!). We're still fighting over who has to take on the Becker job.

There's no problem with your sick leave or medical benefits (Eva checked), so there's really nothing for you to do but concentrate on getting back to 100%.

Best wishes from all of us and

Niels

February 7, 1999

Dear Ruth,

I've just this minute heard that you are in the hospital. I think you are wise to find out once and for all what's been causing your problems and get it over with.

I hope that by the time this note reaches you, you'll have a diagnosis, a treatment plan, and will be feeling a great deal better. I expect that it won't be long before you are entirely and completely yourself again.

Love,

Elvira

Dear Fitzwilliam,

We were sorry to hear of your accident. We are all still wincing and shuddering each time we think of it. As soon as you are back home and feel up to having visitors, let us know, will you? In the meantime, your family's been good about keeping us updated.

If I understand the situation, you are looking at several months of recuperation followed by a period of physical therapy. You'll want to discuss details with someone in the Benefits Department, but the gist of it is that you seem to be fully covered for the interim and can expect to resume your job when you've recovered. For the time being, we will probably divide up your more complicated work among us here and hire someone from a temporary agency to take care of the rest.

You don't need to think of any of this right now, but I thought it might be reassuring to know that things are taken care of. Concentrate on getting well. I hope you're not too uncomfortable and that you surprise everybody by healing faster than expected!

Best wishes!

Darcy

Hey Don!

Just a quick note to cheer you up—well, to try to cheer you up!—while you recover from the extraction of your wisdom teeth. Did you have to do all four at once?

Let me know when you feel up to losing a game of pool to me!

Rose

> Illness is a convent which has its rule, its austerity, its silences, and its inspirations.
>
> —ALBERT CAMUS

Dear Lavinia,

I've just heard that you're back in the hospital with complications from your surgery. It sounds as though things will soon be mended, but I'm sorry you have to go through this.

Instead of more flowers or another house plant (I think you received plenty when you had your surgery!), I'm sending you a book of coupons good for ten movies. Knowing how much you like seeing the latest films, I thought this would give you something to look forward to once you're up and around again!

I'll be in touch.

Catherine

Convalescence is a sort of grown-up rebirth, enabling us to
see life with a fresh eye.

—Margaret Prescott Montague

RELATED TOPICS

Acknowledgments

Belated

Family and Friends

Sensitive

Sympathy

Thank You

23

Goodwill Letters

INTRODUCTION

In the broad sense, every business letter should be a goodwill letter, that is, a letter that sells the reader on the company's friendliness and fine reputation. In the narrow sense, a goodwill letter has as its sole function to encourage present customers to stay with the company and to buy more of its products, to solicit new customers, and to persuade former customers to reactivate their accounts.

Stephen Wilbers, Minneapolis *Star Tribune* business columnist, says, "If the only time people hear from you is when you are making trouble for them, how eager do you think they are to open your mail? . . . Try mixing in two or three positive communications every ten times you write."

Goodwill is probably best defined as a feeling of confidence in a company, an attitude of friendliness toward them, which makes a person loyal to that company rather than to another. Goodwill letters are written to customers, but also to suppliers, to the general public, and even to employees.

Every goodwill letter needs an "excuse" for being written. Although you can write a letter saying, "Hello there! We're still here, you know!" it is more effective to send the message wrapped in birthday or anniversary greetings; congratulations; holiday good wishes; letters of thanks or appreciation (for their business, referrals, recent purchases, payments, helpful suggestions); a welcome to newcomers in the community; an announcement (change in policy, personnel); a get well message; an apology (late delivery, order mix-up); or an invitation (to an open house, special event).

See also the appropriate chapters for each type of letter (for example, Appreciation).

> **It is not enough to collect today's profits, for your competitor is collecting tomorrow's good will.**
>
> —THE SYSTEM COMPANY

DO

- Open with a friendly or complimentary remark.
- State the purpose of your letter briefly: congratulations, thank you, appreciation, keeping in touch, happy holidays, "just wanted to see how you're doing."
- Expand on the message ("I'm particularly grateful because . . ." or "You've been a delight to work with because . . ." or "I hope the New Year is a happy and healthy one for you and your family").
- Focus on the other person's situation, interests, concerns; this is a "you" letter.
- Close with pleasant wishes for success and your confidence in future or continued contact.

> **As much goodwill may be conveyed in one hearty word as in many.**
>
> —CHARLOTTE BRONTË

DON'T

- Don't include a discernible sales message in a goodwill letter. Mention your products or services only lightly or not at all.
- Don't ask for anything—or imply that you want something.
- Don't dilute the impact of a goodwill letter by including business news, requests, or comments. Save them for another letter.

- Don't be too effusive; use a natural, informal, sincere tone that conveys a genuine friendliness.

> Of cheerfulness, or a good temper—the more it is spent, the more of it remains.
>
> —RALPH WALDO EMERSON

HELPFUL HINTS

- Goodwill gifts—samples, trial sizes, the first in a series, something the customer can keep regardless of any other purchase—are sent with a cover letter expressing appreciation for the recipient. The sales message is negligible. A few weeks later a follow-up letter may be sent with an overt sales message.

- A survey or questionnaire about the customer's use of your products or services is not only helpful to you, but can serve as a goodwill letter; most people like being asked for an opinion and thanked for their help. For it to be a pleasure instead of a burden, the survey must be brief, easy to complete, and returnable with a postage-paid envelope.

- Remember to send goodwill letters within your organization. Although it is never mandatory to congratulate an employee on a service anniversary, for example, you encourage good morale and company loyalty by doing so.

- Take advantage of routine announcements (new type of billing statement, new address, meeting notice) to develop a goodwill letter (thanking customers for their business or employees for a good year).

- The end-of-the-year holiday season is a good opportunity to send a goodwill letter, but do mail it as early as possible so that it doesn't get lost in all the other December mail and so that customers haven't already spent their gift budget elsewhere. Remember employees, colleagues, and other business associates with a goodwill message too.

> Kindness is always fashionable.
>
> —AMELIA E. BARR

GETTING STARTED

To show our appreciation for the responsible handling of your account, we are raising your credit limit to $20,000.

To thank you for being one of our best customers this past year and to introduce you to our new refillable permanent ink markers, we are enclosing markers in three of the most popular colors.

Congratulations on the tenth anniversary of Stanley Graff Real Estate—it has been a pleasure serving all your stationery needs!

Periquillo Clinical Equipment Services now has a special toll-free customer hotline.

We've missed you, and to remind you how easy it was to use our award-winning catering services, we're enclosing an updated brochure and a certificate good for 20% off your next order.

All of us here at Winterset Structural Package Designers send you our best wishes for a happy, healthy, prosperous new year!

In the past several weeks, you have kindly referred Harvey Birch, Frances Wharton, and Judith Hunter to the Cooper Architectural Group. We are grateful!

I enjoyed visiting with you last week when you stopped in to pick up some brochures at Spina Travel Consultants.

I read with great pleasure the news in last night's paper about the award you received for your work in food microbiology. All of us here at Quentin Durward Financial Planning extend our congratulations to you.

William de la Marck Interior Designs is having a one-day customer appreciation day for a few of our longtime clients, and you're invited!

Enclosed is a complimentary brochure on high-performance, low-risk funds that we thought you'd like to see.

Please come help us celebrate our twenty-fifth anniversary at an Open House on Friday, June 15. We have a small gift for you to show our appreciation for your past and present business.

Thank you for your interest in Mayo & Owen Capital Management Associates. You have our assurance that we are committed to maintaining the type of relationship necessary for your continued confidence and goodwill.

I once read a survey that said the moment in the daily routine that people look forward to most is opening the mail.

—Nancy Berliner

MODEL LETTERS

Dear Ms. Judique,

Two months ago you bought some shelving and panel systems from us, and we hope you are enjoying them. We know you will continue to appreciate them for years to come because all Simplex Office Furniture products are built for durability.

If we can be of service to you again, please keep us in mind, especially because from time to time we are able to offer special prices—currently, for example, every task chair in stock is 30% off.

Thank you again for choosing your office furnishings from us.

Sincerely,
Fulton Bemis

Dear Sasha Bhakaroff,

You've been such a faithful subscriber to our opera series over the years that we can only assume you love opera as much as we do. Like most opera lovers, you probably enjoy sharing your enthusiasm.

Enclosed are two coupons good for 15% off any opera ticket during the 1999-2000 season. They are for any two of your family members, friends, or neighbors. Just so you don't wish that you too were a newcomer to the opera scene, we're also enclosing a certificate made out in your name, giving you a 10% reduction on the price of the season subscription series you choose for next year.

We hope that your enjoyment of opera only grows with the years.

Sincerely,

Dear Chung Hi,

We thank you—as always—for choosing Levi-Ponsonby Office Products for all your business office needs. You regularly receive our big catalog, the one that puts 20,000 office products at your fingertips.

We're proud of being able to supply every office product made. But we began to wonder if we weren't offering almost too many products!

Today I'm sending you a smaller catalog containing *only* our bestselling items. A select group of customers is receiving this special catalog. If it seems to be helpful to our customers, we may begin publishing smaller catalogs every few months while reserving the big catalog for once a year.

I hope you enjoy seeing what other businesses consider the most essential office products.

Sincerely,
Peter Levi
Levi-Ponsonby Office Products

Dear Mr. Purdie,

We are pleased to have you enrolled at Okinawan Karate ("The Ultimate in Self-Protection and Self-Perfection") for the fall season. Welcome back!

For your convenience, we're enclosing a bookmark with our hours and telephone numbers. You might note on the back our standing invitation to take any other class on a trial basis, free of charge!

Feel free to stop in at the office any time and say hello!

Dear Jacy Picken Florister,

Congratulations on being honored with the Service to Humanity Award—what a stunning accomplishment! I saw the news in this morning's paper and wanted to let you know how inspiring it is to the whole community to have individuals like you among us.

Julian Doffield
City Councilor, Fourth Ward

Dear Pearl Lester and Lou Bensey,

We are pleased to have received the signed contract for your kitchen remodeling project and we are looking forward to starting work on June 6.

We pride ourselves on our professionalism and on the dispatch and precision with which we complete our projects. Even so, we sympathize with clients whose kitchens are disrupted while we work.

We're enclosing a coupon good for dinner for two at the Grand Café. Some evening, when you need to get away from what we're doing to your kitchen, have dinner somewhere else on us!

Dear Mr. and Ms. Mowbray,

We have noticed renewed interest among our RONAN'S JEWELRY customers in the charming old tradition of sending specific gifts for specific anniversaries. (Everybody knows it's silver for the 25th and gold for the 50th, but do you know what the 10th is, or the 20th?)

We thought the enclosed handy chart listing anniversaries and their suggested gifts might be useful to you. And it is one way of saying, "Thanks for being a good customer!"

P.S. The 10th is diamond and the 20th is emerald!

Dear Claude Mulhammer,

It's a little embarrassing tooting our own horn, but you've been a loyal customer for a long time and we thought you should know what good taste you have!

We are pleased to announce that Eggerson's Sporting Goods has been awarded the Greater Cincinnati Outstanding Small Business Award!

The next time you're in the store, bring this letter with you and we'll give you a free pocket compass. We realize that our award is also a tribute to our steady customers and we want to show our appreciation.

Dear Burchell,

I was offered the opportunity to subscribe to the enclosed monthly financial newsletter on behalf of my clients—and I jumped at it! I think you'll enjoy it as much as I do. I'll be mailing it to a select group of clients who (in my opinion) will appreciate the articles on investing, the stock market, bonds, retirement savings, estate planning, tax deductions, and other financial issues.

I appreciate doing business with you, and this is my small way of showing that appreciation.

Let me know if you see anything of interest to you in the newsletter that you and I have not yet discussed.

Best wishes!

Dear Mr. and Ms. Monakatocka,

With the ice beginning to break up on the river, all of us here at Landless Marina are looking forward to seeing you again before long.

We've made some changes in our hours (we'll be opening earlier and closing later, which is what customers requested) so we're sending you a refrigerator magnet imprinted with the new hours to help you keep track of them!

We will again this year have for rent or for sale: boats, motors, sailboats, canoes, pontoons, houseboats, personal watercraft, wind surfers, trailers, and marine accessories. We've modernized some of the storage spaces, slips, docks, and lifts, and we've got an exciting new inventory of this year's top line of watercraft.

See you soon!

Always set a high value on spontaneous kindness.

—Samuel Johnson

Dear Vivian Howard,

We are pleased to note that the Hutchinson Maintenance Experts have been cleaning your office carpets four times a year for six years now. As a business executive yourself, you know the value of faithful, longtime customers.

To show our appreciation, we'd like to pass on to you a sample of an effective carpet spot cleaner that we recently discovered. Note that we are not selling this product nor do we make any recommendation for it other than that we ourselves like it. When we had a chance to buy some samples, we thought of our favorite customers and decided to let you know about it.

Enjoy the spot cleaner, and I hope you continue to look forward to our thorough, deep-cleaning process that leaves your carpeting looking like new!

> Politeness may be nothing but veneering, but a veneered slab has the advantage of being without splinters.
>
> —MARY WILSON LITTLE

RELATED TOPICS

Appreciation

Congratulations

Get Well

Holidays

Neighbors

Sympathy

Thank You

Welcome

24

Holiday Letters

INTRODUCTION

With the growth of commercial greeting card companies and holiday-oriented retail sales events (Memorial Day Sale! July Fourth Sale! Presidents' Day Sale! Labor Day Sale!), we are now conscious not only of such holidays as New Year's or Christmas or Passover, but also of Halloween, Thanksgiving, Hanukkah, Kwanzaa, Valentine's Day, Martin Luther King Jr. Day, Purim, Rosh Hashanah, Veterans Day, Yom Kippur, St. Patrick's Day, Easter, Mother's Day, and Father's Day.

Businesses wanting to send goodwill letters to customers, colleagues, and employees can choose any holiday as a reason for writing. Family and friends are more likely to send serious greetings and newsy letters no more than once or twice a year, most often around the end of the old year or the beginning of the new one. Fundraisers also know that people are more willing to give during holidays and therefore schedule some of their most important appeals in the late fall. It is not surprising that first-class canceled mail peaks substantially in December.

> The choice and nature of our holidays is more perhaps than anything in our lives an expression of ourselves.
>
> —ALEC WAUGH

DO

- Begin with an expression of the appropriate seasonal greetings.
- Inquire about the other person and relate your own news if it is a personal letter. For a business letter express appreciation for the other person and the hopes of being of service in the future.
- Wish the person happiness, success, health, prosperity.

> Here's to your good health, and your family's good health, and may you all live long and prosper.
>
> —WASHINGTON IRVING

DON'T

- Don't send an aggressive sales message in a holiday letter (which is essentially a goodwill letter). An exception is when there's a logical connection such as florists and Mother's Day or candy and Valentine's Day.
- Don't send holiday cards whose only personal touch is your signature. If you have nothing to say to the person beyond the sentiments of a mass-produced greeting card, it is possible the gesture is meaningless; most people are disappointed to open a card and find no personal message.

> A holiday gives one a chance to look backward and forward, to reset oneself by an inner compass.
>
> —MAY SARTON

HELPFUL HINTS

- Because some "holidays" are also "holy days" for some people, businesses need to respect customers' beliefs. This means avoiding religious cards and sentiments unless your audience is carefully selected and well known to you. Do not casually bring religious elements into your goodwill letters; it will be perceived as hypocritical and self-serving. You may want to consult with adherents of different faiths to see how your message appears to them.

- Not every household is a happy one. Among your customers, co-workers, and friends are people who have lost loved ones, who have financial worries, illnesses, and other burdens. Except for mass-produced business holiday letters, from which nobody expects great sensitivity, choose seasonal greetings that are low-key and can convey your good wishes without an insistent and perhaps offensive cheerfulness.

- Those who send personal holiday greetings can piggyback other news onto them: the announcement of a new address, an engagement, a baby, or a new job. In the case of divorce, for example, when informing one's acquaintances might be difficult, it is convenient and tactful to append the news to year-end letters. (Mail your greeting early to save friends the minor embarrassment of sending their greetings to you as a couple.)

- When one member of the household sends holiday greetings on behalf of the whole family, it doesn't matter if they put their name first or last.

- Effective businesses find that sending seasonal greetings to employees on behalf of company management, firm officers, or the board of directors generates goodwill and company identification. After wishing the employees personal and professional happiness, the letter might offer congratulations for the good year just past and appreciation for the employees' contributions.

- Holiday letters from businesses are generally typed, although some companies send greeting cards, postcards, or specially printed letters with colorful graphics. A letter can be made more personal than a greeting card, can carry more information, and is less expensive. You might want to keep an idea file of some of the clever seasonal creations other businesses have used over the years. Eye-catching letters are not appropriate for all purposes; banks, legal firms, and insurance companies, for example, may not be helped by overly creative letters.

- The biggest category of customer goodwill letters is probably the year-end greeting. If your message is a general calling-to-mind letter or card (insurance agent, publisher, bank), send it anytime. But if December is an important sales or fundraising month for your organization, mail your greeting early in the month before people have already shopped or allocated their charitable donations.

- Some people (and letterwriting authorities) find social form letters completely unacceptable, while others (including yet other letterwriting authorities) enjoy writing and receiving them. Whatever one thinks of them, they are unlikely to disappear in the foreseeable future. They provide a practical solution for people who must choose between sending a form letter during the holidays and not writing at all. People used to live and die in the same town; their pool of friends and acquaintances was small and did not require written communications. Today's family might have hundreds of names in its address file: friends from elementary school in one town, from high school in another, from college, from a junior year abroad, from the first three cities in which they worked, neighbors who have moved away, friends of their children, as well as aunts, uncles, and cousins on both sides. Form letters don't have to be boring, and many aren't. In the polycopied part of your letter, tell your general news: the year's highlights, changes in your lives, travels, work and school happenings. You can organize your letter chronologically or by giving each family member a paragraph or by topic. Your letter will be more interesting if you discuss ideas as well as activities: your concerns about the environment, a book you recommend, a lecture you attended, the state of television today, even your political views. You can also include anecdotes, quotations, photocopied clippings of interest, or snapshots. In the handwritten part of your letter (which is really a "must," even if it's only a line or two), speak to the concerns of each of your readers, commenting on their last letter, asking about their lives. If you receive a number of form letters in your year-end mail, you are probably safe sending one yourself. If none of your correspondents use this form, it's possible that you are marching to a different drummer—which may also be why they like you. Ann Landers' final word on whether to write a form letter is: "When in doubt, go ahead. Those who aren't interested can toss 'em." And in any case you can comfort yourself that you have never won Mary Sweeney's annual contest to select the worst form Christmas letter. "Last year's entries," she reports, "were pretty dismal. One of my real estate friends submitted her brother's incredibly boring letter on tax reform in America accompanied by an audiocassette with a tax speech on it. It wasn't funny at all, but it won because it was so bad. Tax reform? At Christmas?"

> We each have a litany of holiday rituals and everyday habits that we hold on to, and we often greet radical innovation with the enthusiasm of a baby meeting a new sitter. We defend against it and—not always, but often enough—reject it. Slowly we adjust, but only if we have to.
>
> —ELLEN GOODMAN

GETTING STARTED

This is just a note to say we're thinking of you at Thanksgiving.

This Thanksgiving, as you reflect on your blessings—and perhaps even on some of the challenges that have helped you to grow—take a minute to consider those who have few blessings to count, those whose "challenges" have overwhelmed them.

Thanksgiving is a good time to count our blessings—and good customers like you are chief among them!

I hope the New Year brings you health, happiness, and small daily joys!

We send our warmest wishes for health and happiness—and to borrow my Irish grandfather's blessing: "I hope we're all here this day twelve-month."

Anaïs Nin once wrote, "Each friend represents a world in us, a world possibly not born until they arrive, and it is only by this meeting that a new world is born." We're grateful for the worlds in us that you've made possible, and the New Year seems a good time to celebrate this.

As we at the Park Jiwon Corporation look back over the year just past, we remember with appreciation our friendly, faithful customers.

On Rosh Hashanah it is written . . . On Yom Kippur it is sealed.

Everyone here at Jacobs & Gladstone sends you their best wishes for health, happiness, and prosperity throughout the coming New Year.

Skip this part if you are allergic to form letters, if you don't care *what* we've been doing, or if you can't remember who we are.

The best part of this beautiful season is keeping in touch with special friends like you.

Warm wishes to you and your dear ones this holiday season.

To start the New Year off right and to show our appreciation for your patronage last year, we're enclosing a certificate good for a free car wash with your next fill-up.

> The holidays are welcome to me partly because they are such rallying points for the affections which get so much thrust aside in the business and preoccupations of daily life.
>
> —George E. Woodberry

MODEL LETTERS

Dear Jane and John Greystoke,

We sincerely hope you have many blessings to count this Thanksgiving. If you do, you may be feeling grateful and wondering how you can share some of your good fortune with others.

Feeding hungry people is a fairly basic way to do this—and hunger is a critical issue in our area.

You may have more time than money. If you do, please come help serve the meal at the Seaforth Shelter on Thanksgiving Day. Or you may have more money than time. If that is true, won't you please send a check to help buy food for the meal?

If you lack both, we will accept gratefully your good wishes and hope to see you next year!

Seaforth Shelter Council

P.S. The Seaforth Shelter is located at 1837 Tappington; servers should arrive for the Thanksgiving meal by 11:30 a.m. Call Caroline at 555-1234 to let her know you'll be there. Send checks to: Seaforth Shelter Council, 1837 Tappington, Charles City, NC 28601.

Dear Homeowner,

It's not too late! If you haven't put in your shrubs and trees and perennials yet, Verrinder Garden Center's big Memorial Day sale will make you GLAD you didn't get around to it!

Enclosed is a checklist of our complete tree, shrub, perennial, and annual stock (helpfully marked to show sun/shade requirements) so that you can walk around your yard and note what you need. Bring the list with you and you won't forget a thing! Not only that, but when you check out, show your checklist and you will receive a 10% discount on your entire order!

Have a safe and happy Memorial Day weekend!

Happy Holidays from the Spangs!

Welcome to Christmas 1997, the year when we will learn what "accessories sold separately," "batteries not included," and "some assembly required" is all about. As we look forward to holiday baking, visits from family, and after-Christmas sales it is once again time to reflect on 1997, and write "Ye ol' tacky Christmas form letter."

Thankfully Jeff and Debbye remained employed over the past year. Looking for a reason to purchase new power tools, Jeff decided to build a deck. He spent hours in the "design stage," meticulously drawing the location of each board. A special thanks to the friends and family who helped us with the construction despite the heat and Jeff's relentless drive for perfection. We are pleased that Jeff was able to complete this project without the need for professional help, or the loss of any fingers.

In our quest to find free babysitters, we spent vacations this year with family. Mason is a very active fourteen-month-old. He is at that wonderful age that understands what you tell him to do but doesn't know enough words to talk back.

Toby, our seven-year-old black Lab, has felt a little neglected this year. We are happy to have remembered to let him back in the house each night, and he is grateful that Mason is a messy eater dropping lots of food his way. Toby enjoys the attention having company brings, so come and visit us at our home in Pewaukee!

May the knowledge of Christ's birth bring you joy, love, and hope this Christmas season.

Jeff, Debbye, and Mason

No matter how many Christmas presents you give your child, there's always that terrible moment when he's opened the very last one. That's when he expects you to say, "Oh yes, I almost forgot," and take him out and show him the pony.

—MIGNON MCLAUGHLIN

Dear Mrs. Gorsand,

If you're a kindergartener, Halloween can be scary. If you're a homeowner, it can also be scary—if you've gotten that far into fall without finishing your yard chores!

The MORGAN RENTAL BARN has everything you need to prepare for winter: leaf blowers, power rakes, lawn vacs, aerators, trimmers, chippers, shredders, drop spreaders, tillers—even lawnmowers if yours didn't make it through the season and you don't want to give a new one house room over the winter!

(And if you did finish your chores in time and want to celebrate Halloween with the kids, check out our rental party supplies!)

Dear Carol and Cecil,

We're remembering you at Passover and wishing you happiness always!

Alison, Jordan, Rebecca, and Jeremy will all be home next week and both sides of the family will be coming here for the Seder.

When are you coming to visit? We miss you!

Dear Mr. and Mrs. Burdock,

Will you be entertaining family and friends over the Fourth of July weekend?

How about inviting just one more to the celebration? Galbraith Catering—a full-service, licensed, insured caterer—can provide you with box lunches, a full multi-course buffet, or anything in between. If you want to make the main course, we'll bring salads, breads, and desserts. Or vice versa!

Feel like a guest at your own party! We provide servers, clean-up crew, tables, chairs, linens, dishes, and expert advice and assistance.

We are glad to supply references, and as a concerned member of the community, we recycle all papers and plastics, and we donate extra food to the Vane County Food Shelf.

For special events, you may want to make an appointment to come taste some of our specialties and choose the ones you think your guests would like. For simpler events, you are only a phone call away from trouble-free hospitality!

Happy Fourth of July! And, remember, we can help with everything but the fireworks!

December 1997

Dear Favorite Cousin,

Happy Holidays from our home to yours! We hope this letter finds you in good health and surrounded by laughter, family and friends, and a warm fire.

This past year has been filled with growth. Maddy, Norman, and Ed all gained 10 pounds! Fortunately Maddy's weight is complementary to her 36", 220 volts, and almost four-year-old body. She continues to challenge both her dads with a "take no prisoners" negotiation style. Put simply, dessert is sanctioned by God, and don't even try to mess with it.

On a serious note, Maddy continues to grow more beautiful each day. Her love for us continues to be a reward and blessing. She is surrounded by her grandparents, cousins, aunts, uncles, and many special friends. We could not have imagined four years ago that so many simple gifts would be a part of our daily routine.

We are celebrating our 10th year with six programs to date, as well as having watched our first Eighth Graders graduate, all four of them! Great teachers, wonderful parents, and easy-to-manipulate test scores. Bang, you have graduates! Seriously, all the classes remain very busy, infant through eighth grade! "For enrollment information, call . . ." (Oops, sorry, wrong letter!) A dedicated staff continues to bless our accomplishments. Professionally we have both remained active in the area of education and children's issues, Ed on the local front with the County's Children Coalition and Norman in state and national Montessori teacher organizations. It remains a challenge to balance a variety of needs, but somewhere in the chaos we find the time to enjoy many good times.

We are looking forward to a visit from you in the coming New Year! Best Wishes and Peace to you and yours!

Love,

Norman, Ed, and Maddy

Dear Homeowner,

Don't wait until the first cold spell to call for an appointment! Take advantage of our Labor Day Sale to get a jump on winter. We at Eben Merritt Heating, Inc. pride ourselves on our prompt response, but even we can't promise you same-day service once the flood of calls begins in late September.

Call now for your appointment and save 10%! We have thirty years' experience with all residential and light commercial heating and boiler systems. This is a good time to have a new furnace installed, your present furnace cleaned, or your air cleaner checked.

Let us do the labor during this Labor Day sale while YOU save 10%!

December 1996

Greetings Dear Family and Friends,

Seasonal salutations to you! We hope this finds you in good health and spirits and that 1996 has been good to you.

The year has been especially noteworthy for our family. In 1996, we saw Kalli play the clarinet at Carnegie Hall, Lauren's soccer team win the World Cup, Leah awarded the Nobel Prize for Literature, and Paul discover the cure for cavities. Not bad for a year's efforts.

Wait a minute! Wait a minute! Just testing to see if you were *really* reading this. Actually, it has been a fine year, mostly filled with all of the usual family business—school, soccer, piano lessons, soccer, gymnastics, soccer, clarinet, soccer, and softball. Favorite activities included skiing, hiking, swimming, camping, golfing, eating in, and eating out.

Unfortunately, this was not a good year for our pets. Our 16-year-old cat, Wilson, passed away. He died a week after some low-rent raccoon broke into our sunroom and digested our 5-year-old turtle, Boji. We have since "adopted" a clever striped kitten named Zoey, and have come to realize how much a part of our lives our pets are.

As the wonderful holidays approach, we want to take this opportunity to send you our best wishes. Even though in miles you may be far away, in spirit you're close to our hearts.

All the best to you and yours in 1997!

Lots of love,

Paul, Terry
Kalli, Lauren, and Leah

Dear Ms. Fanning,

At this time of year, our thoughts turn gratefully to good customers like you. All of us here at Tynan Hair Designers wish you and your loved ones a wonderful Holiday Season and a New Year of health, happiness, and prosperity.

Please accept as our small gift to you the enclosed certificate good for $15 off any of our line of hair-care products.

Happy Holidays!

> When Christmas bells are swinging above the fields of snow,
> We hear sweet voices ringing from lands of long ago,
> And etched on vacant places
> Are half-forgotten faces
> Of friends we used to cherish, and loves we used to know.
>
> —ELLA WHEELER WILCOX

RELATED TOPICS

Congratulations

Friends and Family

Fundraising

Goodwill

Sales

25

Letters Requesting Information

INTRODUCTION

Uncomplicated inquiries and requests for information are usually better taken care of by telephone. Most companies have toll-free numbers; some make available postage-paid reader reply cards.

A letter is indicated if a phone call would be intrusive (for example, asking a researcher for a bibliography of his articles) or if you need detailed information or if your request is a delicate one—it is often easier to be tactful in a letter than on the telephone. In some instances, a letter may be faster than a telephone call, even when the question is simple, because of the time spent on "hold" or being passed from person to person before reaching the appropriate one. A letter also generally has more impact.

For other types of requests, see Requests. For assistance in replying to letters seeking information, see Responses.

> Knowledge is of two kinds. We know a subject ourselves, or we know where we can find information upon it.
>
> —SAMUEL JOHNSON

234

DO

- Use a subject line to quickly orient your reader:

    Subject: cellular phone service

    Subject: horse transporting

    Re: piano tuning rates

    Re: time clock ribbons

    For simple, businesslike requests, no salutation is necessary; the subject line can stand alone.

- Begin with a courtesy phrase like "Please send me . . ." or "May I please have . . ."

- Be precise about the information you want: mailing instructions for the return of a hard drive, how to petition a county court for a legal name change, availability and rates for the high season, absentee figures for the period from January 1 to June 30. The more information you give, the more accurate the information you will receive.

- Be brief, avoiding unnecessary explanations or asking the same question in two different ways. Reread your letter to see how easy your questions are to answer. Most people sitting at information-supplying desks have too much mail and too little time.

- If you have several questions, number and place each one on a separate line.

- Tell where to send the information or where to telephone with a response.

- Give a date by which you need the information, if appropriate.

- Tell why the person might want to send you the information, if appropriate.

- Briefly tell why you want the information, if that will help the person send you precisely what you want.

- Offer to cover any costs of photocopying, postage, or fees for the information.

- Restate your request in the last paragraph if your letter is long or complicated.

- Include a self-addressed stamped envelope (SASE) when asking someone to make an effort on your behalf. When requesting information of companies who hope to make a sale to you, it is not necessary.

- Close with an expression of appreciation ("I appreciate your help" or "Thank you for your time and attention").

- Acknowledge information you are sent, if it involves anything but a routine response.

> Knowledge is the prime need of the hour.
>
> —Mary McLeod Bethune

DON'T

- Don't simply request "information." Narrow your request to the specific kind of information you need. Some companies have hundreds of brochures dealing with their products and services. A vague request for "information" may or may not net you what you need. If you don't know what other information might be available or useful, you can add, "I would appreciate any other information you think might be helpful."

- Don't be apologetic (unless the information you are asking for is time-consuming or difficult to supply). Avoid such phrases as "I hope this is not too much trouble" and "I'm sorry to inconvenience you."

- Although several letterwriting authorities object to ending this type of letter with "thank you" or "thanking you in advance" (because they seem to signal an end to the exchange), both are commonly seen and have become a social convention not too heavily laden with meaning. More expectant of future action are phrases such as "I appreciate your time and attention" or "I look forward to hearing from you."

> It is of equal importance with the discovery of facts to know what to do with them.
>
> — MARY PARKER FOLLETT

HELPFUL HINTS

- To compare different services (office maintenance, lawn care, driving schools, carpet cleaning) send the same letter asking for information to all such services in your area.

> The fact that *TV Guide* has been known to make larger profits than all four networks combined suggests that the value of information about information can be greater than the value of the information itself.
>
> — NICHOLAS NEGROPONTE

GETTING STARTED

I would appreciate receiving information about the clinic for athletic injuries mentioned in your article.

Will you please send me your packet for prospective students, including a course catalog for next year, admission procedures, an application form, and financial aid information?

We will be spending the month of July in Sundering-on-Sea and would appreciate receiving a map of the area, train schedules, a calendar of local events, and anything else that would help acquaint us with your area.

I am preparing a report for which I need annualized total returns for one, three, and five years through December 31. Can you furnish these by March 15?

Please send me information about your preventive maintenance program.

Would you be kind enough to send us the following information as soon as possible?

Please send me a copy of your current foam- and sponge-rubber products catalog along with information on bulk order discounts.

Will you kindly send me information on changing the beneficiary of my life insurance policy?

I am interested in learning more about hypnosis. Could you suggest a reading list of books you consider sound?

Your order forms, prices, and ordering instructions are oriented toward institutions—can you tell me how an individual can obtain your materials?

I'm writing to ask for any information you might have—brochures, fact sheets, hotlines—about osteoarthritis.

Would you please forward this request for information to the appropriate person?

Please send information about your hearing rehabilitation center.

I'd appreciate receiving information about your chemical dependency programs for adolescents.

I would like to know how one goes about getting on your talk show.

May I please have any free informational materials you have on furniture care?

I would like to ask you, if this is possible, for the names and telephone numbers of people who have successfully completed your stop-smoking program.

Can you please explain how your attorney referral program works?

Is it true that it's possible to have stars named for people and, if so, how does one go about it?

I am interested in receiving whatever information you have on lymphedema.

> It is well for us to realize that the great increase in knowledge in the world does not necessarily make us better or wiser. . . . A clever monkey may learn to drive a car, but he is hardly a safe chauffeur.
>
> —JAWAHARLAL NEHRU

MODEL LETTERS

November 30, 1922

Dear George,

Zilla Riesling told me you and Paul just got back from a trip to Maine. Will and I want to visit some cousins there. Do you have any information about sights to see, where to stay en route, most picturesque itineraries, etc.? We'd appreciate your help.
Thanks!

Carol

Dear O'Neill Exhibits, Inc.,

Two summers ago in July, your animated dinosaur exhibit visited our zoo in Cabot, Pennsylvania. Our son, Simeon, was then three years old and too terrified at the sound of the roaring and sight of the lunging dinosaur robots to venture beyond the threshold of your ever-so-realistic exhibit.

Now that he is five, Simeon is filled with remorse (to the point of tears) that his fears at age three prevented him from experiencing the thrill of a lifetime.

I've learned from the zoo administrators that your exhibit travels around the country and I'd like to find out where it will be this next summer from June 1 to August 30. We would make a vacation of it—even driving several hundred miles if necessary—to see your exciting dinosaur show.

Would you please send me your itinerary as well as the phone numbers and addresses of your upcoming exhibit halls?

Thank you very much from a family of dinosaur fans!

Sincerely,

TO: Owner/Manager of Loding Lake Lodge

Please send me your brochure and a schedule of rates for this summer along with information on handicap accessibility. We would be interested in a two-bedroom cabin during the first part of August.

Thank you.

Dear Henrietta Stackpole,

I am writing to find out if you have plans to publish again your Pet Peeve column in the *Archer County Record*. I loved your column and it peeves me that it is gone.

I would like to contribute to your column if you bring it back to life. I have an overabundance of pet peeves, for example, people who leave Christmas wreaths hanging on their houses until springtime (isn't a brown and brittle wreath with a garish red bow hanging there in the middle of May just an ugly and unfestive sight?). This is only one of about a million peeves I have.

Please let me know at 555-1234 if the column will ever reappear and I'll be glad to supply you with material to last you months.

Sincerely,

Dear Ms. Baird,

The next issue of the newsletter will focus on the annual fall conference. You chaired last year's conference, and I'm wondering if you can supply some information to give readers an idea of what to expect.

How many attended?
What were some of the high spots?
Do you have any quotable remarks from the conference evaluations?

I'd welcome any other details of last year's conference that you think would be appealing.

The last date for receiving copy for the newsletter is March 1. I hope you are able to get something to me by then.

Mark Stainer

P.S. Did I tell you it was the best conference we've ever had?

Dear Dr. Copeland,

Thank you for your call yesterday about my blood levels. Is there any possibility that switching to the generic blood thinner would have had anything to do with this? I know that in theory it shouldn't make any difference, but I thought I'd mention it in case you've encountered this with other patients. My health insurance began requiring the use of generics three months ago. Since my blood levels have been absolutely steady for the past two years, I can't help but wonder if this new medication was responsible for the change. If so, what does one do?

You do not have to respond to this letter unless of course you want me to change medications or dosages.

Thank you, as always, for your good care and attention.

Dear Ms. Blanchard,

I am interested in Camp Augusta for my daughter. I have seen your brochure, and would like some additional information:
1. How many campers do you take each session?
2. Is financial aid available?
3. How much of the campers' time is spent on the special art curriculum you offer?
4. Do campers have a choice of the arts area they work in, or is it the same course of study for everyone?
5. What arrangements are made for medical emergencies?

I would appreciate receiving this information in the next two weeks.

Thank you for your time and attention.

Dear Cutler Pest Control, Inc.

Since you are in the extermination business I am wondering if you have any information or statistics on the possibility of sewer rats venturing through pipes and entering homes through basement toilets.

I have recently moved into a basement apartment and have developed a fear of encountering a rat climbing out of my toilet bowl. This fear has begun to make life somewhat miserable for me. Perhaps getting the facts from you is all I need to put my mind at ease.

Have any such incidents occurred in our area? If so, where and when? Please send any relevant literature or statistics to the address shown in the letterhead above. If there is a fee for the materials I will send you a check by return mail.

Thank you for your time and concern.

Sincerely,

TO: Ordering Department

I need a replacement keyboard drawer for my Roscoe Computer Desk. However, I don't see this item offered separately in your catalog. I'm not interested in buying the complete unit. Is there some way to purchase just the keyboard drawer?

Thank you.

To: Membership Secretary, Southwest Builders Association
From: Bibbs Sheridan
Re: Membership information
Date: October 18, 1999

Please send me membership information on the Southwest Builders Association. I was a member of the Upper Midwest Builders Association but have recently relocated. My mailing address is below.

Thank you.

> The paradox, of course, is that you can never have enough information, but you cannot gather information forever.
>
> —PRISCILLA ELFREY

Dear Dr. Sangrado,

My mother, who is 87 years old, lives with us. She gets flu and pneumonia shots every fall, and she of course sees you when she has any serious symptoms.

However, we are wondering if you could give us some guidelines on how to tell a cold from the flu from pneumonia. Perhaps you have an informational brochure you could send (enclosed is a self-addressed stamped envelope).

Thank you.

Dear Lolly,

We're planning to redo the living room this spring, and I wonder if you'd mind if I did the copycat thing and used the same wallpaper you have in your living room. You will remember that when we visited you last year, I simply fell in love with it.

(Does this remind you of when we were little and I copied everything you did?)

If you can handle seeing your own living room wallpaper when you come to visit us this summer, could you let me know the brand, color code, and style number?

Don't they say that imitation is the sincerest form of flattery?

> Everybody gets so much information all day long that they lose their common sense.
>
> —GERTRUDE STEIN

RELATED TOPICS

Acknowledgments
Requests
Responses
Sales
Thank You
Travel

26

Letters of Instruction

INTRODUCTION

Individualized letters of instruction have largely been replaced by form letters, package inserts, owners' manuals, product brochures, drugstore printouts about your medication, and other computer-generated or preprinted materials. Such instructions include equipment or appliance operating instructions, safety instructions, assembly instructions, and installation instructions as well as instructions on how to dispute a credit card charge, apply for admission, sign an enclosed contract or lease, return merchandise, obtain a refund or exchange, or order replacement parts. Because commercial instructions deal with matters involving possible injury, loss of money, damage, and of course customer goodwill and repeat sales, they must be precisely crafted.

Many businesses occasionally need to write an individual letter of instructions, generally in response to a customer query. Letters of instruction are also written inside a company, most often in the form of a memo.

They are also written to the couple staying with your children while you are out of town, the patient following a specific care regimen, the neighbor child who waters your garden, the day-care provider, the carpenters working on your house.

Letters of instruction are often similar to letters of information; see the Index for related references.

> When all else fails, read the instructions.
>
> —AGNES ALLEN

DO

- Begin by thanking the person (if you are responding to a letter, phone call, or in-person query) or by stating the purpose of your letter or form ("The following instructions will help you care for your instrument so that it will give you optimum performance pleasure").

- Number or otherwise set off each step in the instructions.

- Be brief. After writing the instructions, go over them and pare them down to the essentials.

- Be specific. If you say "soak contacts overnight," note the appropriate number of hours in parentheses as "overnight" could mean anything from six to twelve hours. If you state that an appliance needs to be cleaned regularly, describe the products and procedures that work best for cleaning it and tell what "regularly" means. Explain or graphically identify parts, in case readers are not familiar with industry terminology. Even someone who knows what "housing" or a "coupling" is may not recognize it in its present form in the machine at hand.

- Be clear and intelligible. When preparing a form letter that will be used thousands of times, ask other people outside your department to read it for clarity. Some of the worst instructions have been written by experts; because they know their field so well they do not understand the mind of the uninitiated well enough to adequately explain anything.

- Be diplomatic and polite. Some requests for instructions may appear inane to you and the answers so obvious you hardly know how to phrase your response. But people's brains work in wonderfully odd and divergent ways, and the person may actually be looking at the situation in a way very different from the way you ordinarily see it. Then, too, even if it is a "stupid" question, good public relations demands that you treat it as politely and helpfully as any other question.

- If appropriate, give a phone number, contact person and address, or other resource where further help can be obtained.

- End with a pleasant statement of appreciation or thanks or with a mention of future business or enjoyment of the new product.

> Explanations grow under our hands, in spite of our effort at compression.
>
> —JOHN HENRY CARDINAL NEWMAN

DON'T

- "Don't give instructions in the negative" is a negative statement. "Word your instructions positively" is a positive one. Use the positive form. When you find "don't" and "never" and "should not" in your instructions, rephrase the sentence to read positively.

- Don't use words like "simple" and "obvious." Invariably, these words preface something that is neither simple nor obvious to readers, and they feel rebuked for not understanding something that apparently everyone else does.

- Don't use patronizing, insulting, or condescending language. For example, sometimes a "broken" appliance is simply not plugged in. The first in a list of troubleshooting instructions generally advises checking to see if the appliance is plugged in. State this neutrally so that the customer doesn't feel too dumb if that is the problem.

> I am the enemy of long explanations; they deceive either the maker or the hearer, generally both.
>
> —JOHANN WOLFGANG VON GOETHE

HELPFUL HINTS

- Assembly, installation, operating, and safety instructions are generally included in an owner's manual. However, you might like to accompany the manual with a cover letter emphasizing special cautions ("Please particularly note the section on fire hazards").

- It is often helpful to explain *why* as well as *how*. For example, "Do not use this compound when there is danger of rain followed by temperatures below 32°F." Many people will accept this instruction without question. But others will wonder what rain and cold have to do with anything, and still others will ignore it, thinking it unimportant. If you add, "because the compound will absorb the moisture, freeze, expand, and probably crack," users are far more likely to follow the instruction—and you will receive fewer complaints.

- Any document that must be signed (contract, lease, stock transfer) should be accompanied by a letter explaining where signatures are needed, if the signatures need a medallion or notarization, which copy to retain for the person's files, where to send the other copies.

- Instructions are often included in cover letters accompanying a sample, a contract, or a product, telling the recipient how to interpret or use the item.

> People will do things differently. Your instructions will probably be misunderstood. What you say is likely to be different from what they hear.
>
> —PRISCILLA ELFREY

GETTING STARTED

We are pleased to enclose the instructions you requested.

The following guidelines should be helpful.

Please read and save these instructions.

When using electrical appliances, especially when children are present, basic safety precautions, including the following, should always be observed.

Before you use your appliance, please read the important safety instructions.

Please read all the operating instructions before plugging in your unit.

Caution: read rules for safe operation and instructions carefully.

Please read the assembly instructions before unpacking the parts.

Attached are instructions for the use and care of your nonstick skillet.

Below are our easy-to-follow, illustrated instructions for trimming hair at home with your Clark Clippers.

Your Dewhurst Travel Iron will provide you with a lifetime of faithful use if you follow these care instructions.

As I am not sure which model of the Evesham you have, I am enclosing instructions for all of them.

You don't need special tools to install this fixture, but be sure to follow the steps in the order given.

Replacement parts are available for one year from date of purchase and may be ordered by following these instructions.

If you plan to have your baby at Marquand Memorial Hospital, please note the following instructions for pre-admittance.

To register to vote in Dickerson County, follow the five steps listed below.

Here are the instructions for making Joey's formula.

> When driven to the necessity of explaining, I found that I did not myself understand what I meant.
>
> —Maria Edgeworth

MODEL LETTERS

Dear Orin Mannon and Hazel Niles,

Congratulations on the beautiful Everlasting sod you've just had installed.

Newly laid sod requires a thorough watering every day until it has formed new roots that bond it to the soil. If it is allowed to dry out, especially when the weather is hot, the strips of sod will shrink, resulting in unsightly gaps.

Newly seeded areas need to be kept evenly moist at all times, which may require light sprinkling more than once a day. Your diligence will pay off in terms of better and faster germination.

Call us if you have any questions, and enjoy the lush new look of your yard!

Adam Brent Landscaping, Inc.

Dear Ms. Martin-Belième,

I'm pleased that you are able to spend a month with us in Fiesole. You asked about a passport. You might want to doublecheck with your local passport office, but I believe this is what you'll need:

a certified copy of your U.S. birth certificate
a driver's license or military identification
your Social Security number
your parents' birth names, birthdates, and places of birth
two recent passport pictures
a check or money order for $45
a separate check for $15 or $15 in cash.

Sincerely,

Vivian Bell

Attention: New owners of the Fanshawe Electric Toothbrush

To reduce the risk of electric shock, burns, fire, or injury:

1. Always unplug the appliance immediately after use. To disconnect, turn all controls to the OFF position, then remove plug from outlet. Always unplug it before you clean it and before taking it apart.

2. Close supervision is necessary when this appliance is used by, on, or near children or other vulnerable individuals.

3. If the appliance has a damaged cord or plug, if it is not working properly, if it has been dropped or damaged, or dropped into water, return it to a service center for examination and repair.

4. To reduce the risk of electric shock, the polarized plug to this appliance has one blade that is wider than the other. The plug will fit in a polarized outlet only one way. If the plug does not fit properly in the outlet, reverse the plug's blades. If it still does not fit, contact a qualified electrician to install the proper outlet. Do not tamper with the plug in any way.

5. Keep the cord away from heated surfaces.

6. Do not use outdoors.

7. Do not operate where aerosol (spray) products are being used or where oxygen is being administered.

Dear Deborah and Derek,

Thank you for taking care of the yard while we're gone. We'd appreciate it if you would:

1. Cut the grass once a week. If we've had a storm, be sure to pick up any fallen branches before you start mowing.

2. Check the front porch every day to make sure there aren't any flyers or newspapers lying around.

3. We have a lot of wascally wabbits this year and they are eating all our beans and pansies and carnations. It looks as if they have their own tiny lawnmowers, but I know it's just their teeth at work. The wwetches. Anyway, would you check every day to be sure the protective netting doesn't come loose over those plants?

4. Have your parents call us (they have the number) if there are any special problems.

Tommy and Tuppence Beresford

TO: Compson Company Laboratory Personnel
FROM: Joanna Burden
SUBJECT: Safety and Loss Prevention
DATE: September 10

On September 6, Lucas Burch and I examined all laboratories as part of a company-wide effort to identify ways to improve safe operations and to minimize loss of equipment and supplies.

The lab areas were generally very well maintained. We were impressed. Areas in which there are some opportunities for improvement include:

Storage of solvents: Each lab should have its own approved vented flammable solvents storage cabinet. There were too many cases of solvents stored next to strong acids. We also noted some materials past their expiration dates.

Storage of acids and bases: Most of the labs stored these—in fiberglass trays or tubs—away from solvents and separated from each other. However, a few labs did not.

Experimental materials: These must all be labeled with the "Experimental Materials" tags. Most labs are already doing this.

Equipment panels: When these panels are removed to facilitate repairs, employees may be exposed to high voltages or currents. Please post warning signs to indicate the possible hazards of missing equipment panels.

Fire extinguishers: Several labs had blocked extinguishers. This should be easy to fix.

We have an excellent safety record, and I thank each of you for that. Following up on these suggestions will allow us to continue to have a safe and enjoyable place to work.

TO: All employees
FROM: Buildings and Grounds
DATE: July 6, 1999
RE: Parking lot resurfacing

The north parking lot will be resurfaced beginning July 15. This means the lot will be unavailable for employee parking July 15-17. We ask that, if at all possible, you share rides to work on those days. For those three days only, parking will be allowed along the east side of the access road and in the visitor parking places in the east lot (visitors will be able to park around the entrance circle). The Lerrick Mall management has also agreed to let us use the row of parking along its east side (that is, next to Morgan Road) July 15-17. We ask that you do not use any other spaces in the mall parking lot. As a last resort, use the Lerrick parking ramp and take city bus # 78 (there is a bus every 12 minutes) or plan to walk (about 7 minutes). Thank you.

Dear Mrs. Howard,

You asked about flying your daughter's cats to her in California. While I would be happy to make the reservations for you, we often suggest that clients make their own arrangements for shipping animals because of the special responsibilities involved.

Pets must be healthy enough to travel (most airlines require a recently signed certificate of health from a veterinarian). The kennel must be clearly marked with both the sender's and recipient's name, address, and telephone number. Reservations must be made in advance, and animals may not be shipped COD unless the shipper guarantees return of freight. Verify drop-off and pick-up times when you make the reservation.

Dogs and cats must be at least eight weeks old (and, if applicable, weaned for at least five days). They should eat no solid food for six hours before the flight, but should be given a moderate amount of water and taken for a walk just beforehand.

In addition, it is a good idea to accustom the animal to the kennel in advance of the trip. Occasionally a veterinarian will prescribe a tranquilizer.

The airlines are usually helpful and clear about these procedures. I hope all goes well.

> Find out how to give directions and yet to allow people opportunity for independent thinking, for initiative.
>
> — MARY PARKER FOLLETT

Dear Dr. Break,

I'm delighted to hear that your dining room set is already bringing you so much pleasure. There is something very warm and appealing about older furniture.

As you know, the set's surfaces were refinished and the drawer pulls all replaced, so it will never be considered valuable to antique collectors. Maintaining it then is a matter of common sense. I suggest you clean the pieces thoroughly with paint thinner or with a weak ammonia-and-water solution. Loose joints should be glued (don't use nails or screws).

For more specific help, contact R.K. Marlake (555-1234), a professional furniture restorer. His prices are reasonable and his work is outstanding. I've referred many customers to him—and they all thanked me afterwards.

Dear Ms. Firmin,

You are not the only customer to have requested clarification of your Merton cordless phone's speed-dialing function. The manual accompanying all new cordless telephones is currently being rewritten.

To store phone numbers:

1. Press the "program" button (PGM).

2. Press a number from 0 to 9. This will be the number you always press to speed-dial the number you are about to enter.

3. Enter the phone number you want to store.

4. Press the "speed dial" button (SPEED). You'll hear a beep indicating the number has been properly stored.

To make calls with speed dialing:

1. Press the "talk" button (TALK).

2. Press the "speed dial" button (SPEED).

3. When you enter your chosen number from 0 to 9, you will be connected to the desired number.

I hope these instructions help. We have thousands of customers who love their Merton cordless phones. Soon we'll have an instruction manual as outstanding as the phone!

Dear Ms. Jibinsky,

We are happy to send you the enclosed revised contract. After reading it carefully, please sign all four copies, initial each page in the indicated circles, and return all copies to us.

A countersigned original contract will be sent to you by return mail.

Thank you.

I wish he would explain his explanation.

—George Gordon, Lord Byron

RELATED TOPICS

Advice

Information

27

Letters of Introduction

INTRODUCTION

The old-fashioned letter of introduction, with its rigid protocol and demanding obligations (illness, a death in the family, or some other serious obstacle provided the only acceptable excuses for failing in this social responsibility), has all but disappeared. Today most people use the telephone or social or business networks to manage introductions easily and quickly.

Although some letters introducing people to each other are still seen, today's letter of introduction is more casual and less socially binding than it used to be. More common are letters introducing new stores, divisions, products, or services. For assistance with this type of letter, see Sales Letters, since that is essentially what they are.

For help turning down a request to look someone up or to entertain someone, see Refusals. To introduce yourself to a prospective employer, see Applications. To introduce your store, products, or services to a newcomer in the area, see Welcome. To introduce someone for club membership or to introduce a suggested guest speaker, see Clubs.

Letters of introduction are related to references and recommendations in that A is vouching for B to C. You may want to see the chapter on References. However, a letter of introduction is more like the superficial introduction that takes place at a large party, whereas the recommendation is more like a serious talk about someone your friend wants to employ.

> I look upon every day to be lost, in which I do not make a new acquaintance.
>
> —SAMUEL JOHNSON

DO

- Begin by stating your reason for writing: to introduce yourself, to introduce a friend, to suggest that the person you are writing look up someone visiting or new in their area.
- Give the person's name, title, position, or some other identifying label.
- Tell something about the person to be introduced—whether it is yourself or a third party—that will make your correspondent want to meet or help the person ("she has collected paperweights for years, and I know this is a great interest of yours"). Mention interests they have in common, people they both know, work or school connections. The object is to provide both people with a way of beginning a conversation or a friendship.
- Mention the relationship between you and the person you are introducing.
- Be specific about what you would like the other person to do: invite your friend to dinner; make introductions in the neighborhood; explain work opportunities in the area.
- Suggest how best to contact the person: the reader can contact the other person (include address and phone number); the person will call your reader; you are inviting them both to lunch.
- Close with an expression of respect or friendship, and your thanks or appreciation ("I will be grateful for any courtesies you can extend to Chadwick").
- Write a letter of thanks or appreciation to anyone who has written a letter of introduction on your behalf. You will also be writing to thank the person to whom you were introduced for any courtesies extended to you.

> Chance acquaintances are sometimes the most memorable, for brief friendships have such definite starting and stopping points that they take on a quality of art, of a *whole* thing, which cannot be broken or spoiled.
>
> —WILLIAM SAROYAN

DON'T

- Don't organize introductions lightly. They set in motion responsibilities, demands on time and energy, and consequences involving several people, and they can sometimes work a hardship on your distant friends. Reserve your introductions for very special cases.

- Don't ask for a letter of introduction; unlike a letter of reference or recommendation, which may be requested, the introduction must be offered. You may tell someone you plan to be in a certain area or that you are job hunting, but you should then wait for the other person to suggest introducing you to friends or colleagues.

- Don't make the person feel obligated to accommodate you. Unwilling hospitality or grudging meetings do not have good outcomes. Allow the person room to maneuver and provide a way to save face if they must refuse you ("I realize you may not be free just now").

> Never claim as a right what you can ask as a favor.
>
> —J. CHURTON COLLINS

- Don't act as though you are doing the person a tremendous favor by arranging this introduction. Although you will want to imply in a low-key fashion that the person could benefit from meeting the other person, the request may be a burden at this particular time or may not turn out as well as you would like it to.

- Don't be too insistent that the two people must meet and will like each other very much. No one can predict who will take to whom. Emphasize instead what they have in common so that your reader can decide what, if any, interest there might be in meeting the other person. Putting two people in touch with each other is risky; it is not impossible that they will both end up resenting you if it was your idea and you pushed it too hard.

> Make it a point never to write a letter of introduction unless you know both persons intimately and well.
>
> —LILLIAN EICHLER WATSON

HELPFUL HINTS

- Form letters are acceptable when the same message of introduction must be sent to a number of people and when the message is not particularly personal (introducing a new service or new billing procedure to thousands of customers, or introducing new officers or board members to a large organization).

- When new employees, business associates or representatives, or personnel are introduced by letter to those with whom they'll be working, only a paragraph or two is needed. Include a few highlights of their professional background and a general description of their future responsibilities.

- When you would like A to offer hospitality to B, write A directly. This spares B the embarrassment of presenting a letter of introduction only to be rebuffed by A because of lack of time or interest. It also spares A the awkwardness of being caught off guard and perhaps pressured into an undesirable situation.

- Most companies write to introduce a new sales representative to customers before the first visit. This smoothes the representative's way while it also serves as a good-will letter, telling customers that headquarters takes a personal interest in them. The letter should leave customers feeling that they know a little about the new representative and reassured that the company has every confidence in the person's abilities.

- When introducing customers to a change in billing, ordering, or other routine procedures, explain why you initiated the change. Focus on the value of the change to the customer, not its value to you. If you express your appreciation for the customer's business and say that the change will improve service, your letter of introduction becomes a goodwill letter or even a sales letter.

- All letters dealing with introductions can be typed. You may want to handwrite social introductions, but it is not necessary. In some work-related introductions, you may want to include your business card.

> Do you suppose I could buy back my introduction to you?
>
> —Groucho Marx

GETTING STARTED

I am giving Berenice Fleming, a very dear friend of mine, this letter of introduction to you.

A very good friend of mine will be visiting Atlanta next month and I'm wondering if the two of you wouldn't enjoy meeting each other.

I would like to introduce to you Conrad Barnabas, a superb molecular biologist known to me for many years.

Some very good friends of ours, Maggie Verver and Lambert Strether, are going to be in Taos during the month of June.

You've heard me talk about Eugene Witla for years.

My cousin—the one who competed in the luge events at the last Olympics—will be in Kansas City next month.

I normally hesitate to put two of my friends in touch with each other because too often it doesn't seem to work out, but I think this is a very special case.

Osmond Dental Supply is pleased to introduce Isobel Archer, your customer service representative as of April 29.

I would like to introduce myself as your new sales representative from Casterbridge Art and Design, and to take this opportunity of asking if you have received our spring catalog.

We are pleased to introduce the newest member of our practice, Dr. Edmund Darrell, a board-certified ophthalmologist and former resident of Marsden.

May I introduce myself? I'm Maria Gostrey and I want to be your next mayor.

I've just been told that you are writing a book on Deaf culture and, as someone who is doing similar work, I would like to introduce myself.

We would like to introduce you to volunteer vacations around the world.

This will introduce a whole new concept in buying focus funds.

Thank you for the lovely letter of introduction you wrote to Sir Ralph Bloomfield Bonington on my behalf.

> **Why is it that the person who needs no introduction usually gets the longest one?**
>
> —MARCELENE COX

MODEL LETTERS

Dear Tom,

This letter will introduce Lettice Watson to you. She is Chief Operations Manager at our Houston office and is making visits to several branch offices to study their operations. We had originally thought to set up appointments, but with everyone racing toward the April 15 deadline, I didn't want work to come to a halt so everyone could prepare for her visit.

If some of your people are unavailable, or if she doesn't get as complete a view as she hoped because of the lack of advance preparation, that's all right too. Just point her in the general direction of the operations office and she'll do the rest.

I appreciate your welcoming her.

Dear Winnie,

You know I don't believe in foisting people on each other, so this is uncharacteristic for me: A dear friend of mine, Elinor Presset, is going to be in Oklahoma City for a week visiting her family. And she is—guess what!—a dollmaker.

I can't imagine two longtime dollmakers being in the same vicinity and not wanting to talk to each other. I took the liberty of giving her your telephone number, but I know you're as good about saying "no" as you are kind about saying "yes," so I wasn't too worried about imposing on you.

Her parents' number in Oklahoma City is 555-1234 if you'd rather call her (June 13-19).

I am, of course, hoping you will both fall on my neck with glad cries of gratitude (because I really do think you'll like each other). But if not, not.

Love,
Myra

Dear Madame de Cintré,

When Felix Young heard that I would be in Paris for the next three weeks, he suggested that I call on you to convey to you his warmest regards and to reintroduce myself to you. You will probably not remember as I was only one of a group, but we met some twenty years ago in Rennes. Felix was insistent that you and I would enjoy such a meeting—probably because we are both doing research on atrial fibrillation. (I am enclosing several papers published recently in case they would interest you.)

Felix and I have been good friends for many years and I generally like to take his advice, but I hesitate to disturb you. Everyone who passes through Paris must want to see you, and I imagine it becomes difficult.

Should you have the time and wish to see me, I am at your disposal (Hôtel Henri IV, 25 place Dauphine, 43.54.44.53). I also expect to be in Paris this fall, so we could always try again later.

With very best wishes to you, I am

Sincerely,
Clifford Wentworth

Dear Phil,

I ran into your old coach, Mr. Pope, the other day. I'm not sure you ever met his son, Ted, but it turns out he has just transferred to the University for the second semester. If it's hard to go to a new school where you don't know anybody, it's even harder to do it mid-year.

I know you're tremendously busy but I also know you've got a kind heart. Will you give him a call, meet him for coffee, or just in general see how things are going for him? He's living off-campus at 191 Wells St., Apt. 3F. His phone number is 555-1234.

Thanks!

To: All employees
Re: Avisa Pomeroy, Director of Global Strategy
Date: August 1, 1999

The Board of Directors and the management of Vixen Tor International are pleased to introduce to you the new Director of Global Strategy, Avisa Pomeroy. She has been with Vixen Tor since 1985, bringing her talents and energy to the advertising and sales departments before being named Director of Overseas Sales, in which capacity she has spent the last four years in our Bonn office. She attributes the successes of the Global Strategy department to the retiring director, Ives Brown, and says she hopes to consolidate and build on the gains he has made.

Dear Hugh,

This letter will introduce to you a former student of mine and an extremely talented photographer, Charity Lamb.

She is relocating to the Albuquerque area, and I thought it might be beneficial to both of you to meet and to discuss your areas of common interest. I've suggested she bring her portfolio with her—I think when you see her work, you'll thank me for this introduction!

I look forward to returning this favor some day. I hope all's well with you and the family and the company.

Dear Lewis,

How are you? Why do I write only when I have an agenda?

An acquaintance of mine, Albert Sanger, is moving to Tyrol and I imagine he will end up in your congregation. As a choir director constantly on the lookout for new talent, you'll want to know that he has a fabulous voice. He's also reserved so if you wait for him to approach you, you may miss out on months of a truly delightful addition to your choir.

You can thank me for this later. . . !

Dear Esther,

My brother and sister-in-law, Richard and Ada Carstone, are moving to Woodcourt at the end of the month. I don't think they know a soul there. Would you be willing to show them around a little at first? I don't have a phone number for them yet, but I'm writing to ask if I may give them yours.

Richard is an accounting technician and Ada is a medical records clerk. The big loves of their lives are their two cats: a white Persian named Pippa and a black Persian named Jonah. Among other things, they play bridge and Ada collects vintage clothing. What with cats, bridge, and collectibles, I thought you might have enough in common to enjoy meeting them.

Let me know, will you? And thanks!

There are people whom one loves immediately and for ever. Even to know they are alive in the world with one is quite enough.

—NANCY SPAIN

Dear Bret,

The son of a dear friend of mine is moving to Minneapolis and will be looking for work in public relations. Would you be able to give him a little advice? Wan Lee is talented and hardworking, and I think you'd enjoy meeting him.

I've given him your telephone number, knowing that if you don't have time for this, you know how to say "no" with grace and charm.

If you manage to make time for him, I thank you!

From: hisp@email.com
To: rls@email.com
Subject: A little competition
Date: Mon, 14 Jul 1999 16:31:31

Hi R.L.! A friend of mine, Tom Redruth, is being transferred to your office, and I think you'd enjoy looking him up. All you need to know about Tom at the moment is that his last marathon time was 3:19! I think he could give you a run for your money!

> The single drawback to being a good correspondent is that when finally you see the person to whom you've written for quite some time, he may find you rather less enchanting in person than you seemed on the printed page.
>
> —Mrs. Falk Feeley

RELATED TOPICS

Announcements

Applications

References

Refusals

Requests

Thank You

Welcome

28

Invitations

INTRODUCTION

Marcelene Cox once said, "Invitation is the sincerest form of flattery." Modern society must be a complimentary group as a whole because we issue millions of invitations every year—to parties, dinners, banquets, receptions, and weekend visits; bris, christenings, bar mitzvahs, bat mitzvahs, first communions, and other religious ceremonies; business meetings, workshops, conferences, trade shows, book fairs, and exhibitions; baby showers and housewarmings; anniversary, birthday, holiday, and retirement celebrations; school events and class reunions; benefits, recitals, and performances. We even "invite" people to come to a store opening, to accept a trial membership, or to open a new charge account.

This chapter deals with invitations and acceptances of invitations for all social and business events except weddings (see Weddings). When you cannot accept an invitation, see Refusals.

A balanced guest list of mixed elements is to a successful party what the seasoning is to a culinary triumph.

—LETITIA BALDRIGE

261

DO

- Name the occasion: awards banquet, anniversary celebration, dinner dance, open house, retirement party.

- Give the date and time: month, day, year, day of week, a.m. or p.m. (In formal invitations, the time is written out: "Seven o'clock in the evening"; "a.m." and "p.m." are never used.)

- Give the address. If necessary, add instructions on how to find it or even a map.

- Mention refreshments, if appropriate.

- State the charge, if any (for a fundraiser, for example).

- Enclose an engraved or printed reply card and envelope for a formal invitation ("R.S.V.P." is noted on the invitation). Slightly less formal invitations may have in the lower left corner of the invitation "R.S.V.P.," "R.s.v.p.," "Please respond," or "Regrets only," followed by an address or phone number. Informal invitations may also request a response and give a phone number.

- Give a date by which you need a response, if appropriate.

- Indicate the preferred dress (black tie, white tie, formal, informal, casual, costume) in the lower right corner, when appropriate.

- Let overnight guests know when you expect them to arrive and leave, what special clothes they may need (for tennis, swimming, hiking), whether they will be sharing a room with a child, sleeping on the floor, or need a sleeping bag, and whether there will be other guests. Ask whether they can tolerate animals, cigarette smoke, or other potential nuisances.

> The most charming visitor may linger one day too long. The best time to go is when everybody's asking you to stay.
>
> —Eliza C. Hall

- Additional information might include parking facilities, alternate arrangements in case of rain, and an offer of transportation.

- Express your anticipated pleasure in seeing the person. In a formal invitation, this is taken care of in the opening lines with "cordially invited" or a similar phrase.

- With formal invitations add in the bottom left corner "R.S.V.P" or "R.s.v.p." (*"Répondez s'il vous plaît,"* the French for "Respond if you please"). This tells your invitee that a reply is expected. You may also use the slightly less formal "Please reply" or, if you want to hear from people *only* if they cannot attend, "Regrets only." If it is unclear where people should send their response, or if a reply card is not enclosed, give an address or phone number directly beneath the "R.S.V.P." If the zip code is included in that address or on the envelope, it should not appear in the body of the invitation.

- Enclose in your invitation a response or reply card and a self-addressed, stamped envelope. This encourages a prompt answer and is essential when you need to know the number of expected guests. Made of the same paper, style, and format as your invitation, the response card is enclosed with a small envelope (at least 3-1/2 inches by 5 inches to meet postal requirements) that is stamped and printed or engraved with your address. The card is printed with a simple formula: "M _____ [guest's name to be filled in] __ regrets __ accepts [respondent checks one] for Saturday, November 20." In some cases the words "accepts" and "regrets" stand alone, and the guest is to cross out the word that does not apply or circle the one that does. Printers have samples and can advise you on the format that best fits your situation.

- Always respond, and respond promptly, to an invitation marked "R.S.V.P." or "Please reply." This is mandatory, obligatory, required, compulsory, imperative, and essential. If you do not plan to attend, the same is true for "Regrets only."

> Guests are the delight of leisure, and the solace of ennui.
>
> —Agnes Repplier

DON'T

- Don't use "request the honour of your presence" as this phrase is reserved for wedding invitations.
- Don't use abbreviations in formal invitations except for "Mr.," "Mrs.," "Ms.," "Dr.," "Jr.," and sometimes military ranks. Either supply the name for which an initial stands, or omit the initial altogether. In very formal invitations, write out "Second" and "Third" after a name, although you may use Roman numerals: Jason Prescott Allen III. There is no comma between the name and the numeral, although there is a comma between the name and "Jr." State names are spelled out (Alabama, not Ala. or AL) as is the time ("half past eight o'clock").

> Avoid giving invitations to bores—they will come without.
>
> —Eliza Leslie

HELPFUL HINTS

- Formal invitations are generally engraved or printed on fine-quality notepaper, use a line-by-line style, and are phrased in the third person ("Saunders Meiklewham requests the pleasure of your company at a dinner-dance in honor of his daughter . . ."). They may also be handwritten, using the same format and phrasing. The expression "requests the pleasure of your company" is appropriate for all invitations. Each invited person is mentioned by name and honorific ("Mrs.," "Ms.," "Mr.") either on the invitation envelope or on the invitation itself. All words, state names, and numbers less than 100 are spelled out; abbreviations are not used. Telephone numbers are never given in formal invitations. Formal business invitations (awards banquet, for example) are issued in standard formal invitation format.

- Informal invitations use either commercial fill-in cards or are handwritten on informal stationery or foldovers in usual letter style (first person, run-in format). Informal business invitations may be sent on letterhead stationery. In-house invitations may be issued via memo, even sometimes by e-mail. State the occasion (guest visitor or speaker, retirement party, service anniversary); time, date, place; whether refreshments will be provided and whether a collection is being taken up (both optional); an extension number to call for confirmation or information. For sales or business invitations, informal invitations are especially appealing as they let people know they can just drop in without getting dressed up for the occasion.

> It is bad manners to contradict a guest. You must never insult people in your own house—always go to theirs.
>
> —MYRTLE REED

- Invitations are issued by the host or hosts. It is no longer true that all but the most formal social invitations are issued and replied to over the wife's signature even when both husband and wife are hosts or guests. Longtime etiquette uses the "Mr. and Mrs. Rupert Johnson" format when issuing invitations. However, you are not bound to identify yourself by a form you don't normally use. "Jill Wickett and Rupert Johnson" is equally clear and polite, as is "Jill Johnson and Rupert Johnson" or "Jill and Rupert Johnson." The underlying principles are that your invitees recognize your name, that you are comfortable with the way you style yourself, and that there is an appropriately parallel construction for co-hosts. How to address a woman in an invitation (by married name, business name, or birth name) is fairly simple: the woman uses the name she prefers, and the prospective host or guest also uses it. If you are unsure of her preference, call her office or home and ask. In a business invitation, hosts may have their titles and company names after their names. Friends may issue invitations together. Even groups ("The Central High School senior class invites you . . .") may issue invitations.

- Mail invitations to an important event involving out-of-town guests as early as 6 months ahead. Other approximate guidelines for mailing invitations include: 4-6 weeks before a formal dinner, ball, dance, charity benefit, reception, or tea; 2-4 weeks before a reception or cocktail party; 3 weeks before a bar mitzvah or bat mitzvah; 2 weeks before a casual dinner or get-together.

> The fact is, the cocktail party has much in its favor. Going to one is a good way of indicating that you're still alive and about, if such is the case, and that you're glad other people are, without having to spend an entire evening proving it.
>
> —PEG BRACKEN

- When issuing invitations to a fundraising event, be clear about what is expected of those who accept ("$100 donation suggested" or "Tax-deductible contribution of $500 per couple suggested"). Your wording may be limited by the allowable meanings of "tax deductible" and "donation." Enclose a postage-paid reply envelope to make it easy for people to buy their tickets. If you do not include a reply envelope, indicate where to send the check and how to obtain tickets. Some fundraisers fail because potential donors are busy people who can't take the time to read the small print or guess how they should handle the request. Invitations to benefits, public charity balls, and other fundraisers do not require a response; your purchase of tickets with filled-in response card constitutes acceptance.

- When issuing an invitation to a single person or to someone whose personal life is unfamiliar to you, indicate whether the invitation (1) is intended for that person only; (2) includes a friend; (3) can be taken either way as long as you are notified ahead of time.

- When issuing an invitation to a family with young children, list each child by first name on the envelope underneath the parents' names; never add "and family." Adults living in the family home should not be included in their parents' invitation but should receive their own. Children approximately thirteen and up also receive their own invitations.

- When dress is indicated, the following formulas are used. White tie is the most formal dress: men wear a white tie, wing collar, and tailcoat while women wear formal gowns. Black tie or formal means, for men, a tuxedo with soft shirt and a bow tie (a dark suit is not acceptable) and, for women, dressy dresses, cocktail-length dresses, or long evening wear. Semiformal means sports jackets or suits for men and dresses or dressier tops and pants for women; it never includes jeans or T-shirts for either.

- Some sit-down dinner invitations specify the time you hope to see your guests arrive and the time you expect to dine. These are usually sent by people whose previous dinner parties have been spoiled by late arrivals.

- When inviting a guest speaker, the invitation includes: the name of the event and sponsoring organization; the date, time, and place; the type of audience (size, level of interest, previous exposure to subject); the kind of speech wanted; the length of time allotted and the approximate time the speech will begin; equipment available for use; accommodation and transportation information or directions to the meeting site; whether there will be a question and answer session; a description of the program; meals available; name of the contact person; details of the honorarium; an offer of further assistance; an expression of pleasure at having the person speak to your group. You might also request biographical information from the speaker to use in the program.

- Sales letters are sometimes phrased as formal or informal invitations to a special showing, sale, open house, or demonstration or to become a member, account holder, or subscriber. Others use the phrase "you are invited to . . ." in the first paragraph, and then go on to develop the sales message.

- It is absolutely inappropriate to suggest in an invitation the kind of gift one wants (by mentioning where one is registered or by specifying that money is the gift of choice, for example). However, people often want to specify, for one reason or another, that gifts not be given. Readers of Ann Landers' column provided two additions to an invitation that she found acceptable: "Your friendship is a cherished gift. We respectfully request no other," and "We request your help in compiling a book which recalls memories from our parents' first fifty years of marriage. On the enclosed sheet, we ask that you write one memory or event that you have shared with them and return it to us by April 26. We believe that the loving memories they have shared with you, their friends, would be the most treasured gift they could receive; therefore, we request that no other gift be sent."

- Invitations to a daughter's début are issued by the parents, whether married, widowed, divorced, or separated: "Mr. and Mrs. Renny Whiteoak request the pleasure of your company at a dinner dance in honor of their daughter Adeline. . . ." When simply receiving, the invitation can read: "Mrs. Alayne Archer Whiteoak and Miss Adeline Whiteoak will be at home Sunday the second of June from five until half past seven o'clock, Fifteen Roche Lane."

- To cancel or postpone an invitation, follow the original invitation closely in format, style, and quality of paper. If there is time, the announcement is printed or engraved as the invitation was. Otherwise, handwrite the note, using a formal or informal style depending on the original invitation: "Mr. and Mrs. Vernon Whitford regret that they are obliged to recall their invitation to dinner on . . ." or "We must unfortunately cancel the dinner party we had planned for . . ." Urgent situations, of course, require the telephone.

- To cancel an invitation that you have already accepted, call your host at once and then follow up with a note apologizing for the change of plans. Stress your regret and offer a believable excuse. When you cancel at the last minute or when your cancellation is an inconvenience, you may want to send flowers along with your note.

- Responding to an invitation is the easiest correspondence task there is (once you have made up your mind whether to accept it). Reply within several days of receiving it. State clearly that you will be able to attend and repeat the date, time, and, possibly, the place and kind of event. (To send regrets to an invitation, see Refusals.) Simply mirror the invitation, using the same format, and almost all the same words. If you have cards with your name or personalized stationery, you can simply write under your name "accepts with pleasure the kind invitation of . . ." and complete the information. It is mandatory to respond to an invitation marked R.S.V.P. (*"Répondez s'il vous plaît"* or "Please respond"). A modern epidemic of failures to respond is resulting in horror stories of empty places at wedding feasts, huge overpayments for no-show guests, or guests showing up with uninvited children or friends in tow; it is the number-one complaint of people who send invitations. If the invitation is marked "Regrets only" followed by a telephone number, you need respond only if you are unable to attend; the assumption is that otherwise you will be there. Invitations to political rallies, fundraising events, business cocktail parties, or other large gatherings generally don't include an "R.S.V.P." or a "Regrets only," and you are not obliged to respond. Certain other invitations (wedding, bar mitzvah, bat mitzvah) and announcements (engagement, graduation, birth, adoption) require a response, but if you do not attend the event or celebration you are not expected to send a gift.

- White House invitations include the phone number of the Social Office where you may telephone your acceptance and where you can ask questions about protocol, where to park your car, what to wear, and how to respond in writing to the invitation. General guidelines are: send your reply within a day of receiving the invitation; write the reply yourself (do not have an assistant do it); handwrite your reply on plain or engraved personal stationery; use the same format and person (first person or third person) to reply but insert "have the honor of accepting"; if the invitation was sent to you from the President's or First Lady's secretary (in the case of an informal invitation), reply to that person ("Would you please tell . . ."); if the invitation is addressed to the woman in a married couple (as is sometimes the case in traditional, formal invitations), she writes the acceptance but says, "My husband and I will be delighted to accept . . ."

> Giving a party is like having a baby—its conception is
> more fun than its completion, and once you've begun,
> it's impossible to stop.
>
> —JAN STRUTHER

GETTING STARTED

You are invited to an open house at the Desert D'Or Arms Condominiums to see the comfort, convenience, and beauty of truly affordable luxury housing.

As one of our Preferred Customers, you are invited to save 20% on your next family photo at Helstone Photography.

We cordially invite you to a private evening showing of our new collection of Baroudi Oriental Rugs

You are cordially invited to a pre-opening benefit of the Science Museum's exhibit on the gray wolf on Saturday, March 16, at 7 p.m.

You are invited to the 8th Annual Old-Fashioned Barbecue sponsored by the Union for Peace.

It is with great pleasure that I invite you to the 10th Annual Cosmetic Dentistry Conference to be held at The Debonair Hotel in Deer Park, New York, October 21-25.

This is your personal invitation to have your own biographical entry included in the 3rd edition of *Who's Who in American Inventors*, which is scheduled for publication September 1.

Marcella Boyce and Aldous Raeburn request the pleasure of your company for dinner and an evening at the theater on Saturday, the seventeenth of June, at half past seven o'clock.

I'm having a small luncheon here at noon on Saturday, July 24, and I would love it if you could come.

Will you lend us Abbie for a week this summer? Sarah would love to have another eight-year-old in the house!

Dear Aunt Priscilla and Uncle George, Will you join us this year for Thanksgiving dinner?

I've asked a few friends to stop by after work on Friday the 31st—can you join us?

Gerda and Peter Mannheim regret that a previous engagement prevents their acceptance of Alice and Harrison Quinn's kind invitation to dinner on Saturday, August 29.

It has lately been drawn to your correspondent's attention that, at social gatherings, she is not the human magnet she would be. Indeed, it turns out that as a source of entertainment, conviviality, and good fun, she ranks somewhere between a sprig of parsley and a single ice-skate.

—DOROTHY PARKER

MODEL LETTERS

The children of
Anna and Henry Mynors
request the pleasure of your company
at the Fiftieth Anniversary
of the marriage of their parents
on Saturday, the twenty-third of January
Nineteen hundred and ninety-nine
at eight o'clock
Bennett Plaza Hotel
Des Moines, Iowa

Mr. and Mrs. Seymour Glass
joyfully invite you
to worship with them
at the Bat Mitzvah of their daughter
Muriel
Saturday, the tenth of July
Nineteen hundred and ninety-nine
at ten o'clock in the morning
Mount Zion Temple
1300 Summit Avenue
Colorado Springs, Colorado

Owing to the illness of a family member
Blanche Hipper and Loftus Wilcher
are obliged to recall their invitation
for Saturday, the seventeenth of April
Nineteen hundred and ninety-nine

Mr. and Mrs. Percy Munn
request the pleasure of your company
for dinner
at eight o'clock
on Friday, the twentieth of August
Nineteen hundred and ninety-nine
Warren Inn
R.S.V.P.

Dr. and Mrs. Adam Stanton
accept with pleasure
the kind invitation of
Mr. and Mrs. Percy Munn
for dinner
at eight o'clock
on Friday, the twentieth of August
Nineteen hundred and ninety-nine

The Addison-Steele Companies
cordially invite you to an
open house
celebrating
their Fiftieth Anniversary
Friday, the tenth of November
from five to half past eight o'clock
Nineteen hundred and ninety-nine
Fourteen Sealand Boulevard
Bevil, Indiana

Please join us to celebrate
Colin, Frieda, Henry, Michael, Patricia, and Stephen's
graduation from kindergarten
(all six six-year-olds on our block)
at a bonfire and S'mores feast
7:30 p.m., Saturday, June 10
at the Lambert Park fire pits

Dear Preferred Customer:

Bowles Appliance Headquarters cordially invites you to a floor sample clearance sale on September 15, from 9 a.m. to 5:30 p.m. Admittance during those hours will be limited to customers presenting this invitation at the door.

Because of your tremendous response to last year's floor sample clearance sale, we would like to show our appreciation by adding additional discounts of 10% for purchases over $1,000, 15% for purchases from $1,001 to $2,000, and 20% for purchases over $2,001.

No special orders, catalog orders, or service contracts will be available at the sale prices. All sale items must be picked up or scheduled for delivery ($50 charge) within two weeks after the sale. Please bring blankets for pick-ups.

We're looking forward to seeing you on the 15th!

> **Each time the need gripped her to give a dinner party for twelve, or an informal party for fifty, she filled a bag and took a bus to Regent's Park where, on the edge of the bird-decorated waters, she went on until her supplies ran out and her need to feed others was done.**
>
> —Doris Lessing

You are cordially invited
to an open house celebration of
Hmong Language and Culture
sponsored by the Neighborhood Alliance
Coffinkey Community Center
1818 Scott Street
Friday, April 16, 7 - 9 p.m.

Refreshments
Exhibits
Entertainment
For more information, call 555-1234

Dear Jancis,

I hope you are planning to attend our 25th college reunion the weekend of June 10.

The reception on Friday night will be over by 7:30, with no other event planned for that evening. Since I live so close to the College, I thought it would be fun for as many of us as I can gather to spend the rest of the evening here. Can you come?

You don't need to let me know. Just show up. I can hardly wait to see you again!

> What is there more kindly than the feeling between host and guest?
>
> —AESCHYLUS

RELATED TOPICS

Acknowledgments

Anniversaries

Birthdays

Clubs

Refusals

Responses

Sales

Thank You

Weddings

29

Letters to the Editor

INTRODUCTION

For many people, letters to the editor constitute some of their favorite reading. Knowing this, almost every newspaper and periodical prints a limited number of letters in each issue. A daily newspaper might publish 30% to 40% of the letters it receives, whereas a national weekly newsmagazine might publish only 2% to 5% of its incoming letters.

Letters to the editor serve several purposes: to provide corrections to previously published material; to allow the writer to reach many people with information of possible interest; to provide readers with an opportunity to agree with, disagree with, or give an opinion about a story, article, cartoon, news item, editorial position, or previous letter.

> It were not best that we should all think alike; it is difference of opinion that makes horse-races.
>
> —MARK TWAIN

DO

- Check the area surrounding the letters-to-the-editor column for guidelines; most publications have a paragraph giving their requirements. If you are unsure about length limits or some other particular, call before writing.

- Address your letter "To the Editor," rather than to the person responsible for the article, cartoon, or letter you're writing about.

- Tell what you're writing about in the first sentence so that readers immediately know what the issue is ("Your May 8 editorial commending storm clean-up crews neglected to mention the contributions of three neighborhood groups").

- Make your own position clear: "I support . . . ," "I object to . . . ," "I question . . ."

- Be brief in explaining your position (300 words is a good length). Most publications have word limits for their letters to the editor; if you exceed them, editors may trim your letter in ways you don't particularly like.

- Offer supporting factual material (statistics, studies, articles, quotations) whenever possible. Letterwriters with specific knowledge or some professional connection with an issue should so identify themselves; this often makes publication more likely. Including inaccurate information or half-truths will, on the other hand, make publication unlikely; editors often check the facts in your letters.

- Be sure your topic is timely; editors rarely run letters about issues that are weeks or months old. To better your chances of getting published, write immediately after seeing the item you want to respond to.

- Limit yourself to one topic, to one main thought. If you don't stick to the point, your letter will probably be edited so that it does.

- Let readers know what action (if any) you would like them to take (form neighborhood block watches, call legislators, boycott a product, sign a petition, stop littering.

- Close with a startling, memorable, or powerful sentence, if possible—something that will make the reader want to go back and read your letter again.

- Include your name, address, and daytime phone number. Almost all publications insist on this. If you prefer not to have your name published, state that the letter is to appear only with "Name Withheld" or a comparable label. (You might want to call first to determine if this is possible.) When letters to the editor are signed by a number of people, usually only one or two of the names are published (followed by a note "and 16 others"); most publications prefer to use that space for opinions, not lists of names.

> It is all right to say exactly what you think if you have learned to think exactly.
>
> —MARCELENE COX

DON'T

- Don't submit poetry, lost-and-found announcements, or personal messages ("I'm trying to locate any descendants of Jenny Treibel").

- Don't expect newspapers or magazines to print letters that are thinly disguised advertisements for your business or your group. If you want local newspaper readers to know about some nonprofit, community-wide event, editors are generally willing.

- Don't begin by writing, "You won't dare print this letter." Editors generally remove such beginning sentences because, in fact, they dare to print a wide range of opinions, including letters that are highly critical of their own paper.

- Don't end your letter with "Think about it!" According to one editor, this line shows up often and is just as often deleted. Wanting people to think about the letterwriter's point is implied in the very fact of writing.

- Don't indulge in personal attacks. Dispute the issue, disagree with the opinion, dismiss the conclusions, but don't disparage the person. Name-calling is not an argument; it indicates a lack of logical and persuasive reasons as well as an impoverished vocabulary. Pejorative adjectives ("stupid," "ridiculous," "redneck," "bleeding heart liberal") and indefensible generalizations ("what can you expect from a lawyer," "labor unions have always looked out for themselves first," "another anti-male feminist") mark the writer's discussion as weak and ineffectual. Margaret Thatcher once said, "I always cheer up immensely if an attack is particularly wounding because I think, well, if they attack one personally, it means they have not a single political argument left."

- Don't use threatening or bullying language. It is not only ineffective and offensive, but it indicates a weak position.

- Don't write anything that can be proved to be malicious (even if it's true) and don't write anything that can't be proved (even if there is no intent to harm); publishers will not print anything libelous.

> Where all think alike, no one thinks very much.
>
> —WALTER LIPPMAN

HELPFUL HINTS

- Editors prefer typewritten letters. If you handwrite a letter, it must be legible.

- Editors seem to prefer letters that are of probable interest to other readers, opinionated letters dealing with a controversy, letters that reflect a unique point of view on a broad topic, and letters that are clear, entertaining, and thought-provoking.

- If you are deeply concerned about an issue and plan to write a letter to the editor, it is often helpful to get others to write too. It shouldn't look like an orchestrated letterwriting campaign, but a dozen or so letters to the editor submitted over a period of a week or two may persuade the editor that the topic is of serious interest. The resulting column with a number of letters on the topic will be more influential than your letter alone.

- If you write the letter in a spirit of anger, you may want to rethink it the next day before mailing it. Even relatively mild letters take on a different personality when printed in cold ink among other letters in a newspaper or periodical read by your family, neighbors, and co-workers. You may want someone else to read your letter to be sure it has the effect you want it to have.

- Write letters to the editor commending civic groups or individuals who have contributed to the common good in ways that may not be known to everyone. Letters like these not only add welcome relief to the usual fare of a letters-to-the-editor column, but they build positive community feelings and often engender more of the same productive activities. Note, however, that laudatory "nice" letters don't often get published; this kind of letter needs an extra dash of humor, wit, or color.

- Publications have varying policies about repeat letterwriters; some limit letters by the same individual to one letter per three or four months; others have no restrictions.

- Letters-to-the-editor columns become especially popular just before elections. Before writing, be sure you know the publication's policies: some print letters that support one candidate or criticize another; others ban election-related letters during a period immediately preceding an election or on Election Day in order to avoid being used to launch last-minute offensives. Blatant politicking usually never makes it to the printed page; editors have learned to spot letters that are thinly disguised publicity efforts or those that are part of an effort to create a bandwagon effect.

> 'Tis with our judgments as our watches, none
> Go just alike, yet each believes his own.
>
> —ALEXANDER POPE

GETTING STARTED

I am writing to express my disagreement with Judge Gamaliel Bland Honeywell's editorial (Jan. 25).

There was an error in your otherwise excellent June 5 article about the reopening of the Blue Delft Candy Shop.

Most of the recent letters discussing the proposed hockey arena seem to be missing the point.

Two important pieces of information were omitted in your April 9 article on Seneca Doane's mayoral candidacy.

A November 8 *Advocate-Times* article on selling cigarettes to underage buyers presented only one side of the story.

Has anyone else noticed that city street-cleaning efforts seem to have dwindled to nothing?

Society editor Elnora Pearl Bates seems unaware of many of the social changes that have taken place since she began her job thirty years ago.

Congratulations on your impressive November issue featuring the history and contemporary uses of Tarot cards.

I strongly object to your printing letters with swear words in them—is this necessary?

I must take issue with a February 7 letterwriter who claims that her property taxes have risen twenty-fold in the last five years.

How can anyone believe, as apparently Dorinda Oakley does (Dec. 28 editorial), that nursing is a dying profession?

Jason Greylock's column on day-care centers was not only one-sided and insulting to all reputable day-care providers, but erroneous in several respects.

I read with interest the September 15 article relating the delayed closing of city swimming pools to increased rates of school absenteeism.

Your October 26 front-page article on welfare "reform" was a blatant case of editorializing masquerading as news.

Many thanks for your unpopular but eminently sane editorial stand on gun control (July 2).

If you want a recipe for disaster, look no further than Charlie Bentham's letter (Oct. 12) on shortening the school day.

> I disapprove of what you say, but I will defend to the death your right to say it.
>
> —VOLTAIRE

MODEL LETTERS

To the Editor:

So the tax collectors and money changers in rural Wayne County are persecuting Amish woodworker Sam Swartzendruber because he will not get a permit for his outdoor privy. They have fined him and charged him with over 100 offenses, one for each day he uses the privy without a permit. Now he will probably go to jail for his refusal to bend his beliefs to those of the bureaucrats who cannot come up with a reasonable way to regulate outdoor privies.

On my farm in a residential zone in Story County, I could build an unlined earthen sewage cesspool with more than 2 million gallons of liquid manure, taking in waste from up to 4,166 factory hogs, with no state or county permits. I could pollute the air for miles around, contaminate groundwater, and pile up my dead hogs daily out by the road with no permits. Not only would I not go to jail, but our governor, legislature, and the Iowa Supreme Court would all congratulate me and tell me I was helping to build a better Iowa.

Be a good neighbor, go to jail. But build a hog factory, and you're a hero. Iowans ought to give Sam a medal for reminding us all what it means to stand up for our beliefs. We're jailing the wrong people. Let's pen up the mega-hog factory profiteers and turn Sam loose.

Mark E. Maggio
Box 161, Roland

To the Editor:

Would *Newsweek* subtitle a headline "Did a mysterious Jewish family seduce, fleece, and poison lonely elderly prey?" Is it fair journalistic practice to describe a group as being "a tightknit clan of African Americans with a long history of fraud"?

"A Deadly Kind of Charm" (*Newsweek*, December 1, 1997) did just this with Gypsies (a people whose self-preferred ethnonym is Roma). In no way was ethnicity relevant to this story. By highlighting it, an entire group ("5 million") was besmirched based on the possible criminal activities of a relatively small number.

Chris Dodge

To the Editor:

How many pedestrian deaths does it take to get a stoplight and crosswalk at the corner of Policarpo Blvd. and Galdós St.? One? Three? Ten? The correct answer should be one (better yet: none), but so far we have had three tragic deaths at that corner. Neighbors have logged at least 75 calls to the Department of Public Works. What does it take?

Angel Guerra

To the Editor:

Letterwriters have been arguing the merits of an open-air stadium on the site of the former Febronius Mfg. plant versus a covered stadium to replace the current one.

I would like to rephrase the argument: Does this community need a new stadium at all? Do we need a new stadium more urgently than we need shelter for the homeless, afterschool care and intercity sports activities for children, an improved Metro Mobility fleet, some form of mass transit, or any one of dozens of other critical needs of the community?

The discussion about the kind of new stadium needs to be deferred until we are certain we need one in the first place.

Ruth Hofmann

We scarcely credit any persons with good sense except those who are of our opinion.

—LA ROCHEFOUCAULD

To the Editor:

I have noticed an increase in editorials complaining about noise from airplanes. I have a few solutions for those who are unhappy.

First: You can move.

Second: When life gives you lemons, make lemonade. Enjoy those massive steel birds and the technological wonders that they are. Can you imagine what the Wright brothers would think if they saw "their" plane today? Whenever a plane soars overhead, I pause in my conversation and feel the velocity of the winged marvel as it powers over my apartment building.

Third: Consider life without planes. As we found out earlier this month during the pilots' strike, it isn't much fun. We experienced a lot of inconveniences. It makes you appreciate what you have, doesn't it?

Kristina Hoefer

To the Editor:

Three friends and I have been contacted in the last couple of days by a supposed representative of a major credit card. He says he is investigating a series of suspicious-looking charges made to our cards in the Bahamas. Each of us had the same reaction: we balked at giving him our credit card numbers when he requested them, so I'm not sure where he was going with his scam, but the credit card company confirmed that it was not a legitimate request.

If you receive a call like this, don't give out any information, and if you have Caller ID (none of us have it), contact the police with the telephone number if it shows up.

Edgar Lorm

To the Editor:

Your article on area bike paths (May 13) neglected to mention the one beginning at Keeldar St. that parallels the River Road Dr. as far east as Scott Ave., a beautiful, nonstop ride of three miles.

John Bretton

To the Editor:

The article on telephone etiquette (Nov. 3) neglected to mention one of the most common and troublesome issues: telemarketers. What is an effective and polite (or perhaps just effective) response to people you don't know asking how you are (after first mispronouncing your name) and trying to sell you something wildly inappropriate (just think what the proprietor of our apartment building would do if I listed the building with the real estate agent on the phone) at extremely inconvenient times? How do other people handle this?

Laura Fairlie

> Ink-fresh papers, millions of them—ink-fresh with morning, orange juice, waffles, eggs and bacon, and cups of strong, hot coffee. How fine it is, here in America, in ink-fresh, coffee-fragrant morning, to read the paper!
>
> —THOMAS WOLFE

To the Editor:

To those of you who have been expressing yourself in these pages about the presence of wild geese in city parks: Hello! A park is supposed to be natural. It is not meant to be as clean as your kitchen floor. It has messy leaves and gravel and bugs and, yes, goose grease. If you can't handle nature in the raw, there's always your backyard.

Estrella Tavera

To the Editor:

I recently moved back to the city after ten years in another state, and I noticed three dramatic changes from the way things used to be: there is much less litter on public streets and boulevards; residents have taken up flower gardening with a passion, resulting in splashes of color and beauty everywhere; there are sidewalk cafés within walking distance of nearly every neighborhood.

I thought I'd point this out in case those of you who live here haven't noticed the gradual changes. You have a very livable city here! Enjoy!

Colenso Ridgeon

To the Editor:

I wonder if the letterwriter (June 3) objecting to Adalbert Stifter's candidacy for mayor is capable of rephrasing his argument without using the words "stupid," "dumb," and "crazy." When all the name-calling is subtracted from his "argument," not much is left.

Weren't you going to have a policy to limit name-calling and labeling from your letters-to-the-editor column?

Heinrich Drendorf

All I know is what I see in the papers.

—WILL ROGERS

RELATED TOPICS

Appreciation

Complaints

Public Officials

Sensitive

30

Love Letters

INTRODUCTION

In some ways, the love letter is an easy letter to write because we *want* to write it. In other ways, it is the most difficult and frustrating of all letters because we're trying to translate strong and possibly turbulent emotions to a flat surface with the feeble help of words that never seem to do what we want them to do.

The great love letters of history are marked not only by the evidence of a powerful love but also by a certain skill with language. Many of us have all the necessary love to write an outstanding love letter, but we fear we lack facility with the written language of love. Fear no more: if you love and if you can translate your feelings into words simply and sincerely, you can write a love letter that the other person will cherish.

> There's no finer caress than a love letter, because it makes the world very small, and the writer and reader, the only rulers.
>
> —Cecilia Capuzzi

283

DO

- Write from the heart. The most important quality of a love letter is its sincerity.

- Keep the other person in mind as you write. Try to imagine what they are thinking, feeling, and doing at this moment and to picture them later as they read your letter.

- Before writing the letter, jot down some ideas that will lead to sentences or paragraphs in your letter: What is special or unexpected about being in love? What are some appealing things the other person does? What is it about the other person that touches you deeply? What do you miss about them? What would you do if they walked into the room right now? When do you think about them most often? What things remind you of them? What would you like to give them if you could give them anything? Why do you admire them? Why do you love the person? Be specific. Give examples of times you were filled with love.

- Come right out and say "I love you" somewhere in the letter. No one can hear it often enough, and lovers—especially new lovers—have fears and doubts that need frequent reassurance.

- Tell what you have been doing, thinking, feeling. The other person is hungry for news of you; this is not the time to be modest or retiring or brief. Self-revelation is always appealing and will usually elicit something similar from the other person. "I have never told you this before, but . . ."; "When I was little, I always dreamed that . . ."; "One thing I'm really looking forward to (besides seeing you again!) is . . ."; "My favorite way of spending a Sunday afternoon is . . ."

- Write about happy times you've had together in the past and about plans for the future that include you both. The present letter is a good bridge for your love from past to future. It's also (to be practical) a reality check when the other person doesn't remember things the way you do or had no idea you were thinking of doing *that* next year.

- Fatten the letter with newspaper clippings or cartoons, a dried leaf or flower, a bookmark, photographs, etc.

> Our first love-letter . . . the dread of saying too much is so nicely balanced by the fear of saying too little. Hope borders on presumption, and fear on reproach.
>
> —L.E. LANDON

DON'T

- Don't use language that isn't natural to you. While you may want to "dress up" your language, the letter will sound false if you get too flowery or high-flown or use too many clichés.

- Don't write the kind of letter about which you must say at the end, "Tear this up as soon as you've read it." Recipients seldom do this. If it's a simple matter of your embarrassment, it may not make much difference, but if the letter could fall into the wrong hands (as in the case of a romance that involves infidelity), you may someday regret having put anything on paper.

> Brevity may be the soul of wit, but not when someone's saying, "I love you."
>
> —JUDITH VIORST

HELPFUL HINTS

- If you expect to write more than a few love letters, you might want to buy a book of quotations on love. They can inspire you while also supplying quotations that perfectly express your feelings. Some are good for discussion: "Do you agree with Antoine de Saint-Exupéry that 'love does not consist in gazing at each other but in looking outward together in the same direction'?" Bess Streeter Aldrich once wrote, "Love is the light that you see by." Aldrich would probably not mind if you wrote, "You are the light that I see by," and then go on to tell why that is.

- For inspiration, study the letters of some of the world's great lovers and find some that reflect your own feelings.

  ♥ For passion and fire, read Juliette Drouet writing to Victor Hugo (in *The Love Letters of Juliette Drouet to Victor Hugo*, Louis Gimbaud, ed., 1914):

  "A fire that no longer blazes is quickly smothered in ashes. Only a love that scorches and dazzles is worthy of the name. Mine is like that."

  "I see only you, think only of you, speak only to you, touch only you, breathe you, desire you, dream of you; in a word, I love you!"

  "I love you *because* I love you, because it would be impossible for me not to love you. I love you without question, without calculation, without reason good or bad, faithfully, with all my heart and soul, and every faculty."

"When I am dead, I am certain that the imprint of my love will be found on my heart. It is impossible to worship as I do without leaving some visible trace behind when life is over."

♥ For a deeply sincere but lighter touch see Ogden Nash's letters to Frances Rider Leonard (in *Loving Letters from Ogden Nash: A Family Album*, Linell Nash Smith, ed., 1990):

"I couldn't go to bed without telling you how particularly marvelous you were today. You don't seem to have any idea of your own loveliness and sweetness; that can't go on, and I shall see that it doesn't."

"Both your letters arrived this morning. Thank you. I had sunk pretty low in the eyes of the elevator man, to whom I have been handing a letter to mail nearly every night and who has evidently noticed that I have been getting nothing in return. I could sense his thinking, 'You have no charm, sir.' But now it's all right again—his attitude today is as respectful and reverent as I could wish."

"I've been living all day on your letter. . . . Have I ever told you that I love you? Because I do. I even loved you yesterday when I didn't get any letter and thought you hated me for trying to rush things. It ought to worry me to think that no matter what you ever do to me that is dreadful I will still have to keep on loving you; but it doesn't, and I will."

"I've been reading your letter over all day, it's so dear. . . . Haven't you a photograph or even a snapshot of yourself? I want to look at and touch, as I read and touch your letters; it helps bring you a little closer."

"Do you know what is the most delightful sound in the world? I'm sorry that you'll never be able to hear it. It's when I'm sitting in your library, and hear you cross the floor of your room and open the door; then your footsteps in the hall and on the stairs. In four days now—."

♥ For insight on a long-lasting, ever-green love, read Winston and Clementine Churchill's letters to each other (in *Clementine Churchill: The Biography of a Marriage*, Mary Soames, 1979):

Winston to Clemmie: "I love you so much and thought so much about you last night and all your courage and sweetness." "You cannot write to me too often or too long—my dearest and sweetest. The beauty and strength of your character and the sagacity of your judgment are more realized by me every day." "The most precious thing I have in life is your love for me." "Do cable every few days, just to let me know all is well and that you are happy when you think of me." "This is just a line to tell you how I love you and how sorry I am you are not here." "Darling, you can write anything but war secrets and it reaches me in a few hours. So send me a letter from your dear hand." "Tender love my darling, I miss you very much. I am lonely amid this throng. Your ever-loving husband W." "My darling one, I think always of you. . . . With all my love and constant kisses, I remain ever your devoted husband W." "Another week of toil is over and I am off to Chartwell in an hour. How I wish I was going to find you there! I feel a sense of loneliness and miss you often and would like to feel you near. I love you very much, my dear sweet Clemmie."

Clementine to Winston: "I miss you terribly—I ache to see you." "I feel there is no room for anyone but you in my heart—you fill every corner." "My beloved Winston, This is a long separation. Think of your Pussy now and then with indulgence and love. Your own, Clemmie." "My darling. My thoughts are with you nearly all the time and though basking in lovely sunshine and blue seas I miss you and home terribly. Tender love, Clemmie." "I'm thinking so much of you and how you have enriched my life. I have loved you very much but I wish I had been a more amusing wife to you. How nice it would be if we were both young again."

> Be my good angel to the extent of throwing me a scrap
> of your beloved writing.
>
> —George Bernard Shaw

GETTING STARTED

Myrtle Reed once wrote, "It is always winter when I am away from you," and I'm finding this is true for me.

There is no moment in the day when I am not thinking of you.

This morning I saw a car just like yours driving towards me down the street and for a moment I got so excited.

You make me so happy!

I've been carrying your last letter around with me everywhere and it's getting quite limp—will you write me another one?

I keep thinking about the afternoon we met.

It is lonely without you!

I wonder if it's the same for you—that leap of the heart when I see a letter from you waiting for me.

You're my first thought in the morning and my last at night.

I wish you were here.

How were we ever so lucky to find each other?

I just had to tell you how much I enjoyed being with you yesterday.

There is nothing I want more to do and feel less able to do than write you a beautiful love letter.

Your letters are the high point of my day.

Eleven days, four hours, and thirty minutes until I see you again!

> Love demands expression. It will not stay still, stay silent, be good, be modest, be seen and not heard, no. It will break out in tongues of praise, the high note that smashes the glass and spills the liquid.
>
> —JEANETTE WINTERSON

MODEL LETTERS

My dearest Shirley,

You know I have many loves in my life. While we've been planning our wedding and making arrangements for our married life afterwards, I've gotten the sense that you worry about being in competition with my other "loves."

You know I love being a physician. I love my team of huskies and dog sledding. I love winter camping in sub-zero temperatures. I love my parents and siblings. I love playing the drums with the Right Brainer Rockers every Tuesday night. I love the cabin. I love the lake. You know and I know that my life is enriched with many loves.

What you do not know yet, precious Shirley, and what I'm feeling so strongly after our two years of courtship, is that I love you more than all the rest of my loves put together. The sum total of the enjoyment I reap from my job and hobbies and family is nothing compared to what you have become in my life. You are my anchor, my angel, my armor.

Believe that I love you more than anything else on this earth.

Graham

My dear Martin,

I miss you so much! I haven't had a single fit of hearty laughter since you left three days ago on your business trip.

Martin, I don't think I ever told you this, but in my book of romance the sexiest trait a man can possibly possess is a funny streak. You know I am a huge fan of those guys on the big screen like Bill Murray and Jim Carrey who make America laugh. But their screen personas are make-believe, merely scripts come alive on film. No one, no one, in real life has ever made me laugh out loud so often the way you do and that has earned you, dear funny guy, the key to my heart.

Remember last Sunday at church? When the fellow next to you asked to borrow a pen so he could write a check for the collection plate, you handed him yours and whispered, "Do you have a spare check I could borrow? I left my checkbook at home and I don't even have a buck for the offering plate." I'm still laughing.

I can't wait 'til you get back from your trip so my funny bone can have a good workout again. And my heart can be happy again.

> Love, love, love,
>
> Molly

Darling Amy,

I never stop thinking about you. And yet when I try to write, I'm wordless. I've been sitting here, pen in hand, for half an hour trying to express what you mean to me. Will you accept some borrowed words? Jeremy Taylor once said, "Love is friendship set on fire." I feel them both, the fire and the friendship. Bless you for bringing them into my life.

> Love,
>
> Edwin

What cannot letters inspire? They have souls; they can speak; they have in them all that force which expresses the transports of the heart; they have all the fire of our passions, they can raise them as much as if the persons themselves were present; they have all the tenderness and the delicacy of speech, and sometimes a boldness of expression even beyond it.

—HÉLOÏSE

Dear Vic,

It's the eve of our first anniversary and I'm so glad we could take this weekend off to go camping—which we haven't done since our honeymoon in the Rockies! You're sleeping soundly in the tent but I can't drift off, not because of the mosquitoes or the waves lapping on the rocks below our campsite but because my heart is so full of gratitude for you that I have to spill some of these feelings onto paper or I'll burst.

I'm writing this by the light of the campfire and I've just added another log so I can see my pen and paper.

Vic, you built this campfire with the logs that you split with the axe you swung with the powerful arm which so often gently hugs, comforts, and caresses me. You are so strong and capable and loving and lovable and intelligent and innovative and creative and funny and fun and sensitive and caring and kind. You are also so devastatingly handsome in your cargo shorts that every time I looked at you today as we fished and hiked and set up camp I felt like dragging you under the nearest pine tree and making love to you.

Oh Vic, my love for you after a year of marriage is still a love on fire. I love you more today than I did 365 days ago! Let's find a secluded pine tree tomorrow.

Amanda

Dear Carol,

Today I found one more reason to be grateful for you.

You don't want to hear the whole sorry tale but my day involved things like oversleeping and then running into Mr. Valborg while trying to sneak into the office; losing irreplaceable data to the computer gremlins; dripping spaghetti sauce on my white shirt (while having lunch with, of course, Mr. Valborg); having to deal with two incredibly irate clients; and finding, when I finally left the office, that my car battery was dead.

Thinking about you was the only pleasant thing in my life today! Thank you for being so wonderful that all by yourself you make up for everything that goes wrong.

Love,

Will

For, you see, each day I love you more,
Today more than yesterday and less than tomorrow.

—Rosemonde Gérard

Dear Juliette,

Scientists seem unable to measure love. I—you will not be surprised to discover this, knowing how talented I am!—have found a way to do it.

When you go to your seminar in Virginia next week, I am going to keep Moxie for you. Now this is despite the fact that I am not, and have never been, a dog person. If I were a dog person, my tastes would never run to Mexican hairless dogs with bat-like ears, rat-like tails, wrinkled snouts, and, in this case, a cast on its leg.

Not only will I keep Moxie (we haven't taken the full measure of this love yet!), but I will let her sleep in my bed, I will be faithful to her finicky feeding schedule, and I will even—once or twice a day—kiss her on the lips. Or near the lips anyway. I will pet her, I will fondle her, I will let her watch football with me and follow me around. I will take her for her daily walks, even though everyone who sees us looks at her cast, then looks at me and thinks, "Ah, a man who abuses dogs!"

And all this because I love you. So, what do you think? Have I found a way to measure love?

Gabriel

Love turns all the wheels of human industry, is the motive power under the world's machinery, makes worthwhile every enterprise on the earth, is coequal with life, outlasts death, and reaches onward into heaven.

—Margaret E. Sangster

RELATED TOPICS

Appreciation

Family and Friends

31

Memos

INTRODUCTION

The memo (short for memorandum—plural is memos, memoranda, or memorandums) grew out of a need to streamline correspondence—to communicate swiftly, directly, and concisely—among employees of the same company. There was little point in using letterhead stationery, "Dear," "Sincerely," and complimentary openings and closings with co-workers, managers, and executives you saw every day and communicated with constantly, and who were well aware of what company you worked for.

Although the business letter is still the preferred format for out-of-house correspondence, the memo has made its way outside the company: for orders, for brief communications with regular customers or suppliers, for transmitting material, and for such routine messages as acknowledgments, confirmations, and inquiries. It is estimated that in many companies up to one in four business hours are spent reading and writing memos.

One of the important advantages to sending a dated memo rather than picking up the phone (or even sending an e-mail) is that with a memo you have written hard-copy confirmation in case of later questions. In addition to its format, the other characteristic specific to memos is that the same memo can be sent to one person—or to hundreds.

> Talk of nothing but business, and dispatch that
> business quickly.
>
> —ALDUS MANUTIUS

DO

- Follow the memo heading format, which always has four items. The most common arrangement stacks all four lines flush left:

TO: Bogan Maddox
FROM: Sadie Burke
DATE: June 14, 1999
SUBJECT: new software

Or, capitalize only the initial letter, thus:

To: Bogan Maddox
From: Sadie Burke
Date: June 14, 1999
Subject: new software

You may also arrange them so that inserted information is lined up:

        TO: Bogan Maddox
      FROM: Sadie Burke
      DATE: June 14, 1999
        RE: new software

Or, arrange them in two columns:

TO: Bogan Maddox   DATE: June 14, 1999
FROM: Sadie Burke   RE: new software

- Carefully select a word or phrase for the subject line that will immediately tell the reader the main point of your memo: "annual picnic"; "year-end salary reviews"; "medical benefits enrollment"; "mailing list update"; "new corporate library hours."

- Begin the body of your message two to four lines below the subject line and flush left. All paragraphs in the body begin flush left and are separated by one line of space (text is otherwise single-spaced).

- State the purpose of your memo in the first sentence.

- Be concise. The whole purpose of the no-frills memo is its directness, brevity, and precision. Make your information immediately and easily accessible to the reader by using short, simple sentences; by itemizing, numbering, or outlining your data; by arranging units of thought in bulleted lists; by using the present tense and active verbs; by underlining key words. Although memos can technically be any length, the one- or two-page memo is the norm, with the exception of report or issue memos (see "Helpful Hints"). The shorter the memo, the more likely it is to be read immediately.

- Close with a request for the action you want, if appropriate: "Please call me"; "Please inform others in your department"; "Send me a copy of your report."

- Sign your name at the bottom of the memo or else put your signature or initials next to your name in the heading.

- Reference initials and enclosure notation (if any) are typed under the memo flush left.

- If sending your memo to more than one person, you may (1) list each name, if you have only a few, after the word "To:"; (2) list the principal recipient after "To:" and the others at the bottom of the memo after "cc:"; (3) list all the names alphabetically in a distribution list on the last page of your memo. After "To:" type "See distribution list on page 3." Names appear without courtesy titles (Ms., Mr.) but sometimes with professional titles (Dr.).

> Anything you can do to creatively jazz up the memos and communications you send will result in more people actually reading them.
>
> —BARBARA A. GLANZ

DON'T

- Don't include salutations or complimentary closings or any of the wind-up or wind-down sentences you would include in a standard business letter. Although you are courteous, you get straight to the point.

- Don't use the memo for official communications (promotions and resignations, for example); those should be typed on letterhead stationery.

> "The horror of that moment," the King went on, "I shall never, never forget!" "You will, though," the Queen said, "if you don't make a memorandum of it."
>
> —LEWIS CARROLL

HELPFUL HINTS

- Memos are not sent on company letterhead. Some organizations have memo stationery with the company name or simply "Memo" at the top or forms preprinted with the four standard headings. With the advent of computers and e-mail, however, memo stationery is seen less often.

- Informality is the hallmark of memos. They are shorter and less complicated than letters. They use plainer, more everyday language; jargon and acronyms familiar to those in the company may be used. "We" is used instead of "Beaumont-Green Foods, Inc."

- An issue memo is a fact-oriented report that summarizes important information so that policy decisions can be made. An efficient organization of material might include some or all of the following: (1) stating what the issue is, putting it in context, providing history or background information; (2) listing available or suggested options or solutions, along with their pros and cons; (3) detailing the costs, fiscal impact, and effects on other programs of the various options; (4) if appropriate and welcome, naming steps necessary to implement the various options; (5) offering your recommendations; (6) suggesting the next step in the process (further study, meeting, vote, management decision).

- In-house events rarely require formal invitations. If the event is held during business hours, the assumption is that it is business-oriented. A memo-format invitation includes: type of occasion (guest speaker, seminar, retirement, going away, or service anniversary celebration); time, date, place; whether refreshments will be provided; if a collection is being taken up; an extension number to call for confirmation or information.

> You simply cannot communicate enough. Experts say that you have to tell the average adult something six times before it is internalized. The challenge becomes communicating a message in such a creative way that it only has to be told once!
>
> —Barbara A. Glanz

GETTING STARTED

Tax forms are available in the lobby from now until April 15, thanks to Courtenay Brundit, who obtained them for us.

Staff lounge cleanup assignments for November are listed below.

Thanks for the new programmable multifunction mouse that you sent over. So far I'm having a good time with it!

Just a reminder about the conference call with Eusabio International Friday at 3 p.m.

I'd like to request that we get more serious about recycling—if you need another brochure on what to recycle, and how, give me a call.

Please mark your calendars: William Denny, industrial engineer at our new high tech data entry facility in Porter, will be explaining the latest technology in Building 201B, Room 43, on Thursday, January 21, at 3 p.m.

There has been some confusion about the new procedures for travel reimbursements—please note the following guidelines.

Does anyone have a current address for Wilfred Chew Law Offices?

Note the new sick leave policy, as outlined below.

We've just been notified that Highway 36 will be closed from July 9-15; you may want to plan alternate routes to work.

You asked if the company store currently has sandpaper seconds: yes, we do.

Effective immediately, there will be no parking in Lot C because of resurfacing.

I am pleased to report that new surge protectors are now available for anyone who needs one.

> It is nothing short of genius that uses one word when twenty will say the same thing.
>
> —DAVID GRAYSON

MODEL LETTERS

TO: All departments
FROM: Human Resources
DATE: March 10
SUBJECT: Design department/reduced schedule

Lily Briscoe will be working a reduced schedule in the design department for three weeks. She will be here on Mondays and Tuesdays only as she is preparing for her gallery exhibit of sculptures made solely from scrap metal. (See the current newsletter for dates and the location of her show.) We all certainly wish her weld . . . I mean well. This schedule is effective as of March 15 and I'll keep you posted on any changes. We will welcome Ms. Briscoe back full-time in April and hope she won't have gotten rusty in the interim. Thanks, everyone.

TO: All employees
FROM: Raymond Berenger, Building Services
DATE: November 15
SUBJECT: Building maintenance

Please be reminded that the building custodian was terminated a week ago, on the day of the merger announcement. I ask that all employees cooperate by keeping your areas clean and picking up after yourselves. Thanks.

To: Delina Delaney Deli counter clerks
From: M. De Maine, Manager
Date: June 15
Re: Soliciting from the homeless/vendor safety

The presence of homeless people in this area of Manhattan is a fact. Occasionally, as you know, a homeless individual will venture into our shop and ask for handouts of food. Sometimes he or she will simply take a loaf of bread or a muffin without asking.

Now that summer is here we see more of this activity and all staff must adhere to our policy: Never say "no" to a homeless person's request for food. Some of these visitors are mentally unstable, some may carry weapons. Give them the food they want and politely escort them to the door. The cost of the food involved is not worth the risk to your safety.

There is always the possibility that we will thus get a reputation on the avenue for having "free" food. If numbers or interference with regular business escalates, we will reevaluate our policy. Until then, please follow our current recommendation.

TO: All employees
FROM: Staffing
DATE: February 5
SUBJECT: Half-time employees

Following is the full list of half-time employees (continuing with, however, full benefits) during the merger transition with Half Moon Press for a period of half a year effective February 8. HALF a good day!

> Anne Frith, editorial
> Eden Herring, editorial
> Maria Lousada, production
> Luke Marks, production
> Hope Ollerton, order fulfillment

TO: Olive Chancellor
FROM: Varena Tarrant
DATE: June 16, 1999
SUBJECT: Patent authorization for:
    "Three-Dimensional Blueprint Acrylic Viewer"

This memo will serve to authorize the preparation and filing of a patent application in the United States Patent and Trademark Office.

The invention provides a method for viewing blueprints that allows ready discrimination of varied elevations.

The inventors and I will provide additional information and any experimentation necessary to file the application. We suggest that this application be filed by outside attorney Basil Ransome (Ransome & Birdseye) who is familiar with the inventors and technology.

Varena Tarrant
Senior Patent Liaison Specialist

To: All employees
From: Jack Boltro
Date: November 30
Re: Updating telephone numbers

As of January 1, all customer 612 area code numbers given on the attached sheet will be changed to 651. Please correct your files.

Note that 612 area codes NOT on this list remain 612.

Also attached is a listing of the three-number prefixes that take 612 and those that take 651 so that you can verify the correct area code for any new numbers.

To: Auto Leasing Dept. employees
From: Charles Tansley
Date: August 3
Re: Death of Gus Carmichael's wife

Those of you who work with Gus Carmichael will want to know that his wife of 23 years died suddenly last night. No other details are known at present. Funeral services will be held on Saturday; for time and place, please check the newspaper. Those of you wanting to send a note or sympathy card can write to him at his home address:

Gus Carmichael
1927 Lighthouse Road
Central City, VA 23452

To: See distribution list below
From: Norman Rivers
Date: Nov. 10
Re: Gas and arc welding lab proposal

A meeting was held on Nov. 2 with Harvey Anderson and Cherry Elwood of Arnott-Bracy Enterprises to discuss Arnott-Bracy's preliminary proposal for the new gas and arc welding lab. Several changes were made and Mr. Anderson sent the first revision of the proposal to me on Nov. 8. I am forwarding copies of this proposal to all team members. We will review it on Nov. 18 at 2:30 in Room 201. I would particularly like Blanche May, Alan Ernescliffe, George Larkins, Tom Ward, and Mary Cheviot to be available for this meeting. If you have a conflict, please let me know. Arnott-Bracy Enterprises is expecting a response from us by Nov. 23. They will then provide a final proposal on Nov. 30.

TO: Millie Crocker-Harris
FROM: Terence Rattigan
DATE: June 19
SUBJECT: Small-diameter sleeve tools

Can you give me some idea what would be necessary to develop the tooling and fixturing needed to form and laser-weld small-diameter sleeve tools for use on the Bowen project and others?

Good things, when short, are twice as good.

—Baltasar Gracián

To: Department of Data Management
From: Dennis Bulgruddery
Date: July 1
Subject: Project Plans

The attached outlines cover projected work through the end of the year. The outlines have been generated in consultation with each of the key people involved. We will review progress on the first of each month and adjust the work and timelines accordingly.

You will note that we are highly interdependent in this department so we need the interlocking pieces to fit comfortably. Please review the scheduled work and let me know your opinion, particularly of the feasibility of project goals and deadlines.

> Haste is the enemy of politeness.
>
> —DRUSILLA BEYFUS

RELATED TOPICS

Acknowledgments
Announcements
E-mail
Information
Instructions
Reports
Requests
Responses

32

Letters to Neighbors

INTRODUCTION

The search for harmony among neighbors is as old as human society. And there's been no dearth of advice on how to achieve it. In a much-consulted etiquette book written in 1902, *The Correct Thing*, Florence Howe Hall writes, "It is not the correct thing to take offense if a neighbor states civilly that he would prefer your children should cease from breaking his windows." Of course! Why didn't we know that?

Most troublesome issues between neighbors can be handled with common sense and goodwill. As Judith Martin points out in *Miss Manners' Guide for the Turn-of-the-Millennium*, "The challenge of manners is not so much to be nice to someone . . . as to be exposed to the bad manners of others without imitating them." Thus, although one is tempted to record the barking dog at 2 p.m. and play it back under the neighbor's window at 2 a.m., one really shouldn't.

A good part of correspondence with neighbors is of a much happier spirit: offers of help or thanks for help, appreciation of those who keep the neighborhood safe or clean, congratulations on a personal achievement or public award or new baby, birthday and anniversary notes, invitations to social events, announcements of family or business news.

> While the spirit of neighborliness was important on the frontier because neighbors were so few, it is even more important now because our neighbors are so many.
>
> —Lady Bird Johnson

DO

- Get in the habit of sending thanks, appreciation, congratulations, or a note to say "just thinking about you" to your neighbors. This lays the foundation for good relationships. Then, if there is ever a problem, it is already half solved. Notes can be hand-delivered or sent by mail or even e-mail. Build a sense of community with invitations to an annual block party or picnic. Prevention is the best solution to potentially sticky neighbor problems.

- Decide whether a letter is the best way to handle a complaint. If you have already had several unproductive in-person or telephone discussions about the issue, it probably is. Dealing with a problem face to face keeps it a little smaller; once the discussion escalates to a letter, the problem escalates too.

- State clearly what you are asking for: stay off your new grass, trim trees that extend onto your property, contribute toward repairing a common fence.

> Of course the grass is greener on the other side of the fence. Why do you think the neighbors put up the fence?
>
> —Teresa Bloomingdale

DON'T

- Don't make accusations. They will only put your neighbor on the defensive, a position that rarely admits, apologizes, or changes. Use an indirect construction. Instead of "You never put the lids on your garbage cans properly—no wonder it all ends up here!" say, "I'm finding garbage in the alley every Thursday morning." Instead of "Your wind chimes are driving us crazy," say, "We are having trouble sleeping at night because of the wind chimes."

- Don't generalize ("you always park in front of our house" or "you never shovel your walk"). It undercuts your position from the start.

> Those who have given themselves the most concern about the happiness of others have made their neighbors very miserable.
>
> —ANATOLE FRANCE

HELPFUL HINTS

- In any dispute, try to see the issue from your neighbor's viewpoint. The more you are able to see the other person's side, the more effectively you can frame the discussion so that your neighbor derives some benefit or saves face in some way, thus paving the way to a solution or a compromise.

> To get a roaster clean, send something like baked apples in it to a neighbor. Neighbors always return pans spotless, and you won't have to use a blow torch on it like you usually do.
>
> —PHYLLIS DILLER

GETTING STARTED

Thank you for keeping an eye on our place while we were away. We came home to find everything shipshape.

Would you have time some evening to come over for coffee and dessert—and a discussion of what kind of a fence we would both like to put along the lot line?

Here is a key to our back door—I'd really appreciate you keeping a copy in case I get locked out again!

You are invited to a neighborhood meeting to discuss the use of the greenspace.

Thank you for helping us clear away the damage from the storm last week. We couldn't have done it alone.

I am going to be the "Safe House" this year for children walking to and from school, and I just wanted to explain how this works.

I'd like to ask Seraphina and Angelica to feed our hamsters every day while we're gone—I know they'd be very responsible—but I wanted to make sure you approved the idea before I talked to them.

Thank you for the garden bounty. The tomatoes were a special treat!

Hi Neighbors! We have corn coming out of our ears (and, oddly enough, ears coming out of our corn)—if you can use some, please go directly to the garden and help yourselves.

This is to let you all know that Barry is having a graduation party for about twenty of his friends Friday night, but we will be here. If it gets too loud, just give us a call (I hope you won't need to do that!).

Barbary Deniston is in the hospital—I'm wondering if the five families on this block want to go in together on a plant for her.

Since we spoke about the boys setting small fires in the alley, I've noticed them doing it again and thought perhaps I should let you know.

Could you speak to the tenants on the first floor about the strollers, bicycles, and skateboards they keep in the entryway?

> Give the neighbors' kids an inch and they'll take the whole yard.
>
> —HELEN CASTLE

MODEL LETTERS

Dear Ms. Abbott,

This is a long overdue note of appreciation to you for arranging the alley-plowing each winter. Short of taking over for you, is there anything I can do to help out? Deliver the fliers? Contact those who haven't paid yet? Make phone calls? Let me know.

Sincerely,

Jervis Pendleton

Dear Friends,

Samson and I feel so bad about Dan cutting your flowers. It seems somehow worse that his goal was a Mother's Day bouquet for me.

By the time you get this, Dan should have been to see you with his own apology, four-year-old style. We have thoroughly explained to him how wrong this was, and why. I just wanted you to know that we take this very seriously, that he has been spoken to, and that I would be surprised if he ever touched anything on your property again. I think he has learned something, but I'm sorry it was at your expense.

Mali

Dear Mina and Jonathan,

We've been so delighted to have you for neighbors that it's difficult to write this letter. It's because we value your friendship that we're hoping to settle something that's become a problem for us. In a word, Dracula.

This probably comes as no surprise to you since we've called several times about Dracula's barking. We understand that he needs to be outdoors sometimes, but it is difficult to understand why he barks every minute he's outside. As I have mentioned several times on the telephone, he barks incessantly all day long when you are at work. The early morning barking has also been disturbing as we are often up all night with the baby. I can't believe all the neighbors are up by 5:30 a.m. so it must awaken some of them too.

We appreciate your apologies and goodwill, but we are hoping that this time you can figure out some way of solving the problem. Knowing what a good neighbor you are in other respects, I felt that you would want to resolve this without us having to resort to more official means of restoring some peace and quiet to the neighborhood.

With all good wishes . . .

Murray

Dear Mr. Scatcherd,

My name is Mary Thorne and I live around the corner from you at 1858 Anthony Street. During my occasional dog-walking alley visits I noticed that you have a large pile of red bricks and a stack of old picket fence sections in your backyard. If you have no use for them and are planning on getting rid of them, I would love to take them off your hands and use them for my own backyard and garden.

I will tap on your door and introduce myself in the next day or two. Otherwise I would be happy to hear from you (555-1234). I understand that you may have your own plans for the bricks and picket fencing or they may already be spoken for. Perhaps you had planned to sell them? But if not and if I may have them, I would be grateful.

Thank you very much!

Sincerely,

Dear Mr. Marullo,

For as long as I can remember, your market has been a part of the neighbor-hood—and of our lives. You know that my husband and I are in several times a week and my three boys visit the store almost daily during the summer to buy ice cream treats.

Because I'm the mother of three impressionable pre-teenagers (well, what chil-dren *aren't* impressionable?) I'm writing to express my concern about the number of cigarette advertisements on the walls and on display at the counters. I'm also concerned about your candy selection of bubble gum "chew" and candy "cigarettes." I would like to see the advertisements and the tobacco-related candy eliminated. Studies show that exposure to nicotine ads increases children's tendency to smoke and I don't want my boys being influenced like this when they spend so much time in your store.

I will call you next week to see if we could find a time to discuss this.

Sincerely,

True politeness is to social life what oil is to machinery,
a thing to oil the ruts and grooves of existence.

—Frances Ellen Watkins Harper

Dear Mr. Tsi-Puff,

I've been asked to approach you about your nightly routine of riding your exer-cise bike while watching videos. It appears that in order to hear the movie over the noise of the bike, you have to turn the volume way up.

You're very popular with the other tenants, so nobody wanted to complain, but apparently the problem is severe, especially for those who retire early, for renters on either side of you, and for those one floor up and one floor down. The general think-ing is that you do not realize how very loud the sound is.

Nobody wants to curtail your admirable exercise program, but there is a simple solution: headphones.

Let me know what you think of this. I'm particularly eager to see if this works because the sense I got was that a number of your neighbors were quite taken with the idea of exercise bikes and old movies!

Hey Neighbors!

I'm ordering trees to replace the ones we lost in the storm. I've found a great nursery in Wisconsin with the healthiest trees and the lowest prices of any place I've checked. There's a discount for bulk orders so if any of you are also thinking of buying trees now, check out the attached list of trees and prices available. If some of you order at the same time as I do, we'd all save on delivery charges plus we'd get a more favorable rate.

No pressure, OK? I just thought it might be handy to let you know about this.

Dear Neighbor,

You are probably aware that the City is planning to add two lanes to Turner Road and turn it into a link between the two metro-area interstate highways. What this will mean for our neighborhood in terms of increased traffic, pollution, and noise is almost incalculable.

Oddly enough, the EIS (Environmental Impact Statement) seems to think the environment would best be served by converting this quiet road to a heavily trafficked one.

It's going to take a concerted effort to defeat the City's proposal. If you are also concerned about this new direction for our neighborhood, please come to an informational and organizational meeting Friday evening, September 3, 7:00 p.m. in the Bates Junior High auditorium.

Dear Polly,

Thanks for your comments on our new sod last week—it's about time we did something about the yard!

I have a small sod-related problem. I need to water it almost constantly these first few weeks, so I've got the sprinklers going most of the time. Johnny and Emma have discovered how much fun it is on these hot days to ride their bikes through the sprinklers. However, that means they are riding on the new sod, which can't take the activity.

By the time I get outside, they're off and away, and anyway I hate to be the Bad Guy here, so I was wondering if you could say a word or two to them about how fragile new sod is.

Thanks!

Dear Neighbors,

As you know, the fire last week at Alice and Roddy Wicklow's was pretty destructive. Their most urgent needs right now are warm school clothes for the kids, blankets and bedding, and kitchen utensils. If you have anything you think would be useful, give me a call—I have a list of their sizes as well as a sense of what they most need.

Thanks!

Dear Neighbor,

The list of items missing from our neighborhood is growing: 3 bikes, 2 car CD players, 1 electric drill, 2 aluminum ladders, 2 lawn mowers, 6 lawn chairs, 1 glider, 1 well-stocked toolbox, 6 garden hoses, 1 birdbath. For a number of reasons, the police—and most of us—feel the responsible person is someone in this area. There are a few steps we can take to protect ourselves against further thefts. If you're interested, you're invited to our place Saturday afternoon at 4:30 for lemonade and fresh-picked corn on the cob—and a little discussion.

> In summer, when doorstep life dominates, the natural quality of the neighborhood comes out.
>
> —MARY KINGBURY SIMKHOVITCH

RELATED TOPICS

Anniversaries

Apologies

Birthdays

Congratulations

Invitations

Requests

Sensitive

Thank You

33

Letters Dealing with Orders

INTRODUCTION

Standardized order forms, purchase forms, and requisition forms, along with 24-hour toll-free order lines, have almost entirely done away with letters placing an order. Acknowledging or confirming commercial orders is also done with boilerplate forms, either by standard mail or e-mail—or not at all, thanks to the speed with which most ordered goods are shipped. However, letters must still occasionally be written to accommodate special requests, to ask for additional information, to notify of a changed delivery date or other problem, to refund an overpayment. Customers may want to cancel an order, inquire about a missing order, or even occasionally place an order by letter.

To complain about an order, see Complaints. For drawing up instructions to customers on how to order or how to return merchandise, see Instructions. For errors, see Apologies. For order-related credit issues, see Credit.

> Good merchandise finds a ready buyer.
>
> —PLAUTUS

DO

- Include (if ordering without a form): the name of the item; its catalog, style, or model number; how many of the item you are ordering; the color, size, monogram, or other distinguishing features; the price for each item; a listing of any applicable discounts, sales tax, or shipping and handling charges; the total amount due; the payment (check or charge card number, expiration date, and signature); the delivery date (if applicable); the method of shipment (parcel post, two-day, overnight); the order date; terms, purchase order number, and signature of authorized person (if applicable); your name, address, zip code, and telephone number; and the address to which the merchandise is to be sent (if different from the billing address).

- Arrange your order on the page so that it can be read at a glance. Instead of a long sentence ("Please send me twelve Halifax printer ribbons at $7.95 apiece, a one-pound box of assorted rubber bands at $2.39, and a dozen rolls of Fletcher masking tape at $1.89 per roll"), type the information in units of information, each on a separate line. Use Arabic numerals ("12 rolls of Fletcher tape") instead of writing them out; they are more quickly read.

- Specify if the items must be delivered by a certain date. By stating the importance of the delivery date in your letter, you will generally be able to cancel the order without forfeit if you do not receive it in time; the letter serves as an informal contract.

- Refrain from discussing other business in your letter (reference to an earlier order, request for a new catalog). It may delay your order.

- When returning merchandise, include in your cover letter: your name and address; a description of the item; a copy of the sales slip, invoice, or shipping label; an explanation of why you're returning it; your request for a refund, credit to your account, or replacement merchandise; an expression of appreciation. If returning the merchandise is difficult because of its large size or fragility, write first and ask how it should be returned. Request reimbursement for your shipping costs.

- When canceling a prepaid order or asking for a refund, include: order, invoice, or reference number; date of order; description of merchandise. Specify whether the amount of the merchandise should be credited to your account, credited to your charge card, or returned to you as a check.

> The propensity to truck, barter and exchange one thing for another . . . is common to all [people], and to be found in no other race of animals.
>
> —ADAM SMITH

DON'T

- Don't forget the niceties. It is tempting in the nuts-and-bolts world of ordering to forget that real live people are reading these letters. Those placing an order can close their letter with, "Thank you for your prompt attention." The supplier should always say, "Thank you for your order."

> Whatever is clearly expressed is well wrote.
>
> —LADY MARY WORTLEY MONTAGU

HELPFUL HINTS

- In all correspondence to customers about orders, indicate your readiness to be of service to them and an appreciation for their business; these letters serve as goodwill letters when they are helpful and courteous.
- Simplify all aspects of dealing with orders by creating standardized forms for the original order, problem orders, refunds, returned merchandise, and any other type of correspondence that occurs frequently.
- If your first order was not received and you need to order the same items again, emphasize that it is a duplicate order. It sometimes happens that the first order turns up later and is also filled.

> Commerce is the great civilizer. We exchange ideas when we exchange fabrics.
>
> —R.G. INGERSOLL

GETTING STARTED

Please send me the following items.

This will confirm my telephone order of this morning for the following items.

Please bill us for the following at our usual terms.

Please cancel my order #HG3002 for the Deever paper shredder—the six weeks' delay is unacceptable.

If the water softener cannot by delivered by November 20, please let me know immediately.

Will you please check on the status of my order #54-1143 dated August 10?

Thank you for your order.

We acknowledge with thanks your order of February 5 for six serviceberry trees.

I am writing to confirm a March 23 delivery date for the mantel clock and curved-front china cupboard.

> As with most fine things, chocolate has its season. There is a simple memory aid that you can use to determine whether it is the correct time to order chocolate dishes: Any month whose name contains the letter a, e, or u is the proper time for chocolate.
>
> —SANDRA BOYNTON

MODEL LETTERS

Subject: #CHS275

This will confirm receipt of your purchase order dated August 19 for three tenor saxophones. They will be shipped by priority mail on August 23. If you need to contact us again about this order, please use our reference number, 4977-1012.

Dear Customer Service,

I am a senior at the University of Connecticut majoring in performing arts. I am designing the costumes for a film being produced by a group of us for our senior project. The script involves aliens invading the earth—which leads me to your contact lens production company. I understand that you manufacture special-design contacts. I would like to order several pairs of contacts with day-glo pupils and lemon-yellow lenses. I think these colors would give the aliens the high degree of creepiness as well as funkiness that I hope to achieve visually in this film.

Please let me know if this design is available and what the cost would be per pair. I would appreciate a call by March 10 (651/555-1234).

Thank you.

Re: purchase order # K12291944

Thank you for your purchase order of July 9 for the Bascomb stairway elevator. Your order has been forwarded for fulfillment, and your Purchasing Department will be contacted with information about terms and shipping dates.

November 13, 1995

WCIL—Banners
P.O. Box 92501
Los Angeles, CA 90009

Dear Friends,

Would you please send seven (7) highway safety banners to:

Mrs. Margaret Erlynne
1187 Goodrich Avenue
Middletown, OH 45042

Enclosed is a check for $30:

$5	first banner
$24	six additional banners @ $4
$1	postage and handling per order

Thank you!

Re: Order # _____

Thank you for your order, which we have received today. We are unable to ship your merchandise immediately because

___Payment has not been received.
___We no longer fill C.O.D. orders—please send a check, money order, or credit card information.
___We do not have a complete shipping address for you.
___We are currently out of stock—may we ship later?
___We no longer carry that item—may we send a substitute at the same price?
___We need to know the size (quantity, style, color, etc.).
___Your payment did not include shipping and handling charges.

Please include the order number given at the top of the page when you respond.

Thank you for doing business with Brinsley Brothers, where your satisfaction is always guaranteed.

September 4, 1996

Sales Department
Pearson Candy Co.
2140 West 7th Street
St. Paul, MN 55116

Re: Nut Goodies

Could you please send a case (24 bars) of Nut Goodies to:

>   Araminta Dench
>   Apt. # 3F
>   548 W. 113th Street
>   New York, NY 10025

Enclosed is a check for $13.50. Thank you so much for making this service available to customers. A friend of mine became very attached to your Nut Goodies during a visit here and thinks about them often in New York, where she can't get them!

Sincerely,

If it is good and I want it, they don't make it anymore

—ELIZABETH C. FINEGAN

To: Order Department

Enclosed is your standard order form, which I have completed.

I would like to call your attention, however, to the fact that the glass block windows I'm ordering have the same catalog number as one of the chandeliers on p. 167.

Will you please check into this and make sure I receive the glass block windows and not a chandelier?

Thank you.

To: Universal Coin Co.

As per your classified ad on p. 189 of *Home* magazine, I would like to order:

> 3 sets of the Lincoln/Wheat-Ear penny collection 1934-1958 @ $8.80 including postage and handling.

Enclosed is my check for $26.40.

To: "On the Road" Travel Videos

I would like to order the following travel videos:

> Thailand
> China
> Japan
> Korea

Enclosed is a check for $41.80, which includes shipping and handling.

Your ad offered a free bonus video on Russia, but only to customers who ordered by phone. I tried your 800 number hundreds of times over a period of four days (using the automatic redial feature on my phone). It was always busy.

I am interested in receiving the free bonus video. Can you advise me if you expect the 800 number to be available or if there is some other way I can obtain the bonus video?

Dear Home Fittings, Inc.,

I am ordering your garage door opener, catalog # A6774 or # A6775 (order form attached).

Although the catalog copy discusses both chain-drive openers and screw-drive openers, I can't tell which catalog number is for which. I want the screw-drive opener. I am assuming it is the more expensive opener and am enclosing a check in that amount, but would you please doublecheck this for me?

Thank you.

> Never buy what you do not want because it is cheap; it will be dear to you.
>
> —THOMAS JEFFERSON

RELATED TOPICS

Acknowledgments
Adjustments
Apologies
Complaints
Credit
Instructions
Refusals
Requests

34

Pen Pals

INTRODUCTION

Although the term "pen pal" suggests primarily youthful letterwriters, it includes not only dedicated young correspondents but thousands of adults who write with great enthusiasm and delight to people they've never met. A better term might be "pen friend."

If you don't like writing letters in the first place, you won't want a hobby like this one. For people who do love writing letters, however, there is nothing to equal it. In *Gift of a Letter*, Alexandra Stoddard writes, "An inspired letter can be as riveting as a stare. It can move us to tears, spur us to action, provoke us, uplift us, touch us. Transform us. When written from the heart, letters are dreams on paper, wishes fulfilled, desires satisfied."

One of the most devoted and prolific letterwriters in history was Lady Mary Wortley Montagu. As Agnes Repplier describes her in an essay, "The Correspondent," Montagu "wrote more letters, with fewer punctuation marks, than any Englishwoman of her day; and her nephew, the fourth Baron Rokeby, nearly blinded himself in deciphering the two volumes of undated correspondence which were printed in 1810. Two more followed in 1813, after which the gallant Baron either died at his post or was smitten with despair; for sixty-eight cases of letters lay undisturbed. . . . 'The dead no longer write,' said Madame de Maintenon hopefully; 'but of what benefit is this inactivity, when we still continue to receive their letters?'"

For additional ideas and assistance on writing letters to pen friends, try reading some of Lady Mary Wortley Montagu's letters, or see the chapter on Family and Friends.

September 22 is Pen Pal Day, a good time to check into some organizations that may help you get started:

The Letter Exchange
Steve Sikora
P.O. Box 6218
Albany, CA 94706

Devoted to promoting the theory and practice of private correspondence, this publication (nicknamed LEX) for letterwriters seeks "to make sense of our experience and our ideas by telling them to someone else and by listening to what others have to say back to us in response." Its 1,500 subscribers have diverse interests but share a taste for the simple pleasure of letterwriting.

The Student Letter Exchange
211 Broadway, Suite 201
Lynbrook, NY 11563-3265
516/887-8628
516/887-8631 FAX
http://www.pen-pal.com

For girls and boys ages 9-18, this is a well-organized pen pal group that charges $1.25 per address (15 or more pen pal addresses are $1.00 each).

World Pen Pals
P.O. Box 337
Saugerties, NY 12477
914/246-7828

For those ages 11 and up who want a foreign pen friend; fee is $3 plus a self-addressed stamped envelope.

The Letter Enjoyers
Jerry L. Hill
P.O. Box 33214
Minneapolis, MN 55433-0214

Clearinghouse for letter information and letterwriting. Mr. Hill is available only by letter and includes no phone number in his correspondence. Include a SASE if you write him.

International Pen Friends
P.O. Box 65
Brooklyn, NY 11229

Based in Dublin, Ireland, this group has over 300,000 members of all ages; for information, send a self-addressed stamped envelope to the foregoing address.

Pen Pals
1507 Dana Avenue
Cincinnati, OH 45207

A feature of the *Writer's Digest Book Club Bulletin*, the Pen Pals column is designed for members who want to make writing-related connections.

Skywriters
Tall Clubs International
P.O. Box 1964
Bloomfield, NJ 07003-1964
888/468-2552

This pen pal program for those under 21 is sponsored by an organization for tall people.

> Is there anything in the world more suggestive of interesting possibilities than a mail box? Whether it be the iron box beside the door knob, the gilded drawer at the post office, the open row of boxes behind a hotel counter, or just the Valentine box on the teacher's desk, it suggests the exciting possibility of a new friend, an important message, or even, perhaps, the promise of a new experience. . . . The romance of the mail box is an old romance.
>
> —LUELLA B. COOK

DO

- Tell something about yourself, particularly ideas or activities that interest you.
- Ask questions about the other person's life. Try not to sound like an interviewer, however.
- Be discreet in telling personal information. Begin with the standard facts that most people know about you. Reserve more private details for much later in the correspondence.

> Do let me hear from you even if it's only a twenty-page letter.
>
> —GROUCHO MARX

DON'T

- Don't worry about "the rules." What matters is finding someone with whom you can comfortably exchange letters. Where one person might be put off by a ten-page letter from a new correspondent, another person would be delighted. The person who talks only about self-centered news would fascinate one person, bore the next. The letterwriter who never tells anything personal would be considered discreet by some, too uptight by others. The solution is to be yourself. That way, you'll find those who like you as you are.

> The life of literacy declines. It will not long survive as a dynamic force in our culture if we amateur readers leave all our writing and thinking in the hands of a few professionals. In order to do at least some of the writing for ourselves, I can think of no better means than that of private letters. To that end, personal correspondence seems the very best form of literature I can think of.
>
> —STEVE SIKORA

HELPFUL HINTS

- You may want to include a self-addressed stamped envelope (SASE) the first time you write someone in the United States. (An overseas correspondent cannot mail a letter to you stamped with U.S. stamps.) You are much more likely to get a response. After the first exchange of letters, however, this is no longer necessary.
- If you're running out of topics to write about, consider discussing or asking your correspondent's views on: music, books, hobbies, games, sports, history, politics, art, movies, religion, philosophy, travel, daily life, education, health, psychology, work, family, pets, humor, nature, gardening, genealogy, holidays, metaphysics.

> Our correspondences have wings—paper birds that fly from my house to yours—flocks of ideas crisscrossing the country.
>
> —Terry Tempest Williams

GETTING STARTED

Hello! My name is Henry Earlforward and I'm a bookseller by vocation and a bibliophile by avocation and I hope you like books as much as I do.

I've never written to anyone I didn't know before, so let's see how this goes!

For this first letter, I thought I would tell you a little about myself and ask a few questions about you.

Thank you for your letter—I can already tell I'm going to enjoy our correspondence!

> There is nothing quite as personal in today's busy world as someone else's handwriting addressed to you. When you go home, just like a child, the first thing you do is run to the mailbox. You look for handwriting, not for bills.
>
> —Fran Mathay

MODEL LETTERS

Dear Duncan,

I'm so programmed now that the minute I see articles about model trains, I reach for the scissors! Here are three more for you that I found recently.

I never forget how we started corresponding either, so I'm also enclosing a copy of a journal article on cataract surgery—had you heard about this new technique?

Thanks for the photographs you sent last time. I'm returning them in this letter along with some I took when we visited my folks' ranch in Wyoming. Don't the kids look about twice as big as they did in the last photos?

What's happening to your plans to come here for a visit sometime? Can you arrange a professional conference or something? I'm still keeping Scotland in the back of my mind—I've got a whole computer file full of notes, places to visit, sample airfares, etc. One of these days we'll meet—either there or here. Until then, happy reading, and don't forget to put some different stamps on my next envelope—I've already GOT the everyday ones!

Dear Wu Sung,

This is my first experiment with writing to someone I've never met. It's a good thing that you speak (and write) English or this wouldn't be possible. Unfortunately I don't speak any other languages, not even Spanish, which I took for two years in high school.

To help us get to know each other, I'm sending you a few things that show my little corner of the world: a road map, postcards, a small travel book about Chicago, some pages from this morning's newspaper that tell what's going on in Chicago these days, and some pictures of my family, my apartment, and my cat, Mulch.

I work in a bank, so in my next letter I'll send a picture of the bank, some brochures describing its features, and tell you a little about what I do there.

I look forward to hearing about you and your corner of the world!

> Half the world does not know how the other half lives, but is trying to find out.
>
> —E.W. HOWE

Dear Patalamon,

Once my mom said she'd pay the postage, I had a lot of fun gathering stuff for your school report on Texas. Most of the brochures and booklets were free—I got them at the airport when we were out there last week. We've moved around in Texas a lot, so we have pictures of different parts of the state. I'm sending you some, but you have to *promise* to send them back. I bought you the road map with my own money and there are some pressed Texas wildflowers in the plastic package so be careful when you open it.

If you get an A on your paper, can I have half of it? Ha ha!

Write me soon.

Kerick

Dear Pen Friend,

Here's another postcard for your collection—it is from the most *insane* place, called The House on the Rock. It is going to take me a whole letter to tell you about it. We bought a book there and I'm going to photocopy some of the pictures so you can see what I mean. Bye for now!

Alice

> Sometimes I think letter-writing might be an expression of that universal childhood desire to be invisible: to meet people without having to deal with the physicality of it all, suspending space and time, to a degree, in our relationships with others.
>
> —SUSAN WOLFE

Dear Maja,

Your son Jussi, whom I met at work, said you were interested in practicing your English. Since I am trying to learn Finnish, I am hoping you would be interested in exchanging letters, half in English, half in Finnish.

My parents were Finnish but never spoke the language in front of us, thinking it was better for us to learn English, so I am a real beginner.

I am 42 years old, a chemical engineer like Jussi, have been married for 16 years, and have three children.

I hope you will be interested in writing back. Best wishes to you!

> A letter is water you can drink when you are thirsty.
>
> —ELIZABETH YEMO

RELATED TOPICS

Family and Friends

35

Letters to Public and Government Officials

INTRODUCTION

Many times a telephone call will serve you well when you have a request for a public official or want to convey an opinion to a lawmaker. However, if you have ever spent too much time on "hold" or being transferred from one person who can't help you to another who can't help you, you may find that writing a letter is more convenient in the long run.

When you are seeking information from government officials, see Information. When you have a complaint, see Complaints.

> The first thing to be said about government agencies is that the people who staff them are nervous, harassed, overworked, and underpaid, and they are frequently confused, inadequate, and tardy in their correspondence. In short, they are exactly like the rest of us.
>
> —LASSOR BLUMENTHAL

DO

- Begin with a subject line so the other person knows immediately what the issue is:

    Re: absentee ballot

    Re: HR 735

    Subject: proposed property tax increase

    Subject: greenspace hearings

- Your first sentence or at least the first (brief) paragraph should elaborate on your subject line ("Please send an absentee ballot to the following address").

- Depending on your objective in writing, give details of the problem, reasons for your stance, or the heart of your message. If appropriate, use bulleted lists of your points.

- State what you expect of the other person: information, voting a certain way, action on a problem, answers to a question, referrals to someone who can help.

- Focus on one issue per letter. When you bring up several items, it is too easy for the letter to end up in a "miscellaneous" pile.

- If you have any expertise or credentials that bear on the issue, mention them (but public officials tend to discount vague reports of how "influential" a letterwriter is).

- Include photocopies of relevant documents.

- Close with an expression of appreciation for the person's time and attention.

> I have learned that in order to bring about change, you must not be afraid to take the first step. We will fail when we fail to try. Each and every one of us can make a difference.
>
> — ROSA PARKS

DON'T

- Don't demand or insist; it is counterproductive. And don't threaten to throw the bum out of office at the next election. This is a trite and fairly idle threat and, again, counterproductive.

- Don't ask lawmakers to commit themselves on bills that are still in committees or hearings. However, it is useful both to them and to you to state your views at that point in a reasoned and persuasive manner.

- Don't depend on form letters or orchestrated letter campaigns to sway legislators or public officials. They take these with a grain of salt. A single, well-written letter is often more effective. As Florynce R. Kennedy once said, "Unity in a movement situation can be overrated. If you were the Establishment, which would you rather see coming in the door: one lion or five hundred mice?"

> It is so much easier sometimes to sit down and be resigned than to rise up and be indignant.
>
> —Nellie L. McClung

HELPFUL HINTS

- When writing to lawmakers or government officials, check in the reference department of your local library for listings in *U.S. Government Manual* (new edition every year), *Who's Who in American Politics*, and various state and federal handbooks and directories. *Federal Information Centers*, which lists centers across the country to contact when you need assistance from the federal government, is available free from: Consumer Information Center, Pueblo, CO 81009. Also available free from that same address is *The Consumer's Resource Handbook*, which lists—among many other things—federal agencies as well as state, county, and city government consumer offices; state agencies on aging; insurance regulators; state banking authorities; state utility commissions; state vocational and rehabilitation agencies.

- When writing to branches of the U.S. military, to the Department of Veterans Affairs, or to military-related organizations, include with your request: your name, the branch and dates of your service; discharge date and rank at time of discharge; your service number or your Social Security number; all other relevant names, dates, and identifying numbers. The more information you give, the better your chances for getting the information you want. Your chances are also better if you write to the appropriate person; this is often done by trial and error, but you can send the same letter (not a photocopy as that's likely to be ignored, in the hopes that the other person will take care of it) to several people.

> When dealing with the bureaucracy, the man you are talking to is never the man you have to see.
>
> —James Baldwin

GETTING STARTED

I've noticed that temporary "no parking" signs are nailed into the trunks of living trees. Is there not a better way to post these signs?

I am writing to oppose your stand on laws regulating homeopathy.

The purpose of this letter is to voice my support for the proposed planetarium.

Please send me your *Request for Earnings and Benefit Estimate Statement.*

I'm writing because of my profound concern about three accidents in the past year at the corner of Dean and Jollifant Streets.

Will you please send me, in the enclosed SASE, a passport renewal form and guidelines for applying?

Please correct your records to reflect the following change of address.

My daughter is interested in applying to the U.S. Air Force Academy—can your office tell us how we should begin this process?

This is to notify you of the death of my husband, Jared Otkar (Social Security # 555-55-5555).

I understand that you will be holding hearings on lowering the legal drinking age.

There is an urgent need for driver education in this area about the fact that bike lanes are just that—for bikes only.

Enclosed is a completed form disputing the assessed value of my home at 17 Salamanca Boulevard.

All the undersigned wish to express their heartfelt appreciation to the city street crews who worked around the clock to open streets blocked by downed trees during the disastrous storms last week.

I would be happy to have your campaign sign in my front yard (my street is heavily trafficked) if someone from your re-election committee would like to install one.

I want to state in the strongest possible terms that I object to your being elected mayor and then spending all four years of your term of office running for governor.

Can you please send me a list of Medicare-approved physicians and facilities in the metro area?

I would like to see the issue of sibling preference in our magnet schools put on the next school board meeting agenda.

> Change in a democracy can be brought about quickly or slowly. The speed depends on its people's honesty of mind, their values, their humility and knowledge and insight; and, above all else, on the will to act, once they realize the need for action.
>
> —Lillian Smith

MODEL LETTERS

TO: Germain Zoning Commission
FROM: M. Rudolph
DATE: Dec. 16, 2001
RE: Zoning File 11811, Fleur Day Care Center

I am writing in favor of the Special Condition Use Permit sought by the Fleur Day Care Center. We live directly across the street from the proposed Center, and would be one of those most affected by any increased activity in the area. It is my considered opinion that the Center, as currently proposed, would not adversely affect residents of the neighborhood.

Dear Faith Paleogos,

I want you to know that you have my vote and financial backing in your gubernatorial race. I would like to offer campaign support in another way as well: my brother, Hervey Allen, owns a hot-air balloon company in Wisconsin and I would like to see you team up with him (at my expense) for a publicity stunt to give your campaign a colorful liftoff.

I know that several columnists have lambasted you this summer for being "full of hot air," but you've made light of this tag and have even seemed to enjoy the negative publicity in a good-humored way. I'm sure your lighthearted response has only served to win you more votes.

What I picture is a 30-second television campaign spot showing you taking off in a hot-air balloon and flashing your well-known grin. I think this visual would be effective and memorable and would help your campaign really "take off."

Let me know if this interests you. And good luck!

Sincerely,

TO: Social Security Administration
FROM: Arístides García Babel
DATE: June 30, 2000
SUBJECT: Effective date of retirement

This will serve as notification that my last day of work is August 31, 2000. I would like you to activate my Social Security benefits as of that date.

Enclosed are the necessary signed and dated forms. Also enclosed is a self-addressed stamped envelope in case you need anything else from me in order to ensure that benefits start promptly on September 1.

TO: Villette County Jury Coordinator
FROM: Caroline H. Helstone
DATE: July 29, 2000
SUBJECT: Request to report for jury duty dated July 26, 2000

I am planning to be married on August 15, and thus am not available for jury duty beginning on that date. Enclosed is a photocopy of the announcement of my wedding that appeared in the paper. Please let me know what I need to do to regularize my situation with respect to jury duty.

Dear Ms. Links,

We are interested in buying, either from your office or from the successful bidder, the old stone jail building behind the courthouse. We understand the city council has voted to sell it.

We are a family of studio artists and would like to turn the old jail into a gallery. We know what a difficult property this building would be to develop, given its physical limitations and its location in the heart of the historic district, adjacent to the river and having only alley access. However, it is a challenge we would enjoy. My husband has been on the Historic Preservation Commission for fifteen years. Two of my sons are contractors and have developed remarkable properties in the historic district: the hotel, the museum, and the Wain Building.

We would appreciate all applicable information about the purchase procedure, necessary zoning changes (and our chances of obtaining them), building permits, and any other city requirements.

Thank you.

Dear Public Works Department,

I am writing to inquire about the portable toilet that has been parked on the boulevard directly in front of our house from the beginning of May through this week of July. In our immediate neighborhood, where all the streets are being replaced this summer, we are the only house with a biffy on our front lawn, and there is always a steady stream of workers going to and from. This is a distraction I could do without as my terrier barks insanely and my three young daughters think it would be much more fun to use it than our own bathroom.

I would like the biffy to be moved onto the vacant lot on the corner of Jerningham and Forest so that my family can enjoy a "potty break" for the remaining two months of this construction project.

I look forward to hearing from you—or to the absence of the portable toilet. Thank you.

Dear Senator Brander,

Re: television violence

Thank you for your valuable work as Chair of the House Subcommittee on Television Violence. I would like to be counted among those who strongly oppose violence on television. Violence cannot help but encourage and produce violence. The cumulative effect of watching violence is to create an insensitivity toward violence.

As a screenwriter myself, I would like to add that television violence is also stupid and unnecessary. The writer who needs violence to create the illusion of action and suspense is the poorest and lowest sort of writer. On-screen violence is never necessary to advance a plot. Violence substitutes for emotion and thinking; we are not only creating a more violent nation via the television screen, we are also creating an impossibly stupid, insensate, and unthinking population.

I imagine others have quoted this, from Harriet Beecher Stowe, *Uncle Tom's Cabin* (1852): "Whipping and abuse are like laudanum; you have to double the dose as the sensibilities decline." What we have in this country at present is a galloping case of declining sensibilities. TV viewers no longer weep when someone dies, no longer gasp when someone is raped or killed, no longer react in any way to what they are seeing except perhaps with the knee-jerk laugh, wrung from them by means of nudging laugh tracks or broad, witless humor.

I hope to see some concrete results of your deliberations, in the direction of discouraging violence on television. Until then, I and my family will continue to boycott commercial television and the sponsors who bring it to us.

To: Traffic Violations Department
From: Garnet Bowen
Date: March 2, 2000
Re: Traffic ticket # 1255-46-980

The enclosed ticket was issued for failure to have a resident parking sticker while parked in a resident-parking-only zone. The vehicle identified did in fact display a Fenway resident-parking sticker when the ticket was given.

I found the ticket only minutes after it had been issued so I drove around the neighborhood until I found the officer who had written it. I showed him the sticker, and he said to simply send you the ticket along with an explanation.

A records check will show that I have had a resident parking sticker since Dec. 15, 1999.

> If you are not part of the solution, you are part of the problem.
>
> —ELDRIDGE CLEAVER

To: District Council 14
From: Lydia Protheroe
Date: May 17
Re: Summer Jobs Program

I hope you are continuing the Summer Jobs Program you've sponsored the last few years. I'm attaching the names, addresses, and phone numbers of high school students who would like jobs this summer (I work in the Counseling Office at the high school), as well as a list of some homeowners who expect to need help with house and yard chores this summer.

This is a wonderful service, matching the needs of both groups. I hope you have continued success with it.

Dear Representative Battchilena,

Please count me among those of your constituents who support gun control laws. My reasons are the same as your stated public views, so I don't need to say more, but I wanted you to know you have my backing on this issue.

All progressive legislation has always had its genesis in the mind of one person. . . . One can do much. And one and one and one can move mountains.

—JOAN WARD-HARRIS

RELATED TOPICS

Complaints
Information
Requests
Thank You

36

Query Letters

INTRODUCTION

A query is a brief, well-written letter that sparks an editor's interest in publishing your article or book and ideally results in a request to you to submit the proposed or finished work. A query letter can also be sent to persuade a literary agent to represent you or to arouse someone's interest in a business proposal. It is a combination request letter and sales letter.

Editors like the query letter because it allows them to decide quickly if the idea is suitable for them and interesting enough to pursue. If it is particularly well-written, the letter helps editors sell the idea in turn to their colleagues. Reading query letters requires a great deal less time than reading manuscripts or outlines and sample chapters, and thus speeds up the selection process.

For unagented writers, the query letter is the only way to approach publishers who no longer accept unsolicited manuscripts. And it may be a good way to approach even those publishers who do accept unsolicited material. Once an editor responds to your query letter with a "Send your manuscript along," you can mark the package "Requested Material" and your manuscript will not end up marking time in the slush pile; in general, you can count on it being read earlier than if you had sent it without first querying.

The query letter has been used traditionally in connection with nonfiction works, but it is also being requested today for works of fiction. In those cases, the query letter is actually a cover letter, and an outline or synopsis and sample chapters are enclosed. For fiction, follow the guidelines below except that plot, characters, conflict, and resolution are described in the paragraph outlining your story or novel.

> A query letter is really a sales letter without the hype.
>
> —LISEL EISENHEIMER

DO

- Direct your query to the appropriate editor. This means familiarizing yourself with the periodical or publishing house so that you are certain your material is suitable for them. It also means obtaining the correct name and title of the editor currently receiving queries for your type of book or article. Even if you find a name in a marketing book, call first and verify that the person is still there, that the name is spelled the way you have it, and that the person's title is still current. (Do not speak to the editor; an operator, receptionist, or editorial assistant can answer your questions.)

- Begin your letter with a strong hook—something that will keep the editor reading. Many query letters open with a lead taken from the first paragraph of the proposed article or book.

- Tell what kind of a book or article it is (reference, biography, children's), how long it is, its title, and its intended audience. In a few sentences, outline the book in such a way that the editor will be eager to read it. This paragraph must be your best writing.

> There is no security, no assurance that because we wrote something good two months ago, we will do it again. Actually, every time we begin, we wonder how we ever did it before.
>
> —NATALIE GOLDBERG

- Tell why your article or book is different from any others on the same subject, why you are the best person to write it (mention any relevant expertise or knowledge), and why you chose this particular publisher and editor for this particular project.

- Indicate the probable length of the article or book, the estimated completion date, whether photographs or other materials are available, and a list of your other publications.

- Convey your enthusiasm for the material.

- Be brief. A query letter should not be more than one page—two at the most.

- Include a self-addressed stamped envelope (SASE). Always. Every time.
- Close with a direct request to submit the manuscript for the editor's consideration. Thank the person for their time and attention.
- Proofread your letter as many times as it takes to be certain there are no spelling, punctuation, grammar, or usage errors; they are usually fatal.

> A well-written query is crucial, for it gives us an indication of how the writer thinks, tells a story, and writes.
>
> —ANNIE STINE

DON'T

- Don't discuss payment, royalties, rights, or other business issues in the query letter; it is not appropriate at this stage of the process.
- Don't include any personal information (age, marital status, hobbies, education) unless it is highly relevant to the proposed work. You do, of course, include your full name, address, and telephone number.

> A query letter is like a fishing expedition; don't put too much bait on your hook or you'll lose your quarry. Be brief and be tantalizing!
>
> —JANE VON MEHREN

HELPFUL HINTS

- Know how the publisher or magazine likes to be contacted. While query letters are preferred in most instances, some publishers request a query (which then becomes a cover letter) along with an outline and sample chapters.
- Associate editors and assistant editors are often more approachable and more likely to read your letter themselves than the executive editor or editor-in-chief.
- A clever, memorable, or intriguing article or book title can go a long way toward catching an editor's attention. It doesn't have to be your final title; select a working title or one constructed solely for the purposes of querying.

- John Wood (*How to Write Attention-Grabbing Query & Cover Letters*) says query letters should be vital, enthusiastic, and full of conviction: "write them in such a way that the fortunate recipients recognize, from the opening line, that you're on to something startling and that you're not the typical hack."

- A query letter is not normally accompanied by work samples, but on occasion this is appropriate.

- A common fear among unpublished writers is that someone at the publishing house will steal their idea after seeing their query letter. This is an exceedingly rare and undocumented occurrence. In any case, there are no new ideas. What is always new—and saleable—is the way the idea is clothed and presented. Even when two people work on the same idea (there are supposedly only thirty-six dramatic situations), their works will differ significantly from each other. Then, too, how will you get published if you don't send a query letter?

- For in-depth assistance on writing great query letters, see John Wood, *How to Write Attention-Grabbing Query & Cover Letters*, and Lisa Collier Cool, *How to Write Irresistible Query Letters*, both published by Writer's Digest Books. There are also sections on query letters in books such as *How to Get Happily Published*, 4th ed., by Judith Appelbaum, HarperPerennial, and *Into Print* by Poets & Writers, Inc., Quality Paperback Book Club.

- Multiple submissions involve sending the same manuscript to several editors at the same time. There is still little agreement among authors and editors about the advisability of multiple submissions, but there is no problem about querying several editors at the same time about the same project. A decision about submitting multiply will have to be made only if several editors reply to your query letter by asking to see the manuscript.

- A book proposal, which is usually the next step after a query letter, consists of a synopsis, outline, sample chapters, marketing information (competing titles, intended audience, uniqueness of this project), specifications (length, available date, your credentials), and some expression of your passion for your material. A book proposal may be sent instead of a query letter if you have reason to think the proposed manuscript is a good match for the editor. As it can run to thirty or more pages, a book proposal does not qualify as a letter, so check with some of the many excellent guides for writers on the best way to present your material.

> The manuscript may go forth from the writer to return with a faithfulness passing the faithfulness of the boomerang or the homing pigeon.
>
> —Rose Macaulay

GETTING STARTED

Would you be interested in seeing a 40,000-word mystery for children set in the 1920s in one of Upper Michigan's Finnish settlements?

Do you still believe in the existence of high-yield, low-risk stocks? You may not be as naïve as you think!

Francesca Lia Block once wrote, "Love is a dangerous angel," and added, "Especially nowadays." Would you be interested in seeing an 80,000-word manuscript on the physical, emotional, intellectual, and spiritual dangers of sex today, supported by research I am currently involved in?

A man with amnesia trying to negotiate the tricky steps of the life he is told is his— a familiar story? Not in this novel.

If education is not a preparation for life but life itself (John Dewey), why does today's education so little resemble the real world . . . and what would happen if it did? Would you be interested in considering for publication a 75,000-word manuscript about a real-life experiment in education with exciting possibilities for today's world?

Can the market stand one more book on weight control? If it's this one—written by a physician with thirty years' success in helping patients lose weight—it can!

> All inquiries carry with them some element of risk.
>
> —CARL SAGAN

MODEL LETTERS

Dear Rachel Laskin,

Thank you for sending the submission guidelines for *Peaceful Parenting*. Having studied the guidelines and having also been a subscriber to your informative, entertaining, and thought-provoking magazine for more than five years, I believe the article I want to submit to you is new yet highly appropriate to your readership.

What happens to romance and modes of positive communication when you have a baby? What can you do before the baby arrives to ease the situation? What skills and strategies can strengthen your relationship after the baby arrives?

As a family counselor with a new baby, I have been collecting anecdotes, quotations, studies, and first-hand stories to help your readers answer these questions.

I could deliver a 5,000-word article by September 1. Enclosed is a SASE for your response.

Thank you for your time and consideration.

TO: Editors, Aviation History
FROM: Marcel Cordier
DATE: September 7, 1996
SUBJECT: article query: Marie Marvingt

On November 27, 1910, Marie Marvingt set the first women's world record in aviation. Earlier that month she had obtained her pilot's license, the third woman in the world to do so and the first to pass the test without damaging her plane.

I would be very surprised if your readers ever heard of her.

Marie Marvingt (1875-1963) was licensed to pilot planes, gliders, seaplanes, dirigibles, helicopters, and balloons (in 1909 she became the first woman to cross the North Sea in a balloon from France to England). What she most wanted to be remembered for was her invention of the ambulance airplane and her work in air rescue. Daring, colorful, and extraordinarily active, she was one of those whom Amelia Earhart referred to as the real pioneers in women's aviation, a pioneer, however, who has been almost totally overlooked in the annals of aviation history.

I have been fascinated with Marie Marvingt for over fifteen years and have published a French-language biography of her, *Marie Marvingt: Femme d'un siècle* (Sarreguemines: Les Éditions Pierron, 1991). I am also the author of a dozen other books.

For background and to show you the sorts of illustrations that are available I'm enclosing a copy of "The Fiancée of Danger" that I wrote for *Women's Sports and Fitness* and a three-part article that appeared in *Cricket* magazine. Since these were published, Marie Marvingt has been inducted into the International Women's Sports Hall of Fame.

It seems to me that a shorter rather than longer article would be appropriate for your publication since aviation in these earliest days was often more sport than science, more anecdote than rigorous recordkeeping. I'm not sure how much of the rest of Marie Marvingt's life you'd be interested in; although the focus of this article is her contributions to aviation, readers should probably be told that she was also an outstanding athlete (in 1910 the French government awarded her a gold medal for being expert in *all* sports), nurse, inventor, traveler, and the most decorated woman in the world.

Enclosed is a SASE for your reply. Thank you for your time and attention, and best wishes to you.

Dear Rob Angus,

Would you be interested in seeing an 85,000-word novel, *The Boarding House?*

Wealthy, intelligent, and isolated, Marshall is a house divided against himself. Denying important and life-giving facets of his self from an early age, he surrounds himself with shadows formed by his projected unacceptable imaginings. In this literary exploration of the divided self, Marshall struggles to resolve the four basic human conflicts—between freedom and security, right and wrong, masculinity and femininity, and between love and hate in the parent-child relationship. It is in daring to love with maturity and without reserve that he is finally able to deal with the boarders living in his house and to trade his mask for a real face.

I can send the complete manuscript or, if you prefer, sample chapters and a detailed synopsis.

I am also the author of a number of short stories, one of which won the Abinger Prize last year, and I was recently awarded a grant by our state arts board based on a sample from this novel.

Enclosed is a SASE for your reply.

Dear Ms. Treginnis,

It's a question we'd all like answered: Is there life after death?

In April of 1998 I was pronounced clinically dead. As you might suspect, the diagnosis was correct only up to a point.

My experience fed a fierce curiosity in me to know how "normal" such experiences are. And what they mean. And whether they might be proof of anything.

Since that time, I have interviewed 247 people who have also been to the "other side" and returned.

Not since Moody's *Life After Life* has there been such a diverse collection of anecdotal evidence that there is indeed more to life than life.

Would you be interested in seeing some or all of this 70,000-word manuscript? Enclosed is a SASE for your reply.

Thank you.

Dear Ms. Kepple,

We met at a writers' conference in Los Angeles last month and briefly discussed the point at which a writer might need an agent.

I believe I have reached that point. I have had four books published (*The Greatest Adventure*, 1994; *The Jury*, 1996; *The Long Story of a Short Life*, 1997; and *Living Fire*, 2000). All of them have earned back their advances, and the last one has sold over 50,000 copies so far.

I am currently working on a novel and a nonfiction work, with three other projects outlined and waiting. I don't think I have been very effective at marketing my work and at vetting my contracts. In addition, I would rather write than tend to the business side of things. From my perspective, working with an agent seems like a good idea. From your perspective, I can only say that I seem to have a good many books in me yet and my track record so far is decent.

May I send you copies of my books and sample chapters from my current projects?

Enclosed is a SASE for your response.

Dear Mr. Havill,

My family and I have just spent two months on a small island with no human company but our own. The strange story of why we went there and what we did while we were there is one that I think would interest your readers.

Each one of us—48-year-old husband/father, 49-year-old wife/mother, and 17-, 15-, 12-, and 10-year-old children—had a highly individual reaction to the experience and left the island changed in small and large ways.

Would you like to see a 5,000-word article, "Islands Within Islands"?

Although I am an architect, I have had articles published in both professional journals and consumer magazines.

Enclosed is a SASE for your response.

> I didn't set out to become an unpublished writer,
> it just happened.
>
> —NORA BARTLETT

Dear Ms. Dakers,

As the curator and principal scientist at the Leys Marmot Living Museum, I am in a unique position to write about the little-known but fascinating marmot (some species of which are more familiarly known as woodchucks). Studying them has given me a sense of the uncharted boundaries between so-called human and animal behavior.

I think the readers of *Animal Life* would be interested in the daily routine of a yellow-bellied marmot family, from the moment they wake up in their single-family dwelling to the moment they signal whichever family member has been guarding the door that it's time to come in and go to bed.

I am thinking in terms of a 10,000-word article with several sidebars on the folklore of the marmot. I can supply high-quality color slides.

I'm enclosing a SASE for your reply and I look forward to hearing from you.

Dear Geoffrey Farrant,

I've been a season ticket-holder for the past three years and have thoroughly enjoyed your company's vitality, intelligence, and creativity.

I am also a playwright with a script that I think is particularly appropriate for your ensemble.

Would you be interested in seeing a three-act farce for a cast of 23 that leaves as much or as little room for actor interpretation as you like?

Mary McCarthy said, "Bureaucracy, the rule of no one, has become the modern form of despotism." What happens to love in a bureaucracy? to death? to friendship? to art? *One, Two, Three* turns on the unexpected, an unexpected development itself in the rigidly structured bureaucracy of a hospital where bureaucracy—although not always the human life it purportedly serves—depends on expecting the expected.

I'm enclosing a SASE for your response.

Dear Ms. Ryder,

I am a regular customer of Ryder Exercise Equipment, Inc. I am also the owner of three juice bars in the metropolitan area.

It occurred to me that a small line of take-home health foods and juices might be welcomed by your customers.

Enclosed are some articles on the growing popularity of juice bars and a summary of my own stores' financial health.

At this point, I am interested simply in exploring the possibilities of such an arrangement.

Would you like to discuss this sometime? Perhaps we could meet at my Mulcaster Avenue store, which is not far from you. I'd especially like to see what you think of our Apple-a-Day juice.

Sincerely,

Contrary to what many of you might imagine, a career in letters is not without its drawbacks—chief among them the unpleasant fact that one is frequently called upon to actually sit down and write.

—Fran Lebowitz

Dear Mr. Wyndham,

An alumnus of the University, Louis Soltyk, has recently been honored for his successful efforts in saving two neighbor children from a fire. In addition, last year his masonry company was named Small Business of the Year by the local business council. In his personal life, he and his wife, Anastasya Vasek, have four children, all adopted.

Would you be interested in a profile of Mr. Soltyk for the University alumni/alumnae magazine? I'd like to focus on his drive and energy—where do they come from? How does he see himself?

My articles and interviews have been published in local, state, and national publications (see attached list).

If you are interested, let me know word length and deadline.

Enclosed is a SASE for your response.

> The writer's way is rough and lonely, and who would choose it while there are vacancies in more gracious professions, such as, say, cleaning out ferryboats?
>
> —DOROTHY PARKER

RELATED TOPICS

Cover Letters

Reports

Requests

Sales

37

References and Recommendations

INTRODUCTION

It is a rare person who has never had to request or provide a letter of reference or recommendation.

A reference vouches for a person's general character; it lets a third party know that the person is a responsible, functioning member of society. A reference is primarily a report, a verification: "Yes, I know this person." A recommendation is more specific and focuses on the person's professional qualities. It is often written by someone who knows both the other parties (applicant on the one hand and prospective employer, college, club, awards committee on the other hand). A recommendation is an endorsement: "Yes, this person would be an excellent candidate for your program."

A letter of commendation, written to commend a person on an achievement, is a variant of a letter of appreciation with a touch of congratulations; see Appreciation and Congratulations.

To refuse to write a letter of recommendation, see Refusals. To request or provide credit references, see Credit. For additional assistance with that last important letter—the thank you—to those who have written references or recommendations for you, see Thank You.

> The only kind of support that means anything comes from those who believe in you to the hilt. The ones who go the whole hog. Let there be the slightest wavering, the slightest doubt, the slightest defection, and your would-be supporter turns into your worst enemy.
>
> —HENRY MILLER

DO

- Give the person's full name at the beginning of your reference or recommendation. (Later refer to the person as Ms., Mr., or Dr. plus the last name for the first reference in each paragraph and as "she" or "he" after that. Never use the first name alone.)

- State your connection with the person (former employer, teacher, supervisor, adviser, associate, neighbor, mentor) and be specific about the circumstances ("for five years").

- Focus on the person's character for a general letter of reference (trustworthiness, sense of responsibility, enthusiasm, tact). Focus on job experience and skills in a letter of recommendation (length of employment with you, special abilities and accomplishments, your sense of the person as a prospective employee). As much as possible, support your statements with facts or examples.

- Be brief. One page, or at most two, is sufficient to convey the general picture without repeating yourself, using unnecessary and fulsome phrases, or boring the other person.

- Close with a summary statement reaffirming your recommendation of or confidence in the person.

- Include your name, address, and phone number if you are not using letterhead stationery.

- Give the reference or recommendation to the subject of the letter, leaving the envelope unsealed so the person can read it if they wish. If you've been asked to mail your letter directly to a personnel office, scholarship committee, or other inquiring agency, it is of course sealed and sometimes also marked confidential. Applicants should be aware that closed letters are generally more persuasive than opened ones.

> It's never what you say, but how
> You make it sound sincere.
>
> —MARYA MANNES

DON'T

- Don't use the trite "To whom it may concern" if you can help it. A memo format is appropriate: "To/From/Date/Re." Or, give your letter a suitable heading such as "Introducing Geraldine Dabis," "Recommendation of Fabian Desert," "Letter of Reference for Agatha Calkin."

- Don't use too many superlatives, be too lavish in your praise, or attribute too many outstanding characteristics to the person when writing a letter of recommendation. It tends to undermine your credibility. It is better to focus on two or three qualities and give examples of them.

- Don't tell the prospective employer what to do ("I'd hire him in a minute if he were applying here"; "If I were you, I'd snap this one up"; "I can't think of anyone more deserving of this scholarship"). Most people resent being told their business. You supply the information; they make the decision.

- Don't send letters of recommendation along with your application letter or cover letter and résumé. Wait until they are requested.

> Everybody knows how to utter a complaint, but few can express a graceful compliment.
>
> —WILLIAM FEATHER

HELPFUL HINTS

- When asking someone to write a letter of reference or recommendation for you, give the person enough information to be able to emphasize what will be most helpful to you ("I am applying for a position as a claims examiner"). Allow time (two to three weeks) for the person to write the letter and enclose either a SASE for a return to you or a stamped envelope addressed to the person who is to receive the reference. Express your appreciation. A prospective employer asking someone to provide a reference for an applicant should state the type of employment being sought so that the letterwriter can relate the applicant's background to the position.

- If you can't write a positive letter of reference or recommendation, don't write one at all. You do your reputation no favor by providing a favorable or ambiguous recommendation for someone who doesn't deserve it. And if you state or infer anything negative about the person, you risk legal action (most employee records are accessible to employees so they will see what you've written). Many companies and personnel departments have a policy of either giving information only over the phone (thus, putting nothing in writing) or sending a form letter that acknowledges the person worked there and verifies the dates of employment. Such a form might add: "It is against our policy to discuss the performance of former employees." A survey by the National Association of Corporate and Professional Recruiters showed that nearly half of all companies contacted have such policies against giving references on current or former employees. And with good cause: defending a defamation suit before a jury can be very expensive, even if the company wins the suit. Although the employee has to prove that the statement in the recommendation was both false and made with malice, employers are unwilling to spend time and resources on court cases. Nearly a third of all libel cases are filed by workers who sue former employers about bad references.

- Letters of reference and recommendation are typed, while thank-you notes to those who have written letters for you are typed or handwritten. Recommendations of proposals or policy are typed on company letterhead stationery unless they are sent in-house, in which case a memo format is used.

- After thanking someone for writing you a recommendation or reference, share any news of your job search, membership application, or college admission efforts—or at least promise to let the person know what happens. Even if you don't get the position or choose not to take it, you will want to express your gratitude to the person for writing on your behalf.

- When recommending a service or product, relate your own experience with it, but refrain from giving a blanket endorsement. Provide a few disclaimers: "This is only my opinion, of course"; "You may want to see what others think"; "It may not work for everyone, but we liked it."

- When making a formal recommendation or proposal for a course of action, a policy change, or a decision, include: a subject line or first sentence stating what the letter is about; a summary of your recommendations; factual support for your recommendations; your offer to accept further negotiation, to engage in further research, or to submit additional information. If your recommendation is critical or negative, word it carefully. Point out the benefits along with the disadvantages, stating perhaps that you think the latter outweighs the former.

> The hardest thing is writing a recommendation for someone we know.
>
> —KIN HUBBARD

GETTING STARTED

You once offered to write a letter of reference for me if ever I needed one, and that time has arrived!

Working with you has meant a great deal to me and I'm wondering if I can give your name as a reference when I apply for my first "real" job.

I would be pleased to have you use my name as a reference.

I appreciate your willingness to write a letter of recommendation for me, and I hope that some of the details of our past association that I'm summarizing below will make the letter easier to write.

I am writing to recommend Kathleen Wantage—with the greatest enthusiasm and confidence—for your management internship.

I most highly recommend Morris Rosenberg as a concert violinist—and as a positive contribution to the esprit de corps of any orchestra.

Jack Mason was head of the accounting department at Wright-Sherwin's for seven years and I'm delighted to have the opportunity of telling you how pleased we were with his contributions to the firm.

Charles Mallard has applied to us for a position as a records clerk and has given us your name as a reference.

Catherine Bannister Paget is being considered for a position in our home furnishings store, and has given your name as a reference.

Jack Burden was one of the best journalists I ever worked with. We were all sorry when his wife's work necessitated a move to Pennsylvania.

In response to your letter of April 3, Archibald Carlyle was employed by us as legal counsel from January 3, 1997, to September 15, 1997.

Bernard William Chadwick worked as a sales representative for us from 1987 to 1998.

In response to your inquiry about Michael Condron, we were obliged to let him go because of our own financial difficulties—he was a superior scaler and riveter.

Brigid O'Shaughnessy left our employ for personal reasons; we were completely satisfied with her work.

In response to your request for information about Intercontinental Hydraulics, I can only tell you that we have had excellent dealings with them for the past fifteen years and have great hopes of doing the same for the next fifteen.

Shehaab Fakredeen has asked that I write a letter of recommendation based on the twelve years I was his immediate manager at Canobia Services, Inc.

I would like to recommend Jessica Lovell for membership in the Shore Club.

I'm grateful to you for writing the letter of recommendation for me—it must have been wonderful because I did get the job at Critchlow Pharmacy.

Although I am unable, because of company policy, to write you the recommendation you requested, I certainly wish you every success with your career.

My recommendations on the proposed motorcycle safety program are as follows.

May I recommend Marietta Cignolesi as one of next year's guest speakers? I've heard her presentation on cosmetology laws and she's both entertaining and informative.

> **It is usually in better taste to praise an isolated action or a production of genius, than a man's character as a whole.**
>
> —ELIZABETH WORDSWORTH

MODEL LETTERS

Dear Ms. Comparini,

I know Robert has already thanked you for writing him a letter of recommendation, but I would very much like to add my own thanks.

It was a beautifully written letter, and I am positively awed to think that you write a number of these letters for your college-bound seniors! Color me impressed. The one phrase, "elegant and courteous," was so apt. They say good writing is unpredictable beforehand and inevitable afterwards. In the same way, although I would never have thought of him in such terms, after reading your letter, I thought, "Of course." Because he is both. And you recognized this.

Thank you for being the sort of teacher we parents dream about having for our children.

Best wishes!

TO: Office of Admissions, Bloom Institute of Technology
RE: Martha Clifford, admissions candidate for Fall 1995
DATE: February 15, 1995
SUBJECT: Letter of recommendation

I am writing to recommend most strongly the admission of Martha Clifford to your institution.

I have known Martha Clifford for over ten years—as one of her teachers and as a neighbor—and I think she is particularly suited to the Bloom Institute of Technology for several reasons: (1) her record of academic fitness—which is known to you by her test scores, grades, and attendance at a demanding high school; (2) an uncommon maturity and a delightfully level temperament that allow her to move easily and steadily among people, tasks, and challenges; (3) a family background in which responsibility, achievement, and certain standards of behavior are expected and have so far been nicely lived out by Ms. Clifford and her siblings; (4) a very strong desire to attend Bloom Institute of Technology (we're still hearing about her visit there); and (5) a sharp focus on who she is, where she is going, and what she needs to do to get there.

My husband once taught an afterschool science class. I say "once" because he was so disheartened by the lack of curiosity about what—to my husband—were wonder-filled experiments that he never offered it again. Only Martha Clifford showed the excitement he was looking for.

I worked with Ms. Clifford for two years as part of an independent, small-group spiritual development program. The emphasis was on critical thinking, self-discipline, and taking responsibility for one's own spiritual development. She was a joy to have, both because she is a natural leader and nice "anchor" in a group and because, at an age when most young people are losing interest in religion, she was willing to work on the issues and make some decisions for herself. I was impressed with her inner-directedness and her calm approach to life and its ups and downs. For someone so hardworking and ambitious, she manages to live life very gently.

I find Martha Clifford highly intelligent, ambitious, level-headed, and, perhaps paradoxically, both well-rounded and focused.

Dear Dr. Dell,

I write in support of Nick Ratcliffe's application to your program. Mr. Ratcliffe was a student of mine in several writing classes at Roscoe Central College. He was always one of the top two or three in a group of highly talented writers. His short story, "Like Me, Love Me," is one of the best portrayals of young romance I have ever read. I suggested he submit it for publication and I believe it has been accepted by *The Eagle Review.*

I have recently received a copy of a research paper Mr. Ratcliffe wrote for another class here this semester, "What Is Like? What Is Love?" He has not lost his touch. The paper was powerful and mature, exactly the kind of writing that convinces me that he will do very well in graduate studies.

Mr. Ratcliffe is a pleasure to teach, and will, I believe, bring honor to those institutions that help educate him. I commend him to you most highly and without any reservations whatsoever.

Sincerely,

Dear Ms. Rawlins,

In regard to your request for a reference for Mark Frettleby, who is seeking employment as a driver with Hume Transportation: Mr. Frettleby worked as a clerk for us from May 15, 1998, to July 2, 1998. I believe he left our company due to an inability to get to and from work (his claustrophobia prevented his taking the bus), a transportation problem that developed concurrently with the loss of his driver's license after he was arrested for DWI in June 1998.

Dear Mom,

Because of the work Nora did for you last summer, I'm wondering if you could write a letter of recommendation for her. If you have time to write anything (a half-page or so), we have compiled a short list to help you get started:

Things to include about Nora (compliments of Nora and Matt):

Generally a determined person.
A pleasant disposition.
Loyal as hell.
Good company at the airport.
Very goal oriented.
Include something about the way she apartment-sat for Lizzy.
Maybe say something about the concerts at which you saw her playing her flute—
    being the best at what she does.
Cute as a button.
Has good table manners.
Very appreciative of people who write letters for her.

(We were a little pressed to figure out what you, her boyfriend's mother, might reasonably know about her.)

Love,

Matt

Letter of Reference for Nora Terry

I have known Nora Terry for three years. As a neighbor, friend of the family, and professional writer with connections to her high school, I am fairly knowledgeable about her character and abilities.

From other sources you will be made aware of her excellent academic record, musical activities, and work history. What I can testify to is that Ms. Terry is also a young woman of outstanding character: disciplined, hardworking, trustworthy, loyal, and responsible. She has high standards for herself and worthy longterm goals—and she works steadily and undramatically to maintain or meet them. Her family—she is one of five daughters—is warm, close, and supportive of each other.

Ms. Terry is ambitious and tenacious, determined to be the best at whatever she does (I particularly see this in her schoolwork, flute-playing, and afterschool jobs). When she sets out to do something, it gets done. She is also poised, personable, well-mannered, and surprisingly easygoing given her busy schedule. Relaxed and confident, she makes everything she does look very easy, when I am sure it must involve a great deal of hard work and self-discipline.

Twice in the past year Ms. Terry house-sat for one of my family for periods of one month each. This involved caring for animals, taking care of the mail and money matters (depositing checks, paying bills), responding to business phone calls, driving and being responsible for a brand-new car, and taking care of unexpected problems. It is very satisfying to have her take over because we know she will deal with anything that comes up.

The two things I appreciate most about Ms. Terry are that she can think (I sometimes feel very pessimistic about the level of thinking in this country) and that she is responsible. She seems to know choices have consequences and she apparently lives by a code of ethics that leads her to respect herself, others, and her environment. It is a very real pleasure knowing her.

Dear Professor Byfield,

Thank you for the wonderful and apparently persuasive recommendation you wrote for me. I've been accepted at the St. Ives School of Political Science. Yippie!

If I can ever show one of your students around campus, let me know. And if you are ever in the area, I could arrange for you to stay in one of their charming, nineteenth-century guest apartments.

Again, thank you for the recommendation. I'll send you my new address as soon as I know it. In the meantime, best wishes for a lovely spring.

Dear Ms. Wells,

The George Brumley Travel Agency has been booking all my flights and trips for the past 12 years. I give them an A+ for competence, courtesy, and quick action. I am enthusiastic about the staff there as they have saved me untold dollars, anxiety, delays, poor connections, and other travel horrors.

The only thing I can suggest is that you try them for a booking or two, and see if you agree with my opinion of them.

Happy traveling!

TO: Fred Urquhart
FROM: Mirren Gillespie
SUBJECT: Superconductivity program
DATE: February 3, 1999

I have been helping Meg Ashe on an informal basis with some of her work on potential high-temperature superconducting materials.

I understand that Ms. Ashe is experiencing some difficulty getting management support for her program. Given the enormous potential market for these materials and for products associated with these materials, I believe that her work is valuable in itself and perhaps especially appropriate for Walter Precision Metal Products. We have much expertise in sputtering and sol gel techniques and in handling webs and fibers. Ms. Ashe could enjoy a real competitive advantage here.

Ms. Ashe is the ideal person to coordinate such a program. She has been working on the project for over a year, long before the current discoveries. She knows and corresponds with the leading scientists in this field. I think it is a real tribute to her that she had the foresight to start such a program, and now that there is increased public and industry interest in superconductors, I believe Walter Precision Metal Products should increase its efforts in this area.

Dear Ms. Glyde,

You asked for a reference for Frederick Fairlie. I am the owner of an apartment building at 548 West Collins Street where Mr. Fairlie has been living for the past seven years. I can thus speak of him only in this rather narrow connection.

Mr. Fairlie maintains his apartment in top condition, often doing small repairs himself. In fact, I think of him as my "low-maintenance" tenant. I have never had a single complaint about him for any reason whatsoever in the seven years, nor has he ever been late with a rent payment. When I encounter him, he is invariably well-spoken and courteous. He strikes me as a responsible, stable, productive individual.

I hope this information is helpful.

Sincerely,

Marian Halcombe

Dear Glen,

You asked for my recommendation about the possible merger between Withershins Hydraulics and Dousterswivel Tool & Die, Inc. I know we're being pushed for a decision, but I am convinced we do not yet have enough information and that the time is not right for a move of this magnitude.

Can we take the question back to a session or two with all those involved?

> Praise is always pleasing, let it come from whom, or upon what account it will.
>
> —MICHEL EYQUEM DE MONTAIGNE

RELATED TOPICS

Appreciation

Clubs

Employment

Introductions

Requests

Résumés

Thank You

38

Refusals, Regrets, and Rejections

INTRODUCTION

When you have absolutely no interest in something and, in addition, have an iron-clad excuse to refuse involvement (being out of the country or out of money at the time, for example), letters of refusal, regret, and rejection are quickly and easily written. Otherwise, they can weigh heavily on your mind and be some of the most difficult letters you write.

To send regrets to a wedding invitation, see Weddings. To deny a credit request, see Credit.

> To know how to refuse is as important as to know how to consent.
>
> —Baltasar Gracián

DO

- Be clear in your own mind that you want to say "no"; any ambivalence will make it more difficult to write and may show up in your letter.

- Respond promptly. Most people who are asking for something or inviting you to an event need to know soon. By giving them your refusal early on, you allow them time to find other solutions or other invitees.

- Thank the person for the offer, request, invitation (which you describe or mention specifically) and, if appropriate, agree with the person that the cause is worthy, the proposal well thought-out, the résumé impressive, or the invitation appealing. Make some courteous remark before you arrive at your refusal.

- State your "no," expressing your regret at having to do so.

- If appropriate, give a short, uncomplicated reason for declining (long explanations tend to sound false). When possible, phrase it positively, in terms of what you are doing, not in terms of what you can't do. It is often better to give your excuse before giving your refusal; the reader is thus prepared and the disappointment at the "no" doesn't keep the person from "hearing" your reasons. Instead of saying, "We will not be able to have dinner with you on the 16th because we're going to be in Boston," say, "We're going to be in Boston from the 12th to the 18th, which means we won't, unfortunately, be able to have dinner with you on the 16th."

- Suggest alternative courses of action or other resources the person might try.

- Close with expressions of goodwill and a pleasant wish to be of more help next time, to see the person again, or for success with their project.

> The prompter the refusal, the less the disappointment.
>
> —Publilius Syrus

DON'T

- Don't leave any doubt in the other person's mind about your response; your "no" should be unambiguous.

- Don't feel obligated to justify every "no." One good reason for saying "no" is that you simply do not choose to do something. When you have a specific reason for saying no and want to name it, do so. However, the fact that someone else wants you to do something confers no obligation on you to defend your decision. People who become angry with you for saying no, who try to manipulate you, or who make you feel guilty are confusing requests with demands.

- Don't ever give reasons for a refusal based on an applicant's appearance, personality, or behavior. Even if you think it would help the person in interviews with other companies, you are better off leaving this kind of comment to someone else in the person's life.

- Don't lie. It is too easy to be caught, and you will be a lot more comfortable with yourself and with the other person the next time you meet if you ground your refusal in some version of the truth.

> If you would have the goodwill of all men, take heed that, when anything is asked of you, you don't refuse it point-blank, but answer in generalities.
>
> —FRANCESCO GUICCIARDINI

HELPFUL HINTS

- To decline a formal or informal business or social invitation, use the same format as the invitation itself. If it is handwritten, handwrite your reply. If business letter-head stationery is used, use business letterhead to reply. When the invitation is worded informally, your reply is also informal. When the invitation is formal, your reply uses the same words, layout, and style as the invitation. For example:

Owen and Mona Gareth
request the pleasure of
Olive Chancellor's and Basil Ransome's company
at a dinner-dance
on Saturday, the twenty-third of September
at eight o'clock
Poynton Colonial Inn

Olive Chancellor and Basil Ransome
decline with regret
the kind invitation of
Owen and Mona Gareth
to a dinner-dance
on Saturday, the twenty-third of September
at eight o'clock
Poynton Colonial Inn

If you wish to explain your reason for declining a formal invitation, you may send instead an informal response. Even informal regrets should repeat the date, time, and kind of invitation. When an invitation is issued in the name of more than one person, mention all of them in your refusal and mail it either to the person listed under the R.S.V.P. or to the first name given. Always express appreciation for being invited and, when appropriate, offer an alternate opportunity to see the other person.

- White House invitations include the phone number of the Social Office where you may telephone your regret and where you can ask questions about protocol, where to park your car, what to wear, or how to respond in writing to the invitation. General guidelines are: send your regrets within a day of receiving the invitation; write the reply yourself (do not have an assistant do it) on plain or engraved personal stationery; use the same format and person (first or third person). Specify the reason you are unable to attend (there are only four generally accepted excuses for not accepting a White House invitation: a death in the family, a family wedding, prior travel plans, illness) by saying, "We regret that owing to the recent death of . . . "

- If your organization or government agency has specific procedures for handling bids, notify bidders of your requirements as soon as possible. In rejecting bids, be courteous and supportive, and, when possible, explain briefly why the bid was rejected (especially if it concerned failure to follow directives or to stay within certain guidelines) or why the winning bid was accepted. Information like this is useful to contractors. Close with an expression of appreciation to the bidder and a reference to the possibility of doing business at a later date. You do not need to name the winning bidder or defend your choice.

- Business letters of refusal are typed on letterhead stationery. Personal letters of refusal are most often handwritten. Form letters are used to reject manuscripts, to state that a company is not currently accepting any applications, or to make any other numerous and routine refusals.

- When turning down a request for a raise or a promotion, your letter should (1) show appreciation for the employee's contributions, listing specific talents and strengths; (2) explain why the raise or promotion must be denied; (3) offer suggestions on how or when the raise or promotion might be expected or earned or, if the raise or promotion depends on external factors (budget shortfalls), what changes might affect future considerations. The goal is to offer encouragement and recognition of the person's contributions.

- When rejecting a proposal, manuscript, or other material submitted on speculation, be tactful and complimentary enough not to leave the other person feeling hopeless about their work. You may not want to encourage the individual to apply to you again, but you can state that what is not appropriate for you may be appropriate for another company or publishing house. Assure the person that you have carefully considered their work, thank them for thinking of you, and wish them success in future endeavors.

> Your manuscript is both good and original; but the part that is good is not original, and the part that is original is not good.
>
> —SAMUEL JOHNSON

- Canceling an account, appointment, meeting, order, reservation, service, or social event is handled like a combination refusal and apology: mention the event, date and time; apologize for having to cancel; give a simple excuse for your cancellation; and, for social events, close with your hope that the event goes well, that you will see the person soon, that you will be able to attend the next event.

- If you need to return a gift (your company does not permit accepting them from clients or suppliers, for example, or it is too expensive a gift for you to accept comfortably), thank the person graciously for the thought and choice of gift and assure them you will always remember their kindness, but state firmly that you are obliged to return the gift. Word your refusal so that it does not imply the person was guilty of poor taste or judgment in offering the gift.

- When terminating a business relationship, friendship, or dating relationship, aim for a no-fault "divorce": don't blame the other person or bring up past grievances. Help the other person save face by implying that this is what they want too and by taking responsibility for the separation on yourself. Be as honest as is consistent with tact and kindness. Above all, be brief and unequivocal; over-explaining or "keeping your options open" can be fatal if you sincerely want to end the relationship. Conclude with an encouraging, complimentary remark.

- Sometimes people are extremely persistent about wanting your company, your time, or something from you. When refusing their requests, your note should be unequivocal (the moment you waffle, they are back in the door), firm, and simple. It is best to give no explanation for your refusal ("I am sorry but I will not be able to" is sufficient). The moment you say why you are refusing such a request ("I'm very busy just now"), there will be an immediate response ("It will only take a minute"). When you offer another reason, there will be another rebuttal. Engaging you in wearying debate is part of the strategy; you wouldn't be the first person to say "yes" just to avoid being harangued. "I'm sorry, but no" is most effective.

> Remember that in giving any reason at all for refusing, you lay some foundation for a future request.
>
> —ARTHUR HELPS

- There is no obligation to send a refusal to a mass-produced fundraising appeal. When, however, you receive a personal letter with first-class postage, written over the signature of someone known to you, you may want to respond. Compliment the person on the work the organization is doing, give a plausible excuse for not contributing, and wish them well. You are not obliged to give any more detail than you choose; a vague statement that you are currently overcommitted elsewhere is acceptable. If you are sincere about it, you might mention the possibility of giving at some other time. If you are refusing because you disagree with the organization's goals or policies, you might say so.

- Occasionally, the way you turn down an applicant, proposal, bid, or other business matter can lead to legal problems. If you have any concerns, get expert legal counsel before writing your letter.

> Several excuses are always less convincing than one.
>
> —ALDOUS HUXLEY

GETTING STARTED

We have carefully considered your letter of June 5, but we are not interested in changing suppliers at this time.

I wish I could say yes, but I have already committed myself to contributing to similar organizations.

I know how difficult it was for you to ask for a raise; please believe it is almost as difficult to tell you that it is simply not possible at this time.

I'm certainly sympathetic to your request, but I am unfortunately not in a position to lend anyone anything at this time.

I've talked to both production and shipping and they see no way of moving up your delivery date by two weeks.

Although "Love in the Place Dauphine" isn't quite right for our issue on Paris, we thank you for letting us see it and ask that you send along anything else you've done.

We were impressed with the investment opportunity you offered us, but it is not possible for us just now.

We appreciate your suggesting the workshop to us, and hope that we will have the opportunity of saying "yes" some other time.

There was insufficient enrollment for your community education class on beginning contract bridge so we will need to cancel it for the fall session.

I am grateful for your invitation to join the Discovery Club, but my present schedule doesn't permit taking on anything new.

We are unable to furnish you with the information you requested—have you considered contacting Llewellyn Interplastics?

We have now had a chance to review your indexing software, but must decline to take it on at the present time.

Mr. and Mrs. Maxim de Winter regret that because of a previous engagement they are unable to accept the kind invitation of Mr. and Mrs. Jack Fevell for Saturday, the sixteenth of November, at 8:00 p.m.

Thank you for your kind and complimentary letter asking me to contract for the operation of the Student Services Center, but I must regretfully say no.

Publicity is not one of my talents—is there anything else I could do for the organization?

Because of your short employment history, we are unable to extend credit to you at the present time. Please contact us again in six months.

The last time I lent my grandmother's beautiful punch bowl and cups, some of the cups didn't make it home again, and I resolved never to lend the set again—I'm sorry.

We are sorry to inform you that we have filled the position of traffic manager system integrator for which you recently applied.

Thank you for your letter inquiring about job openings at Tancred, Inc. Unfortunately we have nothing at the moment.

The rent on your apartment at 131 Park Drive is consistent with area rates and with the excellent condition of the building; we are unable to lower your rent.

Much as I'd like to, I'm unable to give you the letter of recommendation you requested. Company policy doesn't allow us to furnish such letters for former employees.

Please accept my sincere regrets at having to say "no" to your request to use my name in your fundraising literature.

I would normally be delighted to support Evans Youth and Family Services with a contribution, but I'm unfortunately overcommitted at this time.

Your printer stand does not, unfortunately, qualify for free replacement as the warranty expired over a year ago.

Although the idea is appealing in many respects, I must decline to serve as chair of the speakers' bureau.

We appreciate your interest in obtaining a franchise, but because of ongoing commitments, we are not offering any new contracts.

Although all of us very much liked your silk ribbon embroidery kits, they do not fit in with our other catalog items. I feel sure that you will be able to place them elsewhere.

We enjoyed your entertaining and informative sales presentation last week, but we have decided that this type of workshop is not a priority for us just now.

> You start by saying no to requests. Then if you have to go to yes, OK. But if you start with yes, you can't go to no.
>
> —MILDRED PERLMAN

MODEL LETTERS

Dear J.T. Bullard,

We thank you for your interest in Marquand Advertising, Inc., and for the time you spent interviewing with us.

We have carefully considered your qualifications and work history. While we are impressed with your accomplishments, we preferred that the candidate for this position have more experience in space sales than you have had, and we have offered the position to someone with over ten years' experience in that area.

We very much liked your energy and credentials, and we wish you continued success in your professional life.

Dear Contributor,

Thank you for submitting your work to us, which has been carefully considered by our staff. I regret to report that it does not fit into our current publishing plans.

We receive too many submissions to allow us to respond individually, to comment on your work in detail, or to suggest other appropriate markets—much as we'd like to.

We wish you success in placing your work elsewhere and ask that you remember us the next time you have something you think we'd like.

> What I have always felt about rejection slips is that their glamour soon wears off.
>
> —P.G. WODEHOUSE

Dear Terence,

I wish I could say "yes" to your request to keep Fraser for you while you're overseas for the next six months.

You're right: I love cats. And you're right: I asked how I could help, and I meant it. However, I didn't realize that Fraser is incontinent because of the steroid shots he gets for his chronic mange. I just had new carpeting put in on the first floor—after waiting years to reach this nice period of life between children and grandchildren.

Can I do anything else to help while you're away?

Dear Burton,

Thanks for your letter asking if I'd be able to transform the old grain elevator on your property into a guest house. Design ideas (circular staircases, retractable sleeping bunks, etc.) are popping into my head already, but unfortunately I cannot take the time to do even an estimate right now because I'm so booked up.

I appreciate all the work you've sent my way these past five years and I remain committed to helping you bring your innovative and fun ideas to fruition whenever I'm available.

If your grain elevator project could wait until next February or March, I'd place it at the top of my Redesign Unlimited's waiting list.

Sincerely,

Dear Facey Romford,

Your request to rezone the house at 1865 Surtees Avenue from residential (RM-2) to business (B2-C) use was unanimously rejected by the City Planning Commission on February 3.

The rezoning was judged to be inconsistent with local land-use plans. It would also have represented spot rezoning, which the City Planning Commission has historically and routinely opposed.

If you have questions about the process or about your options at this point, you may contact any of the City Planning commissioners.

Sincerely,

Dear Parry,

I was flattered to be invited to join your jazz trio as percussionist. I've heard you play several gigs and think we could have worked well together. However, because of commitments I've already made, I can't fit anything else into my schedule for at least the next 15-18 months.

Thanks again for asking. I feel sure you'll find just the right person.

Dear Ms. Crisson,

I apologize if I have not been clear enough about my absolute lack of interest in selling any items in my Occupied Japan collection.

I am flattered by your persistent attention and impressed by the escalating prices you are offering. I am also sympathetic to the fact that several of my Art Deco dancer figurines would complete your set very nicely and ditto for some of my salt-and-pepper sets. However, I have no intention of selling. I've promised my collection to my daughter after my death, and I always keep my promises, so there is no chance that I would change my mind.

I wonder if you might not find some of the pieces you need at the huge yearly antique sale in Dayton. It's a bit of a drive, but it might be worth it to you.

Best wishes!

> **Never explain. Your friends do not need it and your enemies will not believe you anyway.**
>
> —ELBERT HUBBARD

Dear Anna and Henry,

It's true we won't be using the lake cabin the week of July 11-17 because we'll be out East for Charlie's wedding. However, we are unable to make it available to you for your family reunion. Multiple considerations—from insurance to neighbors to inconvenience to some earlier unfortunate loans—have obliged us to adopt a non-negotiable policy of not lending the cabin.

I hope you understand.

Dear Clare,

Your request for a transfer to the Manufacturing Operations Department has been carefully considered. We are sympathetic to your reasons for asking for the transfer and we hope to find a way of accommodating you in the future.

For the moment, however, you are irreplaceable where you are. In addition, the MO Department is in the process of downsizing so there is little likelihood that it would take on anyone else at this point.

I wish the answer could have been "yes." . . .

Dear Mr. Stane,

I've received your request asking me to write a letter of recommendation for you.

I think you would be better served by obtaining a letter from someone who knew you better or who worked more closely with you than I.

I'm sorry I can't help.

Dear Marjorie,

Exciting news! I'm so happy for you! I hope you and Peter have a romantic, memorable engagement period followed by one of the all-time great marriages.

I am touched that you asked me to be your wedding attendant. When we were eleven, didn't we always talk about being in each other's weddings?

I hope our friendship can withstand the fact that I need to say "I can't." There are several reasons—all complicated and personal, none to do with you—that make me unable to accept. Six months ago things would have been different—or perhaps two years from now.

I know we've been out of touch for a while and I will write a long letter bringing you up to date when I can. For the moment, I wanted to let you know my decision right away so that you could make other arrangements.

Still your friend,

> Better a friendly denial than unwilling compliance.
>
> —GERMAN PROVERB

RELATED TOPICS

Credit

Responses

Sensitive

39

Reports, Proposals, and Contracts

INTRODUCTION

Although long proposals, elaborate reports, and legal contracts do not qualify as letters, a letter or memo is often used for shorter, more informal versions of them.

Reports, which can be formal or informal, include progress or status reports; monthly or annual sales or other reports; management, staff, policy, or recommendation reports; technical, statistical, or investigative reports; compliance reports to government agencies; even reports on reports, which are preliminary reports sent in advance of a more detailed study that include the abstract or summary from the longer report.

Proposals can be solicited (someone asks you for an estimate, bid, plan of action) or unsolicited (you want to sell your plan or service or program to someone who has not expressed a specific need for it). In either case, your proposal is a sales tool by which you persuade the other party that you are the best firm for the job (for a solicited proposal) or that it needs the service you are offering (for an unsolicited proposal).

To write a letter proposing an article or book for submission, see Queries. To write a letter turning down the recommendations in a report or proposal or declining a contract, see Refusals. For information on credit reports, see Credit.

> Reports in matters of this world are many, and our resources of mind for the discrimination of them very insufficient.
>
> —John Henry Cardinal Newman

DO

- Begin with a subject line or memo format that concisely identifies the subject of the proposal, report, or contract.

- Give a reason for your letter: you are responding to a solicitation for bids or an estimate or to a request for a report; you are submitting an invited book proposal or an annual or quarterly report; you are outlining the terms of an agreement that has been previously discussed, and this will serve as a contract.

- The main body of the proposal, report, or contract can be as short as a paragraph or long enough to be divided into one or more of the traditional report elements: title page; summary, synopsis, or abstract; a foreword, preface, introduction, history, or background; acknowledgments; table of contents; a presentation of data, options, conclusions, and recommendations; appendix, bibliography, endnotes, references, and notice of any attached supporting documents. When appropriate include costs, specifications, and deadlines.

- Organize the main body of your letter into clear, accessible, logical units of information.

- Credit those who worked on the report or proposal, if appropriate.

- Offer to supply additional information or give the name and telephone number of a contact person.

- Close by telling what action you expect of the person: sign a copy of the contract, respond to the proposal, copy the report to interested others, telephone you, set up a meeting, vote.

- Before mailing the proposal, report, or contract, have someone knowledgeable about the issues or, in some cases, a lawyer read it for clarity and precision. Double-check a proposal to be certain that every item in the original request has been responded to.

> Proposals are a basic part of the way we do business, and a successful proposal can mean money for you or your organization.
>
> —WILLIAM C. PAXSON

DON'T

- Don't include anything that doesn't bear on the main issue; reports, proposals, and contracts are very focused documents.
- Don't use jargon unless you know it is familiar to your readers.
- Don't use legalese to make a contract sound more legal (unless you are a lawyer). It is better to use simple, standard English so that both parties are clear about what is involved.

> Jargon often takes on a life of its own. It degenerates into a private code that is used, not to elucidate and inform, but to define the culture of a particular group and to exclude the uninitiated from the inner circle.
>
> —STEPHEN WILBERS

HELPFUL HINTS

- When preparing a report or proposal, first be certain you know the answers to these four questions: Who will read the document? What is its purpose? What material will it cover? How will the material be presented?
- If it appears that your proposal will be acceptable to the other party, a proposal letter can be turned into a contract letter or binding agreement by adding at the bottom, "Approved by [signature] on [date] by [printed name and title]."
- When writing grant proposals for funding from government or private sources, three guidelines will boost your chances of success: (1) follow directions scrupulously—no allowances are made for deviations from stated formats; (2) the physical presentation of your material must be faultless—clear, readable typeface,

heavyweight paper, generous margins, and no spelling, punctuation, grammar, or style errors; (3) the content must be high quality and slanted specifically to that funding organization—the identical material can seldom be proposed to two different groups. Artist resource groups offer help to grant applicants, and sometimes people in your field will critique your material.

- If you can't respond within a few days to a proposal or report, acknowledge its receipt and tell the sender that you will respond as soon as you have evaluated it. People who have spent time writing a report or proposal are eager for a response, and will be more accepting of a delay if their letter has been acknowledged.

- When writing a letter that will serve as an informal contract: give full names and addresses of both parties to the agreement; state what each party will give and receive; give dates by which the agreement must be agreed to or carried out; state whether and under what conditions it may be broken or canceled. Whether you need an attorney to check such letters depends on the complexity of the contract and the possible outcomes if it is poorly written.

- Until they have been standardized and been proven by years of effective use, some reports and proposals should be examined by your lawyer for any potential problems.

- If timing is important to your agreement, contract, or the cancellation of either, send your letter return receipt requested so that you can verify the date that the letter was received. If your lease requires you to give thirty days' notice, you will be glad to have a receipt stating that the notice was received within the time limit.

- Letters serving as reports, proposals, or contracts are typewritten on letterhead or memo stationery. Forms with blanks to be filled in are convenient for credit reports, school progress reports, weekly production reports, and other reports that depend on numbers or short descriptions.

> A writer's first duty is to be clear. Clarity is an excellent virtue. Like all virtues it can be pursued at ruinous cost. Paid, so far as I am concerned, joyfully.
>
> —STORM JAMESON

GETTING STARTED

I am pleased to send you our quarterly production report.

This report summarizes the proposed changes to the staffing of the conservatory.

This report lists and analyzes in-line skating injuries in the United States during the past three years.

Subject: proposed changes in our service contracts.

Attached please find a 65-page proposal recommending the acquisition of the Barclay Telecommunications Corp.

This letter will serve as a contract between Madge Allen and Cain & Sons for sheetrock and plaster repairs to the property at 35 James Court, with the following conditions and specifications.

Your proposal for a book on Feng Shui is very interesting to us, but several other people will need to read and evaluate it before we present it at our weekly acquisition meeting.

Re: Analysis of average annual total returns for the period ending December 31, 2000.

The enclosed forward currency contract constitutes an agreement to deliver or receive a present stated amount of currency at a future specified date.

I am pleased to provide this financial report on Evanturel Express, Inc., for the year 1999, a year of continuing record growth made possible by a responsive public and our energetic and competent staff.

Our annual report on pollution in the United States reveals both good news and bad news.

East Side Neighborhood Service, Inc., has developed a proposal to make our streets safer and cleaner.

Thank you for giving us the opportunity to review your firm's proposal to construct a deck, patio, and rock garden for us—the 3-D computer-generated layout was very helpful in picturing the end result.

Enclosed is a check for $500, which will serve as earnest money for apartment # 37 in the 131 Park Drive building.

Clause 3a requests the manuscript be submitted on June 1, 1999; I would prefer this to read "August 1, 1999."

Paragraph N in your contract is irrelevant; please delete it.

This letter will serve as an informal agreement between us covering the period from January 1, 1999, to December 31, 1999, for the following services.

True eloquence consists in saying all that is necessary, and nothing but what is necessary.

—LA ROCHEFOUCAULD

MODEL LETTERS

TO: Residents
FROM: Community Council
DATE: April 3, 1996
SUBJECT: Environmental Impact Statement (EIS)

The city administration was given an estimate on an EIS on the proposed changes to Zametor Road of from $600,000 to $1,000,000. We are not sure why the EIS costs this much as similar projects have been done in the $100,000 range. The Capital Improvement Budget Committee recommended a funding level this biennium of $250,000. We will keep you posted on this issue.

Proposal
Marryat Insulation Systems, Inc.
54 Easthupp Boulevard
Frederick, IA 50501

Proposed work:

- Install fiberglass under boards in 900-sq.-ft. attic area of two-story house.
- Remove and replace necessary boards.
- Install wind tunnels.
- Install 2 R-61 roof vents.
- Install fiberglass in sidewalls, approx. 2,000 sq. ft.
- Drill siding and redwood plug, chisel and putty; owner to sand and paint.
- Remove and replace siding, drill above second-floor windows only.
- Install 4 8"x16" soffit vents, 2 front, 2 rear.

We propose hereby to furnish material and labor—complete in accordance with above specifications—for the sum of cash on completion, $2,307.

All material is guaranteed to be as specified. All work is to be completed according to standard practices. Any alteration or deviation from the above specifications involving extra costs will be executed only upon written orders, and will become an extra charge over and above the estimate. All agreements are contingent upon strikes, accidents, or delays beyond our control. Owner to carry fire, tornado, and other necessary insurance. Our work is fully covered by Worker's Compensation Insurance.

Note: This proposal may be withdrawn by us if not accepted within 10 days.

Date: May 3, 1999
Authorized signature: F. Marryat

Acceptance of proposal: The above prices, specifications, and conditions are satisfactory and are hereby accepted. You are authorized to do the work as specified. Payment will be made upon completion.

Date of acceptance: May 6, 1999
Signature: Jack Easy

Dear Donna Lucia D'Alvadorez,

As required by our lease, we hereby give you sixty days' notice of our intention to move from Apartment 14 at 1892 Brandon Boulevard.

If you need to show the apartment, please call after 6:00 the evening before you plan to come by.

As we have not damaged the apartment in any way during our tenancy, we will look forward to receiving our rent deposit of $695.

We have enjoyed our four years here very much, and will be sorry to move.

Sincerely yours,

To: Marketing Department
From: Katherine Carr
Date: August 15, 2000
Re: Report on recent drop in sales

This memo report will serve as a summary of the attached 12-page in-depth report on what I think are the mechanisms and underlying causes of the recent nationwide drop in sales at our restaurant equipment and supply outlets.

Based on these ideas, I'm planning a few experimental modifications to our outlets in Del Mar and San Diego. If you have any opinions on these ideas (especially if you disagree), I would appreciate hearing from you.

The driving forces for sales to restaurants are of course need, immediate availability, accessibility, and price. We have isolated price as the critical factor in the recent downturn. Although our prices are in fact competitive with other suppliers, our prices do not *appear* to be competitive.

The report details the three potential ways of dealing with the perception that we are more expensive than our competitors. Please reflect, both individually and in groups, on our choices.

I will let you know the results of the planned changes in Del Mar and San Diego. In the meantime, I would appreciate getting as much feedback as possible (and as quickly as possible) on the attached report.

TO: Beatrice di Santangiolo
FROM: Peter Marchdale
DATE: June 6
SUBJECT: Buy or rent air compressor?

I've looked into this and it seems far more cost-effective in the long run and convenient for us in the short run to buy a small portable air compressor rather than to rent one as needed. A study of our use of an air compressor essentially redefined the term "infrequent." What may seem infrequent can be effectively "frequent" when we add up the rental charges and lost productive time in not having one immediately available. I suggest buying.

> It may be said of me by Harper & Brothers, that although I reject their proposals, I welcome their advances.
>
> —EDNA ST. VINCENT MILLAY

To: Lalla Rookh
From: Thomas Moore
Date: July 8, 2000
Re: store absenteeism

You asked for a breakdown by store on absenteeism for the past month. Figures are given as a percentage of total expected workdays for all store employees.

June 1 - June 30, 2000:
St. Paul: 4%
West St. Paul: 0%
Minneapolis: 6%
White Bear Lake: 3%
New Hope: 0%
Richfield: 8%
St. Louis Park: 2%
Edina: 0%
Burnsville: 1%

To: Edward Shinza
From: Olivia Bray
Date: January 3
Subject: Library fundraiser

To update you on the fundraiser, the following has been done:

The reception hall has been reserved.
Suggested guest speakers have been invited (no responses yet).
Three caterers are submitting bids.

You will have a draft of the invitation and a guest list by next Monday.

To: Members of the Humphrey Hills Orienteering Club
From: Elisa Minden
Date: Sept. 30
Subject: Mini-Goat Event

If we do say so ourselves, the Mini-Goat was a success. We had twice the number of entrants we had last year (52 compared to 25). Because of that, the modest $3 per person entry fee was enough to keep us in the black on this event. Mini-Goat T-shirts were donated by Orford Sports. We heard from many entrants that the event was a bargain: an afternoon of fun (although non-orienteering friends and family persist in questioning that what we do is "fun"!) AND a free T-shirt for only $3. It was the first orienteering event for many of the entrants. We think the allure of this sport is spreading by word of mouth, and we expect the local Club to keep growing, much as the U.S. Orienteering Federation has.

Note: the next event will be held Oct. 10 at Bowen State Park.

Dear Mr. Golspie,

This letter will serve as an informal agreement between us.

On Feb. 7 from 4:00-5:00 p.m. you agree to provide entertainers for my daughter's birthday party consisting of 1 clown, 1 magician, and 1 facepainter. I understand that the clown and magician portion of the entertainment will last about 20 minutes, and the face painter will remain for the rest of the hour.

I agree to pay you a $50 deposit (check enclosed) and the remaining $200 on Feb. 7. As requested a room will be available for your use. Also enclosed is a detailed map with directions to our home.

We're all looking forward to this, adults as well as children!

C. Dagenham
1956 Macaulay Boulevard
Trebizond, MD 21673
301/555-1234

BOOK PROPOSAL

TYPE OF BOOK: Comprehensive reference work of quotations by women throughout history. The broadest, most complete collection of women's quotations in print, it would be similar to collections that have consisted primarily of quotations by men.

POTENTIAL MARKETS: Libraries, writers, speakers, educators, women's groups, individuals, newspaper and newsletter publishers.

FORMAT: 500-800 pages, with my preference being for the longer length. Hardbound edition to be followed by a softbound edition approximately two years later.

SPECIAL FEATURES: A User's Guide explains why certain quotations containing sexist language (the use of the pseudogeneric "he," for example) are included, with suggestions on how to make use of some of these excellent quotations while deleting, replacing, adapting, or rephrasing their sexist elements.

PROPOSED COMPLETION DATE OF MANUSCRIPT: September 1, 1990.

RATIONALE AND DESCRIPTION OF THE BOOK: A study of the list of similar books both in and out of print today (Attachment 1) indicates that there is room for a definitive and comprehensive book of women's quotations, arranged topically rather than chronologically or alphabetically by name. I would like this comprehensive reference work to be useful to people in everyday situations. Both browsers and people searching for specific quotations would be served by categorizing by topics, within which the quotations would be arranged in essay-like form. I expect to have quotations by women on every conceivable popular topic (those generally covered by traditional quotation books). See Attachment 2: Topical Index. Another axis would be the sources themselves: I would include most of those women who are perceived to have contributed to life and society in some way. See Attachment 3: Biographical Index.

MARKETING: Direct-mail marketing of both the hardbound and softbound editions plus a strong trade marketing push could establish this reference as a classic. It should be marketed in all English-speaking countries, as quotations from British, Australian, Irish, Welsh, Canadian, and other English-speaking countries are included.

> I dearly love to persuade people. There can hardly be a greater pleasure (of a selfish kind) than to feel you have brought another person around to your way of thinking.
>
> —James Hinton

RELATED TOPICS

Cover Letters

Memos

References

Refusals

Sales

40

Requests

INTRODUCTION

Many business and social letters are fundamentally letters of request. General requests (or inquiries) are discussed in this chapter. Specific types of requests are discussed elsewhere: to request information, see Information; to request an interview for a position, see Applications; to request an adjustment, see Complaints; to request donations, see Fundraising; to request forgiveness, see Apologies; to request advice, see Advice; to request a publisher consider a manuscript, see Queries; to request credit information or to request a loan, see Credit; to request a reservation, see Travel; to request a lawmaker to support or vote for your position, see Public Officials.

Most commonplace requests (to change a life insurance beneficiary, to claim insurance benefits, to apply for a VA loan, to purchase a home, for federal employment) are initiated by a phone call and completed with the appropriate forms. Only in the case of disputes or problems are letters required.

For information on answering a request, see Responses.

> The way a question is asked limits and disposes the ways in which any answer to it—right or wrong—may be given.
>
> —Susanne K. Langer

DO

- State specifically what you are requesting of the other person. This first sentence should leave the other person in no doubt as to what you're writing about.

- Explain briefly why you are making the request (if appropriate). Long explanations are rarely required. In most cases you are more likely to have your request answered if your letter is short and to the point.

- Give any details that will help the person send you exactly what you want (reference numbers, dates, descriptions, titles).

- Explain why your reader might be willing to respond to your request. In an indirect way, get the person to understand how helping you will be personally beneficial. It may even be appropriate to offer a reciprocal favor or to offer something in return.

- Tell the recipient where to send the materials or where to telephone with a response (if your stationery does not show this information).

- Specify the date by which you expect or need a response.

- Restate your request if your letter is a long one.

- Express your thanks or appreciation for the other person's time and attention and close with a confident statement that the other person will respond positively.

- Enclose a self-addressed stamped envelope, if appropriate. When the other person is doing you a favor, and one of you must bear the cost of postage, materials, or other assistance, it is, of course, you who should offer to pay.

> Know how to ask. There is nothing more difficult for some people, nor, for others, easier.
>
> —BALTASAR GRACIÁN

DON'T

- Don't use apologetic phrases such as "I'm sorry to bother you," "I hope you don't mind," "I hope this isn't asking too much of you," or "I hope this isn't an inconvenient time to approach you." Indicate in passing your respect for the other person's time, talents, and resources ("I know how busy you are") but don't dwell on the negative. Everyone has requests, and the more matter-of-fact and courteous you are, the better your chances of getting a positive reply.

> To be happy with human beings, we should not ask them for what they cannot give.
>
> —TRISTAN BERNARD

HELPFUL HINTS

- A one- or two-line request for routine materials does not require a salutation. Begin with a subject line so that the other person immediately has key words telling what you need (Subject: airbag safety information; Re: mountaineering and ice climbing expeditions in North America; Subject: recipes using cranberries; Re: job placement assistance).

- Make it easy for the other person to respond to you: enclose a self-addressed stamped envelope, a survey or questionnaire with a postage-paid envelope, or a postage-paid postcard printed with a message and fill-in blanks; leave space under each question on your letter so the person can jot down replies and return it in the accompanying self-addressed stamped envelope.

- Business requests that go outside the company are typed, usually on letterhead stationery. Memo paper is used for brief, casual, routine, or in-house requests. Personal requests may be typed or handwritten, but the more personal the request (advice, favors), the more appropriate it is to handwrite the note. Postcards are useful for one-line requests, and if you make the same type of request repeatedly, you may want to design a printed form letter or memo with a blank space that allows you to fill in the title of the article, type of material, or sample you're requesting.

- When requesting someone to be a guest speaker, give the following information: your organization's name; date, time, and place of the event, with directions or a map, if necessary; desired length and subject of the talk; the reason or focus for the event; a description of the group's interests and backgrounds so the speaker has some sense of the audience; an estimate of the size of the audience; your expectations of when the speaker would arrive and depart; whether you are paying a fee and the speaker's travel expenses and lodging; what equipment (microphone, overhead projector) is available; the name and phone number of a contact person (if this is not you) who can give the speaker additional information.

- Your letter requesting a zoning change will become part of public record, so verify all facts, property descriptions, and current zoning regulations. State your reasons for requesting the change, modification, or variance. Include information showing that, first, a zoning change will not harm the environs and, second, that there are potential benefits to the change. Attach statements from neighbors, petitions, assessments, and any other documents that bear on the issue.

- Several letterwriting authorities advise against ending a letter of request with "thank you" or "thanking you in advance" (because these expressions seem to signal an end to the exchange), but both have become common and acceptable in current usage. More expectant of future action are phrases such as "I appreciate your time and attention" or "I look forward to hearing from you."

- When writing to ask if an unacknowledged gift was received, describe the item, tell when you sent it, and offer a face-saving "out" for the person ("I know you are especially busy just now"). You could say you are inquiring because you insured the package and if it did not arrive, you want to follow up on it, or that you are wondering if you should put a "stop" order on the check. You don't have to give a reason for your inquiry, but doing so is more tactful.

- When you request your physician to release your medical records to another physician, to a hospital, or to an insurance company, write: "Dear Dr. [name], I hereby authorize you to release my medical file to [name of recipient]. I would appreciate this being done as soon as possible. Thank you."

- When requesting permission to reprint copyrighted material, make it easy to say "yes." Include two copies of either a special form or your letter so that the person can sign and date them and return one to you. Include a self-addressed stamped envelope. State precisely what you want to use (title of book or article, page numbers, line or paragraph numbers, first and last phrases of the excerpted material). Tell how you plan to use the material (the name of your book or article, approximate publication date, publisher, price, expected number of copies, and anything else that might reflect the anticipated audience and distribution). Ask for approval of the credit or permission line you will use. Express your appreciation for considering the permissions request and your admiration for the person's work.

- When requesting estimates, bids, or price quotes, be specific: quantities, deadlines (for bid and for completion of work); special requirements; types, model numbers, colors; a list of everything you expect to be included in the total. To ensure that you include all considerations, use the contract that you plan to offer as a model for your bid-request letter.

- When requesting reservations for facilities for conferences, meetings, sales presentations, and other business activities, begin your inquiries with a telephone call to determine rates, date availability, and description of facilities. When writing to confirm your arrangements include: time, date, number of expected attendees, required equipment and supplies, refreshment arrangements, billing information, name of contact person in your organization (if not you), and any other agreed-upon items.

> There are many ways of asking a favor; but to assume that you are granting the favor that you ask shows spirit and invention.
>
> —AGNES REPPLIER

GETTING STARTED

I have a favor to ask you, but I take "no" very well!

Would you please send an official transcript to the following name and address?

Your name has been suggested as someone who would make a wonderful mentor for our award-winning mentorship program, Partners.

Could you please give us an estimate for a cement driveway repair job with the following specifications by July 15?

I am being lent to our base in Greece for three months, and I would like permission to sublease my apartment for that period to a responsible colleague, Lt. Robert Hearn.

Will you please write a medical excuse for Harvey Cheyne so that he doesn't have to participate in gym until he is completely recovered from his pneumonia?

It looks as though we are going to need another two weeks to complete the job—is this acceptable to you?

I am writing to ask not only that you support the handgun control bill, but that you use your rather considerable influence to convince other legislators of its worth and significance.

Do you remember that you once offered to lend me Grandma's pearl ring for a special occasion?

Can you spare me five or ten minutes on the phone sometime next week to answer a few questions about your rubber stamp collection?

I am wondering if you could see your way clear to lending me $200 for approximately three weeks, until I receive my income tax refund (enclosed is a copy of my return, showing the amount I will be receiving).

This is a formal request to you to make some other arrangements for your dogs; your lease clearly states that animals are not allowed in the building.

Will you please send my complete medical records to Dr. Elise Bodkin at the following address?

May I give your name as a reference when I apply for a position as a ballroom dance instructor?

I respectfully seek a zoning change for 907 East Spruce Street from the current residential designation to retail business.

Would you please forward this request to the appropriate person?

We are interested in tuckpointing our foundation and chimney, and would like to ask you to submit a proposal and bid after inspecting the house.

Would you please send me a job application form in the enclosed self-addressed stamped envelope?

May I ask a favor of you?

We would appreciate your taking a few minutes to fill out the enclosed evaluation of the dog obedience class you recently completed.

I will be in Houston July 23-27, and I'm wondering if we could discuss the possibility of bringing your creativity workshop here next spring.

I would like permission to reprint the following material from your book, *Nightmare Abbey*.

I'm writing to ask if you are interested in doing the botanical illustrations for a textbook we plan to bring out next year.

I'm not able to introduce the guest speaker at our industrial electronics conference on the 23rd—would you be willing to do it?

Paul R. Brande is applying for a position at Barnabas Ltd. and has given us your name as a reference; we would appreciate hearing from you about his qualifications.

I would like to review with you my current salary, which I believe no longer reflects my responsibilities and contributions.

The Youth Softball League invites you to be one of our sponsors for the summer season.

Would it be possible to bring my sixth-grade students to your workshop for half an hour or so to watch you as you construct your kaleidoscopes?

Please send a certified copy of my birth certificate to the address below (enclosed is a check for $15).

I understand that you occasionally welcome interested stargazers to join you when you are using your 8" telescope.

We're wondering if we could discuss with you, either in person or over the telephone, some of our concerns about the academic progress of our daughter, May Bracknel.

They always say that when you want something done you should ask a busy person—
and so I'm asking you if you are able to chair our annual awards committee.

You've been so kind about answering my questions in the past that I am writing you
with two more.

Would you be willing to coordinate our clothing drive this year? It would require
about 20 hours of your time between now and October 1.

> The best way to get on in the world is to make people believe
> it's to their advantage to help you.
>
> —LA BRUYÈRE

MODEL LETTERS

Dear Ms. Betts,

I attended your presentation at the state nursing conference last month, and I was as much entertained as I was educated and informed by it. I talked to you briefly there to ask if you speak to smaller groups. Your answer encouraged me to write this letter.

I serve on the program committee of our local nurses group. We are now planning our programs for the next calendar year. Would you be able to come to our May 17 dinner meeting and speak for about 25 minutes?

Please let me know if you are available and would be willing to speak. We are a group of 75 and we would be pleased to offer you an honorarium of $150.

I look forward to hearing from you.

Dear Mr. Ronglien,

My sister gave me your name and address after learning of your connections with The State School. As she told you, I am working on a series of children's books and would be grateful for any anecdotes, recollections, or details of life in a children's home.

I plan to be in your area on Sunday, March 22. Would it be possible to offer you lunch so we could discuss this project?

If you prefer, I could telephone at your convenience and ask you a few questions.

Enclosed is a self-addressed stamped envelope for your reply. Or you could call me collect.

I look forward to meeting you.

Dear Mr. Imhof,

Would it be possible for me to move my desk?

A number of factors about my desk's present location makes concentration difficult at times. The shipping clerk traffic just outside the door adjacent to my desk is unrelenting and distracting, the lighting over my desk is poor, and I have a direct view of an office in which the person spends some time every day tending to matters of personal hygiene.

The spot to the left of the lightboard would be perfect for my desk. I'd need an extension cord to reach an outlet for my computer and desklight, but that should be no problem. If Mr. Wahnschaffe could spare ten minutes to help me move my desk and computer, I'd be all set.

I would really appreciate being able to move. Thank you!

Dear Vernon Royce,

Muriel Snow suggested to me that you might be a terrific Santa Claus for our annual holiday party for the families of hospital employees.

One of the directors has offered us the use of her home Saturday afternoon, December 14. It is a sprawling mansion on Lake Michigan with a fireplace big enough to accommodate a thin adult. That brings me to you.

I understand that you are not only the right size and a professional stunt man, but very cheerful and personable as well. It sounds as if you'd be the ideal choice for our Santa, who would make a real-life entrance down the chimney (suspended, of course, by rope, and having taken all possible safety precautions). I understand that all liability concerns are dealt with through your union.

I've sent a copy of this letter to your agent and I will anticipate a call from her, I hope, by mid-October so that plans can be finalized.

We hope that you will be our Santa Claus this year.

Dear Alf Dubbo,

I am the Activities Director at the Patrick White Adventures in Art Camp. I am also a big fan of your Bead Monkey shop on Main Street and already own several of your beautifully designed necklaces. I know that many boys and girls in the area visit your shop frequently since beadwork is one of the hottest retro rages today.

I'm writing to ask if you might have an hour or so during the third week in June to share your beaded bracelet- and necklace-making artistry with our young people. I could arrange your visit at a time that would be most convenient for you.

Will you give me a call when you can at 555-1234?

Thank you for considering the idea.

Mail Preference Service
Direct Marketing Association
P.O. Box 9008
Farmingdale, NY 11735-9008

Re: unwanted mail

Please remove the following names from direct mail lists in order to reduce the amount of unsolicited mail we receive:

Colonel Abel Pargiter
Eugenie Pargiter
Eleanor Pargiter
Martin Pargiter
1937 Renny Avenue
Morris, OH 45042

Thank you!

Dear Knox Motor Inn,

I would like to reserve a no-smoking room in your hotel for two nights, June 19 and 20.

My husband and I have two sets of twins (ages six months and two and a half years) so we will need four cribs and an extra set of sheets per crib. The room should also have two double beds since I spend much of the night nursing the infants and my husband spends much of the night comforting the toddlers.

We have lots of nighttime crying in our life just now so if you could please give us a room in a secluded wing of your hotel I'm sure your other patrons would appreciate it very much.

Please send confirmation of our reservation to our address shown below.

Thank you!

Dear Morgan,

I can't remember an interdepartmental meeting this past year for which Ellen Montgomery has not arrived late. Can you have a tactful word with her? Because she's in your department I don't like to approach her myself. Also, she is so good-natured and such a terrific asset to the group that it seems fussy to cavil about her tardiness. But then, as Edward Verrall Lucas once wrote, "People who are late are often so much jollier than the people who have to wait for them."

Thanks!

> To ask is no sin and to be refused is no calamity.
>
> —RUSSIAN PROVERB

Dear Manager, Hannasyde's Market,

I teach a City University class on nutrition, which is held Tuesday and Thursday evenings at 8:00 p.m. at the high school one block from your store.

Would it be possible for my class of 14 students and me to visit your store during class time some evening so they could gain experience reading food labels and making food choices?

We would be unobtrusive and orderly. Although each student will probably be buying only one or two items (they are to choose a healthful food they normally do not eat), the benefit to you would be in terms of increased familiarity with your store and follow-up visits.

Thank you for considering this request.

Dear Ms. Capsas,

The E.F. Benson Company is holding a small reception in the 8th floor lounge on October 12 for a group of international visitors. We would like to provide some quiet background classical music during the reception.

The hotel management informs us that the only piano on that floor is the one belonging to Mavromichales, Inc.

Could we possibly borrow the piano on the evening of October 12, from 6 p.m. to 9 p.m.? There are, it seems, large double doors between the lounge and your company's suite, which makes it so convenient that I couldn't help checking with you before trying to arrange to have a piano brought to the 8th floor.

We would naturally be very protective of it. If you did agree to the loan, how could we show our appreciation?

Sincerely,

> A letter is a risky thing; the writer gambles on the reader's frame of mind.
>
> —MARGARET DELAND

RELATED TOPICS

Credit

Fundraising

Information

Introductions

Orders

Refusals

Responses

Thank You

41

Responses

INTRODUCTION

Every letter is in some respect a letter of response—to an event, situation, need, or someone else's letter. General response letters are discussed in this chapter. Specific types of responses are discussed in other chapters: Adjustments, Apologies, Congratulations, Refusals, Sympathy, Thank You. For information on responses to invitations, see Invitations.

> I was gratified to be able to answer promptly. I said I didn't know.
>
> —MARK TWAIN

DO

- Respond promptly, especially to customer inquiries, which need to be handled routinely, quickly, and efficiently.
- Begin by mentioning what you are responding to so the other person knows immediately the reason for your letter.

387

- Let the other person know you appreciate them and are pleased to be responding.

- State or enclose the requested information; explain what is being done to respond; or direct the person to other sources of assistance (give names, addresses, and phone numbers). In most cases, avoid giving more information than your reader has requested. It is costly and unproductive.

- For a complicated response, organize your letter elements using numbers, bullets, or asterisks and leave plenty of white space.

- Close with good wishes, an expression of confidence in your product or service, or a remark about future contacts.

> It is not every question that deserves an answer.
>
> —PUBLILIUS SYRUS

DON'T

- Don't misspell a customer's name when responding to an inquiry; this small slip is often paid for in lost sales.

> Children ask better questions than do adults. "May I have a cookie?" "Why is the sky blue?" and "What does a cow say?" are far more likely to elicit a cheerful response than "Where's your manuscript?" "Why haven't you called?" and "Who's your lawyer?"
>
> —FRAN LEBOWITZ

HELPFUL HINTS

- Customer inquiries provide you with an unparalleled opportunity to promote your goods and services as well as your company. Reply in a neutral, respectful manner even to letters that you consider offensive, uninformed, inane, or a waste of energy. Over time, this businesslike attitude builds your company's reputation. Answer questions as completely as possible and enclose supplementary lists, articles, reports, brochures, flyers, or catalogs. Make it easy for the customer to follow up (place an order, find a local distributor, call a toll-free number for more information). If you cannot respond at once, acknowledge receipt of the letter.

- The format for a letter or note of response is simple: do as you were done unto. If the letter was typed, type yours; if it was handwritten, handwrite yours.

- Forms are useful when responding to certain routine matters. Requests for information, materials, or samples can be handled with a printed card saying, "This comes to you at your request" or "Thank you for your inquiry. Enclosed are informational materials." If you leave space on printed forms, you can personalize the note or add information when necessary. A checklist of available publications can be used to indicate which of them are being sent. You can also design a form with blanks ("Thank you for your inquiry about _____") or with a listing of all possible responses ("Your order has been sent"; "We are temporarily out of stock"; "Please reorder in ___ days"; "This is a prepaid item, and your payment has not yet been received"; "Please indicate a second color choice") so that you can check off the appropriate one.

- If you are unsure about responding to a fundraising letter because you are unfamiliar with the sponsoring organization, you can obtain up to three reports on individual agencies free on request by writing to: National Charities Information Bureau, 19 Union Square West, New York, NYC 10003-3395. It is a nonprofit organization so please enclose a #10 self-addressed stamped envelope.

- When you are offered a position that you want, write an acceptance letter that expresses your enthusiasm and pleasure and that confirms the details of your employment.

> He had a way of meeting a simple question with a compound answer—you could take the part you wanted, and leave the rest.
>
> —Eva Lathbury

GETTING STARTED

Thank you for your letter of April 9, requesting information about our Learning Readiness Program.

The information you requested on utility stocks is enclosed.

We are always happy to hear from our customers and pleased to be of service to them.

In response to your inquiry of March 4, I am sorry to tell you that we no longer carry the eyeshade-green gooseneck lamp.

Thank you for your interest in our employer subsidy program.

We are pleased to report that we are able to welcome your small group of students on a tour through our topographic mapping department.

I appreciate very much (and accept!) your generous apology.

We were impressed with your proposal and would like to discuss the possibilities of your working with us.

Thank you for your kind letter of January 9.

Please find enclosed the complete schedule of the "Music in the Parks" concerts that you requested.

Here are the fax paper samples you requested.

Thank you for your request for an estimate on the ceramic tile installation for your two bathrooms.

We no longer offer a free booklet on refinishing hardwood floors, but we have available a similar publication for $4.95.

Thank you for your telephone call of April 23 offering me the position of security officer at Stawarth Space and Communications, Ltd.

This is to let you know that we have received your résumé and will be calling you with a response before August 3.

Thank you for allowing us to clarify the contract terms for you.

As you requested in your letter of September 6, we are asking one of our sales representatives, Elizabeth Endorfield, to call on you next week.

Your letter to Fakrash el'Aamash was received, but as he is away from the office until October 16, his response to you will be delayed.

I was pleased to write the enclosed letter of recommendation for you.

Enclosed is my contribution to the Samuel Bulpitt Scholarship Fund—do you have a matching gifts program?

Thank you for requesting a free sample issue of *Artiste!*

> The impulse to ask questions is among the more primitive human lusts.
>
> —ROSE MACAULAY

MODEL LETTERS

Dear Mr. Chipping,

I am pleased to accept your offer of the position of assistant director of the Hilton Working Family Center.

I very much enjoyed the discussions with you and Ms. Wickett and I look forward to being part of this dynamic and important community resource.

The salary, hours, responsibilities, and starting date are all agreeable to me.

Until Monday, January 30, I am

> Sincerely yours,
>
> Katherine Bridges

Dear Mr. Lennox,

As the newly crowned Dairy Princess of Freeland County, I would be delighted to appear at your malt shop for an autographing on Saturday, August 12, from 7:00 to 9:00 p.m., during what you described as the post-dinner ice cream rush.

I look forward to spending that evening with a group of dairy fans.

> Sincerely,
>
> Mary Blake

Dear Ms. Mantalini,

We are pleased to inform you that your proposal for a travel grant to Peru has been accepted by the Dotheboys Foundation. Congratulations!

Enclosed please find two copies of the Agreement. Sign both copies and return one to our office. Also enclosed is a booklet outlining what you can expect from us and what we expect from you upon completion of your travel. If you have any questions after reading the material, please call me at 555-4421.

The Dotheboys Foundation is pleased to be able to support the unique and important work you are engaged in.

> Sincerely,
>
> Newman Noggs

Dear Dr. Proudie,

I would be happy to perform twenty minutes of magic tricks at the Hiram Children's Hospital silent auction to be held on Saturday, April 24.

> All the best,
>
> Septimus Harding

Dear Newland Archer,

In response to your letter of November 16, yes, you may have a two-month extension on the loan of the slides showing scenes of our amusement park for use in your corporate slide show, with the purpose of adding, as you said, "a bit of amusement" to your corporate meetings.

This extension will be at no cost to you, with our compliments.

Sincerely,

Ellen Olenska

Dear Fergus Fadden,

Thank you for your interest in our correspondence screenwriting course, which guarantees that you will complete a full-length feature film script by the end of the six-week course.

As the enclosed course description states, you will swiftly learn all the tricks of the trade—everything necessary within just six short weeks to produce a script ready to market.

So don't delay. Send along your check and completed forms today!

Best wishes,

Dear Philip Norman Danby,

We have received your letter of complaint about the rats on the property adjacent to yours on Winter Street. We have contacted the property owner who insists that you are seeing a litter of rabbits which she raises as pets. However, we will send a crew to inspect the premises for rats within the next week. If rats are found, and extermination undertaken, you will be notified.

Thank you for your vigilance.

Sincerely,

Dear Mr. and Mrs. Bunting,

Thank you for your inquiry of June 19.

Our organization does not consider you over the suggested age limits for adopting a child.

I'm enclosing some informative materials on adoption and specifically on our organization. When you have read them, you may want to call for an appointment to speak to one of our counselors.

Dear Mr. Highworth Foliat Ridden,

Thank you for your letter inquiring about The Masefield Home. The situation you and your mother are facing following her surgery is a familiar one to us.

The Masefield Home is designed to meet a variety of needs, from short-term care suites for those needing a higher level of care during recuperation (like your mother) to long-term assisted-living apartments.

I'm enclosing a pamphlet describing our facilities, services, and fees. If you feel your mother is a good candidate for The Masefield Home, please call my office to set up an appointment to tour our facilities and grounds. If you or your mother would like to speak to our residents, several have been kind enough to offer their time to answer questions about the Home.

With all best wishes to you and your mother, I am

Sincerely,

Dear Ms. Belmont,

Yes, we are the band who played for your cousin Digby's wedding. We are pleased that you liked us well enough to track us down.

The details he gave you are correct; we are still a five-piece band and our prices have not changed.

Please call so that we can discuss date, time, place, type of music, and any other concerns you might have.

Dear Sam,

I know it was difficult and uncomfortable for you to write and tell me that you'd seen Lucy at a bar with an obviously false ID. Nobody likes bringing that kind of news to doting parents, but in this case, instead of shooting the messenger, we prefer sending you our love and a big hug.

We have begun to get some issues out on the table here, thanks to you.

You're a good friend.

Dear Amelia Sedley,

Thank you for agreeing to speak at the XXV State High School League Conference on March 3. We are delighted, and are very much looking forward to hearing you.

In your letter, you referred to April 3. We have you scheduled for March 3. Please let me know if we are in agreement on the date.

A contract will be sent to you in the next week or so along with a letter with information on your airport arrival host, your hotel accommodations, and details about the program the evening you will be speaking.

Sincerely,

> Bromidic though it may sound, some questions *don't* have answers, which is a terribly difficult lesson to learn.
>
> —KATHARINE GRAHAM

Dear Norman,

I wish I could help you, but divorce law is way beyond my ken. I understand how hard it is to find an attorney you are comfortable with in a new town where you don't know anyone yet. Why don't you call a local attorney referral service?

These are often run by or affiliated with a bar association (ask about that). Sometimes you pay the attorney they refer you to, and sometimes you pay a fee to the referral service (some offer low-income fees). What they'll do is put you in touch with an attorney specializing in divorce law.

At your first meeting, ask questions like these:

How long have you been practicing in this area?
How many divorce cases have you handled?
What were the results of these cases?
What are your fees?
What might I expect court costs to run?
What about filing fees and photocopying fees?

Consider:

How comfortable are you with this attorney?
Do you feel listened to and respected?
Do you have confidence in the person's competence?
Could you work with this person over a period of time?

These are just guidelines—I hope they help. Let me know how things go, OK?

> The mind gives us thousands of ways to say no, but there's only one way to say yes, and that's from the heart.
>
> —SUZE ORMAN

RELATED TOPICS

Acknowledgments

Adjustments

Apologies

Follow-up

Goodwill

Instructions

Pen Pals

Refusals

Sensitive Issues

Thank You

Résumés

INTRODUCTION

Although Henry Ford supposedly said that it was all one to him whether a person came from Sing Sing or Harvard since he hired people, not histories, he probably was unique in his view. Most employers are very interested in your history—and the better organized and prepared it is, the more interested they will be.

A résumé provides prospective employers with a written summary of your qualifications and work history. Its main purpose is to convince the reader that you are a good candidate for the position and should be called for an interview. Although it lacks most of the features of a sales letter (few employers are dazzled by extravagant claims and catchy language), the résumé is essentially a sales letter in which you are both the seller and the product. Reread your résumé with this in mind: would you want to talk to the person who wrote this?

Before writing a résumé, assemble two kinds of information: facts about yourself and facts about the job you want. Whether you are offered or refused a job depends not so much on your education, experience, and skills as it does on how closely you match the prospective employer's needs. To emphasize this match, you need to learn about the company and to target your résumé directly to it. Call the company to ask questions. Research the company at the library. Speak to people who work there or who know the company. Although you cannot change the facts of your employment history, you can emphasize certain skills and qualifications if you know that this is what the employer is looking for. When prospective employers come across a résumé that has obviously been written especially for them, they will give it more than the sixty seconds that most résumés get. By presenting as clear a picture of yourself as you can in terms of the employer's needs, you make it easy to determine quickly whether there is a possible match.

To write the cover letter that always accompanies a résumé, see Cover Letters. If you want to combine a cover letter and a shortened version of your résumé, see Applications.

> A résumé is neither an autobiography nor a memoir. It is a personal advertisement, and the facts it presents must emphasize your accomplishments and abilities. Its purpose is to get you an interview.
>
> —JUVENAL L. ANGEL

DO

- Place your name, address, and daytime telephone number at the top right or in the top center of your résumé (avoid the top left position because it may get stapled or punched).
- For a centered heading, use "Résumé," "Summary of Work History," "Professional History," "Skills, Education, and Experience," "Experience," your name, or no title at all.
- State the specific job or kind of job you are applying for.
- The heart of the résumé is the summary of your work experience and job skills. There are two basic approaches. (1) The traditional reverse chronological employment format starts by listing your most recent position and going back through time. Put the dates of employment on the left side of the page. Beside each date, list the name of the company where you worked during that period. Underneath give the title of your job there and a brief job description. This is the easiest format to use, but it has its weaknesses if there are gaps in your job history, if you're new to the job market, or if your previous jobs don't seem to relate well to the one you are seeking. The emphasis here is on external facts: how long you worked somewhere, job titles, list of duties. For this type of résumé, include: dates of employment, name and full address of employer, job title, job duties, and reason for leaving (readily accepted reasons include moving, returning to school, seeking a better position). It is not necessary to mention the reason for leaving; if the employer wants to know,

this will be brought up in the interview. (2) The nonchronological, skills-oriented, or functional résumé stresses your skills, accomplishments, and relevant qualifications in a way that allows a prospective employer to determine whether you are what is needed. In this résumé you group job experiences according to a specific skill. For example, under "Leadership Skills" you might write, "Supervised night shift at Hooper & Co. for two years." Under "Interpersonal Skills" would be, "As the mayor's troubleshooter, I was often called upon to intervene in disputes, negotiate contracts, and otherwise deal with constituents, politicians, and city personnel under difficult circumstances." "Organizational Skills" might include: "I was hired at Arnold-Browne to reorganize the accounting department, which was barely functioning at the time due to staff turnover, low morale, lack of department guidelines, and poor use of office space. At the end of two years, I was commended by the company president for 'unparalleled organizing skills.'" ➤ You can also combine the chronological résumé and the job skills résumé. Under each job listed in reverse chronological order, group skills used in that job. Or slant your résumé directly toward the job under consideration by listing the general qualifications and specific qualifications you have for it.

- Whichever format you choose, make all listings parallel in form ("I directed . . . I supervised . . . I increased . . .").

- Give the essential facts of your education: name of school, city and state where it is located, years you attended, the diploma or certificate you earned, the course of studies you pursued, special training.

- List special skills: familiarity with office machines, tools, equipment.

- List any publications.

- List honors, awards, and scholarships; organizations to which you belong; leadership positions you have held including class offices, hobbies, volunteer work not mentioned elsewhere; and other relevant activities and qualifications.

- State that references will be supplied upon request. (Ask people in advance if you can use them as references so you will be prepared when you have to furnish names.)

- A cover letter always accompanies your résumé. (For information on writing the cover letter, see Cover Letters.)

- In some situations you will attach work samples, publications, or supplementary materials.

Think of a résumé as a sixty-second television commercial: that's probably all the time the reader is going to spend on it.

—LASSOR A. BLUMENTHAL

DON'T

- Don't emphasize what you expect the company to do for you ("I see this position as a wonderful opportunity to learn about merchandise discount retailing"). Emphasize instead what you can bring to the company. Don't present your accomplishments so that they say, "Here is what I've done." Instead, phrase them to say, "Here is what I can do for you." For example, "My experience maintaining and repairing small gas engines will allow you to expand your services in that direction."

- Don't include personal information (age, weight, height, marital or financial status, children, and religious or political affiliation) unless it is pertinent to the situation you are seeking. For example, if you are applying for a position as a political fundraiser, you will note your political party affiliation. To interview for a position as a weight control group leader, a mention of your weight history is probably indicated. Or if you are applying for a position as church organist, it may be helpful—although not always necessary—to mention your religious background. It is often illegal for prospective employers to ask questions about age, sex, race, and religion. Stephen Wilbers, business columnist for the Minneapolis *Star Tribune*, also counsels against including personal information but adds, tongue-in-cheek, "If you're undergoing treatment for work addiction or over-achievement, be sure to work that in somewhere."

- Don't depend on adjectives and adverbs to carry your résumé. On the contrary, remove every "very" you find and such lukewarm words as "good," "wonderful," "exciting." Use instead strong, perhaps even unusual, nouns and verbs.

- Don't use "etc." It is uninformative and irritating and gives an impression of excessive casualness.

- Don't mention salary in a résumé; this is better discussed in an interview (and then try to get your interviewer to mention a figure before you give your salary expectations). When you give your salary requirement or list previous salaries, you lose a small advantage.

- Don't embellish, exaggerate, tell half-truths, or, of course, lie. Many companies have résumé fact-checkers and if you are found out, you will be dismissed, will suffer at the least a great deal of embarrassment and humiliation, and may be liable to civil charges. Trying to make yourself sound better than you are for a position is often a tip-off that you may not be well qualified for it: Would you be happy in such a job?

- Don't be too modest either. This is not the time to play down your accomplishments. You might have someone who knows you evaluate your final draft.

- Don't tell every single thing you've done. Sometimes filler material detracts from a strong résumé. People who throw in all the extras on the theory that it "can't hurt" may be wrong. Don't, for example, give details of childhood or early schooling. You can also omit work you've done in the past that you don't want to do again (unless this would leave unexplained holes in your résumé).

- Don't use jargon, long, involved phrases, a bookish vocabulary you don't normally use, or acronyms (unless the acronym is so familiar in your field that it would be insulting to spell it out).
- Don't staple, glue, or seal your résumé into a binder or folder (unless specifically requested to). The pages should be loose; they are easier to handle.

> When your work speaks for itself, don't interrupt.
>
> —HENRY J. KAISER

HELPFUL HINTS

- Some companies use optical scanning systems to input résumés into computer files; they may specify that only scannable résumés are acceptable. This means avoiding graphics or "artsy" arrangements, using white paper, choosing a standard typeface like Times Roman instead of more picturesque fonts, and including a list of keywords to facilitate searching for matches by employers. Scanners don't care about eye-catching looks; they care about clarity and ease of readability. See, for example, *Electronic Résumé Revolution* by Joyce Lain Kennedy and Thomas J. Morrow, John Wiley & Sons, 1994.
- Your résumé should be only as long as it needs to be. The purpose of a résumé is always to show that you are qualified for the job opening; at the interview you can elaborate on it. Most authorities recommend a one- or two-page résumé. In *The Smart Job Search* Mark L. Makos says, "Unless it is not important to you to get a job, a one-page résumé is your only choice." However, for many academic and professional positions, you may need more than two pages—as many as twelve perhaps, if you have a long list of publications, patents, cases, conference presentations, or other itemizations. Whether one page or twelve, though, your résumé must be tightly written and readable: use simple, short sentences, keep paragraphs short, and leave plenty of white space and ample margins.
- There are three ways to refer to yourself in a résumé: (1) in the first person ("I performed complex CNC turning operations on diversified parts with minimum supervision"); (2) in the third person ("She achieved a 19% capture rate on grants proposals"); (3) without a pronoun ("Helped increase productivity by approximately 25% and decrease absenteeism by almost 20%"). Each style has advantages and disadvantages. The first can be wearying with all its "I's" (omit as many as possible), the second can appear remote and pretentious, and the third may seem

abrupt. Use the style that feels most comfortable to you, regardless of what you perceive as its benefits or disadvantages. In any case, do not refer to yourself as "the writer" ("The writer has six years' experience . . .").

- Some of the headings and divisions that might be useful to you in constructing your résumé include (you will generally have no more than five or six of these):

Job Objective	Communication Skills
Career Objective	Interpersonal Skills
Employment Objective	Leadership Skills
Education	Organizational and Managerial Skills
Training	Supervisory Skills
Overview of Qualifications	Office Management Skills
Summary of Qualifications	New Product Development Skills
Highlighted Qualifications	Office Skills
Background Summary	Systems Skills
Work Experience	Promotional Skills
Professional Experience	Negotiating Skills
Managerial Experience	Special Skills
Technical Experience	Additional Accomplishments
Professional Background	Activities
Professional Achievements	Extracurricular Activities
Editorial Experience	Awards, Honors, Offices
Copywriting Experience	Memberships
Retail Sales Experience	Professional Affiliations
Additional Experience	References

- Use strong, active verbs. Instead of "I did this" or "I was responsible for that," write "I managed," "I developed," "I directed." Other powerful verbs include:

accelerated	approved
accomplished	arranged
achieved	assembled
administered	assisted
advised	attained
analyzed	bought
appraised	built

cataloguued

classified

communicated

completed

composed

conceived

conducted

consolidated

contracted

contributed

controlled

coordinated

created

decreased

defined

delivered

demonstrated

designed

determined

devised

diagnosed

discovered

distributed

doubled

economized

enlarged

established

evaluated

examined

expanded

facilitated

governed

grouped

guided

hired

identified

implemented

improved

increased

indexed

innovated

installed

interviewed

introduced

invented

invested

investigated

launched

led

maintained

mapped

met deadlines

moderated

monitored

negotiated

obtained

operated

orchestrated

ordered

organized

originated

overhauled

oversaw

performed

pioneered

planned

prepared

prescribed

presented

processed

produced

programmed

promoted

proposed

provided

purchased

qualified for

realized

recognized

recommended

recorded

recruited

rectified

redesigned

reduced costs

referred

regulated

rendered

reorganized

represented

researched

reshaped

resolved

restored

revised

saved

scheduled

screened

selected

served

serviced

set strategy

simplified

sold

solved

sorted

spoke

stabilized

started

streamlined

strengthened

structured

studied

submitted

summarized

supervised

supplied

systematized

tabulated

taught

tested

tracked

trained

transacted

transformed

translated

trimmed

tripled

turned around

uncovered

unraveled

upgraded

validated

viewed

widened

won

worked

wrote

- You will probably use two tenses in a résumé: the present tense for categories like career goal ("Desire position with . . .") and skills ("I am fluent in French, Italian, Spanish, and German"); the past tense for categories like work experience ("Headed all major advertising campaigns . . .") and professional accomplishments ("I won a six-state cabinetmaking competition").

- It is impossible to overemphasize the importance of a neat, correctly written résumé. Robert Half, founder of Robert Half International, a large recruiting firm, says that in a résumé, "flippancy, careless errors, tactless remarks, irrelevant or extraneous material and attempts at humor should be avoided at all costs." The problem is that writers don't often see their own careless errors or their own flippancy or tactlessness, and the error that you miss will jump out at your prospective employer. Have someone (or two or three someones) read the final draft of your résumé. (Note that it is never acceptable to submit a résumé on which you have handwritten updated information, corrections, or new material.)

- Use numbers to report successful outcomes of your work. Even if you were only partly responsible for increasing sales, decreasing expenditures, or coming in under budget for the first time in ten years, say so. State how many people you supervised, how many copies of your books were sold, how many projects you oversaw, how much time or money you saved the company, the size of the budget you were responsible for, the percentage reduction in absenteeism in your department, the percentage increase in productivity at your station.

- When you submit an application form for a job, you may always attach a résumé to it.

- Those seeking their first full-time job encounter the classic frustration: They won't take me because I don't have experience, and I don't have experience because they won't take me. It is, however, possible to structure an appealing résumé without a significant work history. Summer jobs show dependability, initiative, responsibility. Extracurricular activities illustrate leadership potential, the ability to complete projects, and your special interests. Awards, honors, GPA, elected offices, and scholarships indicate accomplishments and show that you have been singled out from your peers. Volunteer work, athletics, and organization memberships help define you and give you a profile. This type of résumé benefits from a skills orientation; you state that you are responsible, dependable, hardworking, a quick learner, or loyal and give illustrative examples.

- Emphasize your flexibility and capacity to learn new tasks and adapt to new situations. Resilience is an important qualification in a world where information and technology develop at high speeds. One way to do this is to make your past jobs sound different from each other. For example, if you have worked at several beauty salons, you might want to emphasize under one position your experience with custom hair coloring, under another position your experience with body-wrap treatments, under yet a third your experience with hair-weaving or body waxing or ordering the product lines.

- If you prefer that your present employer doesn't know you are job-hunting, refer inquiries to your home phone or address and ask that references from your present employer wait until you and the prospective employer feel surer of the match.

- When you are asked to furnish a brief biographical sketch for the program notes of a conference, a newspaper article on a recent achievement, or a company newsletter, your résumé will help you write it. A brief bio is always written in narrative fashion, is far, far briefer and less specific than a résumé, and aims to capture the essence rather than the details of who you are professionally.

- All résumés are typed, printed, or machine-produced on good white or off-white bond paper in sharp black elite or pica type (do not use script or other special typefaces). Shades of ivory, natural, and light gray are also acceptable. Résumés should look professional, conservative, and straightforward. In a few fields, a highly creative résumé with graphics, colored inks, and an offbeat design might be effective. However, you need to have some assurance that this is effective—perhaps you know someone at the company who obtained a job that way. This type of résumé gets many admiring glances but is often passed over for the more "stable"-looking résumé. There is only one correct format for a résumé—a logical, readable one. Your name and address may go in the upper right corner or center of the page. Your material may be typed block or indented style. You have great latitude in setting up the material, so choose the format that seems to arise out of the arrangement of your material. White space helps. It's hard for a reader to spot the highlights if a résumé is run together, with no space between job listings, for example.

Think of your résumé as a continuously evolving, multiform document. There are only two permanent statements of what you've done with your life—your obituary and your epitaph. Until then, everything else is a working draft.

—Stephen Wilbers

GETTING STARTED

Objective   To obtain a position in the transportation industry in which I can help further efficient and cost-effective product movement.

Job Goal   To obtain an internship or temporary position that offers a variety of experience in goldsmithing and jewelry repair.

Career Objective   Entry-level management position in the electronics industry earning advancement through on-the-job performance.

Education   B. Mus., Berklee College of Music, Boston, Mass., 1998, with majors in Jazz Composition, Film Scoring, and Songwriting; summa cum laude.

        M.A., University of Southern California, Los Angeles, Calif., 2000, with a major in Film Scoring.

Education   D.V.M., The University of Minnesota College of Veterinary Medicine, 1996.

Education   B.A., Yale University, 1995; majors in anthropology and theater studies; magna cum laude.

        M.F.A., Columbia University Graduate School of Film, 1998.

Work Experience   Postal worker 1989 - 1992
        Automotive Service Technician 1992 - 1998
        Manager, Automotive Services 1998 - 2000

Patents Granted   US 5738939
        US 5366140

Publications

Your Child From Five to Ten
Doorways to Professional Growth
Breakthrough!
Criminal Justice: Contemporary Perspectives
A Laugh a Minute (co-authored with M. Bunion)

Work Experience

Writing: Twenty-six years' experience writing books, stories, articles, and classroom and miscellaneous materials. (See list of publications.)

Editing: Twenty years' experience editing trade, technical, law, religious, educational, and medical materials. (See attached list of edited books.)

Teaching: High-school French, night-school French, religious education, peace work-shops, creative writing for children, handwriting analysis.

Miscellaneous: Translating/French (1966-1989); public relations work for French Consulate General in Chicago (1969); administrative assistant to NDEA Overseas Language Institute, Rennes, France (1965 and 1966); hospital work (1967); proofreading (1968-1970).

Additional Skills: Part of my duties as music director and liturgist involved instru-ment acquisition and maintenance, including revoicing seven ranks of the organ, con-structing small percussion instruments, enlarging the handbell set from sixteen to thirty-seven, and acquiring a new studio piano for the choir. I also obtained estimates and made plans for a major overhaul of the forty-rank 1926 Casavant organ.

References are available upon request.

> We judge ourselves by what we feel capable of doing, while others judge us by what we have already done.
>
> —HENRY WADSWORTH LONGFELLOW

MODEL LETTERS

Stella Summersley Satchell
1913 Wells Avenue   Chicago, IL 60657
312/555-1234

Professional Objective	To apply educational background, acquired experience, and creativity to a challenging position in photography.
Knowledge & Skills	Black and white film development and printing. Color printing and filtration. Medium format and 35mm cameras. Black and white photofinishing and archival processing, including: archival washing and toning, spotting, trimming, and mounting. Alternative photographic processing, including: toning (selenium, sepia, copper, and iron), hand coloring, paper negatives, collage, Polaroid transfers, Liquid Light, solarization, and cross-processing.

Education	B.A. 1990 with photography major, University of Iowa

Experience	*Freelance artist/photographer/graphic designer*

May 1992 to present

Create photographs for promotional, commercial, and educational purposes. Design, create, and layout advertisements, brochures, presentation materials, logos, and newsletters with Quark Xpress, Pagemaker, and Adobe Illustrator. Computer illustration. T-shirt design. Clients include: Ebbsworth Forms, Inc., The Hutton Companies, Costanza Printing Co., Cochrane-Doyle, Inc., and various individuals.

Assistant to the Sound and Visual Collections Curator
Bunker County Historical Society
February to June 1995
Accessioned new photography collections. Learned basic correct handling and storing of photographic archives. Helped coordinate informational mailing and check-in procedure for Society-sponsored statewide photodocumentary conference.

Teaching assistant
Glendower College Art Department
March to June 1995
Assisted in teaching a college-level beginning photography course. Demonstrated photographic techniques to students. Prepared and checked darkroom chemistry. Critiqued and evaluated students' progress and work.

Major Accomplishment	Fulfilled lifelong ambition to circumnavigate the globe. Traveled extensively through Western and Eastern Europe, the former Soviet Union, China, and Southeast Asia (November 1990 to May 1992).

References	References and portfolio available upon request.

PHILIP MELDRUM

Present Address
59 Stang Road
Ames, IA 50010
515/555-2241

Permanent Address
907 Second Ave. N.
Norcross, GA 30092
404/555-2789

OBJECTIVE

To use and expand my skills and interests with an organization in the business community.

EDUCATION

Bachelor of Business Administration, cum laude, May 1999
Iowa State University, Ames, Iowa

Financed 100% of college expenses through work, work-study programs, and grants.

EXPERIENCE

Auditor, Marks Inventory Specialists, Ames, Iowa.
June 15, 1998 to present.

Operate key punch auditing calculator, compute accurately the store's aggregate inventory value, communicate with store owners to help assure accuracy.

Intern, Derwent Distribution Center, Ames, Iowa.
September 1997 to May 1998, 10 hours per week

Ticketed and distributed orders, received and shipped freight, evaluated daily reports, worked with computer systems.

Construction worker, Bowling Construction, Percy, Iowa.
Summers, 1994-1998

Issued work assignments and inspected completed work for crew of six.

STRENGTHS

Communication: communicate well when speaking and writing; able to act as liaison between different personality types; comfortable and effective communicating with both superiors and staff.

Responsibility: self-motivated and willing to set goals and work to achieve them.

Organization: use time and resources effectively; value efficiency, planning, and accountability.

Computer expertise: experienced with most word processing, spreadsheet, and auditing software.

Other: willing to relocate anywhere; have traveled to Europe, Asia, and South America, thus gaining a global perspective on business and politics; subscribe to a work ethic that finds satisfaction and pleasure in achieving work goals; daily reader of *Wall Street Journal* and *New York Times*.

HONORS AND ACTIVITIES

Commissioned Second Lieutenant, U.S. Army, June 1994, Branch Adjutant General Corps

Member, Delta Sigma Phi Fraternity

Member, University Finance Club

Member, Intramural Basketball Team, ISU, four years

REFERENCES

Available upon request.

Leslie Sanders
1939 Anstruther Street
Cleveland, OH 44101
216/555-1234

OBJECTIVE

To obtain a position as an administrative assistant commensurate with my experience, capabilities, and need to be challenged

EDUCATION

2-year degree from Wylie Technical College in office administration, 1989

WORK EXPERIENCE

Carlyon-Seymour Realty, assistant to the president, 1996-present

Ellen Fortune Consultants, Inc., administrative assistant, 1993-1996

McGrath Manufacturing International, assistant to the vice president, 1989-1993

SKILLS

All general office duties

Typing 65 wpm

Extensive experience with Microsoft Word, Access, Excel, Oracle Data Base, PowerPoint, Peachtree Accounting

Good oral and written communication skills

Fluent in written and spoken Spanish

Personal characteristics include being highly organized, able to take a multitask approach to the workday, self-motivated, tactful, discreet

REFERENCES

Provided upon request

JAMES PAWKIE
1822 Galt Road
Woodland, AL 36280
205/555-1234

OBJECTIVE

An entry-level position offering future management opportunity and present learning challenges.

EDUCATION

Bachelor of Business Administration, Alabama University, 1994

Private security office license, Alabama Department of Public Safety, 1993

Certificate: Certified Security Officer, 1993

WORK EXPERIENCE

P. Picklan International, 1998-present. Duties include monitoring inventory of supplies, accounting, purchasing, stocking, clerking, scheduling, supervising five co-workers, and training fifteen new employees.

W.S. Caption Security, Inc., 1996-1998. Duties included enforcing safety and pilferage rules, processing invoices, and data entry.

Alexander Clues Manufacturing, 1993-1996. Duties included assisting manager with inventory control operations, ticketing and distributing orders, receiving and shipping freight, evaluating daily reports, working with computer system, answering customer inquiries concerning inventories.

ACTIVITIES

Scout Master, 1996-present

Member, Rotary International

Commissioned Second Lieutenant, U.S. Army, 1998

Dean's List all four years of college

REFERENCES AVAILABLE UPON REQUEST

> No job is a good job if it isn't good for you.
>
> — BARBARA DE ANGELIS

EMMA WOODHOUSE-KNIGHTLEY
1816 Isabella Trail
Rankin, TX 79778
915/555-1234

Career Objective

Part-time or half-time elementary school teacher, K-6

Education

Elementary Education Certification, Churchill College, 1999

B.A., Churchill College, 1998, English Major, Magna Cum Laude

Student Teaching

Kindergarten, six weeks, Goddard Elementary School, Summer 1998.

Second Grade, seven weeks, Highbury Elementary School, Fall 1998.

Fourth Grade, four weeks, Dixon Elementary School, Spring 1999.

In some or all of the foregoing I taught lessons daily in all subject areas—individual, small group, and whole group; I observed, assisted, developed various curriculum units, lesson plans, and worksheets; I taught intensive remedial math and language skills to bring students up to benchmark levels; I assisted on field trips and was responsible for lunch/playground duty daily.

Work Experience

Writing for Campbell Publishing, 1994-present: I annotate children's books for a national children's literature resource periodical.

Bookselling for the Elton Children's Bookstore, 1998-present: I review current titles for quarterly newsletter, conduct story hours, order stock, write the mail-order catalog.

Administrative Assistant for the Fairfax Public Relations Agency, New York, 1992-1994: I was responsible for production duties, including typing of slide and script copy, maintaining records, photo research, location and prop scouting.

Volunteer Work

Tutor in local literary project, 1994-1996.

Creative Dramatics Teacher and Stage Hand, Bates Children's Theater, 1993-1994.

References

Available upon request.

> Being a specialist is one thing, getting a job is another.
>
> —STEPHEN LEACOCK

RELATED TOPICS

Applications
Cover Letters
Employment
Follow-up
References

43

Sales Letters

INTRODUCTION

Because sales letters are essential to a company's success and one of the most economical and effective types of advertising, many businesses no longer generate their own but use full-service agencies to handle every aspect of their advertising needs, including the development of professional and sophisticated sales letters. You can locate such firms in the Yellow Pages under Direct Marketing, Advertising Agencies, or Public Relations Counselors. If you prefer to write your own sales letters, consult some of the many books that deal specifically with direct mail marketing.

Every letter mailed from your firm is essentially a sales letter. If you are not selling a specific product or service in the letter, you are "selling" your company's goodwill, reputation, and potential for future sales. Courtesy, clarity, correctness, and persuasiveness are found in all letters sent by successful companies.

The classic formula for sales letters is AIDA: get ATTENTION, arouse INTEREST, build DESIRE, impel ACTION. But much of the work involved in crafting an effective sales letter is done before you even begin to write: you need to know everything about your product or service; you need to know as much as possible about your reader; and you must identify and develop a strong central selling point. You may also need to develop a coupon or sample, ascertain the best timing for the letter, and make certain your mailing lists are current and correct. Only when the foundation work has been done can a winning letter be written.

413

> Sales letters are the life blood of most companies.
>
> —Janet Venolia

DO

- Open with an attention-getting statement, question, anecdote, statistic, or compelling sentence.
- Create an interest in what you're selling with a strong central sales message.
- Arouse the reader's desire for your product by using specific, vivid words and images as well as strong, active power verbs. One word that never gets old is "new."
- If appropriate, point out how your service or product differs from similar ones—what does it have that the others don't? Emphasize quality and dependability.
- Make your paragraphs short.

> People will buy anything that's one to a customer.
>
> —Sinclair Lewis

- Convince the reader that responding to your offer is a smart move. Whenever possible, back up your claims for the product or service with "proofs" (samples, testimonials, statistics) of your assertions.
- State the cost of your product or service. Customers ignore sales messages without prices on the assumption that they probably can't afford the item. Cost determines most purchases, and if the customer has to call to find out what it is, the extra trouble is often not worth it when a competitor's cost is available in its sales message.
- Tell the reader how to obtain your product or service.
- Stimulate your readers to immediate action and state clearly what you want them to do: "Telephone now for an appointment"; "Order one for every family member"; "Call today to arrange a demonstration"; "Return the postage-paid reply card now"; "Send for your free copy of the planning guide." Give them a good reason for acting immediately: limited supplies, expiring sale offer, future price increase, early-response discount.
- Emphasize how easy it is to take the suggested action—because you've made it easy with order blanks accompanied by postage-paid reply envelopes, prepaid form

postcards asking for additional information, toll-free numbers for local distributors or ordering, order now-pay later procedures, listings of store hours and locations. (Note that business reply mail, with the mailer paying the postage, has a 10 to 20 percent higher response rate than courtesy reply, where the customer pays the postage.)

- Add a P.S. to repeat your main point, to emphasize an important feature, or to offer a new and strong sales point such as a money-back guarantee, a time limit for the offer, an additional bonus for buying now ("P.S. To offer you these sale prices, we must receive your order by June 30"; "P.S. Don't forget—your fee includes a free gift!"; "P.S. If you are not completely satisfied, return your Arkwright Water Purifier and we will cheerfully issue you a full refund").

> Knowing something about your customer is just as important as knowing everything about your product.
>
> —Harvey Mackay

DON'T

- Don't try to make too many points in one letter. Focus on your strongest one or two sales points, add one in the postscript if you like, and save the others for follow-up letters.
- Don't, in general, use many exclamation marks or exaggerated adjectives such as astonishing, revolutionary, incredible, sensational, extraordinary, spectacular. Describe instead concrete features, benefits, and details.
- Don't make assumptions: that your reader knows what you are talking about, is familiar with an industry term, can picture your product, agrees with your premises. Dale Carnegie once wrote, "I deal with the obvious. I present, reiterate and glorify the obvious—because the obvious is what people need to be told."
- Don't threaten ("You'll be sorry if you don't order now"); it is offputting. However, telling customers that their names will be removed from the mailing list if they don't order soon is sometimes effective because people fear missing out on something.
- Don't preach to customers, chide them, correct them, or write down to them ("you probably don't know this, but . . ."). Have several people read your letter before sending it to be sure that no patronizing or distancing tone has crept in.

- Don't ask questions. You risk inspiring a negative answer ("Can you afford to throw this letter away?" "Can anyone today get along without one?") Questions also derail your reader from the one-way train of thought that leads to a sale. Once you start building toward a certain conclusion, don't interrupt with questions.
- Don't claim that your prices are already so low you don't need sales or discounts. Human nature likes a deal. Offering occasional bargains, sales, clearances, and special purchase promotions creates a sense of excitement and interest in both old and new customers.

> The advertisement is one of the most interesting and difficult of modern literary forms.
>
> —ALDOUS HUXLEY

HELPFUL HINTS

- Everyone agrees on the one best way to begin a sales letter: with a bang! There is no agreement, however, on the type of "bang." Possibilities include: a surprising fact or statistic; a touching, dramatic, or nostalgic anecdote; a case history or personal story; dramatic savings; the offer of a gift, coupon, or booklet; a thought-provoking question or quotation; a joke or riddle; a celebrity endorsement, quote, or tie-in; a who-what-when-where-why paragraph; stating your strongest selling factor; a reference to something you have in common or to a previous contact or purchase; telling readers in a convincing way that they are special; asking or offering a favor.
- Be brief. In some situations, this means a one-page letter; in others, it can mean a ten-page letter. The key is that each word is doing a job, each word sells. A poorly written short letter is not effective merely by virtue of its brevity, and some well-written long letters have enjoyed a high response rate. In general, however, shorter letters are better letters.
- Although appeals to the intellect are part of every sales message, the more effective appeal is to the emotions. You want to show that your service or product will bring the customer love, security, better health, prestige, popularity, pride of ownership or accomplishment, success, more money, improved appearance, more comfort and leisure, social and business advancement, or loyalty.
- Foster credibility by means of testimonials, case histories, research studies, statistics, company reputation, product usage test results, comparison with similar products, free samples or trial periods, celebrity endorsements, photographs of actual use, user polls. Whenever possible, guarantee the buyer's satisfaction in some way.

- Attention-getting devices that may make your message more memorable include: a message on the envelope itself that inspires the person to open it (only about five out of every one hundred mailings are even opened by the recipient and studies show that mailers have about 15 seconds to get customers to open the envelope or they lose them); handwriting part of the message (the P.S., for example); underlining certain words to look as though you personally emphasized by hand the important points; yellow highlighting of key phrases; colored inks and papers; graphics; questionnaire or survey format; boxed information; italics, capital letters, quotation marks, unusual typefaces; design elements such as heads, subheads, white space, short paragraphs, indented material, and bulleted lists. Repetition is helpful in emphasizing a main point, in clarifying complicated material, and in lending an inviting rhythm to your letter. Remember, too, that consumers love free gifts, enclosures, premiums, samples, special offers, discounts, bargain prices, delayed no-interest payments, brochures, free trial periods, and coupons. The overly friendly approach (addressing the recipient by first name, for instance, or sprinkling the person's name throughout the computer-generated letter) is not effective; according to business columnist Louis Rukeyser, "The artificially intimate stuff appears particularly irritating." In addition, attention-getting devices are not always appropriate; to sell bank cards, life insurance, healthcare services, or other "serious" products and services, a more traditional format is called for.

- From start to finish, the focus of a sales letter must be on the prospective customer. Use the words "you" and "your" frequently, and describe the product in terms of benefits to the customers: how it relates to their needs, problems, and interests; how it can improve their lives, save them money, and make them feel more confident. The customer has only one question: "What is this going to do for me?" You need to persuade potential buyers that they need your product not so much because it's a great product, but because it is great for *them*.

- Choose a consistent "voice" that complements your product or service and maintain it throughout your letter: friendly, neighbor-to-neighbor; serious and intellectual; humorous, lively, and fast-moving; brisk and businesslike; urgent and hard-hitting; sophisticated; soothing and reassuring; mysterious; technical or informational; emotional.

- Vary your message. When you believe certain customers are susceptible to your product (because of previous purchases, for example), contact them several times—but with a different letter each time (highlight different facets of your product or service; offer different premiums or deadlines). Or, customers who are buying one of your products or services can be targeted with a sales letter promoting another product or service that they don't "see" anymore. In addition, for the same product or service, you might write six different letters to six different types of customers. The more carefully matched the message and the recipient are, the more successful your mailing will be.

- Sales messages can adopt the forms of other familiar letters: letters of congratulations, thank-you letters, announcements, invitations, letters of welcome, seasonal greetings. When you respond to customer inquiries with information, the cover letter will be a sales letter of the most potentially effective type because you've been given a focused opportunity to sell your product or service.

- One of your most well-written sales letters must be the one asking for an appointment, interview, or meeting to discuss your products or services with a prospective buyer. Use your letter to pique the person's curiosity—make this potential buyer want to see you. But don't tell so much that the person thinks nothing more will be gained by an appointment. Be assertive about making an appointment; if you leave it to the person ("I'd appreciate hearing from you") you may not get a response.

- Most sales letters are computer-generated form letters—either standard form letters or letters in which names, addresses, and salutations are personalized using a mass-mailing merge feature. For a select audience, form letters are printed on good-quality paper, signed individually, and mailed first class.

> Advertising is what you do when you can't go see somebody. That's all it is.
>
> —Fairfax Cone

GETTING STARTED

Doesn't everyone want high-performance, low-risk funds?

It is my pleasure to extend to you a special trial offer along with our invitation to accept two free gifts.

Before you say, "Not another health magazine," wait . . . !

If you have never tried fly tying, here is your chance to do it—with no cost or obligation to you!

Congratulations! You have been preapproved to receive the enclosed membership in the Society for Historic Preservation. To activate your membership, just initial the postage-paid reply card.

For just a few cents a day, you can buy security and peace of mind.

It's never been so easy to give the gift that keeps on giving—and, for a limited time only, to save 50% off the single-copy price!

In the past year I've helped thousands of motorists throughout the state put extra cash in their pockets. How?

You save every time you make a purchase at Jack Butler Hardware.

Do you have any questions about current trends in the local real estate market?

The Almayer Laptop Computer is ready to spoil you with its powerful features and new light weight!

You can now lease a car for far less than you ever thought possible.

Your time is valuable—make the most of it by scheduling a power workout in your own home.

The Mahmet Babalatchi Gallery is proud to announce the private sale of a choice collection of netsuke, jade, and ivory figurines, and amber jewelry.

Are you paying premiums on a homeowner's policy you signed up for fifteen years ago? Have you compared what's available today with what you bought then?

Your name has been proposed as someone who might be interested in tax savings.

To thank you for your interest in Deruchette mailing supplies, we'd like you to have the enclosed sample bubble-lined envelope along with our mini-catalog.

We are proud to introduce the recently completed Mapp Golf Course and to enclose a brochure detailing the pleasures and benefits of membership.

At this low price, every home deserves the maintenance-free beauty of vinyl siding.

We invite you to join the select company of those who know that today's marketplace is a sea of opportunity.

Join thousands of other satisfied travelers who have received their free large-print world map along with our newest tour brochures.

You are cordially invited to an open house at our new store in Tilling—and to pick up the free gift we have waiting for you.

We have gathered together some of the finest orchestras in the world to bring you the most memorable love songs ever written.

How would you like to pay off all your bills right now and then take the vacation you've dreamed of?

There's only one sure way to show you how well our patented drycleaning system works, and that's to offer you the enclosed certificate good for up to $10 on your next drycleaning order.

Are you waiting for your next promotion?

We noticed that you haven't used your charge account recently—we've missed you!

We're making this unprecedented offer to a select group of car owners.

Many of us here at Knight Financial Services have experienced sending our children off to college, so we knew what we needed when we set out to develop our innovative college financial program.

Knowing the real estate market is the key to getting your home sold fast! And nobody knows it like we do.

> Marketing is about being remembered.
>
> —LYNN BERESFORD

MODEL LETTERS

Dear Walter,

You've done an impressive job with your marketing efforts at Paradine Communities. Because of the quality product you build, I think that you could have even more of a market presence, however.

Following up on our interesting discussion last week, I'm enclosing my proposal to represent Paradine Communities and assist in marketing your homes to the general public and to licensed real estate agents and offices in the Greater Cincinnati area.

What you're getting are actually two marketing plans. You can take advantage of either or both. I've paid particular attention to your concerns about close-outs in order to help you market and liquidate any remaining inventory.

We would want to discuss every aspect of the selected marketing plan in detail prior to implementation. And, although I have itemized many elements of an effective marketing plan, there are still several areas in addition to these that we could explore.

I think Paradine Communities would benefit from my services in increased absorption rate and number of sales and in decreased marketing time. The cost would be relatively small with a greater upside potential and a win-win situation for everyone involved.

I'm excited to visit with you further about this. Let's talk soon.

Sincerely,

Dear Neighbor,

Are you running frantically late with dinner party preparations? Unable to squeeze in all those errands before your business trip? A victim of "last minute-itis" at *both* home and work? In need of an extra set of hands *this instant*?

Call 800/555-1234 for COLLEGE CONCIERGE INC. now! It's the next best thing to having yourself cloned!

• Friendly, knowledgeable, hard-working college students are on call right now, waiting and willing to help you out.

• They'll clean, care for children, shop, run errands, mow your lawn, weed your garden, organize, prepare meals, type, walk dogs, feed cats, return overdue library books, pick up drycleaning . . . whatever your overloaded plate demands!

• Computerized maps locate your home or office quickly. Serving the city and most suburbs in the metropolitan area, COLLEGE CONCIERGE INC. guarantees a concierge will be at your service within five to twenty minutes of your call.

• All our concierges have drivers' licenses and cars, excellent references, a typing speed of at least 50 wpm, and a good work ethic.

• Only $15 per hour—*half* the rate of other concierge companies!

• We guarantee stress reduction and your satisfaction with a job well done.

So relax, put your feet up, and hand your stress over to COLLEGE CONCIERGE INC. Let us help you *today*!

Call 800/555-1234 *now*!

Dear Jean Girder,

Thank you for filling out a postcard requesting information and brochures about our individually designed, pressure-treated wood decks.

Knowing that you're interested in adding a deck to your home is exciting news for us. You'll want to comparison shop, of course, but we are confident that after you check out quality, styles, prices, and durability, you'll be ready to sit down with one of our friendly, helpful consultants to draw up some plans. Gibbie Cooper from our office will call you in a few days to answer any questions you might have and to set up an appointment at your convenience.

And your timing is good—any deck ordered through the end of April will be delivered free of charge!

We look forward with pleasure to the moment when your deck is in place and you sigh that sigh of complete delight that we have seen on other faces. . . .

Dear Mr. and Mrs. Machir,

Selling your home in today's market? Let's talk. I'd love to share with you my thoughts and expertise on selling a home today—even if you later decide to sell your home yourself. I know I can be of help and would welcome the opportunity to talk with you.

If you need assistance in determining the asking price of your home, or if you have any questions on the housing market in your neighborhood, give me a call.

I'm enclosing my "Relocation Pack," which I think will be useful to you as you plan your move. I have also enclosed my business card for your convenience.

Sincerely,

Dear C.E. Montague,

Three kinds of people generally don't worry about the security of their homes:

1. Those who burgle others' homes for a living.
2. Those who truly believe, "It could never happen to me!"
3. Those who are protected by FARRELL TOTAL SECURITY SERVICES.

If you didn't find yourself in the above list, you may want to check with us for ways to protect your family, your home, and your possessions. We design security systems tailored precisely to your needs, habits, and activities.

One phone call (555-1234) will bring someone to your home to make a no-obligation, in-depth survey of your security needs. Make that call TODAY! And you won't ever have to worry about the security of your home again.

Dear Homeowner,

We supply our superior-quality, seasoned firewood to many of the homes in your neighborhood. Because multiple deliveries in the same area are so efficient, we can offer you FREE delivery. (There is a small charge for deliveries outside our regular routes.)

Choose from a variety of woods (oak, birch, hickory, apple, oak, mixed woods) and from a variety of types (stacks, bundles, boxes, bags, pallets, kindling, chunks, chips)—all at our reasonable and popular rates.

Call 555-1234 to place your first order and receive a 10% discount (good ONLY on new-customer orders).

Happy Birthday!

On November 8 you will celebrate something special, your 55th birthday. But up until midnight November 7, you can take advantage of our low life insurance rates for 54-year-olds—a significant savings to you.

Please look over the enclosed fact sheet, which shows in unmistakable terms just how much you can save by acting in the next few weeks.

For your birthday, buy yourself something special: security and freedom from financial obligations for your loved ones!

And—did we say it already?—Happy Birthday!

Dear Ms. Mary Vertrees,

Enclosed is a drawing of your office building that you may not recognize at first! The artist has shown the south and west sides of your building as they would look with awnings! Our awning specialists chose your building as one that might benefit from the sun protection and decorative features of our highly engineered, flexible, and fully guaranteed awnings.

One style appropriate to your architecture is shown, but there are dozens of other fabrics, designs, colors, and styles available to you. Awnings are stationary or retractable, and some systems offer automatic timers to shade certain windows as necessary. You can also choose backlit awnings or awnings with graphics or a logo.

Give us a call (555-1234) to discuss our products and services or to set up an appointment for a free estimate.

Dear Neighbor,

If you've ever had to pitch a tent in the backyard to accommodate your guests or had overnighters hanging from the rafters and sleeping in the bathtub, you might like to have a back-up plan for the next time you get the call that says, "We're coming to visit!"

The Beresford Bed & Breakfast, located at 1919 Beresford Boulevard, offers charming bedroom suites (with private bath) in a gracious old Victorian home not far from you! Furnished with quilts and antique furniture as well as with the modern comforts of telephone, television, and Jacuzzi, each bedroom cossets your guests and makes their stay—and you!—unforgettable.

Lavish, homemade country breakfasts are served every morning in the dining room.

With all this, you might expect to pay astronomical prices, but you will be as pleased and surprised by our reasonable prices as you are by our hospitality, charm, and convenience.

Stop by and take a tour of The Beresford Bed & Breakfast before you get that next phone call. Then, when it comes, you can say, "Have I got a treat for you!"

Dear Mr. Ravenswing,

Nobody wants to talk about dust mites. And we wish we didn't have to remind you about something so unpleasant. But dust mites are one of the worst offenders when someone in your home suffers from allergies.

Microscopic dust mites live in your pillows, mattresses, box springs, carpets, and upholstered furniture. Female mites lay 25 to 50 eggs, with a new generation produced every three weeks. And the waste products from these mites—the main substance in house dust to which people are allergic—continue to cause symptoms even after the mite has died.

The answer? MITE-Y BEDDING PRODUCTS. Our zippered, allergen-impermeable mattress, pillow, and box spring covers keep out 100% of all dust mites. You might never have to talk about dust mites again!

> Howard Walker
> Vice President

P.S. Check out the enclosed catalog for more allergy-control products . . . and for the 10% discount being offered until Dec. 31.

> Today's sales should be better than yesterday's—and worse than tomorrow's.
>
> —ANONYMOUS

Dear Neighbor,

Within days you'll be seeing a new phenomenon in your area: drive-through coffee shops! Order your favorite waker-upper from the comfort of your car, only seconds off your route to work or play. We carry 15 blends of regular and decaf coffee plus tea, hot chocolate, and our sparkling cold fresh-fruit drinks.

We probably won't have to tell you about our assortment of homemade baked goods because you'll be able to smell the cinnamon and apricots and fresh bread from inside your car!

If you thought you didn't have time for breakfast or for a pause-that-refreshes, you thought wrong. Now you do! All we ask is that you DRIVE CAREFULLY!

P.S. Enclosed is a coupon good for one free pastry with any order.

> Without salesmanship we could not sell anything. If we could not sell anything we might as well not make anything, because if we made things and couldn't sell them it would be as bad as if we sold things and couldn't make them.
>
> —STEPHEN LEACOCK

RELATED TOPICS

Announcements

Appreciation

Congratulations

Cover Letters

Follow-up

Goodwill

Holidays

Information

Invitations

Orders

Requests

Thank You

44

Letters About Schools and Education

INTRODUCTION

Although the telephone is useful for notifying the school office of a student who won't be in school that day or asking simple questions, such as the date of the next school holiday, nowhere is it less effective than when trying to contact a busy teacher. Your choices are to pull the teacher out of class to speak to you on the phone, to hope they find a minute to return your call between classes or on their break, or to bother them at home in the evening (should you even be able to obtain their phone number).

Brief notes to the principal, instructors, or other staff members help avoid confusion ("Was that Grace Wellborn's mother or Grace Crawley's mother I spoke to?" "Did he say Tuesday after school or Thursday after school?") and better your chances of getting a response.

For help writing letters requesting application forms for a school, transcripts, or special services, see Information and Requests. For complaints about school or university issues, see Complaints. For announcements of school events, parent-teacher conferences, or open houses, see Announcements. For school fundraising efforts, see Fundraising. And for particularly troublesome issues, see Sensitive Issues.

> If you promise not to believe everything your child says happens at this school, I'll promise not to believe everything he says happens at home.
>
> —ANONYMOUS

DO

- Be brief. Nobody in this line of work, from those who work in day-care programs to those who work in doctoral programs, has any time to spare. Your reader will be more favorably disposed to you if you keep it short. After writing your letter, reread it to see how it can be shortened and tightened. The only time you need not be brief is in a letter of appreciation or thanks, especially if it is written at the end of the school year when the person might have time to read it.

- Tell what action you want (a conference with a teacher, a phone call, a meeting with the principal, school records sent to another school).

- Indicate the best way to contact you or respond to your note, giving phone numbers and times of day when you are available. If a note sent home with your child is acceptable, say so.

- Include the dates when you write to excuse a child's past or future absence. And specify dates if you need a response by a certain time.

> A teacher's day is half bureaucracy, half crisis, half monotony, and one-eightieth epiphany. Never mind the arithmetic.
>
> —SUSAN OHANIAN

DON'T

- Don't run interference with school officials for children or adolescents who have not indicated that they need your help. Very young children and lower elementary-school students may not be able to be their own advocates, but as children grow older, school-student interfaces can be dealt with by parents offering support, encouragement, and strategies while students learn to work with the system themselves. Many times this is not possible, but it is wise to get the child's request or permission for your actions and to keep the student fully involved in all that follows.

> Only people who die very young learn all they really need to
> know in kindergarten.
>
> —WENDY KAMINER

GETTING STARTED

Please excuse Phoebe Pyncheon from gym for the rest of this week—she sprained her
   ankle yesterday after school.

Marcelline Detaze needs to leave school tomorrow, May 16, at 2:00 p.m. for a dance
   rehearsal that could be scheduled at no other time; please excuse her.

Constance and Sophia Baines were absent yesterday, February 16, because of the
   funeral of their grandmother; please count this as an excused absence.

Carmen De La Casas was ill yesterday, November 11; please excuse her absence.

Because of a family move, Doris, Micky, and Marlene Connolly's last day at Waugh
   Elementary will be Friday, March 1.

Please send me information about the Woffington School along with instructions on
   enrollment procedures and an application form.

Please send me your financial aid packet.

Could we please schedule, at your convenience, a parent-teacher conference to discuss
   our concerns about Delphine?

Thank you so much for the helpful and positive conference we had last night with
   you about Jimsy.

We have been following your advice about Jacob's study habits, and we are wondering if you are seeing any improvement.

I have several free hours during the week, and I'm wondering if you could use some
   volunteer help in one of the lower grades.

I've just received your note saying you need a room parent for this year, and I'd like
   to apply!

The number of nonfunctioning stations in the language laboratory means that it is
   impossible for an entire class to complete an assignment by the due date.

I am concerned about the harshness, belligerence, and often abusive language of the
   two baseball coaches toward our young athletes.

I'm wondering if you are aware of the dangerous unruliness that goes on every morning and afternoon on the #37 bus.

The undersigned parents request a review of the school's policy on detention for tardiness.

I agree with the necessity of fundraising for the purchase and maintenance of band instruments, but I disagree with the fundraising program adopted for next year.

This is to notify all students and families of a new dismissal time, effective November 15.

Baker Street Elementary would be a very different school without the volunteers who supervise the cafeteria, coach our sports teams, tutor students in reading, and organize major school events.

This will serve as official notice of my change in majors from Jazz Composition to Film Scoring.

> Universities are full of knowledge; the freshmen bring a little in and the seniors take away none at all, and the knowledge accumulates.
>
> —LAWRENCE LOWELL

MODEL LETTERS

Dear Marian Yule,

Willie is adjusting to a new allergy medication this week, so you may notice that he needs two naps a day instead of one. Let me know if you notice anything out of the usual beyond this, however.

Edwin and I are both so pleased with Ryecroft Montessori Day Care. It is a delight to see how happily Willie goes off to "school" every day.

Sincerely,
Amy Reardon

Dear Dr. Craik,

Our son Walter, a student in Phineas Fletcher's third grade, has been kept after school every day for the past two weeks—along with the rest of the class.

Mr. Fletcher's policy is to punish the entire class for any one student's transgression (whether the "culprit" is known or unknown). We have spoken to him three times over the past two weeks about our opposition to this policy (we cannot believe it is either psychologically sound or in any way fair), and we feel that a conference with you, Mr. Fletcher, and interested parents is indicated.

Thank you for your kind attention to this matter.

Sincerely,
Ursula and John Halifax

Dear Ms. Zimmerman,

I am interested in organizing an afterschool photography club at Olinger High School. There would be no cost to the students except for their materials.

I am a professional photographer and have been helping my daughter and two of her friends with their photography hobby. They tell me that at least another seven or eight of their school friends would be interested in such a club.

Al Hummel, who has served on the school board, and Vera Hummel, whom you know as a fine physical education instructor, said they would be happy to speak to you about my qualifications and background.

I would be pleased to discuss this with you over the phone or to meet with you at your convenience.

Sincerely,

George Caldwell

Dear Matthew Bagnet,

We simply cannot say often or loudly enough how much we appreciate all you've done for Woolrich—and for the other students—in the way of getting the best from them and exposing them to the best. You're a rare and fine role model for high school students. Like other parents who are cravenly and abjectly grateful to those who support, encourage, and like their children, we can only say thank you, thank you, thank you.

I wanted to do something grand and glorious for you but this bookstore certificate was the best I could think of. I mainly wanted you to know how much we appreciate you.

I know you can't keep in touch with thousands of former students, but I hope we won't lose all contact with you. I'll stop in at the fall concert next year to say hello.

Until then, I send along our best wishes to you for a summer full of music, sunshine, health, and happiness.

Dear Mr. Shute,

My son mentioned that you were lining up field trips for the class this year. As the editor of the *Morning Record*, I would be happy to have your class come in some morning (10:30 or 11:00) to see how a newspaper is put together.

You can either call at the paper (555-1234) or send a note home with Nevil.

Roger Dickinson

Dear Ms. Coldfield,

Judith told us she has discussed her world history grade with you several times but that she still doesn't understand why her daily work and test grades averaged out to a C.

Could you possibly see the three of us for a few minutes sometime and go over this with us?

I know you are busy and that this probably seems minor to you, but it has made Judith suddenly doubt her own perceptions, her ability to understand requirements, and her academic skills. I think it would help her if she had a clearer view of what has happened here.

Thank you for your time and attention.

Thomas and Ellen Sutpen

May 28, 1994

Dear Master Onat,

My husband joins me in thanking you most fervently for your many kindnesses to Katie during her four years at Yale. It must be rather wonderful to know that you will be remembered warmly by so many for so long. She had a special fondness and admiration for you, as I'm sure you know, and I think she will always associate you with the Calhoun medal, which means a great deal to her.

We are still enjoying the afterglow of the graduation weekend—the happy Calhoun commencement ceremony, your reception the day before, and the several encounters we had with you here and there.

Along with my thanks to you and my regards to your wife, I send my very best wishes to you both for health and happiness.

Dear Ms. Challard,

Since our post-Science Fair discussion the other night, I've been talking to other parents about the possibility of raising money for new equipment for the science lab. I understand that in the past parental fundraising efforts have not been very successful. However, Mr. Graeme had an idea that some of us think is worth discussing.

Could you meet with a small group of us some evening to talk about this? If you can, call me at 555-1234 or send a note home with Barney suggesting some possible dates. Thank you!

> A school should be the most beautiful place in every town and village—so beautiful that the punishment for undutiful children should be that they should be debarred from going to school the following day.
>
> —OSCAR WILDE

Dear Principal Cleishbotham,

We, the undersigned parents of South Central High School students, are seriously concerned about the vacant house across the street from the school. A picture is developing of a site that shields drug-dealing, gang meetings, and other possibly criminal activities.

We would like the school to sponsor an informational and organizational meeting for school staff, students, parents, city officials, and police.

We are willing to volunteer our time and resources to making the neighborhood safer for our children. We feel that the school is in the most influential position to spearhead such an effort.

Sincerely,

Dear Dean Silva,

Neighbors in the vicinity of the College have been filing twice as many complaints this year as last about students using neighborhood parking spaces.

A check of our records indicates that parking tickets have been issued regularly to a number of vehicles appearing to belong to students (for failing to have resident stickers when parked in resident-parking-only areas). Some students have incurred as many as fifteen tickets already.

I suspect that students intend to ignore resident-parking-only signs and then also ignore the tickets, on the assumption that they will have no liability when they return home in May.

I'm enclosing a copy of the pertinent city code and would ask that you bring it to the attention of your students. The City is permitted to tag and tow cars parked illegally. Beginning on February 1, we will begin an aggressive course of tagging and towing in the neighborhood of the College.

If you have any questions, call me at 555-1234.

> You'll find that the things you learned in school will be vitally important to your success, provided that you are a contestant on "Jeopardy." Otherwise they're useless.
>
> —DAVE BARRY

RELATED TOPICS

Appreciation
Information
References
Requests
Thank You

45

Letters on Sensitive Issues

INTRODUCTION

Some difficult situations must be handled person-to-person as they arise. However, lack of preparation and high feelings often result in literally thoughtless responses and impromptu solutions. When circumstances permit, writing a letter is generally more productive. You have time to reflect on what has happened, to inform yourself of related or supporting facts, to choose your words so that they convey exactly what you want to convey— and, in the end, to rewrite the letter as many times as you need to until it represents clearly your position.

> When it comes to bombshells, there are few that can be more effective than that small, flat, frail thing, a letter.
>
> —MARGARET DELAND

DO

- Write promptly. There is nothing that will make a difficult letter more difficult to write than putting it off.

- Begin with a courteous expression of something, however small, that you can agree upon or that you have in common.

- Admit (if this is true) that you are uncomfortable with the situation.

- State the issue clearly and directly. Dressing up your message in big words, roundabout phrases, and conciliatory sentences will only antagonize the other person. If you have trouble writing this part of the letter, practice saying out loud what you're trying to convey as though you were explaining the issue to a sympathetic friend. Boil down your "conversation" to a sentence or two that expresses the heart of the matter.

- Provide facts and details of the issue.

- If appropriate, convey your respect and sympathetic understanding of the other person's position.

- Admit your role in the situation, if there is one. When you take responsibility for your contribution, others are more likely to own up to theirs.

- Examine your position for possible areas of negotiation. Can you trade one point for another? Can you accept anything less than what you originally wanted?

- State clearly what you are asking for or what solution you want.

- Close with a wish to put the matter behind you, with an expression of confidence that the situation will be resolved, with a statement that a satisfactory solution will benefit both of you, or with a sentence conveying your goodwill.

- Ask someone you respect and trust to read your letter before you send it.

> In dialogue, there is opposition, yes, but no head-on collision. Smashing heads does not open minds.
>
> —DEBORAH TANNEN

DON'T

- Don't assume you have all the facts about anything. Before writing, check out your assumptions. Particularly when a number of people are all discussing an issue, things can become muddled.

- Don't use words such as "problem," "argument," "battle," or others that frame a situation as something disagreeable or adversarial.

> ### Give in on small issues. In the long haul, you get more that way.
>
> —Janice LaRouche and Regina Ryan

- Don't make a decision sound negotiable if it is not. It is kinder to be clear that the answer is no, the news is bad, the response is negative.
- Don't exaggerate. When you adopt an extreme posture, the other person will want to go to the other extreme.
- Don't phrase things emotionally (unless you have a reason for doing so). Concentrate on facts instead of feelings. "I don't feel this is fair" does not carry as much weight as saying, "It is unfair that only one out of eight clerks is consistently asked to work overtime—and without overtime pay."

> ### Never give anyone an ultimatum unless you are prepared to lose.
>
> —Abigail Van Buren

- Don't deal with other matters in a letter about a touchy issue; save them for later. Sometimes people try to hide the difficult part of the letter in a jumble of news, offhand remarks, or other distractions. It doesn't work.
- When requesting a favor that makes you uncomfortable, admit it. Recognize that almost everyone at one time or another has had to do this. You will be able to make the request more easily if you can accept "no" for an answer, and make this clear to the other person.
- Don't try to teach people a lesson, to lecture them, or to label their behavior. Keep always before you the outcome you want (the return of a tool, cessation of a behavior, redressing a wrong) and orient your letter toward that outcome.
- Don't attack people or disparage their personality, character, intelligence, or looks. Focus on the behavior, the facts, the central issue. Getting "personal" indicates a weak position.
- Don't put the person on the defensive. Consider whether your letter is going to make the person feel bad, shamed, inept, or weak. If this is what you are aiming to do, fine. But if you want to negotiate or solve a problem, you are short-circuiting yourself; people who feel little and stupid are not apt to give you what you want.

> Magnifying a matter is not the way to mend it.
>
> —Ivy Compton-Burnett

HELPFUL HINTS

- When dealing with strong feelings, letters can be effective because they distance people from each other and from the problem while obliging them to think through their thoughts enough to get them down in some reasonable order on paper. However, letters can also worsen the problem. Written words are not as easily forgotten as words spoken in the heat of anger; they can also be reread many times by a grudge-holder. Words without accompanying gestures, smiles, and apologetic looks are colder and more inflexible. Three cautions will help: think carefully about the temperament of the person to whom you are writing and determine an approach that the person will be able to "hear"; do not write in the heat of your strongest feelings—that is, it is good to write then, but do not *mail* it; reread and rewrite your letter several times over a period of days.

> Anger is not an argument.
>
> —Daniel Webster

- Be clear about your goal. You can more easily write the letter if you finish this sentence: "I want them to . . ." Do you want a rebate, an exchange, repairs? Do you want an apology, a corrected statement, a credit? Do you want something redone? Do you want to convince the person that their facts, statistics, opinions are wrong?
- There is nothing wrong with saying you are angry, disappointed, upset, distressed, appalled, or anything else you might feel. In fact, the more carefully you choose the words that describe your situation, the clearer the communication will be. What is not acceptable is berating, belittling, or abusing the other person verbally. The difference often lies between "I" statements and "you" statements: "I am upset about the dent in my car door" is appropriate; "You are an idiot and they should take your license away" is not—unless, of course, this is your style and you don't care if the person pays for the dent or if you ever see them again. The tone of your letter makes all the difference between being "heard" and not being heard. Strive for a letter that is factual, dispassionate, considerate, and even-handed.

- Consider if there is any good news that can be linked to the bad news. This shouldn't be artificial good news, but if there is any related good news, it helps put the bad news in context.

- Whenever possible, help the other person save face. Set up the situation so that the person will do what you want and at the same time feel generous, gracious, powerful, and willing.

- Although the active voice is almost always preferred to the passive voice, you may want to consider the more tactful passive voice when involved in a disagreement. Instead of writing, "You did this," write, "This was done."

- A profoundly bitter, prejudiced, hostile, accusatory, or hate-mongering letter requires careful handling. If you think the writer could be actively dangerous, consult with the police or an attorney. In any case, you never need to respond to an abusive letter. At the mild end of the spectrum, when the person simply seems to need to let off steam (and you think a response is called for), reply with "I am sorry to hear you feel that way" and suggest any action on their part or yours that might alleviate the situation.

- In the case of a disagreement, begin by referring to the previous correspondence or to the event responsible for the present letter. Outline the two opposing views or actions. Give clear (perhaps numbered) reasons for your stand, using statistics, quotations from an employee handbook, supportive anecdotal material, and names of witnesses or others who agree with you (with their permission). If appropriate, suggest an intermediate stage of negotiation: a reply to specific questions in your letter; further research; a meeting between the two of you or with third parties present; visits to a lawyer, accountant, or other appropriate adviser. If the disagreement has reached the stage where you can effectively do this, finish by stating clearly the outcome you desire. End with your best wishes for a solution acceptable to both of you and a reference to good future relations.

> Anyone who thinks there aren't two sides to every argument is probably in one.
>
> —*The Cockle Bur*

- Sexual harassment consists of unwelcome, unsolicited, nonreciprocated sexual advances, requests for sexual favors, sexually motivated physical contact, or communication of a sexual nature, usually by someone who has power over another; it includes comments, jokes, looks, innuendoes, and physical contact, and emphasizes a person's sex role over any function as a worker. It is also against the law. To a woman whose boss had been sexually harassing her, Judith Martin ("Miss Manners") wrote, "he will undoubtedly claim that he didn't see anything wrong with what he was doing. He was only (he will protest) joking, or complimenting you, or helping you with your image, or being friendly. How was he to know that you would take it amiss? The answer is that his mother, his wife, his daughter, and in fact, the entire society has been trying to teach him that a gentleman does not make indecent gestures to a lady. . . . It has also been made abundantly clear that any romantic overtures, even when they are the polite sort that might be acceptable in social circumstances (where the lady could decline further acquaintance without imperiling her livelihood), violate office etiquette." If you are on the receiving end of such a violation of office etiquette, a good first step is a letter notifying the person that you consider the behavior to be sexual harassment. It used to be that saying anything about another's offensive behavior not only got you nowhere, but got you in trouble. This is no longer quite as true. Depending on your situation, a quiet warning note might be all that is needed. If you are on the doing end of a violation of office etiquette and have been called on it, you may want to do three things: (1) educate yourself about the issues until you feel sure you know where the boundaries are; (2) write a brief note of apology, thanking the person for letting you know and stating that you will comply with the request; (3) never repeat the behavior. Few reasonable people will bring a charge of sexual harassment against a one-time offender who didn't fully realize the original harm done and who is now apologetic and reformed. This subject is far too complicated to discuss here, what with false accusations, fears of retaliation, underreported harassment, and ignorance of what is and what isn't sexual harassment. But this is a sensitive issue where a well-written letter could avert bigger trouble.

- In *Tongue Fu!* Sam Horn offers advice about dealing with angry, rude people. She recommends trying to see things from the other person's point of view: "How would I feel if I were in their shoes? How would I feel if this were happening to me?" Then ask: "Why are they being difficult?" This will help you approach the situation in a way that the other person can understand.

> One of the keys to our present definition of good taste is that it is better to be kind than to be "correct." There is no situation in which it is smart to be nasty.
>
> —MILLICENT FENWICK

GETTING STARTED

I know—and sympathize—with your feelings about the promotion, but it is simply not in the cards at this time.

Thanks for going in on the blues harp for Pierre with me last month—here's the sales slip so you can see what your half amounts to (either cash or check is fine with me).

I hope you will understand that while I am in the early stages of recovery I simply can't be around some of my old friends—wish me well and I will call you when I can.

You don't have to understand where I'm coming from or agree with me or even like what I'm saying, but would you—as my good, dear friend—do me the great favor of not using blasphemous language around me?

We're getting company on the 23rd—could you return the folding cot and the card table and chairs sometime before then?

I can see how much fine work you put into the proposal for a short-term residential crisis support center, but the proposal doesn't answer many of the issues we felt needed addressing.

I know you think very highly of the copyeditor, but she has added over 400 commas to this little story for children and the manuscript looks as though it has the hiccups.

I dislike writing this, but I'm concerned about the renewal of Ms. Cliveden-Banks's rather steady drinking during the workday and her subsequent drive home during rush hour traffic.

I understand you have some thoughts about my work, behavior, and appearance, and I would like to discuss these with you directly rather than hear them second-hand.

I wouldn't ask you this if I didn't trust you to give me an honest "no" if that's what it has to be.

There appears to be a great deal of cruelty, exclusion, name-calling, and other hurtful behavior in this year's eighth grade class—could we have a parents' meeting to discuss this?

The office has been such a pleasant place since you started work here—with one small exception: I have a hard time with the gum-cracking—do you think you could try for a 100% "pleasant" rating?

The language and tone of your last letter are unacceptable to us. Please forward our file to someone else in your organization who can handle this matter.

> Anyone can become angry—that is easy; but to be angry with the right person, and to the right degree, and at the right time, and for the right purpose, and in the right way—that is not within everybody's power and is not easy.
>
> —Aristotle

MODEL LETTERS

Dear Clara and Baxter,

We are still talking about your beautiful wedding! I meant to ask you if the singer was a friend of yours—his voice was stunning.

I'm wondering if you received my wedding gift. As it was rather fragile, I hesitate to pay my Dawes-Radford charge balance until I am sure that (a) you did indeed receive it and (b) it arrived in one piece. I have visions of it having arrived damaged and you not knowing quite what to do about it.

Give my love to your mother when you see her, will you, Clara?

Fondly,
Lawrence

Dear Ms. Burdock,

You may not have noticed the wine stains on my linen tablecloth when you returned it after the club banquet last week. Because they had set, the stains needed special treatment by the dry cleaners.

I feel sure the club has funds to cover the cost of the drycleaning and would want to take responsibility for it. I'm enclosing the bill.

(This will also make me much more likely to lend things for club affairs next time!)

Sincerely,
H. Rimini

Dear Rev. Dawkbell,

I am able to write this letter only because I am sure that you are well convinced of my deep admiration for you. Leyminster Grammar School has become everything a good school ought to be—and you know that I credit you with the fine progress made these last few years.

- Don't assume you know the whole story or have all the facts about anything until you really do. When staff, teachers, students, families, friends, and neighbors are all discussing an issue, it can get very murky and words may be said, or letters written, that are later regretted.

> Education is not a preparation for life; education is life itself.
>
> —JOHN DEWEY

HELPFUL HINTS

- Be sure you are contacting the person most likely to help you. Generally, start with the person closest to the problem (gym teacher, band director, instructor, student's counselor) and go over that person's head only after you see that your efforts are unproductive. In some schools, disciplinary issues are handled by the assistant principal or a dean of students. Call the school for the name of the person who deals with your problem.

- Schools sometimes need to send letters home: a lice situation has been discovered in the fourth grade; the lost-and-found collection has exceeded all efforts at containment—would parents and guardians please encourage students to check for their belongings; parent-teacher conferences are now being scheduled; new rules for afterschool playground use have been drawn up. Each letter home should deal with a single issue, be worded briefly and clearly, and give the phone number of a contact person for those who have further or related questions. (By trying to imagine in advance what those questions might be, and answering them in the letter, you can reduce phone calls to almost zero.)

- The correspondence involved in applying to colleges and universities has its own rules, dictated by the institutions and often consisting of forms. From the moment you request information and application materials, you will be given full instructions on what to do, when to do it, and how to do it. All guidelines should be respected absolutely, as you risk being rejected for failing to follow them. Treat all correspondence with colleges as business correspondence, that is, each letter should be typed neatly and accurately, and the wording should be brief and professional. For information on letters of recommendation, see References. To write the much-dreaded and highly important college admission essays, you will need more help than a letterwriting book can give you. See, for example, such books as Susan Drachman Van Raalt, *College Applications and Essays*, 3rd ed. (1997); Boykin Curry, *Essays That Worked: For Business Schools* (1991); Christopher J. Georges, *100 Successful College Application Essays* (1988).

I am not sure that you are aware that the students have taken to joking among themselves about how noticeable your aftershave lotion is. My own experience is that a person becomes so used to it himself that he rarely notices its effects on others.

We needn't ever mention this again, but I thought you wouldn't mind this little note.

Truly yours,

J.S. Fletcher

Dear Brett,

I was pleased to get your note saying that your divorce is final—pleased because I know this is the way things had to be.

Did you ever see these lines by Elizabeth Cady Stanton? "Such is the nature of the marriage relation that a breach once made cannot be healed, and it is the height of folly to waste one's life in vain efforts to make a binary compound of two diverse elements. What would we think of the chemist who should sit twenty years trying to mix oil and water, and insist upon it that his happiness depended upon the result of the experiment?"

Congratulations on making it through this painful and often inhuman process. Surviving the past two years the way you have shows a strength of character that I know will stand you in good stead as you establish a new, fuller, and happier life.

I am always ready, dear friend, for a cup of tea, a chat, or a visit to the art gallery of your choice.

Love and a hug,

Frances

TO: George Stratfield
FROM: Liane Brooker
DATE: Feb. 10, 1999
RE: Request

I thought you should know that repeatedly touching my arm or putting your arm around my shoulder is inappropriate in a business setting (it would actually also be inappropriate outside the business setting because I do not welcome or encourage such gestures from people I don't know well). In the office, this is considered sexual harassment. I would very much appreciate keeping our exchanges on a professional level.

Knowing how intelligent and quick you are, I feel sure we will never need to discuss this again.

Dear Ms. Lucas,

I think you know I was unhappy with the author's override of almost all my editing suggestions on the golf book. You and I agree that in general the author should have the last word. However, in this case, the final manuscript contains many universally recognized grammar errors, inappropriate capitalizations, spelling inconsistencies, and such a "creative" approach to outlining that even a fourth-grader would notice.

Would you please see that I am not listed anywhere in the book as its editor? I don't mind if the author prefers his version, and I received a check for the hours I spent on the manuscript, so I have no complaints about the work itself. But I would be ashamed to have anyone think that book was an example of my editing skills.

Thank you!

Dear Friends,

Your stay with us at the lake last week was delightful. It made me determined not to let so much time go by before our next visit. I especially enjoyed getting to know James and Camilla—they were toddlers the last time I saw them!

I am assuming (I hope correctly, for the sake of our friendship) that you would want to know this. After you left, I discovered that several of our bottles of liquor were missing, and others had been seriously depleted. I was also missing a half-bottle of anti-anxiety pills and my prescription allergy medication. I have tried to think of all other possibilities (theft, other visitors, misplaced items, etc.) but find none that make sense.

I thought you needed to be alerted to the possibility of a problem, but now that I've done so, I will not mention this again.

I send all our love and remain

Your loving friend,

Mother is rather upset by the number of letters she has had criticizing her speech. I tell her about some of the ones I have gotten and how you can't help getting, no matter *what* you say, a certain amount of the "Dear Sir, you cur" letters.

—ANNE MORROW LINDBERGH

Dear Mr. Torpenhow,

I have received your letter demanding the return of your dog and your mention of taking legal action.

It would be helpful to review the situation. I found the dog in question on July 18 in a ditch off Highway 48, nearly dead of malnutrition and heat prostration. It also had a broken leg. It wore no collar or other identification.

Thus far, I have only your unsupported word that she is your dog.

My veterinarian and her associate have confirmed that the leg was broken approximately six months ago but was not set and apparently received no treatment whatsoever. Since the leg was broken, the dog was bred and gave birth to a litter. They tell me this neglect of the broken leg and continued use of the animal for breeding purposes in spite of it is animal abuse.

I am enclosing photocopies of my veterinary bills. So far they amount to $845.

I would need to be certain that the dog is in fact yours. I would need to be repaid for the veterinary bills, as well as for dog food, vitamins, etc. I would need to be certain the SPCA considers you a fit owner for the dog.

I am sending copies of this letter to my lawyer, my veterinarian, the local Humane Society, and the national Society for the Prevention of Cruelty to Animals.

Sincerely,

Dear Julius,

We are fortunate that in such a large, high-pressure office we all get along so well. You are one of the ones who keep the social temperature at such a comfortable setting. I don't know anyone in the office who is better liked than you.

You can perhaps help with this. The collection of contributions towards gifts for employees' personal-life events is becoming a little troubling. Certainly, the communal sending of a gift is justified now and then. In the past month, however, there have been collections for 2 baby shower gifts, 1 wedding shower gift, 2 wedding gifts, 1 funeral remembrance, 4 birthday gifts, and 3 graduation gifts.

It is not only the collected-from who are growing uncomfortable (and poor), but the collected-for feel uneasy at receiving gifts from people who don't know them outside the office, who wouldn't even recognize their graduating children, their marrying daughters and sons, or their deceased relatives.

It's difficult to extinguish what is essentially a very kind gesture (and one that people think very well of you for), but I think the practice has become too wide-ranging and is inappropriate in today's office setting.

Thank you for understanding.

Dear Sandra,

We feel so lucky to have you as our Babysitter in Chief—the children are crazy about you. We're looking forward to seeing you again this weekend.

One thing: our last phone bill had a number of long-distance charges that we didn't recognize. Upon checking the dates and after speaking with several of the recipients of the calls, we realized they were yours.

I'm enclosing a copy of the bill with those calls circled. I noticed that all the calls were made after 10:30 p.m., when the children would have been asleep. This agrees with my sense of you—that you would not be talking on the phone when the children were awake. Because of this good sense of responsibility, I felt you would want to reimburse us for the calls.

And, now, that's the end of that, OK?

> Unfortunately civility is hard to codify or legislate, but you know it when you see it. It's possible to disagree without being disagreeable.
>
> —Sandra Day O'Connor

RELATED TOPICS

Belated

Complaints

Refusals

Sympathy

46

Letters of Sympathy and Condolence

INTRODUCTION

Condolences are offered only in the event of a death; sympathy may be expressed for a death, but it is also extended to those who have suffered from a fire, flood, storm, or natural disaster; burglary, theft, or violent crime; a lost job, bankruptcy, personal reverses, or other misfortunes.

The condolence letter—and, close behind it, the sympathy letter—is one of the most difficult to write. People who are shocked and saddened and who feel inadequate and tongue-tied are writing to people who are grief-stricken and vulnerable and who feel life is hardly worth living.

The pitfalls of this type of letter are saying too little (sending only a signed card, for example) or too much (offering clichés, advice, or inappropriate comments). However, it is always better to write (even if you feel your note is unsatisfactory or inadequate); it is not easy for friends, families, or business associates to overlook a lack of response to the death of a loved one.

In a *Newsweek* piece, "Just Say Something," Betsy Okonski writes, "I discovered the amazing power of a humble sympathy card to bring me a measure of comfort. . . . One of the most helpful things you can do for a bereaved person is to acknowledge the loss. Don't fear causing pain by bringing it up. It was much more upsetting to me when someone acted like nothing had happened. 'I'm sorry' may feel inadequate, but the truth is that there is really nothing you can say that will take the pain away. Sincerely said, 'I'm sorry' says that you care, and that's what is truly needed. . . . It only takes a few minutes to send a card, and the act itself is much more meaningful than the exact text."

To thank people for their expressions of condolence or sympathy, see Thank You or Appreciation. To sympathize with and encourage someone who is ill, see Get Well.

> The written word often brings great comfort when an individual is coping with loss. Many letters of condolence are cherished and saved for years.
>
> —LEONARD M. ZUNIN AND HILARY STANTON ZUNIN

DO

- Mention the deceased person by name or specify the misfortune.
- Tell how you heard the news, if appropriate.
- Express your feelings of grief, dismay, loss.
- Offer condolences in the form of sympathy, thoughts, prayers, good wishes.
- Be tactful, but don't fear being honest—using the word *death* or *suicide*, for example. Circumlocutions like *passed on, passed away, departed, left this life, gone to their reward, gone to a better life, the deceased,* and *the dear departed* are no longer seen very often.
- Be brief (in most cases). A lengthy letter may be overwhelming in a time of grief. On the other hand, if your letter is lengthy because you are recounting wonderful memories of the deceased person, it may be very comforting. A letter that is lengthy because it includes other news or because it dwells on your own feelings is not appropriate.
- Mention what you particularly liked or loved about the deceased; relate some happy memory, anecdote, favorite expression, or advice they once gave you; mention the virtues, achievements, or successes for which they'll be remembered; tell about something they said or did that touched you. Especially welcome is recalling a complimentary or loving remark made by the deceased about the bereaved person. The more specific you are, the more memorable and comforting your letter will be.

> Memory is the only friend of grief.
>
> —RUMER GODDEN

- Accept that nothing you write will take away the person's grief, grief that is a necessary part of the healing process. Too many people agonize about finding the magic words that will make everything right again. There simply aren't any.

- If you are writing to one member of a family, include the others in your closing.

- End with a general expression of concern or affection or an encouraging reference to the future: "You are in my thoughts and prayers"; "My thoughts are with all of you in this time of sorrow"; "May you find some small comfort in your warm and loving memories"; "May the love of family and friends comfort and strengthen you in the days ahead."

- You might let the person know that you don't expect a response to your note or letter. After writing thank-you notes for flowers, condolences, memorials, honorary pallbearers, and special assistance, there is often little energy left to acknowledge sympathy letters.

> Condolence is the art of giving courage.
>
> —MONICA LEHNER-KAHN

DON'T

- Don't let your discomfort keep you from sending your sympathy and good wishes. At the very minimum, a commercial card with a line or two in your own handwriting is far better than no response at all. And don't hesitate to send belated condolences. The bereaved will appreciate being remembered even if the message is late. It is not difficult to overlook tardiness, but it is almost impossible to overlook being ignored entirely.

- Don't offer to help ("If there's anything I can do, please let me know"). This requires a response from people who are already facing too many decisions too quickly; most people will not take you up on such a vague offer. Instead, just do something: bring food, have the dress or suit the person is wearing to the funeral drycleaned, put up out-of-town visitors, watch children for several hours, address acknowledgments, take over work duties for a few days, cut grass or shovel snow, water the garden, help clean the house. If you are not close to the bereaved, an offer of help will be seen for the empty gesture it is. If you are close, you will either know what is helpful or you know whom to ask (friend, neighbor) about what needs doing.

- Don't focus on your feelings: "I've been just devastated—I can't seem to keep my mind on anything"; "I start crying every time I think of him"; "Why didn't you call me?" In the chapter entitled "P.S. Don't tell *me* how bad you feel!" of her bestselling book, *Widow*, Lynn Caine says most of the condolence letters she received were more about the writer's awkwardness, discomfort, and inadequacies than about her sorrow or their shared loss. She says many letters were "full of expressions of how uneasy the writers felt, how miserable the writers were—as if they expected *me* to comfort *them*." There is a fine line between expressing your sorrow and dramatizing your own reactions.

- Don't indulge in overly dramatic language ("the worst tragedy I ever heard of," "the dreadful, horrible, appalling news"). If you were shocked or appalled at the news, say so—but avoid being excessively sentimental, sensational, or morbid. A simple "I'm sorry" is effective and comforting.

- Don't discuss the philosophy of death or offer religious commentary unless you are very certain that sympathy grounded in a shared philosophic or religious orientation is appropriate for this person. Avoid pious clichés, simplistic "explanations" of the tragedy, or unwarranted readings of God's activities, intents, or involvement in the death.

- Don't hesitate to write to people who are experiencing a misfortune considered socially embarrassing (a family member convicted of a crime, for example); if friends or family are hurting, your warm message of support will probably be welcome.

> In all disappointments sympathy is a great balm.
>
> —ELIZABETH GASKELL

- Don't rely on well-meaning but hurtful clichés, false cheerfulness, and optimistic platitudes. In a *Reader's Digest* article, "An Etiquette for Grief," Crystal Gromer says, "In the context of grief, clichés are simply bad manners. . . . 'At least he didn't suffer,' people say. 'At least he's not a vegetable.' Any time you hear 'at least' come out of your mouth, stop. Creating an imaginary worse scenario doesn't make the real and current one better. It trivializes it." Lynn Caine (*Widow*) wrote, "It infuriated me to have people say, 'I know you'll be feeling better soon.' I wanted people to sympathize with how terrible I felt right then and there." C.C. Colton once said, "Most of our misfortunes are more supportable than the comments of our friends upon them." Avoid the following comments:

  Chin up.
  Be brave.
  Don't cry.
  You'll get over it.

It's better this way.
She is better off now.
Time heals all wounds.
He was too young to die.
Life is for the living.
Keep busy, you'll forget.
I know just how you feel.
God never makes a mistake.
Be happy for what you had.
He's in a better place now.
It's a blessing in disguise.
At least she isn't suffering.
You must get on with your life.
He was old and had a good life.
Every cloud has a silver lining.
I heard you're not taking it well.
She is out of her misery at least.
Be thankful you have another child.
At least you had him for eighteen years.
Don't worry, it was probably for the best.
I feel almost worse than you do about this.
God had a purpose in sending you this burden.
You're young yet; you can always marry again.
It's just as well you never got to know the baby.
You're not the first person this has happened to.
I have a friend who's going through the same thing.
God only sends burdens to those who can handle them.
Life must go on—you'll feel better before you know it.

True friends visit us in prosperity only when invited, but in adversity they come without invitation.

—THEOPHRASTUS

HELPFUL HINTS

- Letters of sympathy are generally handwritten unless you are writing to someone with whom you have only business attachments: another firm, a client, a supplier, or a customer. Commercial greeting cards are acceptable, although it is rarely suitable to simply sign your name under the printed message. Add at least a line or two of your own. Avoid bright colors and bold patterns in stationery or cards.

- In the case of a suicide, offer your sympathy as you would to any other bereaved family. Because many survivors experience feelings of guilt, rejection, confusion, and social stigma, they need to know that you are thinking of them, that you care. Although it is generally appropriate to say you were "shocked to hear about" someone's death, avoid the phrase in this case. Don't ask questions, speculate about how the death could have been prevented, or dwell on the fact of the suicide; what matters is that the person is gone and the family is grieving. Instead, talk about how the person touched your life, share a happy memory, or express sympathy for the bereaved's pain.

- Miscarriages and stillbirths are devastating experiences. Sympathize as you would for the death of any child. Avoid such unfortunately common remarks as: "You already have two lovely children—be grateful for what you have"; "This may have been for the best—there might have been something wrong with the baby, and this was nature's way of taking care of it"; "You're young yet—you can try again." And the worst of all: "Don't feel so bad. After all, it isn't as though you lost a *child*." The person *has* lost a child.

- To ensure that you don't write anything awkward, pitying, or tactless, reread your letter as though you were the one receiving it.

- Responding to news of a divorce or separation can be awkward unless you know the person you are writing very well. In most cases, neither expressions of sympathy nor congratulations are entirely suitable. However, whether the person is "better off" or not, such life changes are never without their losses, and some acknowledgment of the difficult period of adjustment and a message of support may be welcome. If appropriate, let the person know you have confidence in their choices and their ability to move on.

- In the case of business associates, customers, clients, or employees who have lost someone close to them, write as you would for friends or relatives, although your note will be shorter and more formal. Avoid personal remarks; it is enough to say you are thinking about them at this time, extend sympathy on behalf of the company, and convey condolences to other members of the person's family. When you are writing to the family of an employee who has died, you may want to offer assistance in gathering personal effects, discussing the pension plan, or making a referral to someone in the company who can help with questions.

- Those who are grieving the death of a companion animal will appreciate a note of sympathy. This can be a devastating loss to some people; whether one can identify with the feelings or not, expressing sympathy is a loving, respectful gesture.

- When sending flowers to a funeral home, address the accompanying small card's envelope to "The family of Cynthia Drassilis." Insert a plain white card from the florist or your business card with a brief message ("Please accept my sincerest sympathy" or "My thoughts and prayers are with you and the children"). If you make a donation to a charitable organization in the deceased person's name, include the family's name and address as well as your own. The organization sends a notice of the contribution to the family and acknowledges to you that the donation was received.

- For additional reading, see Leonard M. Zunin and Hilary Stanton Zunin, *The Art of Condolence: What to Write, What to Say, What to Do at a Time of Loss* (1991). For more general background reading, see Judith Viorst, *Necessary Losses* (1986).

> A good letter of condolence is like a handclasp, warm and friendly.
>
> —LILLIAN EICHLER WATSON

GETTING STARTED

My heart goes out to you as you grieve the loss of your sister.

I send you my deepest sympathy on Maury's death.

We were both grieved to hear of your loss and we extend to you our most sincere sympathy on Vassili's death.

We are all grieving with and for you.

How sad I was to hear of Margot's sudden death.

It was with a profound sense of loss that I learned of Rudy's death.

All of us at Swann Industries were shocked and saddened to hear of the death of your lovely wife, Odette.

We were stunned by the news that your dear little Toby died after you knew and loved him for only two weeks—you must be devastated.

Please accept my heartfelt condolences on your miscarriage—I know how much you were both looking forward to welcoming this child into your lives.

Today marks the fifth anniversary of Archie's death, and I just wanted you to know that we still miss him and that you are in our thoughts today.

I was sorry to hear about the divorce. This must be a difficult time for you.

We want to express to you our most heartfelt sympathy on the loss of your lovely home in the fire last Saturday.

Just a note to tell you how sorry we are that you lost your beautiful catalpa tree to the storm. As long as we've lived here I've loved that tree.

We've just heard the upsetting news about your financial problems and we wanted you to know that we are wishing you well and hoping for better news soon.

We were so sad to hear that your father is in intensive care. We will be thinking about all of you and hoping for the best.

I want you to know how distressed I was to hear of the vandalism to the temple—do you need people to help clean up?

Everyone at the seminary is grieving Luis's death and we wish to extend our condolences to all of you. We will miss him more than we can say.

All my thoughts are with you as you learn to live with AIDS. Are you free for dinner some night next week?

It was with sincere regret that I heard about what you've been going through—but thank you for letting me know.

I was shocked to hear that you have been laid off, but I hope that someone with your experience and qualifications will soon find something suitable—maybe even something better.

> There is nothing sweeter than to be sympathized with.
>
> —GEORGE SANTAYANA

MODEL LETTERS

Dear Mr. Morel,

Please accept our condolences on the death of your mother, whom we were privileged to have as a dear neighbor for the past twenty years. Many of her friends share your grief, and I know she will always remain very much alive in the memories of all of us who loved, respected, and treasured her.

Please convey our sympathies to other members of your family.

Sincerely,

Clara and Baxter Dawes

Dear Rina,

All of us here at Benjamin Farm Products are shattered by the news of your daughter's death. We send you our deepest sympathies.

I met Hilda only once, at last year's annual picnic, and was impressed with her keen mind and sense of humor—what a delightful young woman. Your loss is inestimable.

It seems insensitive to mention this here, but I want you to know that everything on your desk is being taken care of. Do not give a thought to anything here until you are ready to do so.

My thoughts and sympathy are with you at this sad time.

Sincerely,
Ben

Dear Judge Irwin,

I would like to extend to you my most heartfelt sympathies on the death of your wife. I only knew Lucy in her capacity as one of the most outstanding teachers at Burden's Landing Elementary, but that was enough to give me an appreciation for her talents, warmth, and generosity of spirit. I don't believe I've ever known anyone who had as many friends or who deserved them more. Like so many others who admired her, I am deeply grieved and bewildered by her unexpected death. The members of the staff have suggested to me that we remember and honor her in some concrete way here at the school.

I will always remember Lucy and feel very fortunate to have known her.

I hope that you can find some small comfort in your good memories and in the thought of the happy years you shared.

Sincerely,

Bogan Maddox
Principal

My dear Yvonne,

Thank you for letting us know that you and Geoffrey are divorcing. I naturally have all sorts of mixed feelings—sorrow that it didn't work out, sympathy for all the time and energy you both put into your relationship, and some relief that things will be better for both of you. This is a rough patch, but you are resilient and you will come out on the other side of it before too long.

I'll be out of town for the next two weeks, but could we have dinner together some night after that? I'll call.

Lots of love,
F.

My dear Rosa,

I wish I could give you a big hug—not that it would change anything. It's hard to imagine how much you must be hurting. You and Edwin were always such a pair—I can't picture you without him (nor could I have ever pictured him without you). I send you my love and sympathy and prayers. I'm glad you have the children and their families nearby—you'll all need each other.

I keep thinking of last October when we were all together—the laughter, the good times, the fun, the warmth. Edwin was in top form—a stranger would never have guessed he had so many health problems. You both looked "in the pink" and it seemed as if that world—and the party—would go on forever. It's unbearable to think of the differences between then and now.

You two have always been such a model for me of what a loyal, longterm relationship could be. I loved the look on your face when you looked at Edwin—and he had the same look for you. There was a warmth between you that many people never know. He had a way of looking on the bright side that was contagious—you couldn't be around him without feeling good. He had such an easy, gracious way about him and he made everybody feel they were special to him—I know he always made me feel that way.

This is—and will be—so hard. I hope all the years of love and happy memories will be a comfort to you. All my thoughts and love are with you now and always.

With love,

Dear Micah,

Please accept the condolences of everyone at Dalmailing Chemicals on the death of your father. Although none of us ever met him, we all enjoyed your delightful stories about his many inventions, and we extend to you our sympathy on the loss of a dear father who was also mentor, friend, and fishing buddy to you.

Dear Mr. Ingleside,

I've just heard about the robbery and vandalism you had at the store last night. That is surely one of the greatest nightmares of any small business owner.

Can I help? What do you need? I thought you could use an extra pair of hands, so I'm sending this note over with Kate Beautiman, my assistant manager. She can stay until 5 p.m., helping you with whatever needs doing.

I'll give you a call tomorrow, but if I can do anything for you between now and then, let me know.

Dear Lemmy,

I was sorry to hear that your efforts to keep the new highway from going through your property were unsuccessful. I remember the day twenty years ago when you took me out to see that poor neglected piece of land. You certainly have worked wonders with it.

I hope you can find some way of living with this or maybe even of finding some good in it (I know, I don't see any either at the moment). From studying the paper, I see that most of your place will remain untouched, but that's not very comforting when you're facing the havoc to the rest of it.

I'll stop by one of these weekends to see how it's going.

Dear Masterson,

I've just heard the news about your brother Joseph's death and want to offer you my most sincere condolences. I've always enjoyed your stories of what it was like growing up in such a large, loving, zany family. You'll not only be mourning the loss of your dear brother (Gideon Forsyth tells me you were especially close to him), but also the loss of the complete family as you knew it.

I send my affectionate respects and sympathies to you and your family.

> The sun has set in your life; it is getting cold. The hundreds of people around you cannot console you for the loss of the one.
>
> — MARIA AUGUSTA TRAPP

Dear Grace,

Thank you for letting me know through Carrie why you've been out of touch for so long.

I am very sympathetic. Since we've lived here for only four years, you may not know that ten years ago we went through something similar with our oldest child— all the hard months of knowing something was wrong, discovering the drug problem, and then several years of unsuccessful attempts at treatment.

It's probably not comforting to you when you're in the midst of all the hundreds of small and large burdens this brings you, but our daughter has completely turned her life around. It *is* possible.

I send you and your family all my best wishes. When you are ready to see me again, I'll be waiting . . .

Dear Cicely,

Your phone call telling us about George's suicide was the saddest news we have ever received. Our hearts go out to you.

We both feel a need to talk about George's life, not his death. That his wonderful gifts and graces and contributions—in short, the manner of his life—should be overshadowed by the manner of his death is one more intolerable grief.

Did I ever tell you how we met him? Or about our wonderful road trip the week we all graduated from college? Or the time we had dinner together and none of us had any money with us? You know he helped us tile the bathroom floor, but did we ever tell you about the mix-up between the tile cement and the grout?

Please, when you can, let us find time to be together to tell some of our stories about George.

We'll be in touch. You know you have our deepest sympathy and our love and friendship always.

> What's grief but the after-blindness
> of the spirit's dazzle of love?
>
> —GWEN HARWOOD

RELATED TOPICS

Acknowledgments

Appreciation

Belated

Get Well

Thank You

47

Thank-You Letters

INTRODUCTION

Thank-you notes or letters are sent to express appreciation for: gifts, favors, contributions; hospitality and invitations; information, materials, reports; loans, financial support, or repayment of personal loans; letters of recommendation, reference, or introduction; support, encouragement, kindness, special assistance, or advice; expressions of sympathy and condolence; messages of appreciation and congratulations; get well wishes; volunteer efforts; honors, awards, recognition, scholarships; customer, client, or patient referrals; new orders or business; job well done, effective sales presentations, useful employee suggestions.

You are not obliged to write a thank you under some of those circumstances (although of course it is always in excellent taste to do so, and a gracious "thank you" will greatly smooth and enhance both your personal life and your professional life). A thank you is considered necessary, however, for: gifts received by mail or when the donor is not present, parties at which you are the guest of honor, overnight stays at the home of anyone who is not a close friend or relative.

When in doubt about whether a thank you is "necessary," remember that it is better to express your appreciation too often than not often enough.

For wedding gift thank you's, see Weddings.

> Thank-you letters . . . are absolutely essential to maintaining good relationships, and their neglect can hurt you. It is better to give too many thanks (if that is possible), than too few.
>
> —MARTHA W. CRESCI

DO

- Write soon. It is much easier to find the words when you are feeling grateful than it is later on when your enthusiasm has cooled. It is also more courteous. Most givers don't need your thanks as much as they need to know if the gift arrived and if it pleased you. Some people think a thank-you note should be written within three days of receiving a gift. Certainly two weeks would be the maximum.
- Mention in some detail what you are grateful for. Be specific, avoiding such sweeping remarks as "Thank you for the nice present" or "Thank you for remembering me."
- Say how pleased you are to have the gift. Tell how useful or appropriate it is, how you plan to use it, where you have placed it, or how it enhances your life, home, office, wardrobe, etc.
- Close with one or two sentences unrelated to the object of your gratitude (expressing affection, promising to see the person soon, sending greetings to family members, saying something nice about the donor).

> There's a self-expansive aspect of gratitude. Very possibly it's a little-known law of nature: the more gratitude you have, the more you have to be grateful for.
>
> —ELAINE ST. JAMES

DON'T

- Don't dilute your thanks by including news, information, questions, and comments; save them for another time.
- Don't ask where the gift was purchased so you can exchange it.
- Don't mention receiving duplicate gifts.

- Don't overdo it. "Never express more than you feel" is a good guideline, especially in thank-you letters, where we are tempted to make up in flowery language for what we lack in enthusiasm. A simple "thank you very much" is very effective.

- Don't feel overwhelmed if someone has overspent on a gift for you, entertained you far more lavishly than the situation called for, or given you a gift when you did not reciprocate. Assume that the person must have wanted to do things that way. Don't try to make your thanks commensurate with the gift; concentrate instead on those smaller aspects of the gift or hospitality that pleased you.

> No metaphysician ever felt the deficiency of language so much as the grateful.
>
> —C.C. COLTON

HELPFUL HINTS

- When gifts arrive early for an event, do not write thank-you notes until after the special day.

- Some authorities recommend not mentioning the amount of a money gift. They suggest instead writing about the other person's kindness, generosity, or, perhaps, extravagance. Other authorities recommend mentioning the exact amount and telling how you plan to spend it. Generally, people don't want to hear that you're saving it, unless they know you have a special college, travel, or house down-payment fund. If the donor has indicated some purpose for the money ("I want you to buy yourself a really good pen that you'll have all your life"), be obliging.

- When you are thanking someone for a gift, dinner party, favor, or advice that wasn't at all to your taste, focus on the giver rather than on the gift. Express your appreciation for thoughtfulness and generosity rather than for the gift or favor itself. It is generally possible to find something to say that is both truthful and positive of either the gift or its giver.

- To respond to a congratulatory message that is flattering and enthusiastic about your talents or an achievement, say "thank you" first of all. Then be gracious. Eleanor Hamilton says, "A compliment is a gift, not to be thrown away carelessly unless you want to hurt the giver." It is easier to handle a compliment if you reflect it back to the giver ("how nice of you to write," "your letter touched me," "how thoughtful of you").

- A few letterwriting authorities dislike seeing "Thanks again" at the end of a thank-you note. However, this is a popular and harmless way of reminding the other person of the purpose of the letter. If you like it, use it.

- A thank-you note should be sent for a thank-you gift, if for no other reason than to let the person know the gift arrived.

- When more than one person gives you a gift, personalized thank-you notes are sent to each person. You do not need to do this when you receive a gift from a family (even when all five of them sign the card) or when you receive a gift from a group such as your bridge club, teachers at your school, your co-workers. You can write one letter to the group but be sure that it is circulated or posted so that everyone who contributed to the gift sees it.

- Elizabeth Post, continuing Emily Post's work as an etiquette resource, says the thank-you note is one of the three kinds of letters that should be handwritten whenever possible (the other two are letters of condolence and formal replies to invitations). She excepts typed thanks when they are part of a long, personal letter to family or friends. Business thanks can also be typed, although the handwritten note carries a little warmer message when that is the effect you want.

- When you need to thank many people, it is appropriate (and, in some areas, expected) to insert a thank-you notice in the local newspaper. The nurses, doctors, hospital staff, friends, and family who helped someone through a long and demanding illness are often thanked this way. The funeral of a public figure may inspire hundreds of notes of condolence, which are best acknowledged in a newspaper announcement. Recently elected public officials thank those who worked and voted for them. The wording is simple and warm: "We wish to thank all the generous and loving friends and family who sent cards and gifts on the occasion of our twenty-fifth wedding anniversary."

- An effective job-seeking strategy as well as a gesture of courtesy is sending a thank-you note after a job interview. Write the note immediately after the interview (before a decision is made), mentioning what you liked about the interview, the company, the position. Since most of us have our most brilliant thoughts an hour or so after the interview, you can add them to the thank-you note along with any words that might redeem parts of the interview that didn't go well. Writing the note gives you a chance to emphasize your interest in the position and to illustrate your self-starting and expressive talents. It may also make you a stand-out as many people do not write thank you's for an interview.

- Business entertaining is often taken for granted, but a brief thank you is appreciated and builds goodwill.

> Business people appreciate receiving a thank-you letter because it adds a touch of warmth to the cold world of business.
>
> —Harold E. Meyer

- The guest or guests of honor at a baby shower, birthday party, housewarming, anniversary celebration, or other such occasion thank each friend warmly for gifts as they are opened, but write individual thank-you notes later. The party host receives a special thank-you note as well as a small gift.

- A donation to a charity in your honor or in memory of a deceased relative will be acknowledged by the charitable organization, but you must also write a thank-you note to the donor.

- Following a death, handwritten thank-you notes are written to people who sent flowers or donations; to those who helped with hot meals, hosted dinners, put up out-of-town visitors, lent chairs, or were otherwise supportive; and to all those who sent notes of condolence (exception: those who sent printed cards with only a signature and no personal message). You may use the printed cards supplied by the funeral director if you add a personal note. When the person closest to the bereaved is unable to write immediately, a member of the family or a friend may write thank you's on their behalf. The notes don't have to be long, and don't even have to be sent as soon as other types of thank-you notes; traditionally, you have up to six weeks after a funeral. To keep track of who sent flowers, attached cards should be collected by a family member or funeral home official and a description of the flowers noted on each.

> His courtesy was somewhat extravagant. He would write and thank people who wrote to thank him for wedding presents and when he encountered anyone as punctilious as himself the correspondence ended only with death.
>
> —Evelyn Waugh

GETTING STARTED

Thank you for your warm, funny note—how did you remember it was my birthday?

Thank you for your interest in the El Dorado Inn & Suites, conveniently located one mile from the airport and two blocks from the Mall of America.

You will probably never entirely realize what a difference you've made this year with your many hours of volunteering.

Thank you for your many kindnesses to Benito while he's been in school at the University of San Diego.

Many thanks for remembering my ten-year anniversary with the company.

Your heartwarming get well message and the long, newsy letter were better than medicine!

I can never thank you enough for the way you helped with the children when I was in the hospital.

Consider me deeply in your debt for taking over all my duties for four days while Mother was in intensive care.

We are most grateful to you for agreeing to be our annual fund coordinator, especially since we know how busy you are this year.

On behalf of everyone at Prescott Printing, Inc., I want to thank you for the wonderful job you did organizing the annual picnic.

Although Kino is going to write you himself, I wanted to thank you for knowing just what would please an eight-year-old.

We are still talking about the evening we spent at your house—thank you, thank you!

I wish to express my sincere thanks for your kind hospitality. I will never forget the four days I spent with you in Munich.

Thank you for your comforting words on the death of my brother.

Thank you very much for your kind expression of sympathy.

Your expression of love and concern brought us great comfort during those first awful days after Delia's death.

You were so kind to Mother during those last weeks—we will never be able to tell you how much it meant to us.

On behalf of the Board of Directors of the Edith and Oliver Price Foundation and all those who benefit directly and indirectly from its work, I thank you for your generous contribution.

This is just a note to say thanks for rushing the presentation binders to us in time for our event.

I'm grateful for your excellent advice on used cars. I'm pleased with what we finally bought.

You shouldn't have, but since you did, may I say that your choice was absolutely inspired!

I want to thank you again for recommending Inglesant Tree Specialists—they've been as good as you said they were.

How thoughtful of you to bring me the paperweight from Murano, especially since I know you had to hand-carry it all the way home.

Thank you for referring Fausto Babel to our office.

Belinda and I are most grateful to you for your expertise, patience, and attention to detail as you shepherded us through the purchase of our new home.

I've just opened your package and I have to tell you that even if you were a mind-reader, you couldn't have chosen anything more perfect!

I can't tell you how delighted I was with the subscription to "Stories for Our Times"!

I appreciate your kind words and your confidence in me. They have been a great support during these first few weeks on the job.

I can't thank you enough for getting the radon testing kits here in time. I'm sorry we could give you so little notice.

Thanks for all the chauffeuring last week when we were without a car. I hope I can do something as nice for you some day.

> There shall be
> Eternal summer in the grateful heart.
>
> — CELIA THAXTER

MODEL LETTERS

February 20, 1995

Dear Ginevra,

I'm always thanking you—which means you're always doing something kind and nice. Writing a college recommendation is even more than kind and nice. I truly appreciate your taking time—away from other obligations—to write this for Tom. It was a glowing description. It's wonderful to know someone else sees your child as you do. Other than his father, I think that person has always been you for Tommy.

Marge

March 16, 1997

Dear Momma,

I just wanted to thank you for a truly inspiring and wonderful gift: the ballet. I cannot tell you how much it has added to my life, my spirit, my happiness, my dreams, my memories, and my knowledge. The last performance was tonight, and oh, I could have cried when it was over. I will carry those four performances with me all my life, though. I still remember when you took me to the Nutcracker, or to see Garth Fagan's Bucket Dance Theater. You have nourished my artistic life so well. Thank you. At heart I'm a dancin' girl.

Love,
Katie

Dear Mr. Holroyd,

Thank you for your invitation to submit a plan for an on-site library branch in the Burgess Building. We will have the proposal ready for you September 1. Until then, may I say that we are all very excited about this "novel" idea!

Mr. and Mrs. Elphinstone,

Thank you so much for letting my film crew use your lovely home for the interior scenes of "The Shuttle." We could not have been more pleased with the way things went.

I promised that we would leave everything exactly as you had it. Please let me know if you discover anything misplaced or damaged.

I'm enclosing two passes to a chain of local movie theaters so that you can see this and any other films you like during the next year.

Dear Mr. Farrar,

Thank you for your thoughtful and generous donation to St. Winifred's in memory of John "Dubbs" Daubeny. He would have been pleased, and the family appreciates your comforting gesture very much.

Dear Mona,

Thanks again for the beautiful ring. Indigo blue is the color of the 6th chakra (third eye) which is insight, intuition, intellect, and introspection—good energy for me.

I'm in the fear and loathing stage of moving. Today is my peak packing day and I will move everything to a storage locker tomorrow morning. The real brain damage is organizing, not the physical labor. Who did this to me? My evil twin?

I love the ring! Many blessings!

Jarvis

> Anyone too busy to say thank you will get fewer and fewer chances to say it.
>
> —HARVEY MACKAY

Dearest Marian,

Your letter of November 3 was immensely comforting. I was deeply moved by your love and concern. I especially liked the quotation from Anne Finger, "Part of getting over it is knowing that you will never get over it," because I'm beginning to know that I'll never get over losing Jasper.

All my love to you,

Dora

Dear Lucina Merritt and Eben Merritt:

Thank you very much for your tax-deductible gift of $500 to the Wilkins-Freeman Neighborhood Center. Your gift will help support afterschool care; marital, peer, and addiction counseling; housing, legal, and medical information; courses in independent living skills; and advocacy programs for the nearly 2,000 individuals we anticipate serving during the coming year.

You have invested in an important and effective community resource. On behalf of the board and staff, we appreciate your support of the Center's work.

> Gratitude is something of which none of us can give too much. For on the smiles, the thanks we give, our little gestures of appreciation, our neighbors build up their philosophy of life.
>
> —A.J. CRONIN

TO: Dr. Alexander Manette
FROM: Cardiac-Rhythm Devices Symposia Committee
SUBJECT: Spring Symposium
DATE: Nov. 18, 1999

Thank you for contributing to the success of the Spring Symposium. The Committee was pleased to be able to present so many high-quality papers and poster talks. The Spring and Fall Symposia are among the most important events sponsored by the Cardiac-Rhythm Devices Division. These symposia provide the research community with a means of discussing proprietary work and new ideas on a company-wide basis.

We appreciate your continued enthusiasm and support for these symposia.

1999 Symposia Committee
Dr. A. Pickerbaugh, Chair

Dear Isabel,

Thanks so much for your conversations and moral support over the past two weeks—and the past 38 years for that matter. They mean a lot to me.

Love,
Pansy

Dear Glenway,

Thank you for your timely help with the ion milling and high-resolution transmission electron microscopy of the materials we were working on when our own TEM broke down. Without your generous and capable emergency assistance, we could never have filed a well-researched patent application on these materials under the tight time constraints.

Your willingness to perform these tasks outside normal working hours was deeply appreciated.

Dear Mr. Fleming,

I understand that it was you who nominated Spectre, Inc. for the Outstanding Small Business Award this year. As you know, we were indeed so honored by the Community Business Association.

Please accept our sincere appreciation for your support and interest.

Sincerely,
Ernst Stavro Blofeld

I would maintain that thanks are the highest form of thought; and that gratitude is happiness doubled by wonder.

—G.K. CHESTERTON

RELATED TOPICS

Acknowledgments
Appreciation
Belated
Responses

48

Letters Dealing with Travel Arrangements

INTRODUCTION

Today most routine travel arrangements (airline, car, hotel reservations; requests for tourist, passport, health information; cancellations) are made by phone or e-mail or, increasingly, on the Internet. Occasionally, however, a letter is the best choice—to confirm arrangements, to address special problems, to register a complaint.

Every letter that a travel business writes to customers—even a one-sentence response to a query for information—is a sales or goodwill letter and should be courteous, positive, and presentable.

> A trip is what you take when you can't take any more of what you've been taking.
>
> —ADELINE AINSWORTH

DO

- Doublecheck every letter dealing with reservations to be sure you have included all the specifics: dates; number of nights, people, rooms; kind of accommodation (single, double, nonsmoking, poolside, connecting rooms); extras requested (crib in a room, for example); verification of information about accessibility, availability of pool, HBO, entertaining facilities; type of car, number of days, pickup and dropoff points; record, confirmation, or other locator number; credit card number, if necessary; your address and telephone number; names of guests or passengers, if necessary; mention of deposit sent or coupons enclosed; terms you were given over the phone so that both parties have the same information. Ask for a confirmation number. Sending complete, accurate information is the best way to ensure that everything goes smoothly.

- Be brief when writing about travel arrangements. Aside from standard courtesies ("thank you for your attention"), you need write only the particulars. It is often best to put each unit of information on its own line:

  compact car

  standard transmission

  airconditioning

  3 days, May 11-14

  pickup: New York-JFK

  dropoff: Boston-Logan

> Oh, I realize that not everybody likes to plan every step of a vacation. Some people would rather just grab a backpack and a sleeping bag, stick out their thumbs and start hitchhiking down the highway, enjoying the fun and adventure of not knowing "what's around the bend."
> Most of these people are dead within hours. So planning is definitely the way to go.
>
> —DAVE BARRY

DON'T

- Don't forget to cancel arrangements if you change your plans; if you have given your credit card number, you will be charged.
- Don't assume anything—ask for information if you are not sure about any details.

> Whenever possible, avoid airlines which have anyone's first name in their titles, like Bob's International Airline or Air Fred.
>
> —Miss Piggy

HELPFUL HINTS

- One can hardly say "travel" without thinking "postcards." If you choose the cards carefully, you will already have something to write ("Our hotel is right by this canal" or "We toured this castle yesterday" or "We went to the top of this mountain in a funicular"). A postcard should show recipients something colorful, interesting, or unknown to them. Your message might focus on your pleasure in being there (nobody wants to hear that you've had nothing but trouble). Tell what you've liked best, a food you've eaten for the first time, an interesting fact or bit of history, the impact your trip is having on you.

> Those of us who travel tend to stretch the truth on occasion.
>
> —Susan Allen Toth

- When requesting confirmation or a response from a hotel, resort, travel bureau, or other overseas place of business, especially one on the low-budget end, it can be advantageous to enclose an International Reply Coupon (IRC) to encourage an answer.
- Take copies of all reservations, confirmation letters, etc., with you as you travel, along with notes on all telephone arrangements.
- If you want to get in the mood to write travel letters home, read Rudyard Kipling's *Letters of Travel*, Pierre Teilhard de Chardin's *Letters from a Traveller*, John Steinbeck's *A Russian Journal*, Michael Crichton's *Travels*. From Phillip Brooks' 1893 *Letters of Travel* and Gertrude Bell's 1894 *Persian Pictures* to Freya Stark's 1929 *Baghdad Sketches* to Joanne Sandstrom's 1983 *There and Back Again* and Erma Bombeck's 1991 *When You Look Like Your Passport Photo, It's Time to Go Home*, you'll find letters to inspire and entertain.

Parents needn't bother driving small children around to see
the purple mountains' majesties; the children will go right on
duking it out in the back seat and whining for food as if you
were showing them Cincinnati. No one under twenty really
wants to look at scenery.

—Barbara Holland

GETTING STARTED

Please send information on your overseas house-exchange program—enclosed is a
    SASE.

Will you please send me a brochure and rate information on your dude ranch?

I have several questions about your adventure vacations that weren't covered in the
    material you sent me.

We are planning to participate in your English gardens tour and are wondering if
    there are any health restrictions and what medical care is available if needed.

We are considering holding our annual estate-planning conference in your area and
    would appreciate your sending us information on hotels and convention cen-
    ters, a description of area attractions, and any other material you think would
    be helpful to us in making a decision.

This will confirm our telephone conversation of September 17 in which I reserved an
    automobile to be picked up at the Brussels airport.

This is to confirm the cancellation of our cabin at the Butterworth Family Resort.

Thank you for your interest in staying at the Crackenthorp Inn on the beautiful
    Cumberland coast, and for your deposit check of $200.

It was a pleasure hearing from the Coniston Convention and Visitors Bureau that
    you are considering our hotel for your upcoming family reunion.

Thank you for making Abney Bed & Breakfast part of your travel plans.

We witnessed a distressing incident while traveling on your flagship, the Hatty
    Doran, and we thought you should know about it.

Having received no satisfaction from two telephone calls to your front desk, I am
    writing to let you know about the condition of our room during a recent stay.

Enclosed are all receipts for travel reimbursement from my trip to Dallas October 3-5.

Re: lost luggage on flight #118, nonstop Boston-LA, May 3.

We just wanted you to know that we have never enjoyed such beautiful accommodations accompanied by so much courtesy, kindness, and attention—thank you!

Too often travel, instead of broadening the mind, merely lengthens the conversation.

—ELIZABETH DREW

MODEL LETTERS

Dear Mr. Dallas,

Vivian Grey Hotels International is pleased to learn that you are considering the Burnsley area for your August family reunion. We look forward to an opportunity to extend our warm hospitality to your group for this special event. Although we are not currently holding space for your group, we have accommodations available at this time that meet your needs. Please call or fax your reservations to us as soon as possible.

Monsieur:

I am pleased that you will be able to accommodate us in June. As I requested in my telephone call of February 1, we will need one room with three beds for June 9-18 (10 nights) at 180 francs per night, breakfast included. Enclosed is a check for the first night and an International Reply Coupon for your confirmation.

If possible, I would like to have the room on the second floor overlooking the park that we've had the last two times we stayed at the Hôtel Henri IV.

Re: Rental agreement # AI9946X, dated May 18, 1998

Before returning this car to the rental car return area at the Cairo Airport on June 3, I stopped at a gas station one block away and filled the tank to the brim. My bill indicates that I am being charged for 17 liters of gasoline in addition to the penalty charge for returning a car without a full tank of gas. Please look into this, and refund the inappropriate charges. Thank you.

Dear Family,

I just have to write and tell you where you want to spend your next vacation: Colorado! Even those of you who live there, and you know who you are, can enjoy a vacation in your home state.

The most amazing thing to us out there was (1) NO BUGS and (2) NO HUMIDITY. I am not making that up. The first night I mistakenly left my tennis shoes outside the tent. It took me about an hour the next morning to get over the fact that they weren't wet. It seemed highly unlikely to me that shoes could spend a night outdoors and still be completely dry. This dryness and no bug thing went on for days and days and days—beyond our understanding.

The only wildlife we saw was Kevin's hair in the morning. No, actually, the only wildlife we saw were pocket gophers and birds. You'll be able to appreciate what a great trip it was because if you study our photos carefully, you will notice that there is no humidity and no bugs!

> With love,
> Mary

Signor Gian-Luca Boselli,

I would like to make reservations for October 31 (1 night). We will need 2 rooms for 4 people (each room must have 2 beds).

May we please have rooms with a view of the Temple of the Concord? The last time we had rooms #6 and #15, and they were lovely.

Below is my credit card number to hold the rooms.

I am looking forward to enjoying your lovely hotel once again.

Dear Cousins,

I hope this letter finds you in good health and that my Italian is not too difficult to read. I am still thinking about my last visit with you in 1994 when I was in Camporeale with my daughter. I must thank you again for the book on the history of Camporeale. Not only I but all my family and cousins here have read it.

I am writing to let you know that my father, my mother, one of my brothers, and I are coming to Sicily. My father, who is 83, would like to visit the birthplace of his parents, that is, Camporeale.

Would it be possible to see you on Sunday, October 26, sometime in the afternoon? We do not want to inconvenience you, but my father would certainly like to meet you. We could perhaps meet at the cantina or at a bar—we would love to offer you a drink. If you are busy, however, we will understand.

I will telephone you from Castellammare del Golfo once we have arrived.

I thank you for your kindness, and I send you best wishes for every good thing.

Re: EWA #416 April 4, 1996

My husband and I had tickets on EastWest Airlines flight # 416 due to leave Fort Dodge at 10:55 a.m. on April 4. We were to connect with EWA # 347 leaving Minneapolis-St. Paul at 1:10 p.m. with a final destination of New York-LaGuardia.

Upon arriving at the airport, we were told the flight would be delayed. Later there was another delay and yet another until finally, after much anxious waiting and several reschedulings of the departure time, we were told that the original plane had electrical troubles, that no other plane was available, and that flight # 416 was canceled.

We asked about a later flight, departing at 3:50 p.m., but were told the flight was full. We were rebooked for the following day at 5:10 a.m.

My husband, who is 82, is in excellent health; I am 73 but have some fairly serious medical problems. Although we travel frequently, we never travel casually and we always make careful plans to minimize problems.

A daughter in Minneapolis spoke to your agents there, who said there *were* available seats on that afternoon flight. They also said that in the case of a flight cancellation we would be "protected." Calling directly to the desk in Fort Dodge, she found that there were indeed available seats. At that point a local son, the Minneapolis daughter, and the son in New York whom we were to visit began calling around town to locate us. (It was probably a good thing that the Colorado sons, the Wisconsin son, and the other Minnesota daughter weren't aware of what was going on.) They found us having a late lunch in time to send us back to the airport to catch the 3:50 afternoon flight. Because of further delays en route we didn't get to LaGuardia until 10:20 that night. It was a long, anxious day.

We have flown EastWest Airlines before and have never had a problem. I'm puzzled at the way our situation was handled. I don't know if you've ever been told to go home and come back the next day for your flight, but it is a great inconvenience to say nothing of being disappointing and fatiguing and ruinous to your plans. I also don't know why seats on the afternoon flight were not available and then were available. What it meant for us was a great deal of disruption and an unpleasant beginning of our trip.

I'm writing because I thought this is something you should know.

Sincerely,

Dear Friends,

Having used your guidebooks for the past 15 years, without exception and with tremendous satisfaction, I can't help but think of you as friends.

I recommend you right and left (although if there's a traveler left by now who doesn't know of you I'd be surprised). The accuracy of your descriptions and information is a pleasure.

Under Sicily, San Vito lo Capo, p. 507, you have a listing for the Sabbia d'Oro. I had my first negative experience with one of your hotels here: in late September we rented two rooms and were told they would be 20,000 lire apiece (this agreed both with the price listed on the door and with your figures), thus 40,000 lire a night.

The day before we left I went to settle my bill and was given a total of 160,000 lire for the four nights, which was correct. However, I'd foolishly failed to get small bills at the bank and had only two bills of 100,000 lire apiece (I assumed the hotel would have change). When the signora said she had no change, I wanted each of us to keep 100,000 lire until I returned with 60,000 lire, but she was quite forceful and as she was holding the money at the time, there didn't seem to be much I could do. When I returned with change, she would not trade the 100,000 lire for my 60,000 lire and, in addition, demanded another 40,000 lire because she said the rooms were actually 30,000 lire apiece. She and her daughter both yelled at me and we finally agreed to split the difference by my paying another 20,000 lire.

I speak Italian quite well and know the difference between *venta* and *trenta*. Also, there's quite a difference between the words for 160,000 lire and 240,000 lire. Don't ask me why I caved in, but I dislike scenes so I suppose that was it.

My daughter and I killed several enormous cockroaches in the hotel (what was worse was watching the ones that got away). Nobody cleaned the rooms the last two days we were there and there was no hot water, no seats on the toilets, and doors with faulty locks—all of which is fine at 20,000 lire, not fine at 30,000. I do not expect luxury at these prices; I do, however, expect to pay the agreed-upon price. I have written to the hotel owner, expressing my displeasure and telling her what steps I have taken (warning off my cousin, who was going to stay there; telling friends in San Vito lo Capo not to recommend the hotel to their friends, writing you).

Best wishes!

Phyllis,

Johan Roth, Freya Breitner, and I will represent the Department at the XVI International Meteorological Conference in Tokyo. Convention dates are October 14-18. We'd like to arrive in time to get a good night's sleep, and it would help if the flight home would also allow us to get a night's sleep before returning to work. But do what you can.

Can you arrange for the three of us:

> roundtrip airline tickets
> hotel reservations (see attached Convention brochure)
> a rental car to be picked up and dropped off at the airport
> the current allowable travel cash times 3 (in yen)

Thanks!

> The first axiom of the family vacation is that someone, possibly everyone, will get sick.
>
> —MARNI JACKSON

Dear Jinny,

We've been pleased with the trips you've arranged for us in the past. This one is going to be complicated so I thought I'd better give you some information early on.

We all need to depart from New York on the same flight. If possible, avoid plane changes and layovers for my parents' flights to New York.

Passengers:

Polly Mahony
Richard Mahony
Ned Mahony
Jerry Mahony
Lizzy Timms Kelly
Sarah Turnham
Hempel Turnham

Dates:

June 2-23 (but we are somewhat flexible)

Destinations:

London, Paris, Rome, Venice (4-5 days in each)

Hotels in each city:

1 double room (2 adults, 1 double or king-size bed) with bath
1 double room (2 adults, 2 twin beds) with bath
1 double room (2 children, 2 twin beds) with bath
1 single room with bath

Special needs:

check availability of babysitters at all hotels
car rentals in all cities (airport pickup and dropoff)
sightseeing packages in London, Paris, and Rome
bulkhead seats for Turnhams at least on the long flights

We can discuss details by phone, but I thought it would help to give you an overview. Let me know if I've forgotten something.

> You define a good flight by negatives: you didn't get hijacked, you didn't crash, you didn't throw up, you weren't late, you weren't nauseated by the food. So you're grateful.
>
> —PAUL THÉROUX

RELATED TOPICS

Acknowledgments

Adjustments

Complaints

Information

Requests

49

Wedding Correspondence

INTRODUCTION

All correspondence relating to weddings (including engagements) is located in this chapter. However, you may find further assistance in the chapters on Acknowledgments, Announcements, Belated, Congratulations, Invitations, Refusals, Requests, Responses, Thank You.

Although many wedding arrangements are made by telephone, you may need to write letters of confirmation to the temple, church, or other location where the ceremony is to be held; to the person who will officiate; to the sexton, organist, soloist, musicians; to your attendants, ushers, and others; to the photographer and videotaper; to the florist, jeweler, bakery; to hotels to make honeymoon arrangements; to the caterer or club for the reception; to order gifts for attendants, the aisle carpet, candles, ribbons, decorations. These are all very different letters, but three requirements are common to each: give all possible details; ask everything you need to know at the outset; keep copies of all your correspondence.

When asking friends or relatives to serve as attendants, be clear about what you are asking; spell out firmly who pays for what; offer them a graceful way of refusing so that they don't feel pressured; express your appreciation for their friendship.

I joined a singles group in my neighborhood. The other day the president called me up and said, "Welcome to the group. I want to find out what kind of activities you like to plan." I said, "Well, weddings."

—Lynn Harris

DO

- Announce your engagement—if you like. Not everyone chooses to do this, but those who do can write letters to tell the news to family and friends, have an announcement put in the newspaper, or send formal printed or engraved engagement announcements to those who aren't invited to the wedding or reception. An announcement can also be made by way of an invitation to celebrate the engagement at a dinner party or other event. In a handwritten note to friends and relatives include: the name of the person you are to marry; the wedding date (if known); briefly, how you met and how long you've known the person (optional); some expression of your happiness; a personal comment (that the other person is the first to know, that you can't wait for them to meet your intended). An engagement announcement in the newspaper generally includes: both your full names; hometowns; both sets of parents' names and hometowns; education backgrounds and places of employment for both; date of wedding or general plans ("a spring wedding is planned"). Some newspapers have requirements and deadlines for engagement announcements, and some will run either an engagement or a wedding announcement, but not both, so check beforehand. A broken engagement needs no announcement if no formal announcement was made. However, if you have written family and friends of the engagement, you should write the same type of personal note telling them simply that you have canceled your plans. There is no need to explain why.

- Plan your wedding invitation. Wedding invitations may be engraved, printed, or handwritten. Many papers, typestyles, inks, and designs are available at printers, stationery stores, and large department stores. The more formal the wedding, the more formal the invitations. Formal wedding invitations have two envelopes: the outer envelope is sealed for mailing, carries your return address, and is hand-addressed; the inner envelope, which contains the invitation (face up as you open the envelope), is unsealed (the flap does not have any glue) and carries the names of the invitees on the front. There may also be a loose piece of tissue paper to protect the engraving and enclosures such as at-home cards or reception cards. Reply cards are inserted in envelopes addressed to you (printed or engraved) and stamped, and then placed in the inner envelope. The inner envelope can be omitted; growing concern about the use of paper prompts many people to do this or to use recycled paper for their invitations. Note that the reply envelopes must be at least 5" × 3½" to comply with postal regulations. If you are not using reply cards, include an address or telephone number below the R.S.V.P. so that guests know where to address their responses. Check your invitations for the correct postage; if they are oversized or if they are over an ounce (which can happen with high-quality paper and two envelopes) they will need extra postage. For a small, casual wedding, invitations may be handwritten (perhaps a friend would offer calligraphy skills) on good-quality white or off-white notepaper or foldovers in blue or black ink. You may write in the first-person, in the same way that you would extend any informal invitation. Printed or engraved invitations are rarely sent for a very small wedding. (However, if large numbers of people are to be informed of the wedding afterwards, printed or engraved announcements are sent.)

Your invitation should include: names of bride and groom; date, time, place; mention of hospitality to follow, if any; expression of pleasure at having guests celebrate with you. The invitation, whether formal or informal, may be issued by the couple, by both their parents, by the woman's parents, by the man's parents, or by a relative or family friend—in short, by whoever is hosting the event or whoever is most appropriate. A deceased parent cannot be named in the invitation as though it were being issued by her or him, but the person can be included if the invitation is sent by the bride and groom ("Jean Lucas, daughter of Martha Lucas and the late George Lucas, and Bruce Wetheral, son of Mr. and Mrs. John Henry Wetheral, request the honour of your presence . . ."). Invitations should be mailed at least four weeks in advance. If all guests are invited to both the wedding and reception, you should add, after the place of the wedding on your invitation, "and afterward at . . ." or "Reception immediately following" or "followed by a reception at . . ." When only some guests are invited to the reception, your wedding invitation mentions the ceremony only. To those who are also invited to the reception enclose an invitation (about 3" × 4" and of the same style as the invitation): "Edith Moor and Jolyon Forsyte request the pleasure of your company at a reception following their wedding, on Saturday, the fourteenth of July, Galsworthy Village Inn. R.S.V.P." Note that the phrase "the honour (not "honor") of your presence" is traditionally reserved for a religious ceremony and "the pleasure of your company" is used for civil weddings or for wedding receptions.

Marriage is like twirling a baton, turning a handspring or eating with chopsticks; it looks so easy until you try it.

—HELEN ROWLAND

- Address your invitations. This is an art in itself. On the outer envelope, list full names and addresses, with no abbreviations if possible. On the inner envelope, repeat last names only with the appropriate honorific ("Mr. and Mrs. Heavistone"). If you are inviting young children in a family, do not include them on the outer envelope but list their first names under the parents' names on the inner envelope. (Never add "and family.") Older children (somewhere between thirteen and eighteen) receive their own invitations. You may address one invitation using both full names to an unmarried couple living together. Your return address goes in the upper left-hand corner, unless you are using embossed or engraved envelopes, in which case it is on the back flap. (Note that the U.S. Postal Service discourages placing return addresses on the back flap.) To address the envelopes, use a good-quality fountain pen, felt tip, or calligraphy pen (if its tip is not overly wide). Attach attractive commemorative stamps.

- Reply to all wedding invitations. Use the enclosed formal reply card or, if there isn't one, use the same wording and degree of formality as the invitation to either "accept with pleasure" or "decline with regret." It is not improper to reply informally to a formal invitation. What is absolutely imperative is that you respond. Failure of guests to reply is the number-one complaint of wedding hosts. (You do not need to respond if you are invited only to the wedding ceremony itself.) When accepting an invitation to a wedding reception, you may accept only for those people named on the invitation. If your children are not listed, they are not invited. It is highly improper and awkward, as well as expensive for the wedding family, for you to bring them to the reception. In the same way, if your envelope doesn't have "and guest" written on it, you may not bring someone with you. Ignoring this simple rule causes much outrage and inconvenience to wedding reception hosts.

- Announce your marriage—if you wish. If formal invitations were sent, formal announcements are also sent. They are mailed as near the wedding date as possible (address them in advance), and may include at-home cards. Traditionally the bride's family made the announcement ("Mr. and Mrs. James Gann announce the marriage of their daughter Caroline to . . ."), and there were rules to govern cases in which her parents were divorced or one or both were deceased. Today, couples often make the announcement themselves ("Adelaide Culver and Henry Lambert announce their marriage on Friday, the twenty-fifth of June . . .") or it is made by both sets of parents ("Sondra Finchley and Clyde Griffiths and Carrie and Charles Drouet have the honour of announcing the marriage of their daughter and son, Roberta Griffiths and George Drouet, on Friday, the fourteenth of August, nineteen hundred ninety-nine, Pilgrim Baptist Church, Chicago, Illinois"). The year is included in an announcement where it usually isn't in the invitation.

    Wedding announcement notices to newspapers should be typed, double-spaced. If a photograph accompanies it, identify it on the back in case it gets separated from the announcement (use a return-address label or taped-on piece of paper;

do not write directly on the back of the photo). Most newspapers publish only brief wedding notices, which may include some or all of the following information (in decreasing order of probability that it will be printed): bride's and groom's full names; date, time, and place of wedding; information on the couple's education and careers; name of officiator or presider; names of members of the wedding party and relation to the wedding couple; names, hometowns, and occupations or accomplishments of the couple's parents (and occasionally grandparents); description of the flowers, music, and wedding party's clothes; where the reception was held; the couple's address after marriage. Avoid nicknames and abbreviations. Ask your newspaper for its guidelines on submitting wedding announcements; it may have special requirements. Some newspapers will publish information about weddings only if they have some news value. Others charge a fee for announcements. Some will publish either an engagement notice or a wedding announcement, but not both. And others will not print an announcement if it is "old news"—arriving more than several weeks after the wedding. Or they might want the information at least three weeks before the wedding so that it can run the day after the wedding. In the short announcement-type newspaper notices, marriages were traditionally announced by the woman's parents. This practice has been largely replaced by couples announcing their own wedding, or the parents of both bride and groom making the announcement. Wedding announcements can also be sent to employee newsletters, alumni magazines, or other affiliation publications.

- Send gift acknowledgments. When you can't write timely thank-you notes for wedding gifts (because of a large wedding or extended honeymoon), acknowledge each gift as you receive it to let the person know the gift arrived safely and to say that you are looking forward to writing a personal note as soon as you can. Acknowledgment cards do not replace thank-you notes and should be followed by them as soon as possible.

- Write thank-you notes. A handwritten thank you is sent for every wedding gift, even if you thanked someone in person or if you see the person at work every day. Both newlyweds are responsible for thank-you notes; a good division of labor is each writing to their own families and friends. Whichever one writes should mention the other ("Phil and I are delighted . . ." or "Julia joins me in . . ."). Sending thank-you notes within a month of the wedding is generally considered appropriate, although with large weddings, you may have up to three months. Each note should include: a descriptive mention of the gift ("the silver bread tray," not "your lovely gift"); an expression of your pleasure with it; how you plan to use it, why you like it, or how much you needed it; a sentence or two unrelated to the gift ("so good to see you at the wedding" or "hope you will come see our new home"). It is generally suggested that you don't mention the amount of a money gift in your thank you, but you should tell how you plan to spend the money. Write separate and differently phrased thank you's to friends who sent joint gifts, unless the gift is from a large group, such as co-workers. When a wedding gift is not to your taste, focus on the kindness of the giver rather than on the gift; never ask where a gift was purchased so that you can exchange it, and do not mention duplication of gifts. A wedding book is useful in identifying each gift as it arrives; you will wish you had one if you find several mystery gifts after the wedding. It is preferable to use your own personal stationery for wedding thank you's, but if you do use a commercial foldover, choose the plainest type.

> When two people are under the influence of the most violent, most insane, most delusive, and most transient of passions, they are required to swear that they will remain in that excited, abnormal, and exhausting condition continuously until death do them part.
>
> —GEORGE BERNARD SHAW

DON'T

- Don't use abbreviations in formal wedding invitations except for "Mr.," "Mrs.," "Ms.," "Dr.," "Jr.," and sometimes military rank. ("Doctor" is written out unless the name following it is too long.) In the case of initials in names, either supply the name for which an initial stands or omit the initial altogether. Write out "Second" and "Third" after a name or use Roman numerals ("Rawdon Crawley II"). There is no comma between the name and the numeral, although there is a comma between the name and "Jr" ("Rawdon Crawley, Jr."). The names of states are spelled out ("Alabama," not Ala. or AL) as are dates ("November third") and the time ("half past eight o'clock," "half past five o'clock"). All numbers under 100 are spelled out. No punctuation is used except for commas after the days of the week ("Saturday, the sixteenth of June") or periods after "Mr.," "Mrs.," "Jr." No words are capitalized except for people's names, place names, and days of the week or months. The year is not included on wedding invitations, but is usually included on announcements. The address where the ceremony takes place is not given on the invitation unless it is located in a large city. When either the bride or the groom is a member of the military, the rank is used on invitations unless it is for a noncommissioned officer or enlisted personnel, in which case it may be omitted. List the title before the name for higher ranks ("Major Dorothy Holding, United States Air Force"), after the name for other ranks ("Henry Wellwood, Lieutenant, United States Army").

- Don't use nonparallel forms in your wedding correspondence (and ceremony readings) when referring to women and men. For example, it is never "man and wife" but "husband and wife." "The marriage of Lucy Fountain to Mr. David Dodd" should be either "The marriage of Lucy Fountain to David Dodd" or "The marriage of Ms. Lucy Fountain to Mr. David Dodd" (the former is preferred). Traditionally, honorifics ("Mr.," "Mrs.," "Dr.") are used for everyone in an invitation except the bride. You may follow tradition or you may make all references parallel.

- Don't invite your ex-spouse to the wedding; if you are friendly with the person, call or write with the news. People being as diverse as they are, however, there are possibly individuals who can ignore this rule without making anyone uncomfortable or unhappy.

> I told someone I was getting married, and they said, "Have you picked a date yet?" I said, "Wow, you can bring a date to your own wedding?" What a country!
>
> —Yakov Smirnoff

HELPFUL HINTS

- It is gracious, hospitable, and acceptable to write a note of welcome to a prospective in-law.

- You still occasionally see advice to offer "congratulations" to the engaged man but "best wishes" to the engaged woman; this hoary distinction is based on old inequalities. You may properly use either expression for men or women.

- Shower invitations may be either the commercial type or handwritten ones that include: the name of the bride-to-be, groom-to-be, or couple for whom it's being held; the type of shower (kitchen, tool, bath, garden, recipe, household); the time, date, and place; an R.S.V.P. or "Regrets only"; the name, address, and telephone number of the host. Guests are thanked for their gifts at the shower, but thank-you notes are also sent to each person (even those who "went in together" on a gift) soon after the shower. The shower host receives a small gift as well as an especially warm thank you.

- To inform friends and relatives of your address after marriage or a preferred name usage, enclose an at-home card in your wedding invitation or announcement. It is usually the same style as your other wedding stationery, about $2\frac{3}{4}" \times 4"$: "Julia and Philip O'Grady (Julia Egerton and Philip O'Grady; Julia Egerton-O'Grady and Philip O'Grady) will be at home after the eleventh of July at 1945 Hinton Circle, Waunakee, Wisconsin 53597."

- Announcements of and invitations to commitment ceremonies can be as similar or dissimilar to formal or informal wedding correspondence as you like; as for all such correspondence, budgets and personal tastes will be determining.

- If prospective wedding guests indicate in their acceptance to you that they are bringing their children, whom you have not invited, or an invited guest or visiting relative, write to say you are pleased they can come to the wedding but that the reception is for adults only or limited to those invited because of space. When you invite friends who may not know anyone at the reception, you can either call them for the name of a companion (so you can send a personal invitation) or add "and Guest" to their invitations.

- If you receive a wedding announcement, there is no obligation to send a gift, but it is customary to write your congratulations.

- Some people like to note on the back of their card a brief description of the accompanying gift in case card and gift become separated. This has been useful to more than a few newly married couples trying to determine which of the mystery gifts came from whom.

- Wedding cancellation announcements are similar in style and format to the invitations you sent. If formal wedding invitations were sent, formal cancellation announcements are sent. They should not be as lavish or decorative as the invitations, but they should be approximately of the same quality. The message is simple: "Olivia Telworthy and George Marden announce that their marriage on the twenty-first of April, nineteen hundred ninety-nine, will not take place."

- If you are late with your wedding congratulations, write anyway. Most people will understand and will be pleased that you remembered at all. Apologize only briefly for the delay.

- Allow adequate time for all necessary correspondence: ask friends to be your attendants as soon as you have a date; order printed or engraved invitations at least three months prior to the wedding; start addressing invitations two months or more before the wedding (the envelopes can be picked up earlier than the invitations); mail all invitations at the same time between three and six weeks before the wedding.

> A wedding invitation is beautiful and formal notification of the desire to share a solemn and joyous occasion, sent by people who have been saying "Do we have to ask them?" to people whose first response is "How much do you think we have to spend on them?"
>
> —JUDITH MARTIN

GETTING STARTED

Mr. and Mrs. Ernest Rockage announce the engagement of their daughter Phyllis to Stephen Newmark.

We have so long thought of you as part of our family that it is a real joy to know you are to become officially a part of it.

We couldn't be happier about your and Tatiana's engagement. We already think of you as one of our own.

How good of you to write us about your engagement. We think that Alexandra is a wonderful woman and that the two of you are beautifully matched!

Congratulations and best wishes to both of you on this, your wedding day. May you take with you into the years ahead some beautiful memories of those who love you and of your shining love for each other.

We wish you every happiness as you exchange your marriage vows today. May your love grow every day and be your firm foundation in all things.

Thank you for the beautiful set of leather photograph albums—I can't imagine anything more happy and hopeful than looking ahead to all the photographs of our life together that we'll be putting in them.

Moira and I were touched by the beautiful old family serving tray that you gave us for our wedding. We feel that we are now connected to all the family that's gone before and all that is yet to come.

Gabriel joins me in thanking you for the oil painting you did especially for us—it is our first piece of original art!

How thoughtful of you to remember us with such a generous check. We are going to use it to buy a pair of silver candlesticks that we hope to have all our life—and to use when you next come to dinner.

> Nothing in life is as good as the marriage of true minds between man and woman. As good? It is life itself.
>
> —Pearl S. Buck

MODEL LETTERS

Mr. and Mrs. A.W. Ridgeley announce the forthcoming marriage of their daughter Annabel to Derek Jesson, son of Mr. and Mrs. Hilary Jesson of Filmer. A spring wedding is planned in Den Haag, The Netherlands, where they both teach at the American School.

Truda Rakonitz and Benno Silber plan to marry on June 3, 1999, at Tents of Israel Temple in Austin. The couple's parents are Dr. and Mrs. G.B. Rakonitz and Mr. and Mrs. Benno Silber, Sr., both of Austin. Ms. Rakonitz is a graduate of Columbia University and is employed by Stern Communications. Mr. Silber is also a graduate of Columbia University and is in private law practice.

Dear Eve,

I think you've known for a long time that this was going to happen. Eric and I have finally chosen a date: September 12! But the really big question is: Will you be my attendant?

I know your business is just beginning to take off and you're working around the clock, so maybe you won't be able to get away. I know you'd want to if you could, so don't worry about it. And particularly don't worry about me sitting here, crying my eyes out . . . No, no, I jest. I'd rather keep our great friendship and have someone else in the wedding party than put you on the spot.

Enclosed is a sketch of the dress you'd wear. I'm paying for it, so don't worry about that. And of course you'll stay at the house, but unfortunately our budget won't run to your airfare. Will that be a problem?

I'll call next week after you've had time to think about this. In the meantime, Eric sends his love along with mine.

Iseult

Lucetta le Sueur
and Donald Farfrae
request the honour of your presence
at their marriage
on Sunday, the fourth of June
at seven o'clock in the evening
Casterbridge Gardens
Henchard, Oregon

Reception immediately following

Barbara Medway and Ferdinand Dibble
invite you to share in their joy
when they exchange marriage vows
and begin their new life together
on Saturday the fifteenth of June
at eleven-thirty in the morning
on Pine Island
boat rides to the island begin at 10:30 a.m.
Pine Island boat launch, County Road C and Wodehouse Lane
light lunch immediately following
return boat rides available all afternoon
life jackets provided
Please reply 555-1234

The honour of your presence
is requested at the marriage of
Cecilia Tennant
to
Donald Iverach
on Saturday, the fifteenth of June
at half past five o'clock
Crockett Calvary Chapel
and afterward at
The New Crockett Inn

R.S.V.P.
Cecilia Tennant
20 Robert Lane
Crockett, Nevada 89117

Mr. and Mrs. Charles Vaucaire
request the honour of your presence
at the marriage of their daughter
Helen
to
Mr. Herbert Wilson
Saturday, the fourteenth of June
at half past five o'clock
Makepeace Unitarian Church
Whitelaw, Indiana

Mr. and Mrs. Charles Vaucaire
request the pleasure of your company
at a reception
immediately following the ceremony
at the Whitelaw Country Club

R.S.V.P.
1931 Jacob Boulevard
Whitelaw, Indiana 47374

Miles and I are going to be married at the Armstrong County Courthouse Monday, June 19, at 4:30 p.m. We would love to have the two of you with us there, and to help us celebrate afterwards with drinks and dinner at my mother's, 1933 Standing Avenue South.

Madeline Arnold
accepts with pleasure
the kind invitation of
Nina Leeds
and
Samuel Evans
to their marriage on
Saturday, the fourteenth of July
at seven o'clock
St. Charles Catholic Church
Reception to follow
St. Charles Community Center

Mr. and Mrs. Virgil Adams
regret that they are unable to accept
the kind invitation of
Mildred Palmer and Arthur Russell
to their marriage
Saturday, the eighteenth of August
at half past seven o'clock in the evening

Nancy Lammeter and Godfrey Cass
announce that their marriage
has been postponed from
Saturday, the second of June
until
Saturday, the fourteenth of September
at half past four o'clock
St. George's Church
Raveloe
Reception to follow
Raveloe Town and County Club

Colonel and Mrs. Martin Lambert
announce that the marriage of
their daughter Theodosia
to George Warrington
on Saturday, the eleventh of October
will not take place

Hey pardners, grab your spurs and saddle up yer horse. Gitalong to Santa Fe little doggies 'cause we're gittin' hitched! We'd sure like for y'all to be here to help us celebrate, June 27, 1998.

There's a lot to do and see here in the land of enchantment besides the wedding. You can go fly fishin', hikin', mountain bikin', or saddle up your pony and ride! All within spittin' distance of Rancho Encantado (that's where the ceremony will take place). There are ancient Anasazi ruins at Bandelier National Monument you could explore for 2 hours, or 2 weeks. And there's some right nice shoppin', and good art too. You could visit the Georgia O'Keeffe Museum, the Museum of American Folk Art, or the galleries on Canyon Road.

Saturday the wedding begins at 4:30 p.m. so you have the day to explore. We have rooms blocked at Rancho Encantado (from $115), but if you'd like to stay in Santa Fe, call us for recommendations, 505/555-1234. We're really looking forward to this weekend, and hope you can make it. If we can help make your planning easier, please call.

We'll keep the homefires burning for y'all!

Jodi and Tom

Dear Dora and Charles,

Hugh and I are delighted that you will be able to attend our wedding celebration. There's been a small misunderstanding, however. I think you know how much we enjoy Hilda, Margery, Cynthia, and Nicholas, but we are having only adults at the reception. I hope you can make other arrangements for the children so you can still come. Thanks for understanding.

Love,
Laurel

Mary Lynton and Thomas Trellick were married December 12, 1999, at Conford Presbyterian Church. The Reverend Beatrice K. Seymour performed the ceremony. Parents are Mr. and Mrs. C.R. Lynton and Mr. and Mrs. Thomas Trellick, Sr., both of Conford. Mary Lynton is a medical lab technician and Thomas Trellick is a nurse assistant at Conford Community Hospital.

> **There is no more lovely, friendly and charming relationship, communion or company than a good marriage.**
>
> —Martin Luther

Avisa Pomeroy and Arthur Brown
wish to acknowledge
the receipt of your lovely wedding gift
and look forward to writing
a personal note of thanks
at an early date.

Dear Judge Lockaby,

Thank you again for your time, presence, and guiding words at our wedding—your short talk was memorable, particularly the way you tied our love of skydiving and flying our Cessna into the message. Many people commented glowingly on it at the reception and we ourselves are still talking about it. Would it be possible to have a copy of your words for our wedding book?

Sincerely,
Maggie and Edward Browne

Two persons who have chosen each other . . . with the design to be each other's mutual comfort and entertainment, have, in that action, bound themselves to be good-humored, affable, discreet, forgiving, patient, and joyful, with respect to each other's frailties and imperfections, to the end of their lives.

—JOSEPH ADDISON

RELATED TOPICS

Acknowledgments

Congratulations

Invitations

Refusals

Requests

Responses

Thank You

50

Letters of Welcome

INTRODUCTION

Because you are never obliged to send them, letters of welcome are easier than most letters to write—and more rewarding, because your recipient also knows it is a gracious, but not required, gesture.

Letters of welcome are written to new family members (in-laws, adopted older children); new neighbors; new business customers, suppliers, or employees; new members of a club, organization, temple, church; new school staff or teachers; incoming students; new businesses in the area.

> Come in the evening, come in the morning,
> Come when expected, come without warning;
> Thousands of welcomes you'll find here before you,
> And the oftener you come, the more we'll adore you.
>
> —IRISH RHYME

DO

- Send your welcome promptly; it is most appreciated when the newcomer is still feeling at sea. It doesn't have nearly the impact weeks later when the recipient feels settled and confident.

494

- State how happy you are to have the person join your company, store, division, club, neighborhood, family.
- Find some common ground between you or your organization and the person you are welcoming.
- Tell something positive about the neighborhood, company, or organization the person is joining. If a special event is coming up, or if something new is going on, mention it to give the person something to look forward to.
- Mention a future meeting, a store visit, an invitation to call you, or at least that you are looking forward to meeting sometime soon.
- Offer to help the person become acquainted with their new surroundings, duties, colleagues, neighbors.

> Small cheer, and great welcome, makes a merry feast.
>
> —WILLIAM SHAKESPEARE

DON'T

- Don't refer to negative aspects of the person's new situation, for example, the mountains of unfinished work left by the person's predecessor or the troubles with the roof suffered by the previous owner.
- Don't use the expression "Good luck!" It implies that good luck will be needed.

> There is no beautifier of complexion, or form, or behavior, like the wish to scatter joy and not pain around us.
>
> —RALPH WALDO EMERSON

HELPFUL HINTS

- Sending letters of welcome to new employees takes little time and goes a long way toward getting things off to a good start. New employees often receive packets of information—material about benefits, building regulations, contact numbers. You could include a letter of welcome as the first sheet in the packet. However, a brief handwritten note from a superior, sent separately, will have a much greater impact.

- If you use a welcome letter to attract potential customers, the sales message will be more effective if it is unobtrusive and undemanding. You might enclose a coupon good for a small gift or a discount or a free service. A relatively inexpensive but useful gift to newcomers is information, for example, a card with phone numbers of area services, hospitals, day-care centers, schools, or hotlines.

- If you know that a customer or client is making a first visit to your place of business, follow up with a letter of welcome. You might offer something to encourage the customer to return a second time.

- Some elementary school teachers send postcards with a brief welcoming message to incoming students. They might mention a project that the class will enjoy or say something like, "I think it's going to be a good year!" These notes help students look forward to returning to school in the fall. Unfortunately, this requires money for stamps and stationery, access to class lists, time, and energy. Parents of a child who is not looking forward to the new school year might offer to help the teacher with welcome notes.

- The welcome letter is a fitting place to let the newcomer know in a subtle way about any unwritten "rules" you might have ("Although there's never time to chat during office hours, I'd like to get to know you better over lunch someday" or "We look forward to seeing you once you're settled in—but do give us a call first").

- Letters of welcome can be handwritten (generally those sent to neighbors, new employees, new members of the family) or typed (generally sales or business letters). Postcards are also useful. In the case of a welcome, the format is not as important as the warmth of the message.

> He greeted us with that extra degree of kindness and hospitality which I had noticed in so many Americans; it always gave me the uncomfortable feeling that, no matter how long I lived among them, I should never quite be able to rise to their level of genuine cordiality with strangers.
>
> —Jessica Mitford

GETTING STARTED

Welcome to the neighborhood! We're having our annual block party next Saturday from 3:00 to 7:00 p.m. and we'd love to see you there!

As the parents of three students at Brookfield School, we would like to welcome you in your position as the new principal.

James, I am really looking forward to having you in my fourth-grade class this year—welcome!

Natalia has just told us about your engagement, and I wanted to be one of the first to welcome you to the family.

We want to welcome you to Deakin Computer Services and to thank you for doing business with us.

Thank you for your first purchase at the Chowbok Trading Company, and welcome to our store!

It is a pleasure to welcome you as a new customer.

With great pleasure, we welcome you to Thorold-Ebbsmith Overseas Investments.

All of us at Drinkwater Securities Systems are looking forward to working with you.

Please accept the enclosed brochure with lists of plants hardy to this area as a gesture of welcome to you from the Shangri-La Gardening Center.

It is my great pleasure to welcome you to Dibbitts Chemicals, Inc. as our new Benefits Administrator.

As president of Pym's Publicity, I'd like to welcome you to our payroll management department.

There is a warm reception waiting for you here at the Cuthbert Center for the Performing Arts.

We are pleased to renew your membership in the Banana Fish Club—welcome back!

Welcome to the 16th Annual Regional Biostatistics Conference.

> It's a rare thing, graciousness. The shape of it can be acquired, but not, I think, the substance.
>
> —GERTRUDE SCHWEITZER

MODEL LETTERS

Dear Caroline Walker,

Welcome to Dilworth Imports! I hope you have a good first day on the job, and that it only gets better after that. We're pleased to have you on our team, and hope that you're equally glad to be here. If any of us can make these first weeks smoother for you, don't hesitate to let us know.

Julian English

Dear Peter and Joan Stubland,

Welcome to the Macalester-Groveland neighborhood! We might be a little partial, but we think you made a good choice, and we're proud to be part of a community that cares about its residents, its trees and parks, and its quality of life.

We at Wells Sundries especially want to welcome you and encourage you to check out our wide-ranging inventory and low prices. You'll be amazed to find under the same roof pharmacy, soda fountain, toy store, bookstore, grocery, discount store merchandise, and even a take-out pizza counter!

Bring this letter with you to pick up a FREE 12" pizza. It's our way of saying welcome to the neighborhood, and welcome to Wells Sundries!

Dear Jennifer Dorn,

We hope you enjoyed your first visit to the Hodge & Hazard Book Shop. We are always happy to welcome new customers to what we think is a unique and well-stocked bookstore.

To show our appreciation of your interest, we are enclosing a coupon good for 15% off the hardcover book of your choice. You will be able to choose from among the latest fiction and nonfiction bestsellers, classic mysteries, useful reference books, travel guides, cookbooks, and scores of other engrossing books.

The next time you come in, please introduce yourself to any of us. We are always happy to meet new customers and to discuss the world of books.

Bibliophilically yours,

Elinor Hodge

Dear Hannah and Rod, Dilys, Madoc, Susan and Penry,

Welcome to the neighborhood! I hope you will find that it is a good place to pitch your tent. If I can help with any area information, just ask (for example, recycling pickups are the second and fourth Thursdays of each month at 7 a.m.).

You'd be hard put to find better neighbors than ours. You will always find willing hands to look after the house if you are away or to help in an emergency.

There aren't many children on this particular block, but about three blocks over, you will find a number of families with young children. I have several friends there, so if you want me to walk over there with you some day, let me know.

Rhys Davies

Dear Mick,

Welcome back! We are all so glad you are able to work at *Trade Unionist Leader* again this summer. We missed you while you were away at school, and we especially missed your magic with sick computers!

Sybil

Dear Rachel Wardle,

It is with great pleasure that we welcome you to the Pickwick Association. Enclosed are: a copy of the by-laws, a list of members, a calendar of events, a brochure about the annual fall conference.

If you have any questions, please direct them to me or to Tracy Tupman, who is Membership Secretary.

I am looking forward to enlarging on our acquaintance.

With best wishes, I am

Sincerely yours,
Sam Weller

Dear Mr. Dost Akbar,

We are happy to welcome you to membership in The North American Plastics Council. Enclosed please find copies of a booklet describing the history and organization of the Council, a list of member benefits, a membership directory, a calendar of events, the minutes of our last meeting, and a receipt for your enrollment fee and first year's membership dues.

Please call on me to answer any questions you might have about the Council. Best wishes!

Dear Millicent Chyne,

It's a pleasure to welcome you to the Environmental Services Department. You'll have to decide for yourself, but the general feeling is that this is a pleasant department with many highly qualified, competent, and kind people in it. A great deal of productive and important work seems to get done here in an easygoing and congenial way.

We are all very much looking forward to working with you.

Civility costs nothing, and buys everything.

—Lady Mary Wortley Montagu

Dear Guy Oscard,

We welcome you as a new patient to our dental office.

Enclosed is a bookmark giving our business hours, our regular and emergency telephone numbers, and the names of the dentists, dental hygienists, and receptionists you will meet here.

Our goal is to work with you in the areas of education, prevention, and treatment of dental problems. We hope that, like most of our patients, you will look forward to your six-month checkups because you appreciate the rewards for maintaining good dental health . . . and perhaps because you enjoy—just a little!—visiting our office.

Dear Katherine Climpson,

Welcome to the 23rd Annual Cleaning Equipment Exposition. Enclosed in your "Welcome" packet you will find: a hotel brochure describing amenities available to you; a map of the exhibit hall with list of exhibitors; an Exposition brochure listing speakers and events as well as evening activities; tickets for the two guest speaker breakfasts and the farewell dinner; a name badge.

If you have any questions or need further information, someone from the Exposition Committee will be available from 8 a.m. to 5 p.m. every day in Room 101.

We hope you find this one of the best Expositions ever!

> I have had that curiously *symbolical* and reassuring pleasure, of being entertained with overflowing and simple kindness by a family of totally unknown people—an adventure which always brings home to me the good will of the world.
>
> —A.C. BENSON

RELATED TOPICS

Employment
Goodwill
Neighbors
Sales

Appendix I: Mechanics

Appendix I covers the concrete aspects of letterwriting, for example, types of stationery, letter formats, envelope addresses, and postal regulations. For assistance with the content of your message (its tone, style, language, grammar), see Appendix II.

STATIONERY

Business stationery

Traditionally, business stationery size is a standard 8½" × 11". There is a practical reason for being traditional: odd-sized stationery is difficult to file. White, off-white, cream, light gray, or other neutral shades are acceptable colors.

Twenty-pound rag bond paper is a popular choice for business stationery; for higher quality, go to a higher-weight paper, for example, thirty-pound paper. Textures and finishes—flat, matte, smooth, woven, linen-look, watermarked—are a matter of personal taste; all are acceptable. Many businesses are using recyclable paper, which is good for public relations as well as for the environment. Erasable bond is not recommended as it invariably smudges.

All business organizations and many individuals use a letterhead on their stationery, which includes the name of the firm (or the individual's name); address including zip code (ideally zip + 4); area code and telephone number; optionally, fax number, e-mail address, and telex number. The letterhead can also include a logo, an employee's name and title, a list of board of directors or other governing bodies (if lengthy, this list is arranged along the left edge of the page). A good letterhead is readable, informative, attractive, and not too insistent. Printers can show you many styles of type, formats, inks, papers, and engraving and printing methods. The most formal and conservative choice is black ink on white or off-white high-quality paper.

Your second sheets are of the same quality as the letterhead paper. They either have no printing on them or are printed or engraved with the company's name (but the print is smaller than it is on the letterhead and the address is not included).

Envelopes match your stationery in color, weight, general style, and letterhead. Window envelopes (without glassine, which isn't biodegradable) save the time and expense of printing the intended recipient's name and address. Your return address always goes in the upper left corner of the front of the envelope. The United States Postal Service discourages return addresses on the back flap, because mail is sorted by machines that cannot flip envelopes over to check for a return address on the back.

Personal-business stationery

The size referred to as personal-business or executive stationery is 7" or 7½" × 10". White, off-white, neutral, or very pale shades of good-quality bond paper are acceptable. The letterhead consists of the company name and address with the person's name, or name and title, set underneath or off to one side.

Although its use is declining, personal-business stationery is still convenient for brief notes, when writing to someone as individual to individual rather than as company representative to employee or customer, when the information is casual, or for matters that cross over into the social or personal arena (congratulating a business acquaintance on the birth of a baby, for example).

Memos

Memos can include anything from 8½" × 11" stationery to small pads of printed memo sheets. In white, off-white, neutral, or pastel colors, memo stationery generally matches the firm's regular business stationery but has only the company name at the top. If memos are sent outside the company to longtime customers, suppliers, or colleagues, they are printed with the company name, address, and telephone number. Some memo paper may be labeled "Internal Correspondence" and have "TO: FROM: DATE: SUBJECT:" with a space after each at the top. (For more information on memos, see the chapter Memos.)

Personal stationery

You may need 8½" × 11" paper for some personal uses (complaints, household business matters), but personal stationery is generally 7-8" × 10½" or 5½" × 6½-7½" and is sold with matching envelopes.

Formal stationery (for handwritten invitations, condolences, thank you's) is white, off-white, cream, eggshell, straw, beige, gray, or some other neutral color with a self-border, contrasting border, or no border. For informal use, almost anything is acceptable, although some authorities suggest not using stationery that is perfumed, decorated with tiny objects, ruled, oddly shaped, or otherwise says too loudly, "Look at me!" On the other hand, nobody appears to have ever returned a letter because the stationery had too much personality.

If you use a letterhead, monograms, or other printing on your personal stationery, your second sheets have no printing but are the same color and quality as your first sheets.

One-page notecards and foldovers (at least 3½" × 5" when folded) are of a heavier weight paper than stationery and are popular for thank-you notes, handwritten invitations, replies to invitations, condolences, and other formal and informal messages. They usually come with matching envelopes and may be engraved or printed. If your name, address, initials, or other printing appear on the front panel, write on the inside—beginning at the top of the two panels for a long letter or using the bottom panel only for a short note. Otherwise, you may begin your note on the front panel. Note that the United States Postal Service discourages printing or engraving your return address on the envelope's flap. Letter-Sorting Machines (LSMs) cannot flip a letter to check the other side when it fails to find the return address on the front.

Other

Popular, versatile, and attractive postcards make it easy to keep in touch with family and friends. In the business world they are used to send routine bills, to announce sales and open houses, to send brief inquiries, acknowledgments, reminders, and confirmations. They can be printed with your logo and return address in the upper left corner of the front, and the back can carry a printed form message, perhaps with fill-in blanks.

Commercial greeting cards are useful—especially if you keep on hand a selection of the cards you use most often (congratulations, get well, birthday, sympathy) and do not have to make a special trip each time you need one. A handwritten message is always added to greeting cards.

ENVELOPES

Business

The United States Postal Service says you will get the best service if you use the optical-character-reader (OCR) format for your envelopes, a machine-readable style that facilitates rapid sorting. Type or machine-print all address information in capital letters, using black ink on white paper and sharp, clear print with no overlapping or touching letters (problem fonts include extended fonts, italic fonts, condensed fonts, bold fonts, and stylized script-like fonts). Scanners can read a combination of uppercase and lowercase characters but prefer all uppercase. Type addresses flush left style, that is, the first letter of each line in the address should be directly under the first letter of the line above. Include as much address information as possible: apartment, floor, suite number, zip code or zip + 4. Omit all punctuation (except the hyphen in the zip + 4). Use the two-letter state abbreviations given at the end of this Appendix and the common abbreviations listed in zip code directories (AVE, ST, APT). Leave at least one space between words and two spaces between word groups. Put nothing in the bar code area, which is the area below the zip code line. Allow a bottom margin of at least ⅝" and a left margin of at least 1". If you have an attention line ("ATTN: Hetty Pepper"), it goes on the second line (under the company name). If the address contains both a post office box and a street address, it will be delivered to whichever appears directly above the city, state, and zip code. Hand-stamp or type mailing directions ("Airmail," "Third Class," "Priority") under the area where the postage will go. When necessary, indicate "Personal" or "Confidential" just to the left and about one space above the address.

Personal

For all formal and many informal personal letters, handwrite your own return address (upper left corner) as well as the addressee's (lower right). For less formal personal correspondence the envelope may be typed (single-spaced). Although formal personal stationery is sometimes engraved or printed with the person's name and address on the back flap, the United States Postal Service prefers the return address on the front. For the other person's address, use either block style (each line's left edge lines up with the others) or indented style (each successive line is indented one or two spaces). Formal correspondence traditionally does not use abbreviations for "Street," "Avenue," "Parkway," "Road," or state names. However, the United States Postal Service (USPS) requests that, for optimum sorting and delivery, the address be printed all in capital letters, with no punctuation except the hyphen in the zip + 4, using approved two-letter state abbreviations. The European "7" is not recommended because of the possibility of its being confused by the scanner with f, h, p, or t. The guidelines from the USPS differ from traditional addressing of personal correspondence. When Judith Martin ("Miss Manners") was asked if we must forgo etiquette rules on envelopes, she recommended following the USPS rules to ensure delivery, but suggested that the double envelope system (still used for wedding invitations) allows the writer to send a personal letter that is both prettily addressed and properly delivered.

Zip codes

Both personal and business letters must have correct zip codes in order to be delivered. When you know it, use the zip + 4 number; it indicates local routes and can speed your letter significantly. It helps to use your zip + 4 on outgoing correspondence so that more people use it when writing you. You can buy a national zip code directory from your local post office, or look up zip codes in the directory at the post office, or, for in-town mail, check your local phone book, which very often lists zip codes by street names.

The United States Postal Service prefers that there not be less than one full character space and not more than five full character spaces between city, state, and zip code; it prefers two spaces between city and state, and two spaces between state and zip code.

Note that there should be no information on the envelope below the zip code line. This area is reserved for bar coding.

Folding and inserting

When inserting a sheet of 8½" × 11" paper into a #10 envelope, fold it in horizontal thirds, and insert it with the back of the top third facing the flap so that the recipient who pulls out the letter and flips up that third is ready to begin reading. When you are using window envelopes, the letters need to be folded so that the name and address appear in the window.

When inserting a full-size sheet into an envelope smaller than a #10 envelope, fold it in half horizontally and then into thirds and insert it so that the open end is on the left and the top fold faces the flap. The recipient pulls it out, rotates it a quarter turn to the right, opens it, and is ready to read.

Personal stationery is folded once with the writing inside and inserted into its matching envelope, open edges down. The recipient removes the letter and flips up the top half to read.

When folding any size sheet of paper, the top and bottom edges should not be perfectly even with each other (although the sides should be perfectly even). It is easier to unfold a sheet of paper if one end extends just slightly beyond the other.

No matter what stationery you're using, the salutation (which will be inside the folds) faces the flap of the envelope.

Enclosures

Flat enclosures (checks, folded flyers, business cards) are placed inside the folds of the letter. To safeguard against your reader overlooking them, add an enclosure line to your letter ("Enc.: subscription blank"). When your enclosures are larger, use an appropriately sized manila envelope (many businesses have their own imprinted larger envelopes). If a package contains a letter, the entire package must go first class. When there is no urgency about bulky or heavy enclosures, send them third class and advise your correspondent by first-class mail of the package being sent under separate cover.

WRITING, TYPING, PRINTING

Handwritten

Black or blue ink is preferred to other colors, and pencil is never used. Certain notes are almost always written by hand: thank-you notes, messages of sympathy, replies to invitations, invitations that are not engraved or printed. Write by hand to convey personal feeling or informality or, in the case of an interoffice memo, when you have a one- or two-line message.

Typewritten or computer-generated

Nearly all business correspondence is being word processed in most companies.

Engraved or printed

Acknowledgments, announcements, invitations, and response cards are commonly engraved or printed (engraving is more expensive). Printers can explain the differences between the types of engraving and printing, show you dozens of samples, and offer you a wide variety of papers, formats, typestyles, and inks as well as advice on how to word your message.

ELEMENTS OF A LETTER

Personal letters

DATE: The date is placed near the top of the right side of the page. If the person is unfamiliar with your address and you aren't using stationery with your address on it, start with your address in the upper right corner (usually two lines) followed by the date. The left edges of these three lines line up flush with each other.

SALUTATION: Begin the salutation a few spaces down and flush left. It is followed by a comma ("Dear Jean,"). No inside address is used.

BODY OF THE LETTER: Indent the first paragraph—five spaces if you are typing the letter, about ¾" if you are handwriting it. Indent all other paragraphs the same way.

CLOSING: The complimentary close ("Love," "Sincerely,") is set about one line below your last sentence and to the right, its left edge aligned with the left edge of your date. Your signature is on the line below the complimentary close.

If your letter is more than one page long, generally write only on one side of your stationery.

Memos

The memo has three elements: (1) the to/from/date/subject lines, which replace the letter's salutation; (2) the message or body of the memo; (3) the notation lines, which list enclosures, attachments, or the names of people receiving copies.

The most common ways of arranging the headings on the page are:

```
TO:     John S. Clayton
FROM: Anthea Winterfield
DATE: June 3, 2001
RE:     Authorization of tuition fees
```

```
     TO:  George Hallijohn
  FROM: Francis Levison
  DATE: November 1, 1999
SUBJECT: Currency risk management seminar
```

TO: Jane Coram   DATE: September 3, 2000
FROM: R. Hall   SUBJECT: Missing blueprint

There are no rigid rules for spacing in a memo, but you may want to leave two or three blank lines between the headings and the text, which is single-spaced. Each paragraph usually begins flush left and is separated from other paragraphs by a single line of space.

No signature is necessary on a memo, but people often sign or initial it at the bottom or next to their name in the "From:" line.

Notations such as "Enc.:" or "cc:" are placed flush left at the bottom, as in a letter.

Some memos are arranged in two parts so that the recipient can respond on and return the bottom half.

Business letters

Business letters contain some or all of the following elements.

RETURN ADDRESS: If you aren't using letterhead stationery, use the two lines immediately preceding the date line for your street address, city, state, and zip code. Unless the letter is extremely formal, abbreviations ("Rd.," "Apt.," "NY") are acceptable.

DATE: For dates use this format: "October 12, 2001." The month is never abbreviated, the day is never spelled out, and endings for numbers ("16th," "2nd") are never used. You may also see "2 October 1992," particularly for international or government business. If you are typing in your return address, the date line goes directly beneath it. Otherwise, it is placed two to six lines below the printed address. If you use the shortened date form ("10/12/2001") in a casual memo, remember that this is used primarily in the United States; in other countries the first number is the day, the second the month.

CONFIDENTIAL OR PERSONAL NOTATION: Indicate "Confidential" or "Personal" between the date line and the inside address, with a space between it and the latter.

INSIDE ADDRESS: The number of spaces between the date line and the inside address depends on the length of your letter. The idea is to balance the various elements of the letter so that there is not too much white space above the inside address or below the last printed line. The inside address is always flush left and single spaced. If one of the lines is very long, put half of it on the next line, indenting two or three spaces. The person's name goes on the first line. If there is a brief title, it can follow the name, preceded by a comma. Otherwise the title goes on the second line or, if you need the space, can be omitted. If you're writing to two or more people, list them one to a line in alphabetical order. The company's name is on the next line, and the department or division is on the following line (unless space is a problem, in which case you omit it). Information such as suite, room, floor, or apartment usually has its own line, unless it and the street address are short enough to fit on one line. It used to be standard practice to spell out all words of the inside address, but the use of two-letter state abbreviations has spread from the envelopes (where the United States Postal Service wants to see them) to the inside address, and if the letter is not very formal, other abbreviations ("Ave.") may appear as well. Spell out compass directions that precede a street name but abbreviate those that follow it ("14 North Cedar," "14 Cedar N.W.").

ATTENTION LINE: When you don't know the name of the individual to whom you are writing or you want to direct the letter to a particular person's attention, the attention line ("ATTN: Customer Service Representative") is placed below the inside address, leaving one line of space between them. You can also include an attention line as part of the inside address on either the first or second line (after the company name).

SUBJECT LINE: To indicate the subject of your letter, type "Subject:" or "Re:" (for "regarding") between the salutation and the body of your letter or between the inside address and the salutation. A brief phrase follows it ("Subject: new e-mail address" or "Re: vacation dates"). Many people today are replacing the salutation with a subject line when writing an impersonal letter to an anonymous recipient ("your credit card statement was incorrect," for example). The subject line is popular with people handling stacks of incoming letters, trying to quickly identify the purpose of each. The subject line is not recommended when your letter deals with several subjects.

REFERENCE LINE: When you need to refer to an order number or to a reference number used either by your correspondent or by your own firm, handle it like a subject line and place it between the inside address and the salutation or between the salutation and the body of the letter (leaving one line of space on both sides in each case). It may also be placed between the date line and the inside address.

SALUTATION: Leave one line of space between the inside address (or the subject line) and the salutation. The salutation is followed by a colon (which is more formal) or a comma.

BODY OF THE LETTER: Leave one line of space between the salutation (or the subject line) and the body of the letter. In general, single space within paragraphs and leave a line of space between paragraphs. If your letter is very brief, however, double-spacing (or even 1½ spacing) will make it look better on the page. Wide margins will also balance brief letters on the page just as narrow margins (but not less than 1½") are helpful in long letters. If you indent paragraphs, start in five to ten spaces. If your letter runs to a second page, indicate the name of the recipient, the page number, and the date across the top of the page (about six lines below the paper's edge). If you're writing two individuals, put both names on the left, one under the other, and on the right indicate the date with the page number under it. Then leave three to five lines before resuming the body of the text. There should be a minimum of three lines of type in addition to the signature block to justify a second page.

COMPLIMENTARY CLOSE: Leave one line between the body of the text and the complimentary close ("Sincerely yours").

SIGNATURE: Your handwritten signature goes between the complimentary close and your typed name and title.

NAME AND TITLE LINES: Four spaces (or more, if your signature is large) below the complimentary close, type your name with the first letter directly beneath the first letter of the complimentary close. If you are using a title, it is typed on the line beneath your name, and also lined up with the left edge of your name and the complimentary close. Omit the title if it appears on the letterhead.

IDENTIFICATION LINE: Leave one line of space between the name or title line and the identification line. Type the letter-signer's initials in capital letters flush left, followed by a slash or colon and the typist's initials in lowercase letters ("DCK/jp," "JN:pjm"). Or, since it is obvious who has signed the letter, the typist's initials appear alone. The identification line is no longer much used; if you need to know who typed or machine-produced a letter, records can be kept on hard copies or computer files.

ENCLOSURE LINE: Leave one line of space between the identification line or the name/title line and the enclosure line. Set flush left, this line begins with "Enc.:" and lists any enclosures in the order in which they are found in the envelope, one to a line. You may also use "Encl." or "Enclosures" followed by the number of items enclosed: "Enclosures (4)".

COPIES LINE: Leave one line of space between all other previous material and the copy line. After "cc:" (from the old "carbon copies") list those individuals receiving copies of the letter in alphabetical order, one to a line, either by their full name, initials and last name, or title and last name only. The person's address may also be included. If you do not want the recipient of the original letter to know about copies being sent, indicate "bcc:" (blind carbon copy) with the names of those receiving copies on the office copy of the letter.

POSTSCRIPT: A postscript, preceded by "P.S.," is typed flush left two spaces below the last typed line.

MAILING NOTATION: Instructions for mailing (Special Delivery, Overnight Express) are noted on copies of the letter, but not on the original.

LETTER FORMATS

There is no "best" way to arrange the elements of a letter on the page (unless there is one company-wide style). The most important issues are that you be consistent—if you indent one paragraph, you indent all of them—and that the layout be readable and appealing. The following four formats are the most common, but any arrangement that makes sense, is readable, and is spaced nicely on the page is acceptable.

Full-block letter

The easiest format for the typist, full-block style means that every line begins at the left margin—no exceptions. If you have a second page, the name of the recipient, the page number, and the date are typed flush left, one under the other. Here is a letter set full-block style:

RUSHWORTH FURNITURE RENTAL
1927 Lowndes Avenue
Belloc, WI 53597

March 15, 2000

Confidential

Royce Furniture Rental
ATTN: Julia Royce
1897 George Street
Belloc, WI 53597

Dear Julia Royce:

Re: bad checks

We spoke at the Belloc Business Association meeting last month about exchanging lists of customers who have written at least three unbankable checks. Enclosed is my list.

Yours truly,

[signature]

Miles Rushworth
President

Enc.: list

P.S. I don't feel too bad about passing these names along because I keep this same list posted by my cash register. If you were to come in and look, you could see the same thing. I don't like doing things this way, but I also can't afford to accept any more checks backed by "insufficient funds."

Block letter

The block letter is identical to the full-block with two exceptions: the date line and reference line are typed flush right and the signature block (complimentary close plus signature plus name line and title line) are also set flush right or at least to the right of center. Otherwise, everything is flush left and there are no indentations. This format, which has a more traditional look than the full-block format and which seems to be the most popular one today, is used in perhaps 80% of all business letters. The following is an example of a block letter.

RUSHWORTH FURNITURE RENTAL
1927 Lowndes Avenue
Belloc, WI 53597

March 15, 2000

CONFIDENTIAL

Royce Furniture Rental
ATTN: Julia Royce
1897 George Street
Belloc, WI 53597

Dear Julia Royce:

Re: bad checks

We spoke at the Belloc Business Association meeting last month about exchanging lists of customers who have written at least three unbankable checks. Enclosed is my list.

Yours truly,

[signature]

Miles Rushworth
President

Enc.: list

P.S. I don't feel too bad about passing these along because I keep this same list posted by my cash register. If you were to come in and look, you could see the same thing. I agree with you—I don't like doing things this way, but I also can't afford to accept any more "insufficient funds" checks.

Modified-block

Also known as the semi-block, this format is identical to the block format with one exception: it has indentations. All paragraphs are indented five to ten spaces. The subject line may also be indented. As in the block style, the date line, the reference line, and the signature block are all set flush right or at least to the right of center. This format, which appears a little warmer than the block formats, is probably the second most popular business letter format. The letter below is in modified-block style.

RUSHWORTH FURNITURE RENTAL
1927 Lowndes Avenue
Belloc, WI 53597

March 15, 2000

CONFIDENTIAL

Royce Furniture Rental
ATTN: Julia Royce
1897 George Street
Belloc, WI 53597

Dear Julia Royce:

Re: bad checks

We spoke at the Belloc Business Association meeting last month about exchanging lists of customers who have written at least three unbankable checks.

Enclosed is my list. I'll look forward to receiving yours when you have time to send it along.

Yours truly,

[signature]

Miles Rushworth
President

Enc.: list

P.S. I don't feel too bad about passing these along because I keep this same list posted by my cash register. If you were to come in and look, you could see the same thing. I agree with you—I don't like doing things this way, but I also can't afford to accept any more "insufficient funds" checks.

Simplified

With its streamlined contemporary look, the simplified format is easily identified by its lack of salutation and complimentary close. Like the full-block style, all lines begin at the left margin. But it has a subject line (typed in capital letters) instead of a salutation. The letterwriter's name and title are typed in all capital letters. The letter below is written in the simplified format.

RUSHWORTH FURNITURE RENTAL
1927 Lowndes Avenue
Belloc, WI 53597

March 15, 2000

CONFIDENTIAL

Royce Furniture Rental
1897 George Street
Belloc, WI 53597

RE: BAD CHECKS

As decided at the Belloc Business Association meeting last month, I am forwarding to other stores a list of my customers who have given me at least three unbankable checks.

Enclosed is my list. I'll look forward to receiving yours.

[signature]

MILES RUSHWORTH
PRESIDENT

Enc.: list

UNITED STATES POSTAL SERVICE GUIDELINES

Jane Austen wrote in 1816, "The post-office is a wonderful establishment! The regularity and dispatch of it! If one thinks of all that it has to do, and all that it does so well, it is really astonishing!"

If you are already familiar with the various services offered by the United States Postal Service (USPS), read no further. Otherwise, consider asking for some of its free publications.

The monthly "Memo to Mailers" is particularly helpful to business mailers; a subscription may be obtained free of charge by writing:

National Customer Support Center
United States Postal Service
6060 Primacy Pkwy Ste 101
Memphis, TN 38188-0001.

"Postal Answer Line" explains the automated telephone service that allows you to obtain information on all postal services. The "Stamps by Mail" form permits you to order stamps, commemorative sheets, stamped envelopes, or postcards, without a handling charge. You don't even need a stamp to mail the form. Ask your mail carrier for it, or call your local post office.

Other materials include brochures such as "Creative Solutions for Your Business Needs," "A Consumer's Directory of Postal Services and Products," "Postal Addressing Standards," and its smaller booklet on addressing envelopes (the third edition was titled "Addressing for the 90's"), "Directory of AIS [Address Information System] Products and Services," "How to Prepare and Wrap Packages," "Postage Rates, Fees, and Information," "International Postal Rates and Fees," "U.S. Postal Service Official Zone Chart."

On the Internet, check with http//:www.usps.com and ribbs.usps.gov. The USPS also has a number of videos available for viewing or reproduction. If you are interested in second-class mailings, for example, a video covers requirements for presorting, packaging, sorting and labeling, mailing list preparation, size standards, postage payment, and acceptance procedures. "From Cave to Computer: A Short History of Mail Preparation" is a short overview of interest to lay people and schoolchildren.

Suggestions from the United States Postal Service on improving your mail handling include:

- Ensure that your mail is readable by the Optical Character Readers (OCRs) used in automated sorting: use envelopes of standard size and shape (first-class mail must be rectangular—a square envelope, for example, will be assessed a surcharge); use only white, ivory, or pastels; avoid unusual features like odd papers or bright graphics; type the address IN CAPITAL LETTERS with no punctuation (except for the hyphen in zip + 4 codes), with one or two spaces between words, and with nothing but the address in the lower right part of the envelope.

- Don't use paperclips; they often jam the Letter-Sorting Machines (LSMs).

- Put your return address on envelopes; a surprising number of people fail to do this.

- Use the two-letter state abbreviations and zip + 4.

- Set up a home postal center. Obtain copies of USPS brochures listing postage rates, fees, and information. Invest in a small postage scale, and buy stamps of different denominations to keep in small nine- or fifteen-drawer organizers.

- Attend USPS workshops on such subjects as marketing with direct mail, professional mailroom management, and organizing your mail for optimum service. The seminars are designed to help cut costs and improve efficiency and will try to match USPS programs to your company's needs. There is usually a small registration fee.

- Subscribe to *Domestic Mail Manual* and *International Mail Manual.* They may be too expensive (and unnecessary) for individual letterwriters, but many businesses find them indispensable.

- Use the Business Reply Mail Accounting System (BRMAS), which is available to customers who use Business Reply Mail.

- Bar code your mail. Using zip + 4 and bar codes gives you the largest postal discount available, and the bar coding equipment eventually pays for itself. If you are interested in bar coding your mail, contact an account representative at your local USPS Marketing and Communications office.

STATE ABBREVIATIONS

Alabama	AL	Iowa	IA
Alaska	AK	Kansas	KS
Arizona	AZ	Kentucky	KY
Arkansas	AR	Louisiana	LA
California	CA	Maine	ME
Colorado	CO	Maryland	MD
Connecticut	CT	Massachusetts	MA
Delaware	DE	Michigan	MI
Dist. of Col.	DC	Minnesota	MN
Florida	FL	Mississippi	MS
Georgia	GA	Missouri	MO
Guam	GU	Montana	MT
Hawaii	HI	Nebraska	NE
Idaho	ID	Nevada	NV
Illinois	IL	New Hampshire	NH
Indiana	IN	New Jersey	NJ

New Mexico	NM		South Dakota	SD
New York	NY		Tennessee	TN
North Carolina	NC		Texas	TX
North Dakota	ND		Utah	UT
Ohio	OH		Vermont	VT
Oklahoma	OK		Virginia	VA
Oregon	OR		Virgin Islands	VI
Pennsylvania	PA		Washington	WA
Puerto Rico	PR		West Virginia	WV
Rhode Island	RI		Wisconsin	WI
South Carolina	SC		Wyoming	WY

Appendix II: Content

Appendix I tells *how* a letter should look on the page. Appendix II tells *what* to put on the page, discussing principles of good letterwriting and effective form letters; grammar and usage; respectful, unbiased language; names and titles; salutations, complimentary closes, and signatures; frequently misspelled words; superfluous words and phrases; forms of address.

GENERAL GUIDELINES ON LETTER CONTENT

The following guidelines apply primarily to business letters. For example, where brevity is highly prized in a business letter, it may not be as much appreciated by a dear friend. You are not obliged to state your main idea (if indeed you have one) in the first sentence of a letter to a family member whereas the business reader wants to know immediately what your letter is about. However, most of these suggestions will improve all your letterwriting.

Matthew Arnold once wrote, "People think I can teach them style. What stuff it all is! Have something to say, and say it as clearly as you can. That is the only secret of style." If you haven't time to read further, that advice will stand you in good stead in your business and social correspondence. For refinements, read on.

- Before beginning to write, state in one sentence what the purpose of your letter is: what do you want the other person to do as a result of reading your letter? Gather all the information you need to be persuasive. Think about your readers—the more you know about them, the better you can aim your message. Only when you are very clear about where your letter is going do you begin to write it.

- Be brief. George Burns's advice on a good sermon applies equally well to letters: "a good beginning and a good ending ... as close together as possible." Augustus J.C. Hare received an invitation that read: "Will you be so very kind as to allow me to take the liberty of entreating you to have the kindness to confer the favor upon me of giving me the happiness of your company on Friday?" Although we can feel virtuous for not having written that letter, many of ours could still be pared down to everyone's pleasure. Give brief explanations, instructions, reasons. Overexplaining always appears weak. The reader who needs to know more can always ask. (Do not even think "brief" when you're writing a friendly personal letter.)

- State the main idea in the first or second sentence.

- Use (but don't overuse) the word "you" throughout your letter, and particularly in the opening sentences. Being conscious of "you" will reinforce that most important letterwriting rule, "Keep your reader in mind." "You" helps you phrase your message in terms of your reader's interests, needs, and expectations. It also involves the reader in the letter. The exception to the use of "you" is the letter of complaint or disagreement, in which "you"-statements are perceived as (and often are) accusing and hostile. In those cases, it is better to phrase your message in terms of "I" statements.

- Be specific. Nothing gives writing more power than details—not unnecessary details, but details that replace vague words and phrases. Readers want to know how much, what color, what date, what time, how big, how little. Go back through your letters and question every adjective—is it pulling its weight? Could it be more specific? But don't go overboard on adjectives either—it's primarily nouns you want. Mark Twain's advice was, "As to the adjective: when in doubt, strike it out."

- Avoid slang, jargon, buzz words, legalese, elitist language, and stilted usage like "I shall." Choose the familiar word over the unfamiliar. Also avoid clichés, gimmicks, rhetorical questions, jokes, and "clever" remarks. We are so used to our own manner of writing that we are often unaware of these little tics in our letters. In a place of business where people are supportive of each other and employees have fairly healthy egos, you might want to schedule a one- or two-hour workshop where a few letterwriting principles are given and participants can critique each other's letters (a packet of sample letters with the signatures inked out can be photocopied and distributed).

- Be factual and avoid emotion in business letters (it is fine—even desirable—in personal letters). Your readers do not, unfortunately, really care about your feelings; they want facts, they want to know outcomes, they want results, they want reasons. Feelings are not generally persuasive in the business world; facts and data are. Whether this orientation is a good thing is a topic for another day. For the moment, it appears to be the way it is. Change it if you can, but be aware of the consequences along the way. Avoid exaggerating or dramatizing your message. You will lose credibility with your reader. It is better to mildly understate your case and let the reader take credit for seeing how wonderful it really is.

- Use the active instead of the passive voice ("I received your letter last week," not "Your letter was received last week"). Use strong, direct, action-filled verbs ("is/are," "do," and "make" are not some of them). Use a thesaurus to find dynamic (but not unusual, unfamiliar, or unpronounceable) substitutes for your most overused words.

- Use a lively, conversational tone. Reading your letters out loud for several weeks will help you spot awkwardness.

- Choose a tone for your letter and stick to it. A letter that starts off friendly, grows indignant in the middle, and winds up with a demand will confuse the reader. A letter might be formal or informal, cool or warm, serious or lighthearted, brisk or relaxed, simple or complex, elegant or down home. But it is, above all, consistent.

- Avoid overused words like "very" and "basically." Neither of them means very much, and they are annoying to the reader.

- Make it easy for your correspondent to reply to you: enclose a postage-paid reply envelope or a self-addressed stamped envelope or postcard.

- In your spare time (that is supposed to be humorous), you might read some of the excellent books available just for business writing. A classic is the 780-page *Handbook of Business Letters*, 3d ed., by L.E. Frailey (Prentice Hall, 1989).

FORM LETTERS

Form letters have been one of the most wildly successful innovations in business letterwriting. They have done away with the numbing and time-consuming chore of typing the same letter thousands of times. With the use of word processing and mail-merge capabilities, letters are printed, individually addressed and dated, and mailed out in a fraction of the time it used to take to do half as many. Form letters have been worth their weight in gold in direct sales marketing and in the processing of many routine business letters (confirmations, acknowledgments, cover letters, rejections).

Form letters have a negative side, however. Joseph Heller poked fun at them in *Catch-22*: "Dear Mrs., Mr., Miss, or Mr. and Mrs. Daneeka: Words cannot express the deep personal grief I experienced when your husband, son, father, or brother was killed, wounded, or reported missing in action."

To make the most of form letters, your message should appear to be directed solely at the person reading it. Inserting the person's name at intervals is not the way to do this; spelling errors of names creep in, which is incredibly offputting, and it appears that people do not mistake this cheery and obviously phony friendship for real intimacy. Personalize your letter by using "you," by tailoring your letter to the individual on the basis of mailing lists of specific market targets. When you are writing to members of a list who are all gardeners or who have all contributed to a charity within the past six months, you know how to frame your letter. For important mailings, you can achieve the personal look by using high-quality paper, signing each letter individually (there are people who look first to see if the signature is "real" or not and then either read the letter or toss it), and mailing the letter first class.

In addition to form letters, you may want to keep boilerplate material—paragraphs, signature blocks, addresses, and other bits and pieces of letters that you use over and over. Most word processing systems have a "phrase library" or similar construct so that by typing two keys you can insert whole paragraphs any time you need them.

GRAMMAR AND USAGE

A few of the most common grammar and usage problems in letterwriting are given below. Anyone who writes more than the occasional letter should have close by a dictionary, a basic grammar book, a usage guide, a style manual, and a thesaurus.

- Use **periods** at the end of sentences. Or sentence fragments. A period also follows an abbrev. Ellipsis points are used to replace missing words: three dots in the middle of the sentence, four at the end.

- **Commas** separate items or lists of things. It is correct either to use or not to use a comma before "and" in a series ("Milk, butter and eggs" or "Milk, butter, and eggs")—the only rule is to do it one way or the other consistently. If you don't know when to use a comma, read the sentence aloud dramatically. The place where you pause to group a thought phrase together may need a comma. Commas are used before and after "etc." and academic degrees.

- Don't use **question marks** after indirect questions or requests ("He asked what went wrong" or "Please sweep up here after yourself"). Omit the comma after the question mark in cases like "Do you like it?" she asked.

- Except perhaps for sales letters, business correspondence doesn't need—and shouldn't have—**exclamation marks**. Be stingy with them in personal correspondence as well. J.L. Basford believed that "One who uses many periods is a philosopher; many interrogations, a student; many exclamations, a fanatic." Exclamations give your letters a certain manic look, like people laughing at their own jokes. At first, it will tear at your heart to remove them; by and by, you will be pleased to find that you can get along nicely without them.

- **Quotation marks** are used for quoted words and for the titles of magazine articles and TV and radio shows. All punctuation goes inside the quotation marks ("What?" "Egads!" "I won't," he said). Common sense ought to indicate the rare exceptions. If the punctuation in no way belongs to the quotation, you can leave it outside, as in the following sentence: How many times have you heard a child say "But I'm not tired"?

- **Parentheses** are used to enclose asides to your main train of thought. When the aside is an incomplete thought (incomplete sentence) it is placed in the middle of a regular sentence; the first word inside does not begin with a capital, nor is there any punctuation. (Sometimes, however, your thought is a complete thought, or complete sentence, in which case it is set inside parentheses and has its own initial capital letter and final punctuation.) When using parentheses within a sentence, all punctuation goes after the parentheses: Please order more ribbons, paper (30#), and file folders.

- In general, **hyphens** are used to help word pairs or groups form one easy-to-read thought group. Traditional exceptions are words ending in -ly ("newly appointed") and adjective groups that follow a noun ("well-known telecaster" but "she was well known"). The trend is to one word rather than hyphenated words or two separate words ("headlight," not "head-light" or "head light"). There are a number of rules on hyphenation, but a quick check with a dictionary will give you the correct form for most words.

- Use **apostrophes** to replace missing letters ("isn't" = "is not") and to show possession ("Simon's"). The apostrophe most commonly shows up in the wrong place in "its" and "it's." If you can write "it is" in place of your word, it needs the apostrophe. If you have trouble with this pair, write only "it is" or "its" until you are comfortable with the difference. When more than one person is involved, show the plural possessive by placing the apostrophe after the "s" ("union members' votes" or "the parents' recommendations"). Omit the apostrophe when making plurals of number and letter combinations: Ph.D.s, the 1990s, the '50s, three 100s, IBMs.

- **Colons** often precede a list or a long quotation ("We carry the following brand names: . . ." or "The hospital issued the following apology: . . ."). Do not use a colon when it unnecessarily breaks up a sentence (remove the colon in "Your kit contains: a lifetime supply of glue, four colors of paint, and a set of two brushes"). The colon is also used after a business or formal salutation ("Mr. President:").

- **Semicolons** tend to give a stuffy, old-fashioned look to a letter. However, they are still useful on occasion. When writing a long list that has internal punctuation, separate each element with a semicolon ("New members for January: Constantine Stephanopoulos; Rachel and Darke Solomon of Velindre, their children Peter, Jasper, Ruby, and Amber; Catherine, Lize, and Fritz Steinhart"). You may also separate two independent clauses of a sentence with a semicolon ("In prosperity our friends know us; in adversity we know our friends."—J. Churton Collins).

- The overuse of **dashes** is questionable and indicates a rather slapdash (you see where it comes from?) style. If you are a regular dash-user, check to see if other punctuation might not do as well. Dashes tend to mate in captivity, so once the dash habit takes hold, it only gets worse.

- One of the most common grammar errors involves **noun-verb agreement.** In complicated sentences, where the noun and verb become separated from each other, it is easy to make a mistake. When proofreading your letters, pick out long sentences, find your noun and verb, put them together, and see if they still make sense. Some nouns that look singular ("data") take a plural verb; some that look plural take a singular verb ("a series of books is scheduled for"; "the board of directors is investigating"). What do you do with "None of them has/have voted yet"? When in doubt, reword the sentence ("Nobody has voted yet"; "Not one of them has voted yet") or ask what the sense of the phrase is. If you are indeed speaking of only one person, use "has"; if the sense of the phrase means a lot of people, use "have." "A number of accountants are signing up for . . ." but "The number of accountants is decreasing."

- **Underline** (or italicize) titles of books and movies; other titles go in quotation marks.

- One of the best things you can do for your writing is to become aware of **parallel structures**—from little things like capitalizing or not capitalizing all the words in a list, to making sure each word in the list is the same part of speech. In long sentences, writers often forget that they started one phrase with "to interview . . ." but later used "calling the candidate" and ended up with "and, finally, you could meet with. . . ." A parallel form would have "to interview . . . to call . . . to meet with. . . ." Parallel constructions are used throughout this book; if you are interested in finding other examples, most pages offer some.

- Keep **paragraphs** short. Let each one develop a single idea. You can start with your broadest idea and then support it with detailed refinements. Or you can start with details and lead the reader to your final, topic sentence.

- The easiest way to decide whether you need "that" or "which" is to see if you need commas. Commas and "which" tend to go together: "The file, which eventually turned up on Frank's desk, had been missing for a week." "The file that had been missing eventually turned up on Frank's desk." Do not set off a phrase beginning with "that" with commas, and do set off a "which" clause with commas.

- "Howard and Paul had lunch together before he left." Which "he" left? A common error is forgetting to check pronouns ("who," "she," "they") to be sure the **antecedents** (the persons they refer to) are obvious.

- **Dangling modifiers** consist of words tacked onto a sentence, front or back (sometimes even in the middle), in such a way that the reader doesn't know what they modify. In *Watch Your Language*, Theodore M. Bernstein gives several examples, among them: "Although definitely extinct, Professor Daevey said it had not been too long ago that the moa was floundering around his deathtrap swamps." "As reconstructed by the police, Pfeffer at first denied any knowledge of the Byrd murder."

- "Between" is generally between two people, no more. (And the correct expression is always "between you and me," "between Sandy and me.") "Among" is generally for three or more: "We should have the necessary know-how among the four of us."

- Watch the placement of "only" and "not only"; they should go right next to the word they modify. Instead of "I am only buying one," write "I am buying only one."

- "Whom" and "whomever" do not occur nearly as often as people suppose. Use them only when you can show they are the object of a verb. The most common misuse of "whomever" occurs in a situation like this: "Please mail this file to whoever is elected secretary." "Whoever" is correct here; it is the subject of the clause. If you are troubled by this construction, see a good grammar book; until then, it is perhaps enough to be aware of the problem.

TALKING ABOUT PEOPLE

Stereotypical language assumes all artists are like this or all children are like that. Exclusive language forgets to include certain groups: when you invite customers to an open house and fail to say that the event is accessible, you exclude people with disabilities; when you begin your letter "Dear Sirs:" you forget that a woman might be your reader. When you refer to the "Christian ethic" or the "Judeo-Christian ethic" you exclude large numbers of highly ethical people who are not included in either phrase. Words can exclude, stereotype, and discriminate against people on the basis of sex, age, ethnicity, disability, socioeconomic class, sexual orientation, religion.

For the rationale for using respectful people language, see *Talking About People* by Rosalie Maggio, The Oryx Press, 1997. The quickie rationale is that it is good business; you can't very well sell anything or obtain any information or favors from someone whom you've just offended with an inaccurate word choice. The following guidelines will help keep your correspondence respectful of our human differences.

- "Labels are disabling," says an old maxim. Labels are by their very nature stereotypes: senior citizens, Asian-Americans, unmarried women, cancer patients, teenagers, Methodists, second-generation Italians. When you begin talking about a class of people, you skate on thin ice because psychologically all of us think of ourselves as individuals. No two "young mothers" are alike. Nor are any two "Roman Catholic priests" or "lawyers" or "blue-collar workers." Write to individuals and write of people as individuals. When asked what labels offended them, young people listed "teens," "teenagers," "youth," "kids," "girls and boys," "adolescents," "minors," and "juveniles." What's left? "People" or "young people," they said. In an interview of older people about the best terminology, "senior citizens," "Golden Agers," "the elderly," and more were all rejected. "Could we just be people?" they said. Nobody likes labels.

- The "people first" rule says we are people first, and only secondarily people who have disabilities, people who are over sixty-five, people who are Baptists, people who are Finnish-Americans. In your letters, ask first if you need to mention classifications such as sex, age, race, religion, economic class, or disability. Most often it is not necessary. When in doubt, omit it. Beware of identifying the whole person by a part of the person. Madeline is a person who happens to have paraplegia. Referring to her as "a paraplegic" identifies the whole Madeline by one part of her. Another common error is speaking about someone as being passively "confined to a wheelchair." The correct and active phrase is "uses a wheelchair."

- Think parallel construction: do you mention one person's marital status and not the other person's? One person's race, and not the other's? Identify some people as gay but not others as heterosexual? Is she Mrs. William Gostrey, but he is Ray Parker? (Or he is Ray Parker and she is Sheila?) When in doubt, switch categories around and see if your letter reads as well when describing someone from another group.

- We've made much progress in reducing the sexism in our language. Instead of false generics like "man" or "mankind" we are using words that include everyone: humanity, people, we, us, humankind, persons, individuals, souls, creatures, society, human society, nature, folks, the general public, planet earth, the world, adults, citizens, taxpayers, the general population. We rarely use "he" when we mean "he or she." Instead of "A mail carrier has his work cut out for him today" we use the plural: "Mail carriers have their work cut out for them today"). We rewrite the sentence to use "you" or "we." Sometimes the pronouns "he," "his," or "him" can simply be omitted or replaced with a noun. Using the awkward "his or her" or "she or he" is not recommended. In great numbers people are returning the centuries-old use of the singular "they" ("to each their own"), and this construction (which is found throughout this book) is accepted or endorsed by many authorities: *Oxford English Dictionary* ("The pronoun referring to *everyone* is often plural"); *Chicago Manual of Style*, 14th ed. ("recommends the 'revival' of the singular use of they and their"); *American Heritage Dictionary of the English Language*, 3d ed. ("may be the only sensible choice in informal style"); *American Heritage Book of English Usage* ("The alternative to the masculine generic with the longest and most distinguished history in English is the third-person plural pronoun"); the National Council of Teachers of English ("In all but strictly formal usage, plural pronouns have become acceptable substitutes for the masculine singular"); *Random House Dictionary II*; *Webster's Third New International Dictionary* (their definition of *everyone* reads in part, "Usually referred to by the third person singular . . . but sometimes by a plural personal pronoun" and they give the example of "Everyone had made up their minds"); and Randolph Quirk et al., *A Grammar of Contemporary English*. "However negatively one may react to this recourse, it is of long-established use" (Robert N. Mory, Assistant Research Editor, *Middle English Dictionary*). With a few exceptions ("layperson," for example), words ending in *-person* are contrived-looking and awkward. Good alternatives exist for almost all *-person* words. Why use *spokesperson* when *representative* is punchier and more accurate? Why use *chairperson* when *chair* is actually the older word of the two and quite respectable today?

NAMES

There are very few hard and fast rules about names today. The most basic principle is to use whatever form of their name your correspondent prefers. When deciding which form of your own name to use, be guided not so much by rules (many of which were laid down in earlier times and by means of less congenial points of reference), but by common sense and your own preferences. Research shows that naming has great power, and the power of saying who we are belongs to us alone. Useful guidelines might include:

- Spell your correspondent's name correctly. It is worth the few minutes and the forty cents or so to call long distance to obtain the correct spelling and current title of the person to whom you're writing. In the case of a company name, use it exactly as they have it: if they use Ltd., Inc., Incorporated, Corp., Corporation, Company, Co., you use it. If they use an ampersand (&) in the name, so do you.

- Although in some fields and in some parts of the country people are quick to call each other by their first names, you may do well to write "Dear Mr. Cokeson" rather than "Dear Bob" until you are sure the latter is welcome. Miss Manners says: "To prevent the unauthorized use of her first name, Miss Manners took the precaution of not having one." Miss Manners (Judith Martin) says she is far from alone in cringing when strangers assume the privileges of intimacy by using her first name. If you are unsure about the degree of formality or informality that exists between you and a correspondent, the more formal approach is preferable.

- When ordering business cards or personal calling cards, spell out your full name. Social titles (Mr., Ms., Mrs., Miss) used to precede the name, but they are largely omitted today. Medical specialists use "Dr." or "Doctor" on social cards ("Doctor Christopher Bembridge"), but use "M.D.," "D.O.," "D.D.S.," "O.D.," on business cards ("Muriel Eden, D.D.S."). Either "Joseph Farr Jr." or "Joseph Farr II" is correct. When using "Esq." (short for Esquire) after lawyers' names ("Marian Beltham, Esq."), omit all other titles (Mr., Ms., Mrs., Miss) before it.

- Which social title (also called courtesy title or honorific) to use for a woman is fairly simple: use whatever name and social title she uses (see her last letter or call her home or office to check on the spelling of her name and to ask "Do you prefer Miss, Mrs., or Ms.?"). If there is no clue to her marital status (and remember that you have been addressing men for years without worrying about this), use her full name without a social title ("Dear Florence Churchill") or use "Ms." and her last name. The worst that can happen is that the letter you receive in return is signed by a "(Mrs.)" or a "Dr." or some other title. Now you know. In business, women invariably use their own first names. This used to indicate that a woman was single, divorced, or possibly widowed. Today it just means that that is her first name. Socially, some women use their husbands' names. They may sign a letter "Nelly Christie" but type underneath "Mrs. John Christie." Traditionally, married or widowed women used their husbands' names ("Mrs. Philip Halliday"), while divorced women used their own first name and either their family-of-origin name, their married name, or both. Single women were to use "Miss" or not, as they pleased. This marital coding system is no longer as reliable or as popular as it once was.

- Naming couples also requires common sense and sensitivity. Use the form they use themselves. A few possibilities are: "Mr. and Mrs. Walter Evson"; "Adela and George Norrington"; "Dr. Guy and Mrs. Elizabeth Phillips"; "Katherine Halstead and Frank

Luttrell"; "Dr. Linda and Mr. Arnaud Hallet." When addressing envelopes or typing the inside address, and each name is fairly long, put one to a line in alphabetic order.

- When addressing more than one person, use each person's full name or use a social title plus last name for each. For single-sex groups, you may use "Mesdames" ("Mmes.") for women and "Messieurs" ("Messrs.") for men, although these terms have an old-fashioned ring to them. These titles are followed by the individuals' last names only. When addressing both women and men, use an inclusive salutation such as "Dear Friends," "Dear Co-chairs," "Dear Committee Members," or "To: (list names, one to a line in alphabetic order)."

SALUTATIONS, COMPLIMENTARY CLOSES, AND SIGNATURES

Salutations

The salutation (also referred to as a greeting) is set flush left. The first letter of the first word is capitalized but other modifying words are not ("My very dear Joanna"). All titles and names are capitalized. Use abbreviations for Ms., Mr., Mrs., Dr., but spell out religious, military, and professional titles such as Father, Major, Professor, Sister, Colonel. The salutation generally ends in a comma for personal or informal letters, and in a colon or a comma for business letters.

When possible, obtain the name of the person who is best suited to receive your letter and obtain the correct spelling of their name and verify their current title; call the company if necessary.

When you know the person's name, write: "Dear George Arthur Rose" or "Dear Laura McRaven" (full name with no social title) or "Dear Ms. Dolbie," "Dear Captain Bubbleton," "Dear Inspector Bigglesworth," "Dear Senator Brander" (social title plus last name). The first convention is useful when you don't know the person's sex ("R.F. Daintree") or which social title (Ms., Mrs., Miss) the person uses. Professional or academic titles (Dr., Representative) are always used instead of social titles (Ms., Mr.).

When writing a form letter or when you don't know your correspondent's name, you can still write "Dear..." with nouns like: Neighbor, Subscriber, Friend, Motorist, Reader, Colleague, Student, Customer, Gardener, Client, Employee, Potential Employer, Parishioner, Collector, Cardholder, Concerned Parent, Initiate-Elect, Handgun Control Supporter, Member, Homeowner, Supplier, Executive, Aquarellist, Equestrian, Do-It-Yourselfer. Or try job titles: Dentist, Copywriter, Electrician, Metallurgist, Customer Service Manager. Or use the company's name: Poulengay Upholsterers, Elliot-Lewis Stationers, Handford Lawn Care. You can also use an impersonal salutation like Good morning! Hello! Greetings! The best solution may be to replace the salutation with a subject line. (The old-fashioned "Dear Sir or Madam" and "To Whom It May Concern" are not recommended.)

In a personal letter, greet the person by first name. If this seems too informal, your letter is probably a business letter or a business-social letter and should be formatted accordingly.

Complimentary close

The complimentary close follows the body of your letter, with one line of space between them. It always begins with a capital letter and ends with a comma. Words in between are not capitalized.

The most everyday, acceptable, and all-purpose complimentary closes are: Sincerely (used perhaps three-fourths of the time), Yours truly, Sincerely yours, Very sincerely yours, Very sincerely, Very truly yours. You cannot go wrong with one of these. Miss Manners (Judith Martin) says that business letters should close with "Yours truly": "Can Miss Manners be the only person still alive who knows that?"

For a highly formal letter involving White House, diplomatic, judicial, or ecclesiastical correspondence, use: Respectfully yours or Respectfully. An informal letter in the same instances uses: Very respectfully yours, Yours respectfully, or Sincerely yours. In formal letters to members of Congress, senators, high-ranking politicians and government figures, priests, rabbis, and ministers, use: Yours very truly. The informal form is: Sincerely yours.

For most formal letters—regular business and personal—choose from among: Sincerely, Sincerely yours, Yours sincerely, Very sincerely yours, Very sincerely, Truly yours, Yours truly, Very truly yours, Yours very truly, Very cordially yours.

Informal closes include: Love, With all my love, Lovingly, Lovingly yours, Fondly, Affectionately, Yours affectionately, Sincerely, Sincerely yours, Cordially, Cordially yours, Yours cordially, Faithfully, Faithfully yours, Yours faithfully, As ever, As always, Devotedly, Yours, Best regards, Kindest regards, Warmest regards, Cheers, Your friend, Be well, Until next time.

Complimentary closes somewhere between formal and informal include: With all kind regards, Warm regards, Best regards, Best, Best wishes, With best wishes, With all best wishes, Cordially, Sincerely, All the very best, With every good wish, Warm personal regards.

After studying the above lists, choose one or two complimentary closes that reflect your letterwriting style and use them for most of your correspondence. It's not worth the trouble to fit a special complimentary close to each letter.

Signature

Although there used to be many rules governing signatures, it's fairly simple today: use the version of your name that you want the person to use for you. If there is any ambiguity (for example, the person knows you only under your pen name, birth name, married name, or business name), put the name that might be more easily recognized in parentheses under your signature. Signatures rarely include social titles, so omit the "Dr.," "Ms.," or "Mr." (They may be typed on the name line, however.) In personal letters, your signature stands alone. In business letters, it is followed by your name and title (on one or two lines, depending on length). The name and title lines are typed four lines below the complimentary close—more, if you have a particularly sweeping signature. If your name and title are given on the letterhead, omit them under your signature. When signing a letter for someone else, put your initials just below and to the right of the signature, often after a slash. When you write a letter on someone else's behalf, sign your own name above a name line that identifies you: "Son of Christina Light" or "Secretary to Cavaliere Giacosa."

If your salutation uses the person's first name, sign the letter with your first name (although in a business letter, your full name and title will be printed below your signature). Nonparallel salutations and signatures can be insulting and off-putting. If you write "Dear Fred," and sign it "Dr. Francis Etherington," you have assumed a superior position; writing it the other way around presumes an intimacy that may not exist. Except in very rare cases, the salutation and signature should be strictly parallel: "Dear Rosa, . . . Love, Judy"; "Dear Thomas Eustick, . . . Sincerely, Margaret Kraft."

INTERNATIONAL MAIL

According to a notice in the United States Postal Service's "Memo to Mailers," which is published monthly, "If you are sending mail overseas, it is important that it be marked 'Air Mail' or 'Par Avion.' In many bases, business mailers and corporate mail centers are not properly endorsing international mail. Without the endorsement, the mailpiece ends up in the domestic mailstream, causing delays. Put the endorsement on both the front and back of the mailpiece."

In correspondence destined for other countries, always spell out the date to avoid confusion about whether 10/12/99 is October 12 (in the United States) or December 10 (in Europe, for example).

When writing to people from other countries, keep your sentences and syntax as simple as possible. Avoid slang, jargon, figures of speech, references to facets of American culture, the passive voice, and complex verb constructions. Keep to the present and simple past tenses. Instead of "If we had only known . . . ," say "We did not know . . .". Avoid colloquial terms that are not readily understood by those not living in the United States culture: hit or miss proposition, ballpark figure, sliding scale, no strings attached, across the board, the ball's in your court now, will lend you a hand. Humor often doesn't translate well to other cultures and political, religious, and cultural observations are better omitted from international business letters.

If you can handle them correctly, use social titles from the reader's language ("Monsieur," "Signora," "Herr," "Señora"). Use the address exactly as it is given in the other person's return address; it is most deliverable in that form. Letters from other countries often have ritualized closing sentences that express the writer's respect and good wishes; take your cue from your correspondent's letter and reply in kind. A French letterwriting guide, *Le Parfait Secrétaire*, gives explicit instructions for signing off: to a colleague or boss you give respectful regards; to a subordinate, distinguished will do. A woman writing to a man need convey only her "expression of my distinguished sentiments." But a man is expected to "pray that you agree with my most respectful homage." Electricité de France wrote customers saying rates were going up and signed the letter (which loses a little dignity in the translation), "Resting at your disposition, we pray you to believe, Madame, Monsieur, in the assurance of our most devout sentiments."

FREQUENTLY MISSPELLED WORDS

Bill Nye once said, "The dictionary is a great book; it hasn't much plot, but the author's vocabulary is wonderful." It is also useful for verifying correct spelling.

abscess	beneficiary
absence	benefited
accommodate	Britannia/Britannica
accumulate	Brittany
acknowledge/acknowledgment/ acknowledging	canceled, cancellation
	Caribbean
acquaintance	category
advice/advise	cemetery
all right (no such word as "alright")	colossal/colossus
a lot	consensus
amateur	concur/concurred/concurrence
appall/appalled/appalling	consistency
apparatus	correspondence/correspondent
aquarium	desperate
arctic	discernible
barracks	drunkenness
barrage	elegant/elegance

eligible

embarrass/embarrassment

exhaustible

exhilarate

existence

February

fluorescence

foreign

fulfill/fulfilled/fulfillment

genealogy

grievance

harass/harassment

hemorrhage

hitchhike/hitchhiker

hypocrisy

indispensable

inoculate

in regard to (not in regards to)

iridescent/iridescence

irresistible

its/it's

jewel/jeweled/jeweler/jewelry

judgment

knowledge/knowledgeable

lieutenant

liqueur/liquor

maintenance

miniature

mischievous

missile

misspell

niece

noticeable

occasion

occur/occurred/occurrence

omitted

parallel

paraphernalia

pastime

perennial

permissible

personnel

Pharaoh

precede

prejudice

principal/principle

privilege

proceed

realtor

receive

reference

regardless (never irregardless)

sacrilegious

seize

siege

sieve

stationary/stationery

subtle

threshold

toward

vengeance

FREQUENTLY MISUSED TERMS

If you have any doubts about your use of the following terms, consult a dictionary.

accept/except

adapt/adept/adopt

advice/advise

affect/effect

all ready/already

allusion/illusion

alternate/alternative

among/between

amount/number

anyone/any one

assure/ensure/insure

beside/besides

biannually (two times a year)/biennially (every two years)

borne/born

can/may

capital/capitol

cite/site/sight

complement/compliment

continuous/continual

council/counsel/consul/councillor/counselor

credible/creditable

definite/definitive

disinterested (neutral/not biased)/uninterested (not concerned with/lacking interest)

disorganized/unorganized

each other (two)/one another (more than two)

emigrate (to leave one country to live in another)/immigrate (to come into a country)

eminent/imminent/immanent

farther/further

formerly/formally

imply/infer

ingenious/ingenuous

it's/its

later/latter

less/fewer

lie, lay, lain (to recline)/lay, laid (to place)

personal/personnel

principal/principle

reaction/response

rise/raise

sit/set

stationary/stationery

that/which

their/there/they're

who/that

who's/whose

your/you're

CONCISE WRITING

Thomas Jefferson said, "The most valuable of all talents is that of never using two words when one will do."

The words and phrases below on the left can be omitted or replaced with the more concise term shown on the right. Read through the list several times to get a sense of constructions that are awkward and cumbersome. Mark the ones you tend to use (check your letters against the list for a week or so to see which ones you're fond of) and try to avoid them. Your writing will be easier to read and will have a more contemporary, confident voice. (Note that occasionally a term on the left will be precisely what you need for your particular context; in that case, use it.)

above-mentioned = (omit)

absolutely essential/necessary/complete = essential/necessary/complete

accompanied by = with

accomplish = do

according to our records = we find/our records show/(omit)

accordingly = so

acknowledge receipt of = thank you for

acquaint/apprise = tell/inform/let know

activate = begin/start

active consideration = consideration

actual experience/truth = experience/truth

additionally = also

advance forward = advance

advance planning/preparation/warning = planning/preparation/warning

advise = tell/inform

affix your signature = sign

afford an opportunity = allow/permit

aforementioned = (omit)

aggregate/aggregation = total

a great deal of = much

all of = all

almost similar = similar

along the lines of = like

already exists = exists

a majority of = most

and etc. = etc.

and/or = (often unnecessary)

an early date = soon

anent = about/concerning/regarding

a number of = about

a number of cases = some

any and all = any or all, not both

applicable to = suitable for/relevant/appropriate

appreciate in value = appreciate

appreciate your informing me = please write/tell me

approximately = about/roughly

are of the opinion that = think that

around about [number] = about [number]

as a matter of fact = in fact/(omit)

as a result of = because

ascertain = learn/find out

as far as I am concerned = as for me

as I am sure you know = as you know/(omit)

ask the question = ask/question

as otherwise = otherwise

as per = according to

as regards = regarding/concerning/about

assist/assistance = help

as the case may be = (omit)

as to = about

as to whether = whether

at about = at

at all times = always

at an early/later date = soon/later

at a rapid rate = rapidly

at a time when = when

at hand = (omit)

at present = now

attached please find/attached herewith/attached hereto = attached/
    I am attaching/I am enclosing

attach together = attach

at that/this point in time = then/now

at the earliest possible moment = immediately/very soon

at the moment = now/just now

at the present writing = now

at this (point in) time = now/just now/today

at your earliest convenience = soon

avail oneself of = use

awaiting your instructions = please let me know

aware of the fact that = know

baby puppies = puppies

balance of equilibrium = balance or equilibrium, not both

based on the fact that = because

basic fundamentals/essentials = fundamentals/essentials

be dependent on = depend on

beg to inform/tell/state/differ/advise/call to your attention/assure = (omit)

be cognizant of = know that

be in possession of = possess

be of the opinion = believe

be the recipient of = receive

beyond a shadow of a doubt = undoubtedly

big in size = big

bona fide = genuine

both alike/together = alike/together

brief moment = moment

but even so = but or even so, not both

but in any case = but or in any case, not both

but however/nevertheless/nonetheless = one or the other, not both

but on the other hand = but or on the other hand, not both

by means of = by/with

call attention to the fact that = notify/remind

call your attention to = please note

cancel out = cancel

check into = check

circle around = circle

classify into groups = classify

climb up = climb

close proximity = proximity/nearby/close by

co-equal = equal

cogitate upon = think about

cognizant = aware

collaborate together = collaborate

come to the realization = realize

commence = begin/start

commendation = praise

communicate = write/talk

communication = telephone call/letter/telegram/fax/e-mail

commute back and forth = commute

completely filled = filled

completely accurate/compatible/finished/unanimous =
    accurate/compatible/finished/unanimous

comprised = made up of

conclude = close/end

conclusion = closing

conclusive proof = proof

connect up = connect

consensus of opinion = consensus

construct = make

continue on = continue

cooperate together = cooperate

correspondence = letter

corroborate = confirm/make sure

could care less = couldn't care less

crucial/critical = important

current news = news

customary channels/practice = usual way/regular procedure/practice

deeds and actions = deeds or actions, not both

deem = consider/think

deem it advisable = suggest

definite decision = decision

delinquent = past due

demonstrate = show

deserving of = deserve

despite the fact that = although/despite

determine whether = find out

dialogue = talk

different [two different dresses/several different movies] = (omit)

direct confrontation = confrontation

disbursements = payments

disclose = show

discontinue = stop

disincentive = penalty

dispose of = sell

doctorate degree = doctorate

do not hesitate to = please

drop down = drop

due consideration = consideration

due to the fact that = because/since

duly = (omit)

during the course of = during

during the period of time = when

during the time that = while

each and every = each or every, not both

earliest possible moment = soon/immediately

effectuate = effect/bring about/do

either one of the two = either one/either of the two/either

empty space = space

enclosed herewith is/enclosed please find = enclosed is/I enclose/
     I'm sending you

encourage = urge

encounter = meet

endeavor = try

endeavor to ascertain = try to find out

endorse on the back of the check = endorse

end result = result

engineer by profession = engineer

enter into = enter

equivalent = equal

essentially = (omit)

etc. = (avoid whenever possible)

eventuate = result

exactly identical = identical

exactly the same = the same

exact opposites = opposites

exact replica = replica

exact same = exact or same, not both

exhibit/show/have a tendency to = tend to

existing condition = condition

expedite = hurry/hasten

expiration = end

extreme hazard = hazard

facilitate = ease/simplify/chair the meeting/make easy

fearful of = fear

feedback = comments/advice/reactions/opinions/thoughts

feel free to call/write = please call/write

fellow colleague = colleague

few in number = few

field of anthropology/politics, etc. = anthropology/politics, etc.

filled to capacity = filled

final conclusion/outcome = conclusion/outcome

finalize = end/conclude/complete/finish

first and foremost = first or foremost, not both

first created = created

foot pedal = pedal

foreign imports = imports

foreseeable future = future

formulate = form

for the period of a week/month/year = for a week/month/year

for the purpose of = for

for the reason that = because/since/as/for

frankly = (omit)

free gift = gift

free of charge = free

fullest possible extent = fully

full satisfaction = satisfaction

furnish = give

future plans = plans

gather together = gather

get more for your money's worth = more for your money/get your money's worth

give an answer = answer

give encouragement to = encourage

give this matter your attention = (omit)

good benefit = benefit

grand total = total

grateful thanks = thanks

great majority = majority

have a belief in = believe

have a tendency to = tend to

heir apparent = heir

herein = in this

hereinafter = from now on

herewith = enclosed/attached

homologous = alike

honestly = (omit)

hopefully = it is to be hoped/we hope

hopeful that = hope

if and when = if or when, not both

if it meets with your approval = if you approve

if at all possible = if possible

if you desire = if you wish/want

immediately adjoining = adjoining

I myself personally = I myself

in accordance with = with/as/by

in addition to = besides

inadvertent oversight = oversight

in all honesty = (omit)

in a matter of seconds/minutes/hours/days = in seconds/minutes/hours/days

in a number of cases = sometimes

in a satisfactory manner = satisfactorily

inasmuch as = as/since/because

inaugurate = begin/start

in back of = behind

in close proximity = near

in compliance with your request = as you requested/as you asked

in connection with = in/on/to/(omit)

increase by a factor of two = double

indicate = show

individual person = individual or person, not both

initial = first

initiate = begin/start

in lieu of = instead of

in light of the fact = since/because

in many instances/cases = often

in order that = so that

in order to = to

input = advice/opinions/thoughts/reactions

in receipt of = received

in reference to = about

in re/in regard to = about/concerning/regarding

in relation to = toward/to/about

in respect of = about/concerning

inside of = inside

integral part = part

interface with = meet with/work with

in terms of = in

in the amount of = for

in the case of = of/in/(omit)

in the course of = during

in the event of/that = if

in the final analysis = (omit)

in the majority of instances = usually/often

in the matter of = about/in/of

in the meantime = meanwhile

in the near future = soon

in the neighborhood of = about

in the time of = during

in the vast majority of cases = in most cases

in this connection = (omit)

in this day and age = now

intrinsically = (omit)

in view of = because/since

in view of the fact that = as

invisible to the eye = invisible

invited guest = guest

irregardless = regardless/irrespective

I share your concern = like you, I believe

is indicative of = indicates

is of the opinion = thinks

is when/is where = is the day/is the place

it goes without saying = (omit)

it is clear/obvious that = clearly/obviously

it is my intention = I intend

I wish to thank = thank you

it would not be unreasonable to believe/think/assume = I believe/think/assume

I would hope = I hope

I would like to express my appreciation = I appreciate

joint collaboration = collaboration

join together = join

join up = join

kindly = please

kind of/sort of = (omit)

kneel down = kneel

lift up = lift

literally = (omit 99% of the time)

literally and figuratively = (omit 99% of the time)

little baby = baby

lot/lots/a whole lot = (omit)

maintain = keep

major breakthrough = breakthrough

make a decision = decide

make a mention of = mention

make an inquiry regarding = inquire

make use of = use

mandatory requirements = requirements

may possibly/perhaps = may

meet with approval = approve

merge together = merge

meet up with = meet

mental telepathy = telepathy

minimum = least

misposted/misspelled in error = misposted/misspelled

modification = change

modus operandi = method

month of December = December

mutual agreement/cooperation = agreement/cooperation

my personal opinion = my opinion/I believe that

native habitat = habitat

necessary prerequisite = prerequisite

needless to say = (omit)

never before = never

nevertheless = but

new initiative/record/recruit = initiative/record/recruit

none at all = none

notification = notice

not in a position to = unable to

not to mention = (omit)

notwithstanding the fact that = although/even though

obligation = debt

obviate = do away with/make unnecessary

official business = business

off of = off

of recent date = recent

old adage = adage

on account of the fact that = because

on a continuing basis = constantly/continually

on a daily/monthly/weekly basis = daily/monthly/weekly

on a few occasions = occasionally

on a regular basis = regularly

on behalf of = for

one and the same = the same

only other alternative = alternative

on the grounds that = because

on the order of = about

on the part of = for/among

open up/close up/fold up/settle up = open/close/fold/settle

original source = source

other alternative = alternative

overall = (omit)

overexaggerate = exaggerate

over with = over

owing to the fact that = because

participate = take part

past experience = experience

past history = history

per = a

per annum = a year

per diem = a day

perfectly clear = clear

perform an examination = examine

permeate throughout = permeate

permit me to say = (omit)

per se = as such

personal friend/opinion = friend/opinion

pervasive = widespread

pervasively = throughout

per your request = as you asked

place emphasis on = emphasize

place an order for = order

positive identification = identification

postponed until later = postponed

predicated on = based on

preparatory to = before

prepared to offer = able to offer

preplanned = planned

present a conclusion = conclude

present status = status

preventative/orientated = preventive/oriented

previous to = before

previous experience = experience

prioritize = list/rank/set priorities

prior to = before

provided that = if

purchase = buy

pursuant to = according to/as

quite a = (omit)

quite unique = unique

radically new = new or radical, not both

raison d'être = reason for

rarely ever/seldom ever = rarely/seldom

ratify = approve/confirm

reach an agreement = agree

reason is because = the reason is or because

rectangular in shape = rectangular

reduce to a minimum = minimize

red/yellow/blue in color = red/yellow/blue

refer back to = refer to

regarding = about

reiterate again = reiterate

relating to = about

relative to = about/regarding/concerning

remuneration = pay

repeat again = repeat

requirement = need

reside = live

return back = return

revert back = revert

right and proper = right

root cause = cause

round in shape/round circles = round or circles, not both

same (as in "will send same") = it/them/the items/(omit)

same identical = same or identical, not both

scrutinize = read/examine/look at/inspect

seldom ever = seldom

send an answer = reply

send in = send

separate entities = entities

serious crisis/danger = crisis/danger

shuttle back and forth = shuttle

sine qua non = essential

sink down = sink

six in number = six

small in size = small

so advise us = advise us

so consequently . . . therefore = so consequently or therefore, but not both

spread out = spread

square in shape = square

stand up = stand

state of Alabama = Alabama

still persists/remains = persists/remains

stipulations = terms

streamlined in appearance = streamlined

string together = string

subject matter = subject or matter, not both

submitted = sent

subsequent to = after/following

subsequently = later

successful achievement = achievement

sudden impulse = impulse

sufficient = enough

take and (e.g., "take and read this") = (omit)

take the liberty of/take this opportunity to = (omit)

technical jargon = jargon

terminate = end

the above = (omit)

the better part of = most of/nearly all of

the bulk of = most/nearly all of

the earliest possible moment = soon/immediately

the party = (replace with specific noun)

the reason is because = the reason is or because, not both

therein = in

the undersigned/this writer = I

this is to inform you = (omit)

this is to thank you = thank you

thusly = in this way/as follows

too numerous to mention = numerous

total destruction = destruction

to tell the truth = (omit)

transpire = happen/take place

true facts = facts

ubiquitous = widespread

ultimate = final

undergraduate student = undergraduate

under separate cover = separately

unexpected emergency = emergency

unintentional mistake = mistake

unless and until = unless or until, not both

until such time as = until

untimely death = death

up above = above

up to this writing = until now

usual custom = custom

utilization/utilize = use

vacillating back and forth = vacillating

various different = various or different, not both

verbal discussion = discussion

verification = proof

very = (omit)

visible to the eye = visible

wall mural = mural

we are writing to tell you = (omit)

we beg to advise = (omit)

whether or not = whether

wish to advise/state = (omit)

wish to apologize = we apologize

with all due regard = (omit)

with a view to = to

without further delay = now/immediately

with reference/regard/respect to = about/concerning/on

with the exception of = except for

with the result that = so that

with this in mind, it is certainly clear that = therefore

words cannot describe = (omit)

worthy of merit = worthy or merits, but not both

would appreciate your informing/advising us = let us know

writer/undersigned = I/me

FORMS OF ADDRESS

No letter has ever been returned with the stamp, "Incorrect form of address." However, using the correct form indicates that you have done your homework and that you are respectful of the person's position. It also increases the likelihood of the person responding favorably to your letter.

Use the information below for the inside address and the address on the envelope. Also included are appropriate salutations; when more than one is given, the first is the formal salutation, the second the informal. Where addresses are known and permanent, they are given.

Government Officials

PRESIDENT OF THE UNITED STATES

The President
The White House
1600 Pennsylvania Avenue
Washington, DC 20500
Mr./Madam President: / Dear Mr./Madam President:

The President and Mrs. Dozier
The White House
1600 Pennsylvania Avenue
Washington, DC 20500
Dear Mr. President and Mrs. Dozier:

VICE-PRESIDENT OF THE UNITED STATES

The Vice-President
The White House
1600 Pennsylvania Avenue
Washington, DC 20500
　　or

The Vice-President
Executive Office Building
Washington, DC 20501
The Vice-President: / Dear Madam/Mr. Vice-President: / Madam/Sir:

SPOUSE OF THE PRESIDENT OF THE UNITED STATES

Ms. Hannah Marryat/Mr. Louis Rony
The White House
1600 Pennsylvania Avenue
Washington, DC 20500
Dear Ms. Marryat/Mr. Rony:

FORMER PRESIDENT OF THE UNITED STATES

The Honorable Jasper Petulengro
Dear Mr. Petulengro: / Sir:

CABINET MEMBERS

The Honorable Mark Sabre or Mabel Sabre
The Secretary of Health, Education, and Welfare
(or The Postmaster General or The Attorney General)
Dear Mr./Madam Secretary:

GOVERNOR (STATE OR TERRITORY)

The Honorable Oswald Henshawe/Sarah Denburn
Governor of California
Sir/Madam: / Dear Governor Henshawe/Denburn: / Dear Governor:

> Note that instead of "The Honorable . . ." the correct form in Massachusetts is
> "His/Her Excellency, the Governor of Massachusetts." This form can be used
> for other governors, too.

LIEUTENANT GOVERNOR/ACTING GOVERNOR

The Honorable Ada Herbert/Horace Beveridge
Lieutenant Governor/Acting Governor of Texas
Madam/Sir: / Dear Ms. Herbert/Mr. Beveridge:

UNITED STATES SENATOR

The Honorable Jack Worthing/Gwendolyn Fairfax
United States Senate
Washington, DC 20510
    or

The Honorable Jack Worthing/Gwendolyn Fairfax
United States Senator
(local address)
Sir/Madam: / Dear Senator Worthing/Fairfax:

UNITED STATES REPRESENTATIVE

The Honorable Marjorie Frant/Peter Standish
United States House of Representatives
Washington, DC 20515
    or
The Honorable Marjorie Frant/Peter Standish
Representative in Congress
(local address)
Sir/Madam: / Dear Ms. Frant/Mr. Standish: / Dear Representative Frant/Standish:

SPEAKER OF THE HOUSE

The Honorable Philip Liu/Rebecca Linnet
Speaker of the House of Representatives
United States Capitol
Washington, DC 20515
Dear Mr./Madam Speaker:

SENATE/HOUSE COMMITTEE/SUBCOMMITTEE CHAIR

The Honorable Richard Gettner/Gelda Rosmarin
Chair, Committee/Subcommittee on Foreign Affairs
United States Senate/United States House of Representatives
Washington, DC 20515
Dear Senator/Representative Gettner/Rosmarin:

> Members of Congress-elect and former members of Congress are also addressed as "The Honorable . . ." and "Dear Madam/Sir:" or "Dear Mr./Ms. . . ." Members of Congress holding special positions are addressed as "The Honorable . . . ," followed by their title ("Speaker of the House of Representatives"), with a salutation of "Sir/Madam:" / "Dear Madam/Mr. Speaker:" or "Dear Ms./Mr. . . ."

MAYOR

The Honorable Anna Fitzgerald/Nick Faunt
Mayor of Caldwell
City Hall
Dear Madam/Sir: / Dear Mayor Fitzgerald/Faunt: / Dear Ms./Mr. Mayor:

CHIEF JUSTICE OF THE UNITED STATES SUPREME COURT

The Chief Justice
The Supreme Court of the United States
> or

The Honorable Alvin Belknap/Constance Nevil
Dear Sir/Madam: / Dear Mr./Madam Chief Justice: / Dear Mr. Justice Belknap/
> Madam Justice Nevil:

Heads of State

PRESIDENT OF A REPUBLIC

His/Her Excellency Abdou Diouf/L. Sédar-Senghor
President of the Republic of Senegal
Excellency: / Dear Mr./Madam President:

PRIME MINISTER

His/Her Excellency Lt. Colonel Ramahatra Victor/Gabrielle Ranavalona
Prime Minister of Madagascar
Excellency: / Dear Mr./Madam Prime Minister:

PRIME MINISTER OF GREAT BRITAIN/CANADA

The Right Honorable Julia Lancester/John James Ridley
Prime Minister of Great Britain/the Dominion of Canada
Madam/Sir: / Dear Madam/Mr. Prime Minister: / Dear Madam Lancaster/
> Mr. Ridley:

PREMIER

His/Her Excellency Major Pedro Pires/Luzia Sotavento
Premier of the Republic of Cape Verde
Excellency: / Dear Mr./Madam Premier:

> When writing to officials of another country, check the country's exact name (a
> desk almanac will help) and the correct spelling of the official's name. Country
> leaders include queens, kings, rulers, co-regents, presidents, prime ministers,
> premiers, governor-generals, chancellors, emirs, episcopal co-princes, and sul-
> tans; verify the correct title. For example, in Mauritania, you write to the Chief
> of State and Head of Government, The Islamic Republic of Mauritania. Letters
> are traditionally sent to reigning monarchs via their private secretaries, thus you
> are not addressing a king or queen directly.

Diplomats

AMBASSADOR TO THE UNITED STATES

Her/His Excellency Elizabeth Tenbruggen/Kristian Koppig
The Ambassador of The Netherlands
    or Her/His Excellency the Ambassador from The Netherlands
Excellency: / Dear Madam/Mr. Ambassador:

> Use the full name of the country except for Great Britain; address British representatives as British Ambassador or British Minister. If an ambassador has a personal title, use it before the name ("Her Excellency Lady Catherine De Bourgh"). For an ambassador with a military title, substitute that title for "The Honorable" ("Colonel Jean Albert De Charleu").

U.S. AMBASSADOR

The Honorable Grace Carden/Harold Dakers
The United States Ambassador/Ambassador from the United States
The United States Embassy
Madam/Sir: / Dear Madam/Sir: / Dear Madam/Mr. Ambassador: / Dear Ambassador
    Carden/Dakers:

U.S. CONSUL-GENERAL, CONSUL, VICE-CONSUL, CHARGÉ D'AFFAIRES

Mr. Christopher Pumphrey/Ms. Margaret Hart
Consul-General/Consul/Vice-Consul/Chargé d'Affaires of the United States
    of America
Sir/Madam: / Dear Sir/Madam: / Dear Mr. Pumphrey/Ms. Hart:

FOREIGN CHARGÉ D'AFFAIRES

Mr. Horatio Hieronimo/Ms. H.G. Nuñez
Chargé d'Affaires of Spain
Sir/Madam: / Dear Mr. Hieronimo/Ms. Nuñez:

U.S. OR FOREIGN MINISTERS

The Honorable Nathan Rosenstein/Adèle Rossignol
United States Minister to Pakistan/Minister of France
Sir/Madam: / Dear Sir/Madam: / Dear Mr./Madam Minister:

HIGH COMMISSIONER

The Honorable Waris Dane/Ethel Armitage
United States High Commissioner to Argentina
Sir/Madam: / Dear Mr. Dane/Ms. Armitage:

SECRETARY GENERAL OF THE UNITED NATIONS

Her/His Excellency Anne Menzies/Peter Levi
Secretary General of the United Nations
The Secretariat
United Nations
United Nations Plaza
New York, NY 10017
Excellency: / Dear Ms./Mr. Secretary General: / Dear Ms. Menzies/Mr. Levi:

UNDER SECRETARY OF THE UNITED NATIONS

The Honorable Rose Mei-Hua/Thomas Henry Fould
Under Secretary of the United Nations
Madam/Sir: / Dear Ms./Mr. Under Secretary / Dear Ms. Mei-Hua/Mr. Fould:

U.S. DELEGATE TO THE UNITED NATIONS

Mr. Hans Kleinhans/Ms. Isabella Woodhouse
Chief of/Delegate from the United States Mission to the United Nations
Dear Mr. Kleinhans/Ms. Woodhouse:

U.S. REPRESENTATIVE TO THE U.N. WITH RANK OF AMBASSADOR

The Honorable Arethusa Gaunt/Manuel Chaver
United States Representative to the United Nations
Madam/Sir: / Dear Madam/Mr. Ambassador:

FOREIGN REPRESENTATIVE TO THE U.N. WITH RANK OF AMBASSADOR

His/Her Excellency Pietro Spina/Eline Vere
Representative of Italy to the United Nations
Excellency: / Dear Mr./Madam Ambassador:

Academics

COLLEGE/UNIVERSITY PRESIDENT

Dr. Clare Browell/George Heyling
President, Montague College of the Arts
Madam/Sir: / Dear Dr./President Browell/Heyling:

PROFESSOR/ASSOCIATE PROFESSOR/ASSISTANT PROFESSOR

Professor/Dr./Ms. or Mr. Wat Ollamoor/Joan Heseltinev
    or Wat Ollamoor/Joan Heseltine, Ph.D.
Department of English
Aspent University
Dear Professor/Dr./Ms. or Mr. Ollamoorr/Heseltine: / Dear Sir/Madam:

> "Dr.," meaning someone who has received a doctoral degree and "Ph.D." do
> not appear together; use one or the other. If the instructor does not have a doc-
> toral degree, use a social title (Mr., Ms., Mrs., Miss) instead of "Dr." Do not use
> "Professor."

DEAN/ASSISTANT DEAN

Dr. Frederick Mulliner/Jane Oliphant
Dean/Assistant Dean, School of Veterinary Medicine
University of Minnesota
Dear Sir/Madam: / Dear Dean/Dr. Mulliner/Oliphant:

CHANCELLOR

Dr. Jane Geoghegan/Edward Bronckhorst
Chancellor
Robinson University
Madam/Sir: / Dear Dr. Geoghegan/Bronckhorst:

CHAPLAIN

Chaplain/The Reverend Sarah Brockett/Martin Whitelaw, D.D., Ph.D.
Crowther United College
Dear Chaplain/Dr. Brockett/Whitelaw:

> For a member of the clergy, use the religious title first and put affiliations and
> degrees after the name ("The Reverend Malachi Brennan, S.J., Ph.D." or "Sister
> Mary Beatrice Fitzclare, C.S.J., Ph.D.") and use either "Dear Dr. Brennan/
> Fitzclare:" or "Dear Father Brennan/Sister Fitzclare:").

Members of the Clergy

RABBI

Rabbi Miriam Ephraim/Benjamin Ezra
    or Rabbi Miriam Ephraim, D.D./Benjamin Ezra, D.D.
Temple of Mount Zion
Madam/Sir: / Dear Rabbi/Dr. Ephraim/Ezra:

CANTOR

Cantor Simon Rosedale/Leah Dvoshe
Temple Ben Aaron
Sir/Madam: / Dear Cantor Rosedale/Dvoshe:

CANON

The Reverend/The Very Reverend Esmé Howe-Nevinson, D.D.
Canon of St. Elizabeth's
Reverend Sir: / Dear Canon Howe-Nevinson:

NUN/SISTER

Sister Donna Agnes Rebura, C.N.D.
Dear Sister Donna Agnes: / Dear Sister: / Dear Sister Rebura:

BROTHER

Brother Casimir Lypiatt, O.S.B.
Dear Brother: / Dear Brother Casimir: / Dear Brother Lypiatt:

MINISTER, PRIEST, OR MEMBER OF THE CLERGY

The Reverend George B. Callender, Ph.D./Martha Rodd, Ph.D.
    or The Reverend Martha Rodd/George B. Callender
    or The Reverend George B. Callender, D.D.
    or The Reverend Dr. Martha Dodd
Reverend Sir/Madam: / Dear Reverend Madam/Sir: / Dear Dr./Father/Mr. or
    Ms./Reverend Callender/Rodd:

An Eastern Orthodox priest's title is "Reverend Father Kostes Palamas" and the
salutation is "Dear Father Palamas:".

DEAN (CATHEDRAL/SEMINARY)

The Very Reverend Andrew Montfitchet, D.D.
Dean of St. Philip's Seminary
Very Reverend Sir: / Dear Dean Montfitchet:

MONSIGNOR

The Right Reverend Monsignor John Woodley
Reverend Monsignor: / Dear Monsignor Woodley: / Dear Monsignor:

ABBOT

The Right Reverend Gilbert Belling Torpenhow, O.S.B.
Abbot of Heldar Abbey
Right Reverend Abbot: / Dear Father Abbot: / Dear Father Torpenhow:

FATHER/BROTHER SUPERIOR

The Very Reverend William Falder, M.M.
Director/Superior of The Mission Fathers/Brothers
Dear Father/Brother Superior: / Dear Father Falder/Brother William:

> See the *Official Catholic Directory* if you are unsure whether the individual is a priest or a brother or if he has other titles.

MOTHER/SISTER SUPERIOR

The Reverend Mother/Sister Superior Ellen Mary Montgomery, A.C.M. Convent of St. Joseph
> or Mother Ellen Mary Montgomery, Superior of St. Joseph's Convent
> or Mother Ellen Mary Montgomery, Superior Convent of St. Joseph
Reverend Mother/Sister: / Dear Reverend Sister/Mother: / Dear Mother/Sister Superior: / Dear Mother Ellen Mary Montgomery: / Dear Mother Ellen Mary: / Dear Madam:

> There are also titles such as Regional Superior, Provincial Superior, and President, and salutations like "Dear Religious Leader" are used when writing to large or international orders. Someone within the order might write simply "Dear Sister." For the correct title, check the *Official Catholic Directory*.

ANGLICAN BISHOP

The Right Reverend James Crowther
The Lord Bishop of Oxford
Right Reverend Sir: / Dear Bishop Crowther:

ANGLICAN ARCHBISHOP

The Most Reverend Reginald Kershaw
Archbishop of Salisbury
> or The Most Reverend Archbishop of Salisbury
> or The Lord Archbishop of Salisbury
Your Grace: / Dear Archbishop Kershaw: / Dear Archbishop:

EPISCOPAL BISHOP

The Right Reverend Dinah Morris
Bishop of New York
Right Reverend Bishop: / Dear Bishop:

> The Presiding Bishop of the Protestant Episcopal Church in the United States has that title in place of "Bishop of New York." You can also replace "The Right Reverend" with "The Most Reverend" and address him as "Most Reverend Sir."

PROTESTANT BISHOP

The Reverend George Cassilis
Bishop of Los Angeles
Dear Bishop:

METHODIST BISHOP

Bishop Richard Feverel of the Miami Area
       or The Reverend Richard Feverel
       Methodist Bishop of Miami
Reverend Sir: / Dear Bishop Feverel:

L.D.S. BISHOP

Bishop Roger Dainton
The Church of Jesus Christ of Latter-Day Saints
Dear Bishop Dainton: / Sir:

ROMAN CATHOLIC ARCHBISHOP/BISHOP

The Most Reverend Jean Latour
Archbishop/Bishop of Santa Fe
Your Excellency: / Dear Archbishop/Bishop Latour: / Most Reverend Sir:

EASTERN ORTHODOX ARCHBISHOP

The Most Reverend George, Archbishop of Philadelphia
       or His Eminence George, Archbishop of Philadelphia
Your Excellency:

EPISCOPAL ARCHDEACON

The Venerable Nicholas Broune
Archdeacon of San Francisco
Venerable Sir: / Dear Archdeacon:

CARDINAL

His Eminence James Cardinal Wickham
Archbishop of New York
Your Eminence: / Dear Cardinal Wickham:

ROMAN CATHOLIC POPE

His Holiness, Pope John Paul II
        or His Holiness, the Pope
Vatican City
00187 Rome, Italy
Your Holiness: / Most Holy Father:

The complimentary close is always "Respectfully yours," for the pope.

APOSTOLIC PRO-NUNCIO

His Excellency, The Most Reverend John Sylvester Clayton
Titular Archbishop of Greece
The Apostolic Pro-Nuncio
Your Excellency: / Dear Archbishop Clayton:

GREEK ORTHODOX PATRIARCH

His All Holiness Patriarch George
Your All Holiness:

RUSSIAN ORTHODOX PATRIARCH

His Holiness the Patriarch of Chicago
Your Holiness:

Military Personnel

When writing to officers and enlisted personnel use full rank (may be abbreviated), full name, comma, initials for the branch of service ("Captain Marguerite Evelyn Falconer, U.S.A."). For retired personnel, add "(Ret.)" after the service affiliation. Abbreviations for the service branches are:

Air Force, U.S.A.F.

Army, U.S.A.

Army Reserve, U.S.A.R.

Coast Guard, U.S.C.G.

Coast Guard Reserve, U.S.C.G.R.

Marine Corps, U.S.M.C.

Marine Corps Reserve, U.S.M.C.R.

Naval Reserve, U.S.N.R.

Navy, U.S.N.

Salutations include the rank and last name ("Dear Commander Marlow:") or rank only ("Dear Commander:"). You may write "Dear General:" when addressing a general, a lieutenant general, a major general, or a brigadier general. "Dear Admiral:" includes fleet, vice, rear, and ordinary admirals. The salutation for junior officers, petty officers, warrant officers, enlisted personnel, ensigns, and noncommissioned officers is "Dear Ms./Mr. Marcovitch:".

For chaplains use: "Chaplain," full name, comma, rank, comma, initials of their branch of service ("Chaplain Michael Sabrov, Captain, U.S.A."). In the Navy, the order is reversed: "Captain Michael Sabrov (Ch.C.), U.S.N."). "Dear Chaplain:" is the salutation.

Index